Heidi Blake is a multi-award-winning investigative journalist. She was assistant editor of *The Sunday Times*, attached to the Insight team, until spring 2015 when she became BuzzFeed's UK investigations editor. She lives in south-east London.

Jonathan Calvert has worked for various newspapers in a long and distinguished career as an investigative journalist. He is the longest-serving editor of the Insight team at *The Sunday Times*, having held the role for more than ten years. He lives in west London.

The Insight team have won a series of awards for their work on the FIFA Files, including The Paul Foot Award for campaigning and investigative journalism as well as Investigation of the Year and Sports Journalist of the Year at the British Journalism Awards. They were also awarded the Scoop of the Year prize by the London Press Club and won News Story of the Year at the Foreign Press Awards.

'I would also like to pay tribute to the Insight team at *The Sunday Times* without whose investigations, many of these allegations may never have come to light' John Whittingdale, Secretary of State for Culture Media and Sport

'Allegations of shady dealings have long swirled round FIFA ... never before has bribe-giving been documented in such graphic detail' *Independent*

'[*The Ugly Game*] offers the most comprehensive account of the affair to date, and asks why Blatter continues to support Qatar despite all the evidence against the desert state' *Radio Times*

'There's an urgency about the storytelling as the authors manage to extract excruciating tension from the unpromising materials available to them' *The Secret Footballer*

'An explosive account of the biggest World Cup heist since the trophy was nicked in the 1960s' *Sport*

'By examining how Qatar landed the 2022 World Cup, two investigative journalists, armed with internal documents, take apart the continuing FIFA corruption controversy' *Boston Globe*

'With Sepp Blatter under criminal investigation, this tale of how Qatar bagged the 2022 World Cup is a timely football horror story. At times it is hard to believe how corrupt and dirty football's global leaders were. With every page of this book, we see just why FIFA desperately needs a complete overhaul' *Sun*

'Riveting and insightful ... What is perhaps surprising is just how successfully it has translated from a series of headline-grabbing news stories into a gripping book' *New York Journal of Books*

The Ugly Game

The Qatari Plot to Buy the World Cup

Heidi Blake and
Jonathan Calvert

A *Sunday Times* Insight
team investigation

**SIMON &
SCHUSTER**

London · New York · Sydney · Toronto · New Delhi

A CBS COMPANY

First published in Great Britain by Simon & Schuster UK Ltd, 2015
This paperback edition published by Simon & Schuster Ltd, 2016
A CBS COMPANY

3 5 7 9 10 8 6 4

Simon & Schuster UK Ltd
1st Floor
222 Gray's Inn Road
London WC1X 8HB

www.simonandschuster.co.uk

Simon & Schuster Australia, Sydney
Simon & Schuster India, New Delhi

A CIP catalogue record for this book
is available from the British Library.

ISBN: 978-1-4711-4937-5
Ebook ISBN: 978-1-4711-4936-8

Typeset in the UK by M Rules
Printed in the UK by CPI Group (UK) Ltd, Croydon, CR0 4YY

MIX
Paper from
responsible sources
FSC® C020471

Simon & Schuster UK Ltd are committed to sourcing paper
that is made from wood grown in sustainable forests and supports the Forest
Stewardship Council, the leading international forest certification organisation.
Our books displaying the FSC logo are printed on FSC certified paper.

This book is dedicated to the casualties of corrupt decisions everywhere and the whistleblowers who risk so much to expose the rot in the hope of a better world.

Contents

Prologue

The announcement that the tiny desert state of Qatar had been chosen to host the football World Cup in 2022 was greeted with shock and disbelief in the packed auditorium in Zurich and around the world. The great and the good of international football exchanged incredulous glances in stunned silence as the Qatari royal family erupted into jubilant cheers, clenching their fists in the air.

It was a snowy afternoon on 2 December 2010 in the Swiss city where FIFA, world football's governing body, has its headquarters. This was the climax of years of frenzied campaigning by the nine countries competing to host the world's biggest sporting tournament – worth billions of dollars and priceless prestige to the victor.

How had a minuscule Gulf state, with virtually no football tradition or infrastructure and searing summer temperatures of up to 50°C, beaten established footballing countries with much stronger bids? One man, more than any other in that room, knew the answer. Mohamed bin Hammam, the billionaire Qatari FIFA official, waited modestly for the royal celebrations to subside before stepping forward to embrace the Emir and kiss the young sheikh at the head of his country's bid on the cheek. No casual observer would have guessed that this dapper man, with his mild manner and his neat silver beard, was the true architect of Qatar's astonishing and improbable victory. Even the men who ran the official bid committee would tell you he had nothing to do with their campaign.

Since that day in Zurich, allegations of corruption have swirled around Qatar's World Cup bid. Journalists, private investigators and powerful figures in football have tried to unravel the mystery of how the royals commanding the country's campaign from their desert palaces could have pulled off such an audacious feat. But the hidden hand of Bin Hammam remained a closely guarded secret – until a massive leak of confidential data changed everything.

In the early months of 2014, more than three years after Qatar's triumph, journalists working at *The Sunday Times* Insight team in London received a phone call. The familiar voice of a well-connected source at the top of world football told them a whistleblower from inside FIFA had come forward with what appeared to be a large and explosive cache of documents. The source arranged an introduction and then took a step back. Coming face to face with the Insight team, Jonathan Calvert and Heidi Blake, for the first time in a London hotel, the whistleblower explained nervously how he had developed grave concerns about the way Qatar had won the World Cup and had decided its secrets needed to be spilled.

He led the journalists to a discreet location far away from London where they were shown a treasure-trove of hundreds of millions of documents stored on a network of supercomputers. Many of the files related to the activities of Bin Hammam working secretly to bring the World Cup to Qatar against the odds. The whistleblower himself had barely scraped the surface of the vast mass of information, but he wanted the journalists to dive in. Over the course of the next three months, the reporters worked day and night in a secret data centre with the blinds drawn, surrounded by the whirring of overheating servers and the blinking lights of powerful machinery, all hidden behind the bland façade of a high-street shop front.

The scale of the leak was unprecedented. The whistleblower

had given the reporters the key to emails, faxes, telephone logs, electronic messages, letters, bank slips, accounts, cash chits, hand-written notes, flight records, secret reports, diaries, minutes of confidential meetings, computer hard drives and more. The documents were a portal into the secret command centre from which Bin Hammam waged his campaign to buy World Cup support and later the dare-devil attempt to topple the FIFA president Sepp Blatter which led to his own spectacular downfall. The reporters used forensic search technology to unravel the network of slush funds from which he paid millions of dollars in bribes to scores of FIFA officials and to piece together the backroom deals and vote-rigging ploys which brought him first victory and then disgrace. The man who overcame the odds to bring glory to his country now lives anonymously in his mansion in Doha, the capital of Qatar, estranged from the royal family he once served and sworn to silence as preparations for the World Cup he brought home to his city gather pace around him.

The Ugly Game comes in the wake of 'The FIFA Files' exposé in *The Sunday Times* – a world exclusive that made headlines around the planet when it broke on the eve of the Brazil World Cup in June 2014. It tells the extraordinary story of the most corrupt World Cup bidding contest in history, shining a light into the darkest recesses of FIFA through the portal of Bin Hammam's secret campaign. It is a human drama of personal triumph and disaster, of one man who realised an impossible dream but was brought low by overreaching ambition. It is a tale awash with dirty money but glittering with mystery and intrigue – its characters swept up in the treacherous currents of sport's power politics. Above all it is an invitation to join Bin Hammam as he moves through the corridors of world football greasing palms and striking deals; revealing the ugly venality of the men who control the beautiful game.

One

A Surprising Proposal

The air was thick with tobacco smoke and tension. A small clutch of men in long white dishdashas were craning around their host Mohamed bin Hammam in the dimly lit room. Cardamom-scented steam rose from cups of Arabic coffee freshly poured from a fine golden dallah by robed servants who melted in and out of the shadows. No one was watching the football match flickering on the wall. The Qatari billionaire had a lot to get off his chest, and his guests were listening intently. Tonight, like every other night, Bin Hammam was holding court in his majlis, the male-only sitting room of his Doha mansion where local men came to lounge in exquisite comfort as they smoked and drank coffee or mint tea.

These evenings had once been relaxed and jovial affairs, alive with the hubbub of many voices and shouts of celebration or dismay as goals were scored or saved on the giant television screens. Bin Hammam was known by his friends around the world for being generous to a fault, and he was never without company. At the peak of his success, he had opened his home every night to dozens of men who piled into the sitting room at sunset to talk and watch football before moving through to the dining room to feast on Qatari specialities at his banqueting table. His guests gorged themselves on flatbreads stuffed with marinated shawarma meat, vine leaves, spicy kabsa, zatar pie, tab-bouleh salads, baba ghanoush and ghuzi lamb, all washed down with ice-cold mineral water.

Back then Bin Hammam was away on football business as often as he was at home, but when he was present at the head of the table, his grandchildren skipped around him and he would break off from the dining-room chatter to tousle their hair or press sweets into their palms. Neither his younger wife Nahed, a beautiful Jordanian who dressed demurely in western clothes and spoke French, nor the older Fatima, who covered her face and had been at Bin Hammam's side for many years, were anywhere to be seen when the men were at the table. In his glory days, these gatherings had been lively, crowded occasions, with guests jostling for position for a word with their host. Now all was lost, Nahed had left him and just a few loyal friends remained in the majlis.

This quiet evening, only Bin Hammam's voice could be heard by the newcomer who had been ushered past the football pictures lining the hallway into the splendour of the sitting room, and was now approaching the party through the haze of cigarette smoke in the air. Having slipped off his shoes at the door, the tanned visitor in a crisp open-collared shirt and a dark blue business suit padded across the carpet. He was an unfamiliar face in the room, and the locals eyed this western interloper with caution, but he was greeted warmly by their host. He smiled respectfully as he settled into an ochre sofa opposite Bin Hammam, but something had unnerved him.

It was a few months since the visitor had said goodbye to the Qatari in Zurich, and his friend had changed. It wasn't that he was any less immaculate than usual. His silver beard was tightly trimmed around his strong jaw and the spotless white keffiyeh his servants had pressed that morning flowed over athletic shoulders.

But for all Bin Hammam's finery and the opulence of his surroundings, it was clear that his spirits were tattered. The 62-year-old was admired by all who knew him for his steady poise and dignity. Now his shoulders were hunched and his eyes were circled with dark shadows. His friend was worried. Did Mohamed's hand tremble as he reached for his golden coffee cup, or did he dream it? Did his voice quaver as he spoke? How could he be so altered? This man had forged a long career as a captain of industry at the helm of a multi-billion-dollar construction firm, riding the economic boom that thrust the shimmering metropolis of Doha skywards out of the desert. He had transcended his humble origins and surged through the ranks of Qatari society, becoming one of the richest men in a city of billionaires with a place in the inner sanctum of the Emir's most trusted counsellors. Now he was brought low, and by what? A game.

Bin Hammam's friends, like his family, knew that football had always been his first love. Now it had spurned him. The man who had pulled off the audacious feat of winning the right to host the World Cup in the Qatari desert only months before was now in disgrace and banned for life from the game he adored. Shut out and consigned to silence, there was nothing left for Bin Hammam but to watch as Qatar's plans to host the tournament he had brought home for his country took shape outside. In the weeks and months after his spectacular downfall in May 2011, he sat among the friends who gathered in his mansion each night, going round and round the events leading up to the catastrophe, trying to make sense of how it could have happened.

The billionaire spoke slowly and deliberately, but there was one word that almost choked him with its bitterness every time it spilled from his lips: Blatter. The traitor he had once called his brother. The man who owed him everything, for whom he had been prepared to sacrifice even the last precious moments with a dying son. The man whose presidential crown by rights belonged to him. The man who had destroyed him.

Bin Hammam had been a hero in world football before his career was wiped out in one sickening blast by the bribery scandal that had exploded under the Caribbean sun in the Port of Spain, blotting out all he had achieved. Everyone knew the lurid details of what had happened on that ill-fated junket for a host of small-time local football chieftains whose loyalty he had tried and failed to secure. The world had seen the photographs of cash spilling out of manilla envelopes which had surfaced like bloated corpses, bobbing in the warm West Indian waters, when those traitors had turned on him in the days after the trip.

But there was much about Bin Hammam's demise which continued to mystify even the most knowing onlookers. This was the man who had achieved the impossible by bringing the World Cup to the desert, and his downfall had followed strangely quickly on the heels of that improbable triumph. His visitor was puzzled. Why had Bin Hammam's old friends at FIFA turned so viciously against him? And why were the young figureheads of Qatar's 2022 World Cup Supreme Committee so quick to disown their former mentor? Strangest of all, why had this proud man suddenly crawled away so quietly?

The Qatari football grandee denied the specific allegations against him and he was known to be planning an appeal in the relative secrecy of the Court of Arbitration for Sport (CAS), but on all other matters he was sworn to silence. So the men who gathered in the privacy of his majlis were the only people who would be trusted to hear the whole story. It was these men who sat listening intently that night as Bin Hammam mulled over his ruination. Mostly they were locals, sweeping into the mansion set back from the hot city street as the sun went down outside. Every now and again, they were joined by a friend from Bin Hammam's days in Zurich, like the visitor who had entered this evening:

westerners who flew through Doha from time to time and stopped to see a man they remembered at the peak of his powers. So Bin Hammam told these guests his story. How it all began. How he had turned his boyhood dreams into reality. How it had ended like this.

All his life, Mohamed bin Hammam had been gripped by a peculiar passion for football. The obsession had kept him up at night as a youth, straining to hear the commentary on his favourite team, Liverpool, crackling out of his father's transistor radio from a country far away. Football was a lonely love for a boy from Doha in the 1950s, and Mohamed cut a solitary figure kicking his ball around the dusty streets and scrublands. Many of his friends didn't even know how to play this strange foreign game.

Bin Hammam was born in Doha in 1949 – the same year Qatar shipped off its very first exports of crude oil – when the country was just an obscure Gulf statelet under British protection. This tiny peninsula, which juts out of the Arabian mainland into the Persian Gulf, had a minuscule population of just 25,000 back then. The energy boom was on the distant horizon as the oil started gushing out of Qatar's wells, but the city had not yet started shooting up out of the desert into the gleaming mirage of glass it was destined to become. Back then, the sandy dirt roads where Mohamed played were lined with crumbling single-storey buildings, the sky pierced only by the minarets of the Wahhabi mosques where he and his father went to worship.

This little boy chasing his tattered ball through the dusty streets wasn't only marked out from his peers by his strange love of a foreign sport. Mohamed's wide-set features and tight cap of black curls belied the distant African ancestry that would always set him apart from the pure-bred Arabs who ruled the roost in Doha. His mother was a nurse and his father a local businessman, both of whom had been born Qatari, but way back in the family's lineage was an ancestor from Africa In this tiny country differences like that stuck out, and being different meant never quite belonging.

Mohamed dribbled his ball along the rocky paths leading up the West Bay and ran along the waterfront, ducking between the pearl merchants' rowing boats dotting the unpaved foreshore. He scampered up the jetty, with the cobalt waters of the Persian Gulf glittering all around him, watching the fishermen bobbing on the waves and the lighters chugging out to meet the cargo ships on the horizon. The skyline was speckled with the white masts of dhows carrying fruit, vegetables and barrels of fresh water along the Eastern Arabian shores, and from time to time an oil tanker loomed into view – a harbinger of the vast mineral riches his tiny country was beginning to discover. And with oil, came football. Down by the West Bay, little Mohamed would watch with wide eyes as, all along the shore, foreign oil workers fresh off the boat from Europe played his beloved game. He saw how they threw down their grubby flannel shirts to mark the goalposts, divided into teams and tossed a coin for the first kick. He heard them shouting to one another in strange foreign tongues; clapping each other on the back; cheering in celebration when the ball flew through the makeshift goalposts in clouds of desert dust.

Football arrived in Doha with the foreigners who flocked to the Gulf when Qatar first began spudding its vast oil reserves at the end of the Second World War. The country had come under British protection after the collapse of the Ottoman Empire, and its first onshore oil concession was awarded in 1935 to the Anglo-Iranian Oil Company – the predecessor of BP – and operated by a local firm that would become the Qatar Petroleum Company. Drilling began in the late 1930s, but the war delayed its full development and the first crude exports didn't start until 1949, the year Bin Hammam was born, by which time 5,000 barrels a day were gushing out of that first well.

The foreign riggers brought with them their love of football, and the game they played all along the shore and on patches of scrub throughout the city began to catch the attention of the local population. By 1950, when Mohamed was just reaching his first birthday, Qatar's first amateur football team, Al-Najah, was formed. It fell to the Qatar Petroleum Company to organise the country's inaugural football competition – the Ezz Eddin Tournament in Dukhan – in 1951. The Qatar Football Association was set up almost a decade later in 1960, when Mohamed was 11, and when he turned 21, in 1970, the country's national association was finally recognised by FIFA.

By the time Bin Hammam had grown into a smart young entrepreneur in his early twenties, the country's fortunes were transformed. Qatar threw off the yoke of British protection in 1971 and the ruling Al Thani family took full control of oil operations, cranking up the extraction of the country's energy reserves, pouring the massive revenues into the swelling coffers of its sovereign wealth fund and setting the Gulf state on a fast track to becoming one of the world's richest countries. Bin Hammam's own company, Kemco, was founded in the same year the oil industry was nationalised, 1974, when he was just 25. With the oil money flooding in, building projects were mushrooming all over town, and the young businessman grabbed the opportunity. Kemco began life as an electro-mechanical engineering firm, with the tools and talent required to help build the glass skyscrapers erupting all along the West Bay waterfront. With each new development that sprang up along the shore where he'd watched the oil workers play as a boy, Bin Hammam's bank balance expanded. Before long he was a millionaire.

For all that business was booming, Bin Hammam still found plenty of time to pursue his childhood passion. Aged just 18, Bin Hammam had fallen for a local girl and decided to get married, abandoning any boyish hopes of a playing career. Instead, in the early 1970s he took up the mantle of running Al Rayyan football club – nicknamed the Lions – which had been formed only a few years before as an amateur team run out of a two-bed house in Rayyan town. In 1972 the Qatar Stars League was formalised, and Al Rayyan played in its first season. Bin Hammam proved a talented manager, and he would steer his Lions to multiple championship titles in the QSL during his presidency, all the while keeping a firm hand on the Kemco tiller.

Rayyan was the home town of Qatar's ruling Emir, Sheikh Khalifa bin Hamad Al Thani, and Bin Hammam's transformation of the shambolic local side into a winning team did not go unnoticed. This dapper businessman with his love of the foreign game of football particularly caught the eye of Qatar's heir apparent, Sheikh Hamad bin Khalifa Al Thani, himself an ambitious youth with western sensibilities. Three years Bin Hammam's junior and fresh out of Sandhurst, the young royal had come back to Qatar with all the polish of a British education and big ideas about what his country could achieve. He remembered Bin Hammam as a local boy from his early school years in Doha, before he had crossed the waters to pursue his education in England, and he liked what the self-made multi-millionaire was doing with Kemco and Al Rayyan now.

Sheikh Hamad was a tall man with shoulders like granite boulders and a forbidding military moustache. He hurtled up the ranks of Qatar's emerging military to become commander-in-chief at the age of 25, and took charge of the Supreme Planning Council, which sets the country's economic and social policies, in the early 1980s. Qatar was getting seriously rich, but Sheikh Hamad believed it was not powering forward quickly enough. He wanted his Gulf homeland to become a truly modern country. The crown prince was a keen sportsman who had observed the power of football to unite a nation during his education in Britain. He saw the galvanising potential of the game Bin Hammam loved. The pair became as close to being friends as an ordinary boy of African descent can with a member of the Qatari royal family. Bin Hammam sat with his head bowed in reverence when Sheikh Hamad was in the room – but when he was invited to speak, the crown prince listened.

With the patronage of the royals came certain special privileges, and Kemco began to win more and more major state contracts. It wasn't long before the millions in the bank became billions, and Bin Hammam was one of the richest men in town. By 1992 he had climbed to the top of the Qatari football ladder too, becoming the president of the country's football association. In his first year at the helm, he arranged for Qatar to host the Gulf Cup of Nations and steered the country's national team to victory in the tournament.

By now, Sheikh Hamad was getting restless. His father, the Emir Sheikh Khalifa, had presided over impressive economic growth since he took power after independence, but he was a traditionalist who favoured a stately pace of change. Sheikh Hamad didn't have that kind of patience. Sheikh Khalifa had handed him a growing portfolio of royal responsibilities, including control over the country's oil and gas development programme, but not enough to satiate his thirst for power. By 1995, the crown prince was ready to make his lunge. He waited until his father was away on holiday in Geneva before seizing control of the Amiri Diwan Palace with the backing of the rest of the royal family. Next, he hired an American law firm to freeze his father's international bank accounts and head off any countermoves the old Emir might try to make. The coup was bloodless, but the crown prince had shown he had ice in his veins by freezing his father out of Doha. Sheikh Khalifa endured a decade of exile in France and Abu Dhabi before being allowed to return home in 2004.

With the old guard out of the way, Sheikh Hamad's power in Qatar was absolute and he could begin the rapid modernisation he had been dreaming of for years. Under the rule of the new

Emir, Qatar's natural gas production would soar to 77 million tonnes per year. By 2008, Qatar's gross domestic product had reached $84,812 per capita – making it the world's richest country – and 76.8 per cent of that wealth came from oil and gas. But Sheikh Hamad wanted his nation to become so much more than just an energy-rich Gulf statelet, and he knew he needed to shore up Qatar's position in the world for a future when the mineral reserves finally ran out. He intended to position Qatar as a major global power extending its financial, political and cultural tentacles all around the globe. Property, the arts, industry, media, sport, education – these were the building blocks of a truly modern nation.

So Sheikh Hamad would set up the Qatar Investment Authority to spread $100 billion of the country's sovereign wealth internationally. He would turn the Gulf state into a crucial strategic partner of the US government in the Middle East, allowing his new American allies to construct two regionally pivotal military bases on Qatari soil and inviting several world-class US universities to open campuses in Doha. He founded the Arabic news network Al Jazeera in 1996 and later established the Qatar Museums Authority which transformed the country into the world's biggest contemporary art buyer. And then he would turn his attention to sport. He knew that global glory and prestige attaches to no one like it does to the world's sports superstars. He wanted to transform Qatar into the international sporting capital of the 21st century.

The Emir set about assembling a group of trusted favourites to help him steer Qatar into its glittering future, and his old friend Bin Hammam was an obvious choice to help him realise his sporting ambitions. The billionaire football lover was given a seat on the Emir's 35-man advisory council – his Majlis Al Shura – charged with deliberating on new laws, economic and social policy, cultural development and the general glorification of Qatar.

Bin Hammam had ascended to the very highest echelons of Qatari society that it was possible to reach without royal blood. Charm, nous and determination had carried him a long way from his modest origins, but he could never escape his ancestry altogether. The other courtiers were jealous of this outsider's newfound status and as he passed between the colonnades of the vast white palace on the Corniche, he could hear their whispers. They called him 'The Slave'. However high he climbed, however limitless his fortune, Bin Hammam would always be an interloper in the upper reaches of Qatari society, where pure Arab blood was the only true mark of nobility. He would always be looking over his shoulder; always anxious to jump higher than all the other favourites to please the Emir; always striving for the chance to really put himself and his family on the map of Qatar forever.

By the time he reached his late forties, Bin Hammam was a super-rich businessman who ruled over Qatari football and held a coveted place in the inner sanctum of the Amiri Diwan Palace – but he wanted more. Determined to shore up his status at home and prove his worth on an international stage, he ran for election to the executive committee of the Asian Football Confederation – the body which controlled every member association across the continent from its headquarters in Kuala Lumpur – and won. It was 1996, the same year Bin Hammam joined the Emir's advisory council, and now he had transcended Qatari football to take a powerful position at the helm of the Asian game. It wasn't enough. Next, he extended his gaze far past the Doha city gates, and beyond all of Asia, to the distant European kingdom of FIFA. There was no higher place in football. FIFA dictated the rules of the game and was the keeper of soccer's most sought-after prize, the 18-carat gold World Cup trophy. All the star players that Bin Hammam had so admired in his youth had adorned this glittering tournament. It was the greatest show on earth.

The Fédération Internationale de Football Association controls the beautiful game from its hilltop headquarters in the Swiss city of Zurich. The World Cup is the biggest and best-loved sporting tournament on the planet, and FIFA sweeps the hundreds of millions of dollars that flow in from marketing, sponsorship deals and TV rights into its vast reserves. World football's governing body is controlled by an elite cabal of two dozen men who fly into Zurich from the far-flung corners of the world to meet in secrecy and call the shots on the sport. While FIFA's congress, with a representative from each national football federation, met once a year and voted in the president every four, the ruling executive committee (Exco) of 24 men took many of the most important decisions including which country should host the World Cup. Bin Hammam wanted to be part of their club. He ran for election onto the executive committee in 1996, the same year he ascended to the Emir's advisory council and the AFC, and his winning streak continued. The Qatari football-lover took his place around FIFA's boardroom table and joined in the running of the international game.

This was a very long way from Doha's sandy desert pitches and the gleaming corridors of the Diwan Palace. FIFA was a brave new world where creed and colour were no bar to prestige and recognition. Here, as Bin Hammam would quickly discover, those things were up for sale to the highest bidder.

Six years on, the delegates at FIFA's 53rd annual congress in Seoul, South Korea, were sipping their evening drinks between the tall white columns in the atrium of the Grand Hilton Hotel. It was a humid May evening in 2002, the night before world football's presidential election, and the lobby was alive with chatter and political intrigue. Speculation was mounting. Could the

FIFA president Sepp Blatter hold on for a second term the next day? He was facing formidable opposition from Issa Hayatou, the powerful Cameroonian chief of the Confederation of African Football (CAF). What was more, his authority had been sensationally rocked days before by a legal complaint filed by 11 members of his own executive committee accusing him of abuse of power and financial mismanagement. Surely the president was finished? It would take something pretty spectacular to turn things around now.

Blatter was a small, square-set Swiss bureaucrat in his mid-sixties with silvery tufts of hair at his temples and a sly twinkle in his eye. He had been elected in 1998 when his mentor, the suave Brazilian João Havelange, stepped down after 24 years in power, and by anyone's reckoning that was a tough act to follow. Havelange had transformed FIFA from a small gentlemen's club with just eight employees presiding modestly over the organisation of the World Cup into a global powerhouse with hundreds of staff and billions of dollars in the bank. All this was made possible by a golden alliance formed early in his presidency with Horst Dassler, the Adidas scion, who came to be known as the godfather of sports sponsorship.

Havelange had campaigned in the 1974 election on a platform of expansion, promising to double the size of the World Cup, and he needed money to make it happen. Adidas had plenty of cash to offer, and it wanted to supply FIFA with branded sports gear to market its products to football fans around the world. So the game's first major sponsorship deal was born. Adidas and Coca-Cola were the first big corporations to pile in and pay millions of dollars to slap their branding all over every available surface at the World Cup, and they were closely followed by fast food chains, electronics giants, beer companies and luxury watchmakers galore.

Spotting the television transmitter masts shooting up in every

direction in the 1970s, Havelange had been quick to realise the
riches that would flow from selling the rights to beam the world's
best-loved sporting tournament into homes all around the planet.
The FIFA president packaged up the broadcast rights to future
World Cups into bundles and put them on sale. Soon enough
FIFA was raking in billions from TV, too. Just as Havelange had
promised, the World Cup ballooned in size from just 16 teams in
the final to 32 under his watch. More teams meant more
matches, and more matches meant more broadcast money. With
so much cash flooding in, Havelange had built FIFA its smart
new base in Zurich, and hired an army of full-time staff, spin
doctors and money men to turn world football's governing body
into the slick machine it is today.

Blatter worked for Dassler at Adidas headquarters in the
French commune of Landersheim before migrating over to FIFA
in 1975 to become its technical director in the first wave of
hiring after the sponsorship gold-rush began. A slick PR man,
schooled by the godfather himself in the arts of sports branding,
Blatter had buckets of ingratiating charm, a background in business administration and an instinctive love of money. He was the
perfect protégé for Havelange. The new technical director was
tasked with spending Coca-Cola's millions on new schemes to
create more coaches, referees and sports doctors, and quickly
ascended to become FIFA's secretary general in 1981. When his
master stepped down at the grand old age of 82, he was the natural successor.

Football had turned into seriously big business by the time
Blatter took over in 1998, with the non-US TV rights to the next
three World Cups on sale for $2.2 billion. The new FIFA presi-
dent had a lot to live up to. Sure, he'd earned his spurs holding
the purse strings for 17 years as secretary general, but Havelange
was a giant in the mercenary world of international football and
his were big boots for his small Swiss successor to fill. When

Blatter took the head of the FIFA boardroom table, he looked around the room and asked himself how to win the trust and respect of the men staring back at him. It didn't take long to spot the dollar signs in their eyes that gave him his answer. Blatter was the first president to professionalise his hitherto voluntary executive committee, offering hefty salaries and gold-plated benefits to the men seated around him. Their pay and perks were to be a closely guarded secret, but leaked documents revealed that by 2014 they were pocketing salaries of $200,000 for a handful of days' work a year and topping up their wallets with daily allowances of $700 in cash.

Blatter had paid handsomely for the loyalty of his board, and he had sprayed FIFA's cash around the planet in the form of generous development grants to national associations in his first presidential term. But now, here he was on the eve of his re-election in 2002 facing an insurrection. His own secretary general, Michel Zen-Ruffinen, had lashed out at Blatter's dictatorial style and produced an explosive report accusing him of misleading accounting practices and conflicts of interest, prompting the 11 members of his well-paid executive committee to file a criminal complaint against him with the Zurich courts. How dare they? And as if that wasn't bad enough, his opponent Hayatou was capitalising on the trouble by running on a ticket of transparency, which had won him the backing of the European football confederation, UEFA, and a raft of powerful figures on the executive committee.

Hayatou had a face like a bloodhound on a tall, athletic frame. The former middle-distance runner and basketball player had loomed over football's high politics for two decades, having become president of CAF in 1988 and joined the executive committee two years later. Hayatou was the son of a local Sultan in Cameroon and he ruled over African football with a regal air. He had pocketed the secret salary, bonuses and allowances offered by Blatter with the same alacrity as his colleagues, but now he was promising to publish FIFA's accounts each year and reveal the pay of the president as part of his sudden enthusiasm for transparency. Hayatou was a heavyweight and he did not pull his punches. 'The image of FIFA is becoming very negative, due to the lack of leadership and illegal practices committed by its president,' he told reporters. Heresy! But his pious stance had won him pledges of support across Europe, and he ruled over Africa's 54 national associations whose bosses held more than half of the votes needed to win in the presidential race. He was a mean opponent to have to beat, and Blatter was still reeling on the ropes from Zen-Ruffinen's attack.

The delegates whispering intrigue to one another in the Grand Hilton on the eve of the vote in May 2002 could have been forgiven for writing the president off when they gathered in the lobby for their nightcaps. But something strange was happening in the hotel that night, and suddenly it seemed as though the game was changing.

From the lobby floor, the chiefs of African football could be seen traipsing one by one up the stairs towards a room on the upper level of the five-star hotel's grand atrium. Each would return after a few minutes, then the next would take his turn. Their votes would be crucial to victory. Would it be Blatter or Hayatou? The football officials lounging in wicker armchairs amid the tropical plants on the atrium floor were intrigued. Where were the Africans going? One or two plucky juniors made it their business to find out, and word quickly began to spread that the officials were heading into the penthouse suite of a powerful figure in world football. They went in one by one and emerged a few minutes later with a discreet smile for the next man in line. Which power-broker was holding private audiences with these crucial voters behind that closed bedroom door?

It was none other than Mohamed bin Hammam.

*

The Qatari billionaire had been fleet of foot in forging alliances when he arrived in Zurich to take his place at the FIFA boardroom table back in 1996, and the organisation's powerful secretary general Sepp Blatter was the main target of his attentions. It was clear for all to see that this stocky Swiss pen-pusher, the darling of president Havelange, was waiting in the wings to seize control as soon as his master stepped aside. Bin Hammam had profited once before by befriending a man on the cusp of power, and he used all the same obsequious charm on Blatter that had won him the trust of Sheikh Hamad back in those early boom years in Doha.

When Havelange finally stood aside in 1998, Blatter went head to head with the then UEFA president Lennart Johansson for the top job in world football, with Bin Hammam behind him all the way. The billionaire Qatari bankrolled Blatter's election campaign, supplied private aircraft to fly the Swiss candidate around the world and lobbied vociferously for his victory. The Swiss man quickly discovered that a friendship with Bin Hammam came with royal privileges, and the golden gates of the Amiri Diwan Palace swung wide open. Blatter became well acquainted with Sheikh Hamad, who even gave him the rare honour of using his royal jet on at least one leg of his campaign tour.

Bin Hammam was with Blatter in Paris in the days ahead of the FIFA congress at which the presidents of all 203* member associations would come together to vote in his first election in 1998. The pair were planning the last few visits on the campaign tour, when news of a disaster reached them. Bin Hammam received a phone call from his wife Fatima to say that his son had been horrifically injured in a car crash back in Doha. The young man was close to death and Bin Hammam should rush home to be with him, she said. Bin Hammam did not go.

---

* Some of the associations were ineligible to take part in the ballot and only 191 votes were cast.

His decision to stay and fight beside Blatter instead of hurrying to his son's bedside was a source of great pride, and he would often recount the story of his sacrifice. 'We were in Paris and we were planning a trip to South Africa in a commercial flight, not belonging to or financed by HRH The Emir of Qatar,' he would reminisce in a speech to FIFA delegates after the election. 'The night before we travelled, I received a frantic phone call from my wife with the shocking news that my son, aged twenty-two, had met with a very serious accident and was fighting for his life and his condition was more towards death and was lying in the intensive care unit in a coma. I should immediately return to Doha. I regretted and apologised to my wife, and told her my son doesn't need me but needs the blessing of God and help of doctors, while it is Mr Blatter who is in need of my help now. So I sacrificed seeing my son maybe for the last time.' Fortunately, Bin Hammam's son survived. But his dreadful accident had given his father a valuable opportunity to prove his slavish devotion to his new master – Sepp Blatter.

When FIFA's member associations came together in Paris to vote in 1998, Blatter had triumphed over Johansson with 111 votes to 80. It was a commanding victory, and the new president of FIFA was hugely indebted to Bin Hammam – and the Emir. The presidential crown came with astonishing privileges. FIFA was getting richer by the second, and the president commanded that vast treasure chest from his plush office on the uppermost floor of the organisation's Zurich headquarters. He pocketed a hefty salary but he would hardly ever have to pick up a bill again, because when he travelled the world his first-class tickets, gourmet meals and five-star penthouses all came free as perks of the job. FIFA was now an organisation with truly global power, controlling a game adored by billions of fans in every corner of the planet, so everywhere Blatter went he would be received like royalty by presidents, prime ministers, kings and queens. Yes, he had a lot to be thankful for.

True, though, that the involvement of his wealthy Qatari friend had not been without its complications. Tawdry rumours of cash-stuffed brown envelopes being shoved under the bedroom doors of the African voters at their hotel in Paris in 1998 had taken some of the sheen off his victory, but Bin Hammam had batted those off by insisting he had simply helped pay the expenses for some of the officials to travel to the vote. Blatter said sums of $50,000 had been given out as cash pre-payments of previously agreed grants to struggling African federations. Then Farah Addo, the vice-president of CAF, had caused a stink by claiming outrageously that Bin Hammam had offered him $100,000 and 18 other officials from the continent had also been offered cash to vote for Blatter. He sued Addo for libel and won: the official had to pay FIFA's freshly re-anointed president 10,000 Swiss Francs and was banned from football for two years for the wicked slur on his name. Asked by FIFA's disciplinary committee to provide any evidence that might justify his claims, Addo had handed over a photograph of Bin Hammam at the centre of a group of African officials who he said had signed a declaration alleging the Qatari had paid them to vote for Blatter. The committee was unimpressed, finding that Addo's claims were baseless and he had 'undermined the interests of football as a whole'.

On the eve of the 2002 election in Seoul, the delegates watching the African voters proceeding into Bin Hammam's penthouse had good reason to ask questions about what was going on behind that closed bedroom door. Everyone in the atrium that night remembered the rumours from Paris. Nothing had come of all those accusations of bribery and brown envelopes, but then FIFA's hilltop headquarters was a place where allegations of that sort came to die.

The morning of the vote, Bin Hammam stood at the entrance to the Grand Hilton congress hall in all his flowing white finery, greeting the delegates with the gracious condescension of a royal host receiving visitors. 'We're going to see fireworks today,' he told one passing official. Sure enough, the continent of Africa swung its weight behind Blatter, and Hayatou's candidacy was demolished 139 votes to 56. Days later, the treacherous secretary general Zen-Ruffinen who had tried to foment insurrection with his claims of financial malpractice announced he would be leaving FIFA on 'mutually agreed terms', and the 11 members of the executive committee who had brought the criminal complaint against their president thought better of their disloyalty and agreed to drop the action. All was well again, and Blatter gazed out over the Zurich skyline from his office once more and looked forward to another four years in charge.

Bin Hammam had snatched victory from the jaws of defeat for his master, and the ambitious Qatari had extracted a promise in return. The president had vowed privately that two terms of office would be enough for him. The next election wasn't until 2006. By then he would be 70 and it would be time to reach for the proverbial pipe and slippers and retire to his home canton in the valley of Visp. Once he had stepped aside, he would do all he could to ensure that Bin Hammam would become his successor, just as Havelange had done for him, and the Qatari's dreams of dominance in world football would at last be fully realised.

The same year Blatter was re-elected, Bin Hammam became the president of the Asian Football Confederation (AFC), overseeing its 45 member associations. This was real power, and Bin Hammam ran the AFC like his own personal fiefdom. It was good enough for now, but it would not keep him happy forever. He wanted the top job.

Blatter was so definite about his promise to stand aside and make way for his ambitious Qatari friend at the next election that he agreed to revise the FIFA statutes to limit presidents to just two terms of office. True to his word, when he returned to Zurich from Seoul in 2002 he called in his officials and told them to begin drafting the new set of rules right away. The new statutes would sharpen up the FIFA constitution in several respects: as well as confining the president to two stints in power, there were new regulations governing the status and transfer of players, and the rights of home nations to field national teams. The proposals were to be put to a vote at an extraordinary congress of FIFA on Bin Hammam's doorstep in Doha in October 2003, and Blatter kept a beady eye on his staff's progress in drafting the new statutes as the deadline approached.

Then, at the last minute, something changed. In a meeting with his aides to discuss the new rules, Blatter suddenly railed testily against the mention of the cap on presidential terms. That proposal was being dropped: 'Bin Hammam can wait,' he announced. The congress went ahead in Doha that October, but the new statutes put before FIFA's member associations concerned only player transfers and the status of national teams. Term limits were nowhere on the agenda. Instead, Blatter asked the congress to extend his current term of office by another year, to 2007. They granted his wish.

It was a bitter blow for Bin Hammam. He told himself he was a fool to have trusted Blatter. That sly old Swiss fox had double-crossed him. After all he had done! But by now the FIFA president was building up a formidable power-base all of his own. He knew how to keep the troops happy, and he splashed FIFA's cash liberally around the globe, bumping up pay and bonuses and writing cheques for hundreds of thousands of dollars to national member associations in the name of football development. He was building a solid coalition of support throughout Asia and Africa, with promises of more and more money as FIFA's coffers bulged. It would be suicide to challenge Blatter head to head when the next election finally came round in 2007 – and anyway, that sort of confrontation was not in Bin Hammam's nature. The softly spoken Qatari would have to put his dreams of becoming FIFA president on ice for at least another eight years, until the next term of office ended in 2011. By then, Blatter would be 75. Surely he would be ready to stand aside and let Bin Hammam take his turn?

Sure enough, when the 2007 election arrived, Blatter was returned unopposed. This time around, he didn't need the same kind of leg-up from his wealthy Qatari allies. But the following year, when Blatter celebrated his tenth anniversary in power, he wrote to Bin Hammam remembering what his friend had done to secure those first victories in 1998 and 2002. 'Everyone knows that in football, very few matches are won by one player alone. Therefore I would like to thank you for your support and above all your tireless work back then. Without you, dear Mohamed, none of this would ever have been possible,' he wrote.

And then Blatter asked his friend to lift his chin and think ahead. 'I have absolutely no doubt that we will look to the future with the same drive and commitment and that we will continue to work together in our duty to put football on the right path for the years to come.'

The servant was back, and the men in the majlis held out their delicate golden cups as he poured out some fresh coffee. Bin Hammam was still talking in his low growl. He recalled all he had done for Blatter, and how Blatter had failed to stand aside as he had promised. The old fox had smoothed the betrayal over with lashings of charm, of course. Bin Hammam was a proud man and the letter of thanks for his loyal service to the president, acknowledging in plain black ink that Blatter would be nothing without him, had also gone some way to consoling his bruised ego. But, he said, after the disappointment in 2007, nothing had prepared him for Blatter's next big move.

The FIFA president had jetted into Doha early in 2008 to visit the Emir and Bin Hammam. On the morning of 11 February, he was taken to see Qatar's Aspire Academy for talented young footballers and he made a characteristically gushing speech for the benefit of the television cameras. Blatter had been critical of Aspire in recent months, and the time had come to smooth things over. The academy had been founded by royal decree to talent-spot and train Qatar's most promising up-and-coming footballers in 2004, but on the eve of the FIFA presidential election in April 2007 it had announced a bolder ambition.

The Aspire Africa Football Dreams project would send 6,000 talent-spotters to screen more than 500,000 boys in 700 impoverished locations across Algeria, Cameroon, Ghana, Kenya, Nigeria, Senegal and South Africa. From each country, 50 would be selected to compete in a week of trials. Three victors from each country would then be flown to Doha for four weeks of training, and the most talented players would be enrolled in Aspire and airlifted out of poverty forever. The rest would be packed off back to Africa.

News of the massive talent hunt had discomfited Blatter. Qatar was attempting to buy up future football stars from across the continent to top up its languishing national team with some real world-class athletes. It was all part of the 30-year plan to turn Qatar into a truly modern country and a sporting powerhouse. But Africa was the foundation of Blatter's influence, thanks to Bin Hammam's generosity in 1998 and 2002, and now those Qataris were trying to park their scooters on his lawn. Handily, there was growing disquiet among human rights campaigners who likened the Aspire Africa programme to a human trafficking scheme, and Blatter was not slow to take advantage. In a written reply to five concerned members of the European Parliament, mysteriously leaked to the *Observer* newspaper, he wrote: 'Their establishment of recruitment networks in these seven African countries reveals just what Aspire is all about. Aspire offers a good example of . . . exploitation.'

Blatter's criticisms had stung badly. But now here he was at the Academy on 11 February, slathering the Emir and the Aspire officials with all the emollient charm he could muster. 'This was a wonderful opportunity to see Aspire and to discuss the important role of sport in youth development and education,' he simpered at the TV cameras. 'The essence of football is education, because it teaches teamwork, discipline and respect for your peers and your competitors. The fact that Aspire has been able to combine both education and sport in one institution is remarkable.'

But, hang on: the assembled reporters were confused. Had Blatter not accused Aspire of exploiting poor African youngsters only months before? Quite the contrary: 'This visit has provided me with the opportunity to learn about the Aspire Africa programme first-hand and I have to say that I am very relaxed and supportive about the project now that I understand how it works. Aspire has a balanced plan for youth development, which supports education and sport for Qatar-based and scholarship students from the developing world. This is making a very important contribution.'

So now all was happy and bright again, and Bin Hammam, Blatter and the Emir could celebrate their renewed friendship over a delicious banquet that evening. It was at the meal that Blatter suddenly played his surprise hand. The election was out of the way; the differences over Aspire settled. Blatter was grateful to Bin Hammam for standing aside in 2007, and he remembered all that his wealthy Qatari friends had done to help him win power in 1998 and stamp out the scourge of Hayatou in 2002. It was time, at last, to give something back. Bin Hammam recalled what Blatter had said to him in front of the Emir at that private dinner as clearly as if it were yesterday, he told his friends in the majlis.

He remembered it because it shocked him. It was impossible. It was insane. The president of FIFA had waited for a pause in the conversation, sipped his drink and leaned back in his chair with a twinkling smile.

'We are going to bring the World Cup to Qatar,' he said.

TWO

Brother Jack, *Der Kaiser* and a Man with a Parrot

The drone of air catching on lowered wing flaps shuddered through the private jet as its speed dipped in preparation for landing. From his cream leather seat in the cabin, Mohamed bin Hammam could see a gleaming citadel of glass, steel and concrete across the waters of the Persian Gulf. He was proud of his home and everything that his fledgling state had achieved. But ever since the Emir had made his wish known, Bin Hammam had been gripped by a gnawing anxiety that touching down in Doha in the summer months did little to dispel.

It was early June 2008, and Bin Hammam was returning after FIFA's annual congress in Australia. He came home with far more reason to be worried than when he had left. Sepp Blatter had caught him off guard when he stood up in front of a packed auditorium at the Sydney Opera House and told more than a thousand delegates that Qatar was one of the countries interested in bidding to host the World Cup. Now the genie really was out of the bottle, and there was no way to put it back. By announcing this private ambition so publicly, the FIFA president had left Bin Hammam with no choice but to do everything in his power to make the Emir's pipe-dream a reality. But how could he do it?

Ever since Blatter had set this hare running at that private dinner in Doha in February, Bin Hammam had tried his best to persuade the Emir that the country risked humiliating defeat if it attempted to achieve what the FIFA president had promised. Qatar was simply too hot; it had no international standing as a footballing country; there was only a small fan base; and, to top it all, it didn't even have the stadiums to accommodate the world's biggest sporting competition. If Qatar entered a formal bid, it was guaranteed only one vote on the executive committee which determined the host for the tournament – his own. What if none of his 23 Exco colleagues backed him with support? Wouldn't that bring humiliation and shame upon Qatar? Would that not be an affront to the country he loved so dearly? But it was all to no avail: the Emir wanted the world's best-loved sporting tournament on his doorstep, and nothing Bin Hammam said could change his mind.

As the cabin doors opened onto Doha International airstrip, Bin Hammam slipped on his signature aviator sunglasses and stepped out into the penetrating white light of the desert sun. Alongside him was the familiar figure of Mohammed Meshadi, his constant companion, gopher and confidant. Meshadi revelled in the high life that came from travelling the world with a multi-billionaire. While Bin Hammam kept his figure trim with discipline and a daily exercise routine, Meshadi was losing the chiselled good looks of his youth and, now several pounds heavier, was sweatily lumbering across the airport tarmac carrying the bags behind his master. Within Bin Hammam's close entourage, Meshadi was known as a lovable bear of a man with a twinkle in his eye. The female assistants liked to gossip girlishly about his playful role as the office flirt, but they were also wary of his quick temper. He had a sharp tongue that he used to keep hotel staff and office juniors on their toes. For Bin Hammam, the short walk to his waiting black Mercedes through the searing midday heat did nothing to diminish his nagging doubt about the size of the task ahead of him.

The car purred through the wide avenues passing through streets which were mostly deserted. Doha is not a city where people go out for a casual stroll in the summer. The sun is too unremitting, too cruel. The temperatures average over 40°C and can often climb into the fifties. It is a city that beats to the pulse of a million air-conditioning systems – a hostile desert environment tamed and made habitable by the best refrigeration devices money can buy. People move seamlessly from expensively cooled homes and offices to the comfort and safety of air-conditioned cars and shopping malls, avoiding the harsh rays as much as possible. Stepping out into the open air is a little like opening an oven door. You are hit by a wave of heavy heat – so thick and tangible you could almost grasp it. In such temperatures, pale skin burns within ten minutes.

They sped along the Corniche snaking around the West Bay with the Persian Gulf shimmering in the glaring daylight, then hit the long wide stretch of Al Rayyan Road heading out to the gated compound on the outskirts of the city where Bin Hammam lived with his two wives, 11 children and numerous grandchildren. The billionaire had plenty of time to reflect on the problem he had been wrestling with on the way. The Qatar summer is a brutal climate. He had only to look at the forehead of his stout travelling companion: beads of sweat had already formed after a short exposure to the sun. Yet modern football is a lung-busting high-velocity game. Players can cover more than six or seven miles in the course of a 90-minute match – much of it in bursts at sprinting pace. If it was too hot even to venture outside, surely it was too hot to play the world's biggest football tournament?

Bin Hammam was proud of the rise of the game in his nation since he had watched the oil workers play along the West Bay waterfront as a boy, but he knew it could never really compete with countries hundreds of times bigger where football was almost a religion. The game had come a long way since his days scuffing around with a ball in the Doha scrublands, and as a pioneer of organised football and the former president of the Qatar Football Association, he could take some credit. But it still had a long way to go.

The top dozen clubs in the Qatar Stars League averaged crowds of 4,000, and that was no more than a club like Yeovil Town in the third tier of English football pulled in. For the price of their tickets to the Khalifa International Stadium, the fans came to see the odd fading professional from Europe or South America paid handsomely to bolster the home-grown teams and slog out the dregs of their career under the desert sun. Qatar's tiny population had not produced one single great player of note. Even the native footballers didn't dare play in the summer cauldron: the Stars League season runs from September, when the worst of the heat has died down. Having grown up listening to raucous choruses of 'You'll Never Walk Alone' in the Scouse theatre of Anfield, Bin Hammam was realistic enough to understand that football in Qatar would struggle to match the passion so famously encapsulated by Liverpool's legendary manager Bill Shankly when he quipped: 'Some people believe football is a matter of life and death. I am very disappointed in that attitude. I can assure you it is much, much more important than that.'

The truth was that Qatar had never even come close to qualifying for a World Cup finals and it was unlikely to do so in the near future. Unless, of course, he succeeded in his mission. The team from the country which hosts the World Cup qualifies automatically. Bin Hammam had been successful in bagging the 2011 Asian Confederation Cup to be hosted in Qatar, a big tournament contested by national teams from the region, but that would be played in January when the mercury dips to a more bearable 20°C. It was a sensible solution, but not one that Qatar could propose when bidding for the World Cup. His nation would have been a laughing stock. Every World Cup finals since the competition began in 1930 had been played in the months of May to July.* It was tradition, and an unfortunate one from Qatar's point of view because June, July and August are its hottest months.

But it wasn't just about history. The world's packed sporting calendar had evolved in such a way that those eight or nine weeks every four years in early summer were the only window to hold the tournament. The powerful professional football leagues, especially in Europe which controlled many of the world's top players, were always bitterly resistant to any change to their seasons, which mostly ran from August to May. Weeks lost at the heart of a season equalled millions of pounds lost in gate receipts and broadcasting money. In addition, the major television companies, which were the lifeblood of a World Cup's income, would fight against any attempt to move the competition to a time of year which clashed with events such as the Winter Olympics or American football's Superbowl. It *had* to be June or July. But it simply could not be: not in Qatar. It wasn't safe for the players or fans. Bin Hammam rubbed his silvered chin and stared pensively out of the car window. His task seemed impossible.

But the Emir wanted the World Cup to come to Qatar and Bin Hammam was the only man in the whole Middle East who stood any chance of making his ruler's dream a reality. He had risen out of the desert and through the ranks of world football to become a member of FIFA's ruling Exco, earning the admiration, loyalty and gratitude of many along the way. That was why the improbable task of persuading his colleagues to let him carry off their crown

---

* Some started at the end of May but were mostly played in June, some were both June and July and only two – the inaugural World Cup in Uruguay and 1966 in England – began and ended in July.

jewels to the desert fell to him. To outsiders it might have looked like a poisoned chalice. But, on the other hand, might this be his big chance to put himself and his family at the very top of Qatari society?

Sheikh Hamad had explained to him that hosting the World Cup was a crucial pillar of his plan to turn Doha into the foremost sport and tourism hub of the 21st century. It was all part of the 30-year strategy devised to shore up Qatar's position for a future without the oil and gas that had brought such riches. Four years previously, Qatar had unveiled a $15 billion scheme to transform the country into a centre for sports, tourism, business and culture, and earlier in 2008 the Emir had pumped another $17 billion into the project.

The plan had just suffered a humiliating setback when Qatar's bid to host the 2016 Olympics was quashed, failing even to make it through to the candidate city shortlist. The bid had proposed to hold the Olympics in October to avoid the summer heat, but this was outside permitted dates for the games. The president of the International Olympic Committee, Jacques Rogge, had also privately told his aides that he did not trust his 102 members to withstand the temptation to succumb to the advances of the super-rich emirate, and Qatar's bid had been nipped in the bud. But no matter, Sheikh Hamad had reasoned. The World Cup was an even bigger, more glittering prize. So now Mohamed bin Hammam had a chance to play a pivotal role in securing his country's future. If he failed, he would bring further humiliation upon his homeland. If he won, his family would bask in the victory forever.

By now Bin Hammam was back home again and the sun had begun to dissolve into a dusty horizon. A shamal was gaining potency and soon a desert sandstorm would be whipping up from the winds gusting in from the north-west coast. It was time to close the shutters and attend to his guests who were beginning to assemble in his majlis. His evening ritual was a reminder of the immense wealth and status which was founded on the hard-won patronage of the royal family. Sometimes men would come seeking money or loans, and Bin Hammam would always listen carefully. In Qatar generosity is a mark of honour and if someone asks you for something you are bound to give it to them. If you admired Bin Hammam's watch, he would take it off his wrist and press it into your palm. The Emir wanted the World Cup and it was in his gift to help deliver it. How could he say no?

The World Cup is a colossus dwarfing even the Olympic Games for television viewing figures. For four weeks in a given summer, the competition stirs up a heady mix of joy, triumph and despair among the billions of people who are sucked in to watch the improbable drama of 22 athletic young men in shorts patriotically chasing a small polyurethane sphere around a neatly mown rectangle of grass. A missed penalty can be a national disaster and a hopeful hoof goalwards can be such stuff as dreams are made of. The names of the heroes are writ as large in popular history as the pioneers who first stepped on the moon. Think of the slender 17-year-old Pelé juggling the ball over the head of a bemused defender in Sweden 1958, the much-imitated Johan Cruyff dragback in Germany 1974, or the barrel-chested Diego Maradona skipping past half the leaden-footed England team to score one of football's greatest ever goals in Mexico 1986.

It is an event of such outrageous glamour that countries will fight tooth and nail to be the hosts in the knowledge that nothing else – except war or natural disaster – would attract such a swarm of the world's television cameras to their doorstep. For a ruler or politician, hosting the competition is a way of bathing in the stardust and advertising the capability, organisation, hospitality and, above all, prestige of their nation. It is the ultimate showy dinner party in your lovely home, with the whole world as your guests. So it is perhaps surprising that the decision on where to hold this great showcase, the tournament to end all tournaments, should rest with just 24 people.

Thankfully, Bin Hammam was well acquainted with all of them. After 12 years at the FIFA boardroom table, he had come to call his colleagues on the ruling Exco his 'brothers in football'. This was one advantage Qatar could count on. The Emir's grand plan was in its early stages, but there were only a few months to get the scheme into shape before it would have to be revealed in detail to the world. FIFA was about to open the bidding process for the hosting of the 2018 and 2022 World Cups, and countries who wanted to enter the race would have to register their formal bids by 16 March 2009. Speculation had been mounting for months as to which nations would throw their hats into the ring. Would England put together a credible bid? Would the United States enter the fray? Unsurprisingly no one had even considered that Qatar might be a contender, until Blatter had let the cat out of the bag in Sydney.

Once the candidates were formally declared in March, Bin Hammam would have just over 20 months to persuade his executive committee colleagues to back his country's unlikely bid. The secret ballot to host the next two tournaments would be held at FIFA headquarters on 2 December 2010. Bin Hammam had an intimate understanding of the murky world of football politics learnt at the heel of his mentor, Blatter. He understood what made his colleagues tick and more crucially how to strike deals with them. It took only junior school maths to calculate what was required for victory. Persuade 13 of his brothers – a simple majority – and the glittering prize would be his. The ballot could take several rounds depending on how many countries had entered the race. After each round, the bid with the fewest votes would be eliminated until one of the contenders notched up the 13 or more ballot papers needed to win. In the event of a tie between two final bids, the FIFA president would have the casting vote.

Despite all the difficulties he faced, Bin Hammam had to admit that Blatter had given him a leg-up. The FIFA president had announced in Sydney that for the first time ever he would propose the rights to host two World Cups should be awarded at the same time, meaning the bidding process for the 2018 and 2022 tournaments would be run side by side. In the same congress speech when he outed Qatar as a potential bidder, Blatter had also revealed that England, Spain, the Netherlands, Russia, Japan, Australia and the United States were potential contenders. These were some fearsome rivals, but all the big guns from Europe would surely rush for the closest prize – the 2018 World Cup – splitting the field and leaving the contest for the 2022 tournament relatively open.

The Exco had also sanctioned a new rotation policy which would prevent a country from bidding to host the tournament if the World Cup had been held in their continent in the previous eight years. Since Brazil had already been selected for 2014, the new rules meant that the whole of South America – one of the world's most football-obsessed regions – would be excluded from both ballots. If all went to plan, Europe and South America, the two continents which had produced all the World Cup-winning teams since the competition began in 1930, would not be in the running for 2022. Also, Qatar had only a handful of small stadiums and the 12-year gap between the vote and the 2022 tournament would give the country time to build the requisite eight or nine world-class venues from scratch. Even more crucially, the dual bidding process paved the way for the novel possibility that bidding nations for the respective tournaments could broker deals to rig the ballot by trading blocs of votes. No one was more adept at that sort of politicking than Bin Hammam. There was a glimmer of hope.

Best of all, the ballot was secret, providing the perfect cover for any backroom deals the bidders cared to strike. Secrecy was part of FIFA's culture. While the world of business had moved into a new era of transparency and accountability since FIFA was formed as a gentlemen's club of seven nations in 1904, it suited the men who ran football to cling onto its status as a mere non-profit association in secrecy-obsessed Switzerland. That country's regulators have the tenderest of touches with such bodies, demanding no taxes and placing only the lightest requirements upon them to file annual accounts. The laws are intended to shelter national yodelling clubs or homeless charities from cumbersome bureaucracy, but FIFA is one of several multi-billion-dollar enterprises which have benefited from the peaceful impunity they afford.

The Swiss association is structured in such a way that it allows Blatter, as president, a free hand to run the administration of world football more or less as he likes. There are two checks on his power: one is the congress of all the member associations, which meets only once a year, and the other is the FIFA Exco. A supine committee suited Blatter very well, and in turn the president appeared more than willing to turn a blind eye to anything which did not directly threaten his own position.

A handful of times each year, FIFA's ruling committee waft into Switzerland on first-class flights and are put up in the elegant splendour of the Baur au Lac Hotel, with its lawns rolling down to Lake Zurich. They are treated like royalty. Since 2006 the meetings have been held in a cavernous chamber in the bowels of FIFA's new headquarters where the participants are shielded from prying eyes by huge black-out blinds. Blatter sits at the head of the table and dictates the agenda while the other 23 men eye each other across a big oblong table in a scene eerily similar to the war room in the Cold War satire *Dr Strangelove*.

Many of the men stay silent and simply nod through Blatter's proposals before heading off for dinner in one of Zurich's numerous Michelin-starred restaurants. These were the people that Bin Hammam would have to win over if he was going to fulfil the Emir's wish and deliver the World Cup on a plate to Doha. He would need to call in favours, cut some deals and grease the palms of those who had influence with the voters. There had been a commercially successful World Cup in Germany two years earlier where the final had been watched by more than 700 million people worldwide. The next tournament in 2010 was going to be held in Africa for the first time, fulfilling a long-standing promise from Blatter, whose grip on FIFA depended on his support from the continent's power-brokers. Then Brazil would take its turn in 2014. After that, everything was up for grabs.

A reader of pure heart might be forgiven for thinking that the decision on where FIFA's prize money-spinning tournament should be held might be judged on the quality of the country's stadiums, transport infrastructure and accommodation for the fans. Surely the bidders ought to be assessed on how capable they are of holding a first-class World Cup? Bin Hammam knew it was far more complicated than that.

Previous ballots have been littered with tales of intrigue and skulduggery. A FIFA Exco member was likely to vote for his own country if it happened to be in the running, although even this was by no means certain. Other members would be swayed by regional loyalties, football politics and alliances offering some kind of advantage. Anyone who spent enough time in FIFA's corridors of power would have heard the stories about large cash sums being offered and accepted in the witching hour before the ballot. A sizeable bung, however, was not always a guarantee of support. Since the ballot was secret, an Exco member could take the cash, then sneak off to vote for someone else. Nobody would be any the wiser. Broken promises and double-dealing were the dark heart of a World Cup ballot.

Bin Hammam was a little distracted that evening as he sipped his coffee in the majlis while his guests lounged on his sofas, glued to the football on the television. Perhaps the task set by the Emir wasn't completely impossible after all, he thought. But he needed to devise a way to win over his fellow Exco colleagues, and fast.

For any World Cup bid to be successful, it had to have the support of FIFA Exco member number one: the president, Sepp Blatter. Given his proposal over dinner with the Emir back in February, and considering all that Qatar had done to help him get elected in 1998 and 2002, Bin Hammam could surely count on Blatter's vote. Or could he? While Blatter had blithely uttered the words 'We are going to bring the World Cup to Qatar,' as though the tournament was entirely within his gift and there might as well be no ballot at all, his duplicity over the 2007 presidential election showed he was a man who could not be trusted.

The FIFA president had the charm of a kindly grandfather and could often seem slightly bumbling in public, with his platitudinous utterances about his 'FIFA family' and the 'beautiful game'. But behind the scenes, Blatter's FIFA lair was a world apart from the football pitch that he so frequently eulogised: that open arena where fair play was prized and cheats were punished with a referee's whistle. This was the ugly game. It was not sufficient to be merely an accomplished football administrator, although Blatter was certainly that. You had to be a prince in the style of Niccolò di Bernardo dei Machiavelli. If this meant surrounding yourself with sycophants, purging your opponents and being all things to all people while quietly taking a course which secured your position, then Blatter was eminently capable of it all. He had told the Emir he wanted to see the World Cup come to Qatar. Did he really *mean* it?

By 2008 the 72-year-old Blatter had been the president of

FIFA for ten years, and the decade at the helm of world football's governing body had taken its toll on his private life. There had been three failed marriages, producing one daughter, and plenty of salacious rumours about his private tastes and habits into the bargain. Blatter had once been president of the World Society of Friends of Suspenders – a campaign group pushing for women to abandon wearing tights and go back to saucier stockings – and he kept a succession of glamorous women dangling on his arm, so far as he had time.

But Blatter didn't have friends as such, and he couldn't make these girlfriends stick for long. It wasn't so much that he devoted his life to his work: his work *was* his life. At weekends he could often be found alone busying himself in his grand office at FIFA's headquarters. So much of his time was spent on all-expenses-paid business for football's governing body that he barely needed to draw his salary – rumoured to be several million – although this, like much of FIFA's opaque accountancy, remains a closely guarded secret, kept from even the Exco. His attention to detail was as legendary as his political charm. Members of the Exco were used to receiving his gushing emails celebrating their birthdays or congratulating them on some recent success, such as re-elections which retained their positions at football's top table.

Keeping his grip on power was what mattered most to Blatter, as Bin Hammam knew to his cost. To hold down the job as world football's top administrator you had to keep the support of the Exco and tame the unruly bunch of federations who each had one vote at the organisation's annual congress. It was not sufficient to send out a few fawning emails. Blatter had learnt from his mentor, João Havelange, that the key to success was to use FIFA's ever-expanding wealth to achieve your own political ends.

In the four years leading up to the 2006 World Cup in Germany, FIFA had raked in more than £2 billion which could be distributed to win favours. Three-quarters of the federations had become financially dependent on FIFA, which paid them $250,000 annually, plus a bonus in World Cup years. Without those payments many of the federations would be bankrupt, so they needed a president who kept the cash flowing. Under Blatter, the handouts were expanded to help exactly the type of smaller nations that shored up his presidency with their votes. FIFA's targeted development schemes such as the Goal Project (chaired by none other than Bin Hammam) and the Financial Assistance Programme doled out sums of up to $400,000 a time, which enabled top football officials in impoverished nations to cement their standing at home by building artificial pitches and sparkling new administrative headquarters. Though these were ostensibly laudable objectives, the payments were also a neat way to win friends and influence people.

At the same time, Blatter used his patronage to reward supporters and keep opponents in plain sight by appointing them to FIFA's myriad committees which met a few times a year to discuss everything from sports medicine to beach soccer. A committee member could easily earn $100,000 and more each year from FIFA by claiming generous day rates and expenses. The Exco was by far the most important committee. Blatter had not only doubled their numbers to two dozen, but he had also secretly introduced the six-figure 'salary' for each member, which was a welcome addition to the wages they earned from their day jobs back home. As accommodating as ever, FIFA made the payments available in cash which could be picked up from the finance office in tax-free Switzerland. It was, of course, pocket money to Bin Hammam. When in Zurich he would often send his chauffeur or Meshadi to pick up envelopes from the finance office containing $10,000 or $20,000 in crisp new bank notes. It was money that could be dispersed to friends and underlings.

The only thing Bin Hammam knew for sure about Blatter was: the old fox would do whatever he needed to cling to power.

Nothing more, and nothing less. So if Blatter continued to believe it was in his political interests to lend his backing to Qatar's World Cup dream, that's just what he would do. If for some reason the wind changed, Blatter's promises of support would diffuse like the dust in a desert shamal.

Bin Hammam mixed easily with his other 'brothers' on the FIFA executive committee. At events in Zurich and around the world, he glided effortlessly from handshake to handshake, his serene countenance revealing little of the steely determination that lay beneath. The Exco saw themselves as swashbuckling globe-trotters with wheelie suitcases: toasting each other's honour in some of the world's finest restaurants; propping up the bar in the early hours at five-star hotels; joshing in the hospitality boxes at the best matches; and snoring loudly in their first-class reclining seats on the flight home. For these grey-haired men, FIFA wasn't just a gravy train, it was a truffle and saffron-infused express with gilded carriages. At least a dozen of them were already millionaires and rest were treated by FIFA as if they were. Bin Hammam knew well which members of the Exco old guard had taken bribes and got away with it. He was also close to the double act who were quietly fleecing FIFA for millions.

When sitting down to plot his strategy, it was useful for Bin Hammam to think of his Exco colleagues in regional blocs, because that was how they often voted. It increased their bargaining power. The Exco were drawn from the four corners of the globe: seven from UEFA, the body which controls European football; three from South America's Conmebol confederation; four from the Confederation of African Football (CAF); three from CONCACAF in central and northern America; one from Oceania which covers the Pacific islands and New Zealand; and four from the Asian Football Confederation (AFC), of which Bin Hammam was president; as well as one from the British home nations and Blatter himself. The cornerstone of his campaign would be to win over the Africans and shore up his support in Asia. That would give Qatar almost two thirds of the votes it needed.

Asia should have been straightforward. Bin Hammam had plenty of leverage over the three other Exco members from the continent as the president of its confederation. There were, however, complications. Three other countries from the AFC were planning to enter the bidding race, and as their leader Bin Hammam owed them at least a semblance of impartiality. Australia, South Korea and Japan all wanted to throw their hats in the ring, so Bin Hammam couldn't be seen to be backing Qatar's bid at all costs at the expense of his other members. He was going to have to tread carefully. South Korea and Japan were represented by members of the Exco, and the very rules that Blatter had proposed to effectively disbar Europe and South America from the 2022 contest had stirred up their hopes. The two countries had jointly hosted a modestly successful World Cup in 2002 and their chances of being allowed to snatch the tournament back so soon were slim, but with the big guns out of the running they thought it was worth chancing their arm for 2022.

The South Korean bid was a political ploy by Chung Mongjoon, who vied with Bin Hammam for the position of richest man on the FIFA Exco. He had been adopted into the family that owned the Hyundai Heavy Industries group, and now aged 57 he was the controlling shareholder of one of the biggest conglomerates in the world. Like Bin Hammam, Chung loved sport as much as business. He had been a champion equestrian in his youth and further distinguished himself as cross-country skier. He had become the head of his national football federation partly out of a passion for the game, but also because he saw it as a stepping stone for greater things: his country's presidency. And the World Cup was to be the spring-board for his political ambitions. In the regional politics of the AFC, Chung was not a supporter of Bin Hammam. The two men were wary of each other and Bin Hammam had his work cut out if he was going persuade Chung to vote for Qatar as a second choice once South Korea dropped out of the contest in the initial rounds, as he intended to make sure it would.

The softly spoken Junji Ogura of Japan was a little easier to deal with. His country had half-heartedly thrown in their hat for the 2022 competition alongside South Korea. Few understood why and, like South Korea, nobody expected them to win. Ogura, aged 70, was a quiet, respectful grandfatherly man with floppy white hair who adored football but was more comfortable sizzling up tempura in his Tokyo home. He was one of the Exco who went to Zurich to nod through Blatter's proposals. Ogura, surely, would do the decent thing once Japan was out of the race and vote for its Asian comrades in Qatar? So Bin Hammam's strategy was to deftly tie his AFC 'brothers' into a pact. He needed to persuade Chung and Ogura that their three countries would vote for the last man standing – out of a regional patriotism. If Bin Hammam could find the votes, that would be Qatar.

There was one Asian member left, Worawi Makudi from Thailand. Bin Hammam was all too familiar with the 57-year-old Makudi, whose reign in Bangkok had survived the ever-changing whims of his country's many political regimes. He was primarily a football administrator but he used his position to create a number of lucrative business schemes in his homeland with the help of his sidekick and chief advisor at the Thai FA, Joe Sim, a gambling baron known to his friends as 'The Casino King'. Makudi kept questionable company, and he was known in world football as 'Mr Ten Percent' – a reference to his personal entitlement for the television rights from some of the friendly matches played by Thailand's national team. He was a close friend of Bin Hammam's, certainly, but he always made sure he got his slice from any deal.

In order to ensure Asia's voters backed Qatar when their own countries were out of the running, Bin Hammam would also have to drum up a groundswell of support for his country's bid across all the continent's member associations who mandated their representatives on the Exco. That wasn't a problem: Asia was his power-base, and he knew how to curry favour here. Many of the continent's national football officials were already on his pay-roll. Sewing up Asia would still get Bin Hammam only four votes, however, including his own. He needed 13 to win. Where were the rest going to come from?

Thousands of miles across the ocean were three of the FIFA Exco's most entrenched members. The trio from South America came as a group and between them they had notched up more than 40 years on the executive committee. In any normal organ-isation with robust ethics, they would have been kicked out of their jobs several years ago, but this was FIFA and Blatter had come to rely upon them.

For 19 years Ricardo Teixeira had been in charge of the foot-ball federation that had produced some of the greatest teams, Brazil. A combative, sturdy man with a shock of white hair now aged 61, he had married into the FIFA family years before when he took the hand of Lúcia Havelange, the daughter of Blatter's predecessor. Under the tutelage of his father-in-law, Teixeira had become a multi-millionaire in a country where vast sections of the population live in shanty huts and child malnutrition is rife. Teixeira had been the subject of several investigations by the Brazilian authorities for creaming off a percentage of sponsorship contracts to his federation, but he had managed to survive. Even the country's most adored footballer, Pelé, had accused him of corruption in a dispute over television rights. But there was one scandal that even he could not escape from: one of the darkest moments in FIFA's history. It also implicated his fellow Exco member Nicolás Leoz, the president of Conmebol, the South American confederation.

At the age of 80, Leoz, a former sports journalist, lawyer and history teacher, made even Blatter look like a sprightly young thing as he tottered into FIFA headquarters for Exco meetings. He had been making the same trip since 1998 and by now had the air of an aloof dictator with bulbous face and raised eyebrows that had fixed over the years into an expression of almost permanent disdain. He was comfortably wealthy from his years controlling football in South America, but he still craved recognition in his dotage. In his home country Paraguay, a football stadium and a beach boulevard had been named after him and his lackeys kept a book of his long list of titles. He collected honours like other people collected stamps. Like his close ally Teixeira, he had taken bribes and got away scot-free. In fact, even as the investigation into the kickbacks began, Leoz was awarded the FIFA Order of Merit for his leadership in football. Blatter knew how to keep the old man happy.

The scandal that engulfed Leoz and Teixeira had followed the collapse of International Sport and Leisure (ISL), a sports marketing company that had been awarded contracts by FIFA in the 1990s to sell broadcast rights to the 2002 and 2006 World Cups. ISL had paid several hundred million dollars but had struggled to turn its contracts into profits and collapsed in 2001. A resulting investigation by Swiss prosecutors found that it had won the contracts by paying out more than $100 million in bribes and commission payments – many to FIFA officials – through front companies in Liechtenstein and elsewhere. Leoz had been paid a $130,000 kickback by ISL, but this was dwarfed by the cash paid out to Teixeira, who pocketed a staggering $13 million.

The payments were sweeteners for the contracts which had been voted through by the FIFA Exco. However, thanks to Switzerland's tenderness towards its associations, the acceptance of bribes like these was not considered an offence under the laws of the land and the two men were never prosecuted. It was not even a breach of FIFA's own rules, because world football's governing body didn't have a code of ethics until three years after the fall of ISL.

In any normal organisation Teixeira and Leoz would have been shown the door, but these men were key power-brokers and personal friends of the president. Blatter had knowledge of ISL's dirty payments as early as 1997 when a $1 million payment slip had ended up in his Zurich office by mistake. The named payee had been none other than his own mentor, the then FIFA president Havelange. At the time, Blatter was just the secretary general and he simply passed the payment on to its intended recipient because, as he later tried to explain, he couldn't understand why the money had been routed through FIFA. He didn't think to ask why Havelange was receiving such a substantial sum from ISL. That was his story and he was sticking to it.

The final member of the Latin triumvirate was Julio Grondona, from Argentina, who was virtually untouchable. He commanded FIFA's finance committee and was therefore one of the handful of men in the world who knew how much Blatter earned. Grondona was the most senior of the vice-presidents on the Exco and was, in effect, Blatter's number two. He founded Arsenal Fútbol Club, an Argentinian league side, in the 1950s, and rose through football administration before taking a seat at the executive committee in 1988. Now aged 76, he had a weak heart but that did little to subdue his sharp tongue. Grondona was a politically astute operator who played to the gallery in Buenos Aires by using every opportunity to display his hatred of the English over the 'occupation' of the Malvinas (Falkland Islands). They certainly wouldn't be getting his vote and neither would the United States bid for 2022, because they were England's stooges as far as Grondona was concerned. In any other organisation he would have been sacked for racist comments he had made years earlier. In 2003 he told a journalist: 'I do not believe a Jew can ever be a referee at this level. It's hard work and, you know, Jews don't like hard work.' He repeated his anti-Semitism later, saying: 'Jews don't like it when it gets rough.' FIFA's public stance had always been that it did not tolerate any form of racism, and yet Grondona's jaw-dropping remarks passed unpunished in Zurich.

For Bin Hammam, the South Americans were a challenge which would require all his skills of diplomacy and deal-making. These men were no push-over. What he did know, however, was that both Teixeira and Grondona had problems at home. Brazil was struggling to find the funds to update its stadiums for the 2014 World Cup and the Argentine football league was in a financially parlous state. Might this provide a way in?

You would have to fly 5,000 miles from Buenos Aires to the pearl fishing island paradise of Tahiti in the middle of the South Pacific to find the next Exco member on Bin Hammam's list. The lonely Oceania confederation had claim to just one seat on the Exco, and the current incumbent was the former French league football player Reynald Temarii. At meetings in the Zurich war room, the suave, bronzed Tahitian stood out from the rest of the Exco not least because there wasn't a single grey hair on his head. At 41, he was the youngest member by nearly a decade, having joined the world of high football politics just four years earlier. He may have worn a Hawaiian shirt on occasion, but Temarii was no buffoon. He had returned to Tahiti after finishing his playing career with FC Nantes and became first an advisor to the president, then a minister for youth sport and development. At FIFA he was one of the executive committee's eight vice presidents and frequently rubbed shoulders with Bin Hammam as they both held senior positions on the body that doled out Goal Project cash. What

Temarii needed more than anything was development money to improve the Pacific islands' threadbare playing facilities.

The Europeans were an entirely different proposition for Bin Hammam to ponder. Their federations were mostly rich and they didn't vote as a pack as some of their colleagues around the world were apt to do. They would have to be dealt with one by one. There was a new rising star at the head of European football, and his name was Michel Platini. The Frenchman had enjoyed a stellar career as a footballer, with many rating him as one of the top ten players of the 20th century. He was the type of footballer every fan loved to watch: effortlessly agile with the ball at his feet and capable of conjuring a pass or a shot which was simply sublime. He was a lover of art, a *bon viveur* and perhaps surprisingly, for a man of such rich athletic talents, a smoker. He had played in Italy for one of the great Juventus teams and once wryly observed: 'A Frenchman would drive two hundred kilometres for a good vineyard; an Italian would drive two hundred kilometres for a good game of football.' Platini was undeniably in the French camp. After hanging up his boots in 1987, he managed the national team for four years before moving into football administration as an organiser for the 1998 World Cup in France and joined the Exco in 2002.

It was a charmed life which just kept on getting better. By 2008 he had served as the president of UEFA for a year, after pulling off an improbable and narrow victory against the 16-year incumbent Lennart Johansson – largely due to the efforts of his new patron, Sepp Blatter. He did it with typical aplomb, announcing to an assembled crowd of voters: 'My hair is gone; I've got a big belly; it's time to be president.' Platini seemed unstoppable and a clear candidate for the ultimate job, the FIFA presidency. So where would that leave the Qatar bid? Platini was not the sort of man who would want to see his cherished game played in 40-degree heat. But he was known to be close to the French president Nicolas Sarkozy, who had made it clear he was open to forging alliances with oil-rich Qatar. Bin Hammam might have found his pressure-point.

The other big name from Europe was an equally tough nut to crack, Franz Beckenbauer. The former German footballer would also feature on most people's top ten list of the great players of the last century. While Platini never made it to a World Cup final, Beckenbauer had won the competition as both a player and a manager. His achievements were without parallel. In his playing days he controlled games by sweeping behind the defence, organising those around him and reading the play intuitively. Upright and elegant, he would choose his moment to stride up the pitch in a manner that suggested he knew he was in charge. The Germans called him '*Der Kaiser*' and he had retained his unshakeable self-confidence when he entered management with his national team, and later Bayern Munich.

Beckenbauer was better placed than most to understand the nature of an Exco World Cup vote because he had seen it at first hand when he led his nation's bid for the 2006 competition. It was a highly controversial ballot swung by a typical piece of Blatter chicanery. The president had promised the Africans that the World Cup would come to their continent when he was first campaigning to lead FIFA in 1998. It was one of his tactics to win the continent's support, and he therefore publicly supported the South African bid against Beckenbauer's Germany. However, when it came to the secret ballot for the 2006 World Cup hosts at Zurich in July 2000, Blatter was said to have reneged on his promise. Michel Zen-Ruffinen – the FIFA secretary general who turned on Blatter in 2002 – had collected the votes from each member and later revealed that the president had actually put his tick against the name of Germany, not South Africa. Zen-Ruffinen reasoned that this was because FIFA was already wedded to a financially uncertain World Cup in Japan and South Korea in 2002 and Blatter did not want this to be followed by another high-risk tournament in Africa – despite his pledges during his election campaign.

The vote on the 2006 tournament was closer than anyone could have imagined. Going into the final round, South Africa and Germany were tied at 11 votes each, and England was about to drop out as its support had been cut to two. Then a curious thing happened. Charlie Dempsey, the Exco member from New Zealand, went awol. He had been mandated by his federation to vote for South Africa and did so in the opening two rounds. Then in the final round he had a sudden change of heart and abstained. Germany won 12 votes to 11, and best of all they had done so in a manner which meant that Blatter would not have to reveal his hand by using his casting presidential vote. Quite what caused Dempsey's 11th-hour capitulation has never been discovered, but he was forced to resign by his Oceania committee two days later. The sorry saga did, however, present Bin Hammam with an opportunity. Qatar had given its backing to the German World Cup bid over South Africa and Bin Hammam, ever the deal-maker, had played a crucial role in rounding up the Asian votes Beckenbauer needed to win the ballot. The Germans owed Qatar a debt of gratitude and it was time to call in the favour.

Four of the other European members of the Exco were representing countries which were in the running for the 2018 competition. Although it was against the rules, Bin Hammam could offer his vote to them if they agreed to back Qatar for 2022. England were pushing hard for 2018 after losing out on the 2006 World Cup and they were well equipped in stadiums and infrastructure to host the tournament. But they were not popular among the Exco. They clung to the arrogant belief that England was superior as the home of football and they were loathed by grandees such as Grondona.

They also had a fundamental weakness: their own Exco member (who joined the committee as one of the British home nations, rather than as a member of UEFA), Geoff Thompson, was only half-heartedly promoting their bid. Thompson, aged 63, was as straight as they come: he had been a referee and now worked part-time as a magistrate. He shunned the limelight, preferring the peace and quiet of his Chesterfield home. Behind his back, the England bid called him 'the blazer' and were never quite sure if even they could count on his vote because he seemed so diffident. He had gone from slicing the half-time oranges for his village team to running the Sheffield and Hallamshire FA in the 1960s. Following a spell as general manager at Doncaster Rovers, he climbed his way up the English FA to become its chairman in 1999. Thompson, however, stood down from this role in early 2008 to make way for a favourite of the Labour government, the former minister Lord Triesman. It left him freer to concentrate on his roles at UEFA and of course the Exco, which he had joined two years previously. Thompson presented Bin Hammam with a problem: he was a stickler for the rules, and wouldn't England be more inclined to vote for their big ally, the USA?

Perhaps he had to look to Spain, where a football revolution was taking place thanks to the foresight of the urbane Exco member Ángel María Villar Llona. As head of the country's association, Villar Llona had put in place a youth training system decades earlier which was now bearing fruit. Only that summer Bin Hammam had been present at the Ernst-Happel-Stadion in Vienna to watch Villar Llona spring to his feet as Fernando Torres scored the winning goal for Spain against Germany in the final of the 2008 European Football Championship. It was a rebirth for a country of perennial footballing underachievers who could now pass their way through all before them thanks to the array of young talent which had matured together into an outstanding team.

Villar Llona, aged 58, had been an accomplished midfielder

himself, representing his country on 22 occasions. He studied law after leaving football and was celebrating his 20th anniversary as the head of the Spanish FA. The handsome Spaniard was now fronting his country's World Cup hopes and was negotiating with Portugal to agree a joint Iberian bid which would be culturally and linguistically attractive to the three South American voters. If Villar Llona could pull that off, he would have four votes at his disposal. Of all the European contenders, he had to be the prime target for any vote-swapping deal.

The chubby Belgian doctor Michel D'Hooghe offered an alternative if he could be persuaded that the temperatures in Qatar were not too threatening to players' health. D'Hooghe's home country had made a partnership with Holland and was styling itself as the green bid for the 2018 World Cup – which was slightly misplaced as hardly anyone on the FIFA Exco gave a hoot about environmental issues. Bid teams on bicycles were not going to cut much ice with men more used to chauffeur-driven limousines. The Low Countries bid was unloved and needed votes. Even D'Hooghe would stay at a distance from his nation's well-meaning campaign. While Villar Llona led the Spanish bid from the front, D'Hooghe made it clear he supported his country, but did not get involved.

The jovial 62-year-old loved nothing better than to don his short-brimmed Belgian hat and entertain friends with his accordion. He had become smitten with football as a child when he first walked on to the grass of the Klokke Stadion in his home city of Bruges dressed as a smiling bear mascot in blue and black football kit. After medical school, he was appointed the club's first doctor – a job that launched him on an illustrious career in sports medicine as, among other things, an expert in groin strain. At the same time he took charge of the Belgian FA, and for the last 20 years he had been a fixture on the Exco. As the FIFA medical expert, he understood better than anyone else how extreme heat sapped the performance of elite athletes. Bin Hammam scrawled a question mark against his name.

Russia was a dark horse. Sport had been an instrument for bringing prestige to the state since the days of communism, but prime minister Vladimir Putin was not a football fan. The country's football chiefs were planning to bid for the 2018 World Cup, but would its leader throw his weight behind their efforts and give them the backing of a state apparatus which had tentacles all over the world?

In 2008, Russia's FIFA Exco member was Vyacheslav Koloskov, a long-standing sports functionary who cut deals on the Exco based on national interest, but the leadership of the bid had been handed to Vitaly Mutko, one of Putin's cronies from his days as mayor of Saint Petersburg. It was rumoured that Mutko would take Koloskov's seat on the Exco and that might be a signal of Putin's intent. Qatar and Russia could not have been more different in size and yet they had certain things in common. Both were autocracies with strong rulers whose positions were cemented by an accident of geology which made them the world's biggest exporters of liquefied natural gas. To secure the vote of the Russian Exco member, whoever it might be, Bin Hammam would have to persuade Putin to back Qatar, and perhaps his country's shared gas interests might be a way of getting his foot inside the door of the Kremlin.

The other UEFA Exco members were Marios Lefkaritis from Cyprus and Şenes Erzik from Turkey. The Cypriot entrepreneur Lefkaritis was an unknown quantity when it came to the World Cup vote. He had been a reliable stalwart on UEFA committees for many years, but at the age of 62 was only just getting accustomed to the machinations of the FIFA Exco following his election the year before. He had been born in the port of Limassol, Cyprus's second biggest city, and had made a fortune through the oil industry. His family's company, Petrolina, owned dozens of petrol stations all over Cyprus and supplied fuel to the shipping and aviation industries, with subsidiary firms owning land and property developments across the island. Bin Hammam could not predict how amenable Lefkaritis would be to a back-room deal before the World Cup ballot, but one thing was for sure: when it came to oil and property, he knew how to do business.

Erzik, aged 66, was a multilingual economics graduate who had worked in the pharmaceutical industry and the United Nations before being hired by the Turkish FA. From his office among the minarets of Istanbul, he used his marketing expertise to transform Turkish football and was awarded posts with UEFA in 1994 and then the FIFA Exco two years later. At the time Turkey was the only Muslim country with a representative on the Exco besides Qatar. It was something Bin Hammam could build on.

And then there was the little and large partnership that had been quietly skimming the cream off the FIFA coffers for years: Jack Warner, the president of CONCACAF, and his gargantuan secretary general, Chuck Blazer. CONCACAF had three seats on the Exco, and in any normal ballot you would have expected the trio to pledge their support to the USA, their confederation's only candidate for the 2022 World Cup. But the small group of men was led by Warner, and that meant anything was possible.

The former history teacher from Trinidad and Tobago was already one of the most notorious figures in Blatter's 'FIFA family'. He wielded disproportionate power as president of CONCACAF, presiding over an organisation that had a fifth of all votes at the FIFA congress. Warner's fiefdom included three countries from North America and seven from Central America, but his strength lay in the 31 Caribbean islands which each had a football federation no matter how small they happened to be.

The great footballing nations, such as Brazil (population 200 million) and Germany (80 million), each had one vote at FIFA congress. So did tiny Montserrat with a population of just 5,000 people which formed part of Warner's empire. The joke was that every time a tiny atoll pierced the warm blue-green waters of the Caribbean, Warner would give it a football federation.

Warner was a natty figure in a shiny suit with short lapels. He was quick to grin and crack a joke and played the part of the lovable rogue to perfection. But beneath all the zap and charisma, this was a rapacious opportunist who would bully and browbeat friends and enemies alike in order to get what he wanted. Warner had several money-making schemes, but the most lucrative was the cash he was looting from FIFA using his pet project, the Dr João Havelange Centre of Excellence.

The centre, on the outskirts of Warner's home city of Port of Spain, had lofty ambitions. It was, according to its website, a 'hub of football education, expertise and skills training, catering to the needs of players, both club and national teams, sports officials, referees and other stakeholders, with a mission to achieve a sustained level of excellence in every aspect of the game'. It was also open for weddings, birthdays, rock concerts and Miss Universe contests, in fact, anything that generated cash.

Over the years Warner repeatedly bombarded FIFA with requests for money to develop the centre. FIFA duly obliged, pumping millions into Warner's scheme almost every time he asked. His secret, which he never let on, was that he owned the land the centre was built on, and the CONCACAF bank accounts FIFA were regularly filling were also under his complete control. FIFA never enquired about what happened to the money. The votes Warner controlled at congress were too important. Instead, Blatter tried to keep his Caribbean friend happy, offering patronage in the form of membership of various FIFA committees to 72 officials from Warner's confederation.

Warner's co-conspirator was one of the most conspicuous people on the FIFA Exco. His American comrade, Blazer, was as wide as he was tall. With his perfect rotundity and curly white beard, CONCACAF's secretary general had all the appearance of a cash-crazed Father Christmas. He ran the confederation's operations from a grace-and-favour penthouse in Trump Tower: one of the most expensive pieces of real estate in New York, with prized views over Central Park. Blazer was highly intelligent, but also eccentric. Joggers would turn their heads to watch this man-mountain taking his daily 'exercise' around Central Park on a Segway with a parrot on his shoulder. Even stranger was the fact that the parrot had been trained by Blazer's ex-wife to hurl abuse at him in her own voice. Mrs Blazer had taken temporary custody of the bird after the pair had separated, and spent a year training it to spit out choice insults which she felt summed up her ex-husband's many defects before sending it back to give him a piece of her mind. Blazer was still fond of his parrot which he kept in a giant gold aviary in his penthouse office, but he wished it would stop squawking 'You're a dope' at him during business meetings.

Warner and Blazer came together as a partnership in 1990 when the Trinidadian made an audacious challenge for the presidency of CONCACAF. Warner won against the odds thanks to the support of Blazer, who was an official in the United States soccer federation at the time. Shortly afterwards, Warner made Blazer CONCACAF's secretary general and the pair set about making money. In the ten years before 2008, Blazer misappropriated many millions of dollars from CONCACAF in unauthorised commissions, fees and rent expenses for his apartments in Trump Towers and Miami. Even his giant Hummer was fully paid for by the football organisation.*

In the contest for the 2006 World Cup, Warner and Blazer,

* CONCACAF's Integrity Committee Report of Investigation, 18 April 2013.

along with the third CONCACAF member of the Exco, had initially backed England. They soon proved inconsistent. After voting for England in the first round, they switched their support to South Africa, effectively ending the English bid's chances. Since then, a new third member had joined the Exco. Rafael Salguero Sandoval, a 62-year-old former football player turned solicitor from Guatemala, was a vice chairman of CONCACAF and had been on its executive committee for 22 years. Salguero had been unaware of the huge amounts of money being siphoned off by Warner and Blazer. Bin Hammam was not sure how this new third member would vote, but the way into CONCACAF was undoubtedly through Warner.

The man from the Caribbean was key, and thankfully he described Bin Hammam as 'my only brother in football'. The Qatari was already working hard on locking down Warner's support. A couple of weeks earlier in May 2008, he had emailed his staff at the AFC to ask for Warner's bank account details so he could wire over $250,000 – a sum 25 times the average wage in Trinidad and Tobago at that time. Days earlier, just ahead of the Sydney congress, Warner had been taken to China on Bin Hammam's private jet in his role as the Qatari's 'consultant' on a project to raise the standards of football across Asia. The men were touring Beijing when a massive earthquake hit the Sichuan region, hundreds of miles away. Warner would later claim that the cash from Bin Hammam was to recompense him for 'losses' he had suffered during the natural disaster. He never explained quite what he was carrying in his luggage that could possibly have been worth such a huge round-figure sum – unless, of course, it was a suitcase full of cash.

Last but a very long way from least, there was Africa, Bin Hammam's political heartland – the continent he had learned to navigate extremely well on the campaign trail for Sepp Blatter.

Here, he would have to build bridges with Issa Hayatou, the man he had helped trounce in the FIFA presidential elections six years earlier. For 20 years the French-speaking Hayatou had been the dominant force in African football as the president of CAF, and had served on the Exco for longer than Bin Hammam. He cut an imposing figure in his flowing white boubou – an impression accentuated by his oke headdress which made him look even taller than his 6ft 5in frame. His vote would come with conditions. He would want to know what Qatar could do for Africa and his home country Cameroon. But Hayatou was not unassailable. Bin Hammam, alongside Blatter, had ruthlessly cut his support in half in 2002 and could do so again. If he wanted to stay at the helm of African football, it might be easier for Hayatou to go with the flow this time, especially if his country and his continent stood to benefit.

In contrast to Hayatou, two of the three other members of the Exco from Africa had been voted onto the committee only the previous year. Jacques Anouma, 56, was a quick-witted former accountant for a French airline who had prospered in the Ivory Coast under the ruthless dictator Laurent Gbagbo. In fact, he and Gbagbo were so close that Anouma had been the country's financial director for years while at the same time running his nation's football federation.

The other newcomer to the Exco was the squat Amos Adamu, the president of the Western African football union, who clearly had the Midas touch. He had grown rich as a football administrator in Nigeria, owning at least three homes, including one in London. His critics had blamed him for the millions of dollars that were lost following the 1999 World Youth Championships and the 2003 All Africa Games, but the accusations went no further. Bin Hammam resolved to invite all three men to Doha to show them what his gleaming city had to offer. The fourth African Exco incumbent, Slim Chiboub of Tunisia, was widely expected to be replaced at the next election in 2009, with the former Egyptian footballer Hany Abu Rida looking like a strong contender for the seat. Bin Hammam wasn't going to waste much time on Chiboub until he knew who was going to be in position in December 2010, when the World Cup vote would be decided.

Winning the support of the four Africans was crucial because they were expected to vote as a bloc. That would get Bin Hammam a third of the 12 votes on top of his own which he needed to win for Qatar. CAF was a tight-knit federation under Hayatou, and its member associations knew how to make their voices heard. Bin Hammam knew that if he was to sew up the African voting bloc, he was going to have to drum up a groundswell of support among officials from across the continent who would lean on their Exco members to back Qatar's bid. His campaign in Africa would be two-fold: he would deal directly with the voters and he would buy up an overwhelming coalition of support from across their confederation to make it impossible for them not to support Qatar. He had done it before in Africa, and he would do it again. This was to be the first phase of his campaign and he was going to start right away.

Three

Bagmen and Brown Envelopes: The Campaign Begins

It was bright and early in the morning in Kuala Lumpur, and already the humidity was so high that walking outside felt like stepping into a steam room. This drenching tropical climate was always a shock to Mohammed Meshadi's system, accustomed as he was to the dry desert heat of Doha, and his closely tailored suit wasn't nearly as cool as the loose white dishdasha he wore when he was at home. Anyone strolling under the shady palms outside the Asian Football Confederation's headquarters on that morning in early June 2008 might have spotted the perspiring figure of Bin Hammam's trusted gopher taking the last few drags on his cigarette before heading through the entrance of the glass-fronted building. Meshadi was there on an important errand. He was collecting $200,000 in rolls of crisp dollar bills, withdrawn from AFC accounts controlled by Bin Hammam.

The AFC president's bagman was a favourite among the secretaries who administered his expense accounts, and they looked forward to his visits. Even in his fifties Meshadi still had plenty of rakish appeal. He was almost always in tow when the president swept into the AFC building, and he liked to keep the girls who held the purse strings sweet. He would pop by their desks to feed them chocolates over their mid-morning coffee break or deliver cups of fresh noodles at lunch time. Meshadi wasn't a classic dish but he was broad-chested, slightly thicker round the middle than he had once been, but still a strapping figure of a man. He wore his collar open under his royal blue suit and his hair slicked back. The secretaries liked to giggle and gossip about him. So they were happy to count out $200,000 as he grinned and mopped his forehead on that steamy June morning. He joked and chatted with them as they noted in their ledger the reason he told them he needed the money. The rolls of dollar bills were required, he said, to provide 'cash advances for CAF guests'.

Bin Hammam ran the Asian confederation like an extension of his private office, so he had no qualms about draining its coffers of cash when the occasion demanded it – and this was a special occasion indeed. The Qatari football chief had invited the leaders of 25 football associations from the Confederation of African Football to stop off in Kuala Lumpur on an all-expenses-paid junket on their way back from FIFA's annual congress in Sydney. Days earlier, Sepp Blatter had announced in his speech to delegates that Qatar wanted to bid for the World Cup, so now it was vital that Bin Hammam made a favourable impression on his guests. He knew well that to secure the support of Africa he would have to start from the bottom up, winning the hearts and minds of the federation chiefs across the continent by filling their pockets. That way they would bring their influence to bear on the continent's four voters through the key committee that ran CAF. Phase one of that campaign began today.

Once Meshadi had picked up the cash, he headed up to the president's office to confirm the last few details before the guests began arriving. As they touched down throughout the day, the African officials were picked up from Kuala Lumpur International Airport in air-conditioned limousines and chauffeured to their five-star hotel. They were given envelopes stuffed with spending money and presented with gifts, before being greeted by Bin Hammam. That night, they dined sumptuously on Malaysian specialities alongside their Qatari host. The next day, they were treated to a trip to the historic port of Malacca, where they could stroll along the waterfront, spend their rolls of dollars at the antique shops along the bustling Jonker Street, and even pray for their future prosperity in the richly gilded Cheng Hoon Teng temple, if they were so inclined.

Bin Hammam was charm personified as he moved among his guests. The Qatari was not a garrulous host, preferring to listen than to talk, but he exuded the quiet charisma of a man entirely in command of his situation. He had that penetrating ability possessed by certain powerful people to make each man feel like the only person in the room when fixed with his attention. Bin Hammam had no difficulty in making each of his guests feel special. But he needed a fixer who could talk straight to them. Someone who mixed naturally with the Africans, understood them and spoke their language. Someone who he could take into his confidence, besides Meshadi. Fortunately, the perfect candidate for the job was already at hand.

One of Bin Hammam's key roles at FIFA was to chair the Goal Bureau committee which doled out cash to the less wealthy federations for projects such as building training pitches and administration headquarters. Between 2001 and 2007, the Goal Bureau had employed a Paris-based freelancer called Amadou Diallo to monitor the projects in Africa. A small ebony-skinned man with darting eyes, Diallo had grown up in the West African country of Guinea and spoke fluent French, the most widely used language among the continent's member associations in the continent. He had friendships across the African football fraternity and crucially knew most of its Exco members. Bin Hammam had put Diallo on the payroll as his go-between, and this was his first outing in the World Cup campaign. The fixer surpassed himself: glad-handing the guests as they arrived; laughing and joking with the group as they explored Malacca; taking each man aside for a private word. Diallo's speciality was finding out what the Africans wanted and making sure they got it.

After the delegates left, Bin Hammam ordered his finance staff at the AFC to transfer direct payments to Anjourin Moucharafou, the president of the Benin FA, as well as three other delegates, without saying what the money was for. Moucharafou was key because he was a member of the powerful CAF executive committee, chaired by its president Issa Hayatou, which would play a crucial role in determining how the continent's four voters would cast their ballots.

The junket had exactly the desired effect, and emails of thanks flooded into Bin Hammam's inbox in the days and weeks after everybody flew home. He had not yet shaken off his trepidation about the scale of the task before him, but the gushing gratitude of his African brothers must have gone some way to steadying his nerves. Mohammed Iya, chairman of the Cameroon FA and a close associate of Hayatou, wrote: 'We have really enjoyed the trip and all your staff at all the levels have just been wonderful. All of you left no stone unturned to assure the success of our stay in Kuala Lumpur.' The general secretary of the Ivory Coast FA, whose president, Jacques Anouma, was a key Exco voter, also wrote to thank the Qatari for his hospitality, extending particular gratitude to Diallo. He said he would describe the welcome he had received to Bin Hammam's 'friend' Anouma. Already, Bin Hammam had won the gratitude and loyalty of three men close to the World Cup voters whose support he needed.

Even the formidable Izetta Wesley, then the Liberian FA president who was known to her colleagues as the 'Iron Lady', was uncharacteristically gushing in her appreciation. 'I had a wonderful time and was previledge to sea that part of the world,' she wrote in an email to Bin Hammam after returning to Monrovia. 'I will always cherish these memories. Thanks for all the beautiful gifts.'

The campaign had got off to a flying start. But soon after the delegates returned home, a story broke in the football press which upset Bin Hammam's equilibrium. People had started to gossip about the generous hospitality laid on for his African visitors on their way home from the Sydney congress. They remembered the rumours about how he had sweetened the continent's voters during Blatter's presidential campaigns in 1998 and 2002, and this looked like the beginnings of a similar strategy. What was Bin Hammam up to? Was he laying the groundwork for a FIFA presidential bid of his own, as the internet rumours suggested? But the next presidential election was three years away, and Bin Hammam's sole focus right now was on doing everything necessary to win the World Cup for his Emir. Blatter's support in this was more important than anything else, and if he felt threatened he would surely go on the attack. Bin Hammam had to put the story straight, so he issued a statement on the AFC website. 'It is very clear that I support Mr Blatter who is the current president of FIFA. I do hope that he runs for another term in 2011 and I will support him as I always do,' he insisted. 'I believe that all AFC Member Associations are on the same page with me on this.'

It worked. Within two hours, another grateful email appeared in Bin Hammam's inbox, this time from Zurich. 'Dear Brother, Very good News! Thank you for your trust and confidence. With my best regards, Joseph S. Blatter.' Bin Hammam wrote back: 'My dear President and Brother, Like in the past, you may count on my commitment and loyalty for the present and in the future. Always by your side, Mohamed.'

Bin Hammam had been the overlord of the Asian Football Confederation since 2002, and he ruled with the proverbial iron fist in a velvet glove. At the head office in Kuala Lumpur, he surrounded himself with an adoring coterie of female assistants who did his bidding unquestioningly, but there were others in the organisation who took a more hostile view of their president's autocratic style. For the most part, Bin Hammam's manners were impeccable, but there was no doubt that he was high-handed. He insisted that staff call him 'Your Excellency' or 'Mr President' rather than just plain 'Mohamed'. He was softly spoken, courteous and always over-generous but, if you crossed him, he could also be cruel. He talked down to people in meetings. He refused to have his methods questioned. Sometimes he scolded grown men as if they were naughty schoolboys. His detractors muttered that he was a pedant and a control freak. He was only meant to be an elected figurehead as far as they were concerned, but he ran the AFC like a fiefdom.

Bin Hammam was used to wielding absolute power over the workings of an organisation, having been the sole owner of his multi-billion-dollar construction company, Kemco, since 1985. Back in Doha, he commanded a workforce of thousands of migrants who toiled away dutifully under the desert sun by day and retreated at nightfall to the labour camps where they lived on the outskirts of the city. As their employer, Bin Hammam held their passports so they couldn't return to their home countries – usually Bangladesh, India or Nepal – unless he chose to let them. His power over the Kemco workforce was absolute, and the billionaire ran the AFC like he ran his business. He never relaxed his grip on any aspect of the confederation's management. He acted as president, chief executive, finance director and general secretary all at once, leaving the officials who were paid to perform those roles wringing their hands in frustration. His detractors at the AFC said he had no right to ride roughshod over the work of his colleagues. Who did this jumped-up Qatari think he was? Though maybe they were just jealous that they weren't part of the inner sanctum who really knew what was going on in the secrecy of the president's office.

Bin Hammam had done many laudable things since his election in 2002. He had launched the Vision Asia programme to pump millions of dollars into football development, education and training in each of the 46 member associations. He had transformed the AFC from a financial wreck into a decent money-maker by stepping up the sales of marketing and TV rights. At the same time, however, there were some strange things going on at the confederation under his watch. The president used the organisation's funds interchangeably with his own, moving sums amounting to millions of dollars in and out of his sundry-expense account so regularly that his finance staff struggled to keep track. He often generously topped up the football development funds from his own coffers, but then he took money out of the AFC too, and it wasn't always clear why, or where it was all going. It was an unorthodox approach to running a football confederation, and Bin Hammam needed to know he could trust the people administering his affairs.

The president kept his inner circle tight: there were only three people he really took into his confidence at the AFC. First, there was Jenny Be Siew Poh: a sweet-natured woman in her mid-thirties who worshipped her boss. She was pretty and petite with fine cheekbones and a pointed chin, and she wore her silky black hair in a girlish bob. Be was divorced and raising two young sons on her own. Sometimes life was tough, but she cheered herself up by baking treats like pineapple upside-down cake, banana loaf, lemon meringue pie, blueberry muffins or peanut butter cookies, which she often brought into the office to share. You had to be careful not to mistake her sweetness for weakness. She was the director of the president's office at the AFC and his closest aide in Kuala Lumpur. The head of the inner sanctum, she defended her master like a tigress.

Then there was Amelia Gan, the AFC's director of finance. Gan was in charge of all the confederation's accounts, including the president's. She oversaw the movement of millions in and out of the AFC for Bin Hammam: it was she who had transferred the money to the four African officials after their visit to Kuala Lumpur in June. Like Be, she revered the president and her loyalty to him was unshakeable. If the president's office director was small, his finance director was tiny. Gan was bright-eyed with round cheeks and a pert little heart-shaped face. Her black hair tumbled over delicate shoulders and she had a winsome way of tilting her head to one side and smiling up through her lashes. But she too was a force to be reckoned with when it came to protecting Bin Hammam's interests inside the AFC.

The third woman in Bin Hammam's closest circle was Michelle Chai, the AFC's assistant general secretary and director of the Vision Asia football development programme. Chai was different from the other two: sharper and more boyish with a quick tongue and an impish smile. She wore her floppy hair short and sported round spectacles. She didn't bother with makeup or jewellery and she was happy coming to work in her sloppy AFC polo-shirt, or a blazer if she was out on official business. Chai was a skilled administrator and a genuine football nut. She loved the game almost as much as she loved Bin Hammam, and for that he respected her. The AFC's assistant general secretary was a strong woman and she didn't take any nonsense. But, when it came to Bin Hammam, she was just as hopelessly devoted as Be and Gan.

All three women adored him, and vied for his attention and approval. They spent much of their day chatting to one another over electronic messages, exchanging titbits of gossip, joking about Meshadi or sometimes scratchily competing over who was closest to the president. Mostly their messages were friendly and light-hearted, but at times the rivalries within the group became clear. They were suspicious of each other. They got jealous. And sometimes tittle-tattle swirled around the office which exacerbated the tension.

'Since we are being honest and in a confessional mood,' Be wrote to Chai one May morning, 'I was not jealous of you but was uncomfortable when it seems you were doing my job. I must admit, I was convinced by the rumours. I have always known the president loves you very much, from the start, so I have no reason to be jealous of a fact but I was very worried that I'll lose my job.'

'I have absolutely no intention to do that,' Chai replied. 'You know how it is with boss ... He sees and he asks to do. Doesn't draw the line. And yes, my weakness is, if he ask I cannot say no. This is my problem.'

Be was pacified. 'We all have our weaknesses. But we have many things in common too. One thing for sure. We both love the president very much.'

It was vital to Bin Hammam that the women who oversaw his affairs at the AFC were slavishly loyal and unquestioning, and that they guarded the gates to his private office in Kuala Lumpur jealously. He had been using the AFC sundry accounts as a slush fund for years now, pumping money in and out from accounts controlled by staff at Kemco, back in Doha. The Qatari had learned early on that the way to secure power in world football was to buy it. He had a network of officials across Asia on his payroll, as well as a scattering of football chiefs in Africa who remembered his generosity in the 1998 and 2002 elections and kept coming back for more. This was a power-base he planned to build from substantially for his World Cup campaign, and it was going to be necessary to crank up the cash flow.

When Bin Hammam wanted to slip someone in world football a discreet sweetener, he had a system. Often it was merely a matter of instructing Gan to wire the money from his sundry account at the AFC under some flimsy football-related pretext, but there were times when a less traceable route was prudent. Thankfully, over in Doha his accounts staff at Kemco operated a network of ten funds which provided the perfect cover for clandestine transactions. The accounts were generally marked for commercial mundanities such as 'real estate', 'transport', 'retention' and 'overheads'. Bin Hammam's personal bank account, and another in the name of his adult daughter, Aisha, were also operated by the Kemco staff to make payments to football bosses.

When Bin Hammam wanted to show an influential official some generosity, his clerks would often be ordered to make a transfer from one of these funds directly into the personal account of the individual in question. At other times, the money might go into the account of the football federation the official controlled, or be paid to a spouse, son or daughter. Whatever the route, the reference on these payments was always the same: it went down in the Kemco ledger as 'business promotion'. Once the money had been paid, the accounts staff would email a copy of the bank transfer slip to Bin Hammam's private office in Doha's Olympic Tower. Job done.

The man opening the emails from the Kemco accounts team in the skyscraper on the Corniche was a pivotal figure. This was Bin Hammam's right-hand man, and he was closer to the Qatari billionaire than the trio of women he trusted at the AFC could ever hope to be. His name was Najeeb Chirakal. From the private office overlooking the West Bay where Bin Hammam had once watched the riggers play, Chirakal supervised all of the billionaire's affairs. He was in his fifties, having left his home in the Keralan backwaters of India to come to Doha decades earlier. Just like Bin Hammam, he could remember the dusty old city before the boom. Everybody liked Najeeb. He was small, button-nosed and bespectacled, with a shy smile under his bushy moustache. There was something homey about this quietly cheerful man in flannel trousers and a baggy jacket: you couldn't help but warm to him. He knew his place as a migrant worker in Qatar and he was always humble, but the high degree of trust the billionaire football boss had placed in him lent him a special status in the capital. Chirakal was the gatekeeper. If you wanted to get to Bin Hammam, you had to go through him.

It was a key part of Chirakal's job to oversee the payments that were made to football officials from the funds operated by Kemco, and he kept a tight ship. Once the money had been transferred and he had received a scanned copy of the payment slip, he would forward the document to the official in question as proof that the money was winging its way speedily into their account. Bin Hammam rarely sent emails, leaving Chirakal in charge of his inbox. The scanned payment slips he sent to the officials were always accompanied by some kind words on behalf of his boss.

Chirakal was going to have his hands full now the World Cup campaign was seriously underway, and the sly requests from the African football officials who had so enjoyed their visit to Kuala Lumpur were beginning to trickle in. The trusted trio at AFC headquarters were going to be just as busy: some of the dignitaries were proving particularly persistent in their entreaties. Izetta Wesley had taken to peppering the president with 'urgent' requests for financial help for her federation since being so blown away by the hospitality she received in Kuala Lumpur, but she was far from the most brazen.

That, undoubtedly, was Seedy Kinteh. The president of the Gambian FA had enjoyed visiting Malaysia in June, wandering around Malacca in his satin dashiki, and he had been particularly pleased with the bundle of cash and gifts he received. But at least four of his fellow visitors had done even better out of the visit, persuading their host to ask Gan to wire them extra money after they returned home. Seedy wanted a slice of that pie.

He was saving up to buy a new car to drive around football

projects in the Gambian countryside, and he thought Bin Hammam might be able to help. In an email to a senior official at the AFC on 17 July 2008, he explained that he was writing 'to remind the President through you about our Vehicle problem that we had earlier discussed'. The official was not part of the inner sanctum, so he was flummoxed by Seedy's constant demands. In desperation he forwarded the email to Jenny Be with the note: 'Please see below another reminder (the 5th!) from Seedy Kinteh of Gambia. Kindly advise if the President would like me to reply to him and what should I tell him. He also called me almost every 2 days.' Be told the official to 'ignore it at the moment'. But Seedy would not have to wait long for his pay day.

The first junket in Kuala Lumpur had been such a roaring success that Bin Hammam decided to host a second that October. Meshadi was duly dispatched back to AFC headquarters to flash his most winning smile at the secretaries and extract another stack of dollar bills, this time totalling $130,000. On this visit the African football chiefs had been invited to bring their wives and daughters, with Meshadi instructed to present the guests and each of their companions with packages of $5,000 when they landed on 15 October. A set of gifts was also prepared for all 40 visitors and packed up in Nike hold-alls, which were left in their five-star hotel rooms. This time the delegates were treated to a private cruise on the vast blue expanse of Putrajaya Lake. Moving through the crowd on deck was Amadou Diallo, and time was made for each of the delegates to have a private meeting with Bin Hammam.

The visit was just as effective as the last, and Bin Hammam could once again congratulate himself on having bolstered his alliances with men close to Issa Hayatou, whose backing was essential to victory. The Cameroonian was not there in person on this trip, but his influence was felt. Afterwards, Anjorin Moucharafou of Benin, the CAF executive committee member who had a payment wired to him by Gan after the first junket, emailed his host in French: 'Thank you for all the attention you paid to me during the stay of my wife and I. I was also very flattered by the attention you paid to promoting World football in general and Africa in particular. Your commitment to a partnership for the benefit of Africa alongside President Issa Hayatou gives me a positive feeling in building our future actions.'

Another powerful CAF official, Togolese General Seyi Memene, Hayatou's vice president, also wrote to Bin Hammam later that month. He asked the Qatari billionaire to fund a pilgrimage to Saudi Arabia for himself and his wife. Bin Hammam duly ordered Chirakal to arrange a transfer of $22,400 to cover flights, hotels and living expenses for the general and Mrs Memene.

The requests continued to roll in. The president of the Swaziland FA and former senator Adam 'Bomber' Mthethwa emailed to thank Bin Hammam for an 'unforgettable' visit to Kuala Lumpur. He went on, 'I am in dire need of finance in the region of $30,000. This arises from the fact that I've just retired from politics and my gratuity will only be paid to me when I reach the age of 55 in 2010.' Bin Hammam forwarded the email to Jenny Be. She knew what to do.

Phase one of Bin Hammam's campaign was gathering pace nicely and he was feeling increasingly confident of the support of his African brothers. He would need them to lean on the confederation's four voters on his behalf, but all that could follow in good time.

By the end of 2008, Qatar's intention to launch a bid to host the 2022 World Cup was as good as public, but Bin Hammam was having to practise his poker face. As the president of the AFC, it would be unseemly for him to push his own country's bid at the expense of the confederation's other three contenders – Australia, South Korea and Japan. What's more, he knew that if he was going to win he would have to play dirty and that meant keeping a low profile. The Emir was lining up his handsome young son, Sheikh Mohammed bin Hamad bin Khalifa Al Thani, to front Qatar's official bid committee, and the royals had to keep their hands as clean as their pristine white dishdashas.

So when his old friend Peter Hargitay began to probe him about Qatar's bid, Bin Hammam had to play dumb. Hargitay was a man who was steeped in the mire of FIFA like no other. The moustachioed Swiss-Hungarian lobbyist, spin doctor and fixer had worked for years as a special advisor to Sepp Blatter, and Bin Hammam had employed him in the past too. He was not picky about his clients.

Early in his career in 1984, Hargitay had represented Union Carbide Corporation after the Bhopal disaster in India, in which more than 500,000 people living in shanty towns were exposed to a cyanide leak from the company's plant. It was the world's worst industrial catastrophe and Union Carbide badly needed to clean up its image – though it was less interested in cleaning up the thousands of tonnes of toxic waste in the soil and water which continue to cause terrible birth defects in Bhopal's babies today. He was just the man to make the best of a bad job, and would later joke about how his spin campaign for the petrochemicals giant got his career off 'with a bang'. Next, he went to work for Marc Rich, the multi-billionaire American commodities trader who boasted of busting UN oil sanctions against apartheid South Africa and had been hiding out in Switzerland since the mid-1980s after being indicted for breaking a US trade embargo with Iran and tax evasion on an unprecedented scale. Hargitay liked a challenge, and he had never met a rich and powerful man he didn't admire. It was the perfect assignment.

He prided himself on being able to fish his clients out of difficulty, and he learned from first-hand experience how to get out of a bad rap when he twice got himself acquitted of cocaine trafficking in the 1990s. By the turn of the millennium he had become a master of the dark art of 'reputation management', and he was looking for a new berth. Where better for a man with Hargitay's many dubious talents than FIFA headquarters? He went to work as a spin doctor for Sepp Blatter, helping the president slither through corruption scandal after corruption scandal and come up smelling of roses every time. Hargitay had found his spiritual home in the murky world of football administration.

The lobbyist operated in mysterious ways. He had an army of pet journalists under his spell, ready to attack his enemies or lionise his allies when he gave the word. He knew about how to spy on people, or smear them. He'd take your money to fix votes in an election or spin a disaster into a PR triumph. He was an invaluable asset to anyone trying to manoeuvre their way through FIFA's back-corridors, so he would doubtless play a pivotal role in the World Cup bidding race. The whole business was sure to be flush with consultancy cash, and Hargitay was not one to miss such an opportunity. So he quit his job as Blatter's special advisor in December 2007 and prepared to enter the fray.

England's 2018 bid team had sniffed around Hargitay early on and briefly hired him as an advisor, but the relationship had ended quickly. The rumour was that the spinner had advised them to earmark substantial funds to be used to curry favour with the FIFA Exco members, and the chairman of the bid, Lord Triesman, had baulked at the suggestion and shown him the door. Now he was in the pay of the Australian team, which was about to launch their country's bid for the 2022 World Cup. He might be an old friend, but for the purposes of this campaign Hargitay had become a direct rival. He could not be trusted. But Bin Hammam valued the cunning old lobbyist's opinion, so he read the withering email which arrived in December 2008 with some dismay.

'Dear Brother,' Hargitay wrote. 'Attached a story [about Qatar's World Cup bid] going around the globe right now. I cannot imagine how Qatar can be serious . . . I honestly believe that they should receive honest and straight advice: I fear they have not a chance to win this. The temperatures are just too forbidding.' Hargitay ended by saying he had sounded out a fellow lobbyist, who shared his view that Qatar's chances were 'virtually nil'. He recommended that Bin Hammam advise 'the Emir not to pursue it'. Bin Hammam knew that was not an option. He had continually warned about the temperatures till he was blue in the face, but the Emir was resolute. Qatar's ruler wanted the World Cup come hell or high water, and a little summer heat wasn't going to stand in his way. Of course, Bin Hammam had anxieties about this that he just couldn't shake, but he was not about to share them with Hargitay.

So his response was sphinx-like: 'Dear brother . . . Thank you for the information, but I have no clue!!'

Qatar finally declared its hand officially when it registered a formal 'expression of interest' in bidding for the World Cup with FIFA in February 2009. A fortnight before, Bin Hammam had been in Zurich with Sheikh Hamad bin Khalifa bin Ahmed Al Thani, the president of the Qatar FA, and his bagmen Meshadi and Diallo. Days later, Bin Hammam was reunited with his African brothers when he travelled to CAF's annual congress in Lagos, Nigeria. He had Meshadi at his side, and was also accompanied by Diallo who had €3,000 pocket money transferred into his bank account in the days beforehand. Chirakal took special care to ensure that the bag-man was accommodated in the same hotel where the delegates were staying, for easy access, and it was his job to get the drinks in.

The same month, Bin Hammam reached out to Sepp Blatter. Despite his very public promise in June to support the president in the next election, and the gushing letter of thanks he had received, he couldn't help but feel there had been a cooling of relations in the months since. Qatar had now made clear its intention to campaign for the World Cup and was preparing to submit its formal bid registration form the following month. It would be ruinous to lose Blatter's support at this crucial stage. So Bin Hammam wrote to his old brother-in-arms that February, tentatively enquiring as to whether Qatar could still count on his good will. His message read simply: 'Hi President, I am looking for Friends. Are you still one of them? Kind regards, Mohamed.' History does not relate if he received a reply.

Bin Hammam had other reasons to take heart, though. A month later, when Qatar met the deadline to hand in its bid registration form to FIFA on 16 March, the rewards of the groundwork he had so carefully laid in Africa were immediately apparent. Fadoul Houssein, the president of the Djibouti FA, emailed him the same day, ready to sign up for the fight. 'How much I am pleased with you when I heard this news with our brother Diallo,' he wrote. 'I am ready to go with you to the end. I'm sure that Somalia, Comoros . . . Sudan, Yemen and Djibouti will support us. Count on me I'm already starting the war and I am sure you will win.'

Houssein was right: the football leaders of those countries all became close allies of Bin Hammam and their associations were rewarded for their leaders' loyalty. Houssein himself solicited payments of more than $30,000 from the Qatari to fund an expensive course of medical treatment for his general secretary over several months at a private hospital in Bangkok. The Somali FA had $100,000 paid into its bank account the following year, while the Sudan association asked for help paying for their general assembly, and Bin Hammam's staff asked them to provide their bank details. Yemen was paid just under $10,000, while Bin Hammam's staff arranged another bank transfer to the Comoros.

So by the time Qatar formally launched its World Cup campaign, Bin Hammam had already enlisted the ground troops in Africa who would help march the bid to victory.

Four

A Corrupt Official Called Seedy

Two figures sat hunched forward in the wan glow of their computer screens, their faces furrowed in concentration. Only the pale shafts of spring sunlight slanting through chinks in the blinds penetrated the gloom. This anonymous attic room above a boarded-up high-street shop was the perfect hide-out. No one would think to look here, in this obscure little northern suburb that could have been anywhere. The two figures were Jonathan Calvert and Heidi Blake – together, *The Sunday Times* Insight team – and this attic room was the nerve-centre of their investigation into Mohamed bin Hammam's corrupt World Cup campaign.

Through draughty windows which never quite closed came the comfortable chatter of the blue-rinse brigade of elderly ladies who congregated each morning outside the café across the road. The only sound within emanated from giant computer servers whirring away endlessly in the corner as they churned through tens of thousands of terrabytes of data. It was March 2014, and Calvert and Blake had been camped out in the attic for two weeks already. They were here to trawl through many millions of highly sensitive documents held by a whistleblower from inside FIFA who wanted to lift the lid on corruption in the bidding process for the 2018 and 2022 World Cups. The source was rightly cautious: he had been introduced to the journalists by a mutual acquaintance at a London hotel just a month before, and he didn't trust strangers easily. He wasn't prepared to allow them to access his documents from anywhere other than this secure room, where their activities were monitored by two CCTV cameras mounted on the wall. The documents were to remain on computers controlled by the source and were not to be sent electronically outside of the room until the work was finished.

The deal was clear-cut: Calvert and Blake would spend three months working on the story in secret and they would do justice to the material by publishing a full and detailed account of the investigation in *The Sunday Times* at the end. The source's identity would be protected, and any documents the journalists published on the newspaper's website with his agreement at the end of their work would be redacted and stripped of identifying metadata. If any material leaked before that, if their whereabouts became known or if the source's identity was blown, then the deal was off.

The stakes were high. So the journalists could not tell anyone other than their senior editors and the newspaper's lawyers where they were, or what they were doing. Their families and friends were, for the most part, kept in the dark. Blake and Calvert simply disappeared one morning, and their colleagues at *The Sunday Times* had no idea where they had gone. In their absence, rumours began to circulate back in London that the Insight team had been disbanded. The journalists received concerned phone calls and emails from their fellow reporters, and media bloggers began to get in touch to try to find out what had become of them. But their lips had to stay sealed.

It was wearying work, sitting for the most part in silence with their backs turned to each other, their eyes glued to screens in opposite corners of the room, scouring their secret haul for the single explosive element which would blow the whole story wide open. There were hundreds of millions of documents from inside Bin Hammam's private office in Doha, the headquarters of the Asian Football Confederation in Kuala Lumpur, the offices of the official Qatar World Cup bid and FIFA itself.

It was a physical impossibility to read them all, so the pair had hired a technical expert to set them up with forensic technology which allowed them to run smart searches across the vast database. They could now narrow down the millions of documents by searching multiple combinations of key names and phrases, filtering the results by variables like date-range, author or the location where the document was created. When they found relevant material, they could apply tags to cluster it together so they could navigate back to it quickly. The cache contained emails, faxes, accounts, bank records, telephone logs, letters, electronic messages, minutes of meetings, confidential reports, flight manifests, travel bookings and more. It was a data leak on an astonishing scale. For FIFA and the Qatar World Cup bid, this was nothing short of a catastrophe.

So far, the reporters had read thousands of documents, many of which set their journalistic antennae wagging. Qatar had always claimed Bin Hammam had played no part in its successful World Cup campaign, but there was plenty of evidence here that his role had really been crucial, as the source suspected. There was proof of secret meetings between Bin Hammam and members of the FIFA executive committee at which the voters were showered with lavish hospitality as the World Cup bid was discussed. There were emails from shadowy fixers hinting at dubious back-room deals, and flight records showing Bin Hammam had flown voters across the world on his private jet to meet the Emir. But still the reporters had not yet found the smoking gun they were looking for: the document that proved corruption beyond doubt. Until now.

Calvert was frowning and leaning closer to his screen.

'Huh,' he said. Blake spun round.

'What have you found?' The pair had worked together closely for several years, and they knew each other inside out. Calvert had a cool head and there wasn't much he hadn't seen before. Blake was more readily excited by the first glimpse of a breakthrough. She had learned to read her colleague's reactions, and when Calvert said 'Huh,' she knew he had struck upon something worth hearing about. She scooted across the room on her swivel chair. Calvert was staring at a grainy facsimile of a blue bank transfer slip, dated 18 June 2009. The slip showed that $10,000 had been paid into the personal account of a Mr Seedy MB Kinteh at Standard Chartered Bank, Serrekunda Branch, Gambia. The money had come from the account of an Aisha Mohd Al Abdullah at Doha Bank, Al Handasa Branch.

'Aisha is Bin Hammam's daughter,' said Blake. 'She's come up in the documents before. But who's that she's paying?'

'Seedy Kinteh is the president of the Gambian FA,' said Calvert. 'Or at least he was. I've just Googled him. He was banned from football last year over financial irregularities in the federation.' They looked at each other. Blake was grinning.

'A corrupt official called Seedy! This is basically the high point of my career so far,' she laughed. 'But seriously, what is Bin Hammam's daughter doing paying this guy ten grand the year before the World Cup vote? What possible innocent explanation is there?'

'God knows,' murmured Calvert. 'But I wonder if there are more of these.'

The transfer slip was attached to an email that had been sent to Bin Hammam's closest aide, Najeeb Chirakal, by accounts staff at his construction company, Kemco, after the money was paid to Kinteh. The reporters quickly discovered that Aisha's account was administered by staff at Kemco to make dozens of payments like this one. In fact, it was one of ten slush funds, including Bin Hammam's own account, which the Kemco clerks used to funnel cash to football officials at Chirakal's instruction.

The reporters found that if they ran searches for the standard Kemco email address, they hit a rich seam of emails just like this, with the grainy blue bank transfer slips attached. Over the next few days, they gathered evidence of scores of payments that Bin Hammam's staff at Kemco had made to the heads of football associations across Africa and Asia in the two years before and straight after the World Cup vote. They began compiling spreadsheets of the transactions, noting down the amounts, dates and account details and the content of the emails accompanying the transfer slips. They added each of the payments to a timeline they were building of Bin Hammam's activities, which began to reveal a clear picture of the Qatari's campaign to build up a groundswell of support among football officials across the continents of Africa and Asia.

It was evident that the bulk of the African payments coalesced around a series of junkets which were hosted by Bin Hammam in Kuala Lumpur and later Doha. Days after they discovered the first Kemco payment slip, Blake uncovered AFC accounts documents which revealed how his bagman Mohammed Meshadi had withdrawn hundreds of thousands of dollars in cash to provide handouts to the visitors in Kuala Lumpur in June and October 2008. By the end of the week there was no doubting Bin Hammam's corrupt activity. In the two years leading up to the World Cup vote, he had paid more than $5 million to the leaders of 30 football federations across Africa in cash handouts and transfers of as much as $200,000 from the slush funds operated by his staff at Kemco.

But the reporters were far from finished. Next, they wanted to know whether the officials appointed to head Qatar's World Cup bid committee could be connected to the junkets at which Bin Hammam bought the support of his African brothers.

Five

How to Score Points

FIFA's hilltop headquarters was suffused with milky morning light as the cavalcade of limousines glided down the landscaped drive on the morning of 16 March 2009. The young son of Qatar's Emir gazed out of the window, taking in the futuristic glass and granite edifice of the home of world football rising up ahead. Resting in his lap was the sheaf of documents required to register his country's official bid to host the 2022 World Cup, which he had been sent to hand over to the FIFA president, Sepp Blatter.

This was a big moment for Sheikh Mohammed bin Hamad bin Khalifa Al Thani. Aged just 20, he had been put at the head of the team officially charged with bringing the world's biggest sporting tournament to his home country. Sheikh Mohammed was still an undergraduate, studying international relations at the Georgetown University campus which opened in Doha as part of his father's diplomatic entente with the USA. The Emir had big plans for him once he graduated. When he finished his studies in two months' time, he would be made the assistant director of the Prime Minister's office for International Affairs, and he would spearhead Qatar's World Cup campaign on the global stage as the chairman of its official bid committee. His father was counting

on him. All of Qatar was counting on him. It was a heavy responsibility to carry on such young shoulders.

Sheikh Mohammed was the Emir's fifth child with his second
wife, the dusky beauty Sheikha Mozah bint Nasser Al Missned,
and he was his mother's son. All the young royal had inherited
from his hulking father in the looks department was the little gap
between his front teeth in an otherwise Daz-white filmstar smile.
Like Sheikha Mozah, he was tall with finely carved features, and
a glossy black sweep of perfectly coiffed hair. Sheikh Mohammed
looked every bit the dashing young royal when out on duties in
Doha with his silk robes shining as spotlessly white as the Diwan
Palace. But he was more at ease when abroad, as he was today,
wearing the suits he had hand-woven from rare and exquisite
fibres by the finest tailors in the world.

Sheikh Mohammed wasn't just a pretty face: he had sporting
pedigree, too. As the captain of Qatar's equestrian team, he had
captured hearts across Asia three years before when he emerged
on horseback from underground at the opening ceremony of the
15th Asian Games in Doha and galloped to the top of the stadium to light the ceremonial flame. He played for the
Georgetown University football side and he supported the Al
Sadd team in the Qatar Stars League. There was no doubt that he
was a glamorous figurehead for Qatar's international sporting
ambitions. But how much did this young sheikh really know
about football politics?

The cavalcade passed through the security gates and descended
into the bowels of the building where FIFA's well-paid executives
parked their Porsches and Ferraris. The chauffeurs leapt out to
open the doors and Sheikh Mohammed emerged. Climbing out
behind him was the wiry figure of his new companion. Hassan
Al-Thawadi was the freshly anointed chief executive of Qatar's
2022 bid committee. Al-Thawadi was rake-thin and a touch bug-
eyed with a jaw that jutted so sharply it sometimes gave him a

mean look when he forgot to arrange his face. But he was as smart as a whip, and he wasn't there for appearance's sake. It was Sheikh Mohammed's job to lend the grace of his royal presence to Qatar's World Cup dream; Al-Thawadi would bring the brains.

The bid's new chief executive was only 30, but he was already the legal director at the Qatar Investment Authority, the country's vast sovereign wealth fund which was pushing its financial might around the world through its ballooning property and business portfolio. Al-Thawadi was the son of a former Qatari ambassador to Spain and he had spent much of his youth in Europe. It wasn't all glamour: he took his A levels in the struggling British steel town of Scunthorpe, and went on to study law at Sheffield University. Al-Thawadi came home the proud possessor of a law degree with the gloss of a Western education, but his sojourn in the industrial north of England had thrown a touch of grit into the mix. For all that he was charismatic and articulate, there was something a little scratchy about this fiery young lawyer.

Al-Thawadi's early business career had taken him to live in Houston, Texas, which accounted for his mid-Atlantic accent and his appealing command of slangy American English. But his father had been a friend of the Emir's, and it did not take long for the ambitious young lawyer to be airlifted into positions of power in Qatar. He had worked as a senior lawyer at Qatar Petroleum, the state oil company, and he had taken the job of general counsel to its sovereign wealth fund just a year before. Now he had the chance to be part of making history.

Al-Thawadi had returned from Britain with a case of football fever that he couldn't shake. He still regularly checked the scores of Scunthorpe and Sheffield United, but the teams he loved best of all were Liverpool and Real Madrid. The European leagues held an impossible glamour for him. He had played with distinction as an attacking left-back in Qatar Club's youth team, modelling himself on the great Italian defender Paolo Maldini, and now he was the legal director of Al Sadd club – Sheikh Mohammed's favourite side. But it was all such small beer compared with the gladiatorial clashes between international superstars he had grown up watching in the European leagues. The chance to bring the greatest sporting show on earth to his home country flushed him with tingling excitement. Al-Thawadi would use all his fiery passion and intellect to make the dream come true.

The young chairman and chief executive of the bid were accompanied by an older man with baggy eyes and straggling grey hair long enough to brush his shoulders. He was Sheikh Hamad bin Khalifa bin Ahmed Al Thani, the president of the Qatar Football Association and himself a member of the royal family. This elder statesman of Qatari football with his bristling steel-wool beard was there to lend some gravitas to the youthful delegation. But none of the three Qataris who were now striding through the granite corridors towards Blatter's office to submit their country's World Cup bid had an iota of the international football experience of the one man who was missing from the party.

Mohamed bin Hammam was conspicuous by his absence. The country's most senior football official was a natural choice to join the delegation: he had been there at the inception of the Emir's World Cup dream as Blatter well knew. But his role in pushing Qatar's bid needed to remain under wraps. In submitting their registration documents that day, Qatar signed up to rules of conduct which banned its official bid committee or any of its associates from providing any football official with 'monetary gifts [or] any kind of personal advantage that could give even the impression of exerting influence, or conflict of interest, either directly or indirectly, in connection with the bidding process'. That was exactly what Bin Hammam was doing behind the scenes in Africa on a mass scale – whether or not the new leaders of Qatar's bid knew it. But so long as he was not publicly associated with the official committee, he acted with impunity.

Bin Hammam may not have been present when the bid was formally registered that day, but he was not far away. He was, in fact, also in Zurich, ready to attend a meeting of the executive committee the next day. Najeeb Chirakal, his closest aide, arranged for his chauffeur to pop down to FIFA headquarters shortly after the delegation departed to pick up $25,000 in cash from Bin Hammam's FIFA account. It was just a bit of spending money while the Qatari billionaire was in town, on top of the $16,342 in expenses and daily allowances that he claimed for his three-day visit.

Blatter was typically gracious as he accepted the sheaf of documents which formalised Qatar's World Cup bid that March morning, and wished the young leaders well in their campaign. Beside him was his secretary general, Jérôme Valcke, a handsome, bulky Frenchman in his late forties with a crop of curly chestnut hair and cool blue eyes. Valcke was as much of a power-broker as Blatter had been when he was secretary general under João Havelange. He and the president were as closely conspiratorial as two men who so jealously guarded their own self-interest could ever be. Valcke was no ingénu. He knew that for all the formal presentations and glossy bid books and the scrutiny of FIFA's technical assessment team, the real deciding factor in this bidding contest would be the same thing that had transformed world football's governing body into the global powerhouse it was today. It would all come down to cold, hard cash. And as he eyed the Qatari dignitaries smiling graciously and glad-handing Blatter that morning, he was in no doubt that these were serious contenders.

That same day, ten other contenders entered the running for the 2018 and 2022 tournaments by submitting their bid registration documents to FIFA. The European nations were England, Russia and two joint bids which saw Spain teaming up with Portugal, and the Netherlands with Belgium. It was an open secret that the 2018 tournament would go to a bidder from their continent, but the Europeans initially hedged their bets by declaring their intention to compete for 2022 as well, though FIFA would eventually persuade them all to drop out of the running for the latter.

Indonesia and Mexico also entered the race at first, but soon fell out. The real contenders lined up against Qatar for the 2022 tournament were South Korea and Japan, who represented little threat because they had held the tournament together only six years earlier, and two more formidable opponents. First there was Australia, a sports-mad country which had demonstrated its flare for hosting a major tournament with the widely praised Sydney Olympics. Second, there was the United States which had hosted a World Cup once before in 1994. The US was viewed with suspicion by some in the FIFA Exco because it was not primarily a soccer-loving country, but its bid could not be underestimated. An American World Cup would have pizzazz. Its potential to bring in bumper television revenues, marketing opportunities and a sponsorship bonanza would light up the dollar signs in the eyes of the FIFA Exco.

Qatar's official bid committee had to get serious if was going to beat off that kind of competition, and the young bid leaders knew it. After formally submitting his country's registration documents at FIFA headquarters, Sheikh Mohammed released a statement. 'We believe it is time to bring the World Cup to the Middle East for the very first time,' he said. 'Our bid truly epitomises FIFA's slogan "For the Game, For the World" ... It would allow the rest of the world to gain a true picture of Arab culture and hospitality.' And the young royal acknowledged that he had a mountain to climb. 'We know that we have a lot of work to do before the FIFA Executive Board makes its decision in December 2010,' his statement concluded.

Sheikh Mohammed was right. While Bin Hammam manoeuvred behind the scenes, the new leaders of Qatar's official bid team had their work cut out for them. It was their job to create a compelling case that Qatar was a viable place to host the World Cup, despite all the obvious impediments. They would have to come up with a plan to beat the sweltering heat with the most aggressive air-conditioning systems science could deliver, and devise a way of cramming the giant sporting jamboree into the cramped space available in one of the world's tiniest countries.

They had to persuade FIFA's team of technical evaluators that they were capable of building nine world-class stadiums and all the players' and fans' facilities from scratch in a country with only the scantest football infrastructure. There was no room in Doha: it would be necessary to build a whole new city out in the desert to fit it all in. Not only did they have to convince FIFA's evaluation team, they had to find a plausible way to explain to fans around the globe why Qatar deserved to host their beloved tournament when it had no real football tradition to speak of, no serious professional league and not a single world-class player. The country languished near the bottom of FIFA's world rankings – it would drop to 113th by the time of the vote – and had never come anywhere close to qualifying for the World Cup finals it wanted to host. Bin Hammam had made it his mission to sell the idea of a Qatar World Cup to the relatively small number of influential football officials required to sway the vote, and their loyalty often came with an affordable price tag. The bid committee had to dream up a way of selling it to the world. It was hard to say who had a more daunting task.

Paradise Island in the Bahamas is blessed with brilliant white sand beaches and pale turquoise water warmed by the tropical currents of the Gulf Stream. It is home to the dizzyingly glitzy Atlantis mega-resort, famed for its giant water park rides, buzzing casino scene, lively bars and array of celebrity chef restaurants. The island is linked by two bridges to the capital city of Nassau, with its gracious pink colonial buildings, fish shacks piled high with red snapper, and rum distilleries selling Bahama Mamas for $10 a pop. These streets were once stalked by pirates, looters, Spanish invaders and Prohibition rum-runners. So where better for FIFA's motley crew to gather for their annual congress?

When FIFA's hundreds of officials came together at the Atlantis resort in June 2009, the bidding race for the 2018 and 2022 World Cups was well underway. The billionaire retail property tycoon and Australian FA chairman Frank Lowy had sailed his 74-metre superyacht to the Bahamas and moored it off Paradise Island, ready to host a succession of FIFA Exco members in the lap of luxury as he lobbied them to support his country's 2022 bid. The leaders of England's 2018 committee – its chairman, Lord Triesman, and the London Olympics chief Lord Coe who sat on its board – had also jetted in to Nassau to make their case.

Bin Hammam flew into Nassau on his private jet accompanied by Mohammed Meshadi, ready to step up his campaign to cement the loyalty of his African brothers. He met a string of delegates in private on Paradise Island to discuss their financial needs. Seedy Kinteh from Gambia was naturally first in line. After the congress, he emailed Bin Hammam to remind him about what they had discussed. 'I really need your brotherly help again as per discussed in Bahamas and i hereby provide you with the full bank details that you can use for any transfer,' he wrote. 'While i hope to here from you, please Sir do accept my very sportive regards and fraternal esteem always and my continuos prayers for your well being. Everyours Seedy M.B.Kinteh, PResident, Gambia Football Association.'

The service was quick. Just ten days later, another email dropped into Bin Hammam's inbox from Kinteh. 'Many thanks indeed for your recent mail disclosing to me the transfer of $10,000 Dollars. I must first of all express my profound gratitude to you for this very wounderful brotherly gesture that you have once again demonstrated.' Kinteh said he was sure the money would go a long way to developing the skills of Gambia's players – despite the fact the payment had gone into his own bank account. He signed off: 'On behalf of the entire Football family of the Gambia and indeed on my own humble behalf i wish you a continuos well being and good health as you continue to steer the affairs of your continent football. I have every reason to be grateful and indeed my President and Brother I AM!!!!'

Manuel Dende, the president of the Sao Tome federation, also emailed Bin Hammam after meeting him in Nassau. Dende had visited Bin Hammam in Kuala Lumpur on one of those famous junkets the previous October, and he had been aboard the cruise ship in Putrajaya when the bagman Amadou Diallo had moved between the guests finding out how to make them happy. He knew how beneficent his new Qatari friend could be. So after a second meeting in Nassau, he asked for $232,000 to be paid into his personal bank account, apparently to build artificial football pitches in his country. Bin Hammam was nothing if not a generous man, but he considered such a large request from an official who was not even a member of the CAF executive committee a touch audacious. He decided to scale it back, faxing a copy of the email to Chirakal with the instruction: 'Najeeb: I want to transfer $60,000 to this Federation.' The money was not immediately forthcoming, and when Chirakal eventually emailed Dende in December with news his federation had been paid the lesser sum of $50,000, his response was curt. 'Ok, tks,' he replied.

Liberia's 'Iron Lady' Izetta Wesley was more easily gratified. She received $10,000 into her personal bank account after meeting Bin Hammam* in Nassau in July and responded: 'I've received the transfer. Please convey my thanks and appreciations to

---

* The Liberian FA said it 'has never in any way found any evidence of bribery' and that its former president, Wesley, did not influence the 2022 World Cup vote.

Mohammed. May the Almighty Allah replenish his resources a hundred fold. I am so happy that I have a brother and friend that I can always depend on.' She had written to Bin Hammam before the congress in the Bahamas to report 'a serious problem'. Her letter explained: 'My league have started and I do not have any sponsors. Things are very difficult. Therefore, I have decided to send you a portion of my league budget for assistance.' Her generous Qatari brother had smiled on her request, and she was eternally grateful.

The Ivory Coast FA, home to the Exco voter Jacques Anouma, received $22,000 from one of Bin Hammam's private slush funds at the start of July, earmarked as football aid,* while the president of the Moroccan FA, Said Belkhayat, received a payment straight into his personal bank account.

Bin Hammam was not the only Qatari on manoeuvres in Nassau. Sheikh Hamad bin Khalifa bin Ahmed Al Thani, the country's FA president who had met Blatter in March when its formal bid was presented at FIFA headquarters, had arranged a private audience with the FIFA president. The Emir was determined to have a World Cup on his patch, but some of the naysaying about the improbability of cramming the entire tournament into his tiny country had evidently sunk in. He had decreed that overtures should be made to other Gulf states to mount a joint bid to host the tournament, and the FA president had been deputised to run the idea up the flagpole with Blatter. He had written to the FIFA president in May, and Blatter had responded warmly.

'It is with great interest that I took note of your proposal to include neighbouring Gulf cities into your World Cup bid in order to share the vision of "Bringing the World Together" with

---

* The Ivory Coast FA said the money was a charitable donation for victims of a stadium collapse.

several countries. I would be happy to discuss this matter further
at the upcoming FIFA Congress in Nassau,' he wrote.

The plan to mount a joint Gulf bid did not go ahead because
Qatar could not persuade its neighbours to sign up to take on the
unlikely challenge. The other heads of state had told the Emir he
was crazy even to consider a bid because they were bound to lose.
But the meeting between Blatter and Sheikh Hamad was another
opportunity to cement the ties between the FIFA president and
the Qatar bid he had first encouraged over dinner with the Emir
the previous year.

Now that Bin Hammam had the enthusiastic support of the
influential leaders of African football, it was time to kick off phase
two of his campaign. He needed to begin making his approaches
to the men who really mattered: the 24 voters on FIFA's executive
committee who would ultimately decide on the two hosts of the
2018 and 2022 World Cups in a secret ballot in December 2010.

In August, his aides began making arrangements for a visit
from the only man at the helm of FIFA who really knew how it
felt to win a World Cup. Franz Beckenbauer, the former German
football superstar, was a highly influential figure on the executive
committee and an international icon. He ranked among the
greatest footballers of all time: one of only two men, along with
Brazil's Mário Zagallo, to have won the World Cup both as a
player, in 1974, and as a manager, in 1990. Beckenbauer was
football royalty. He cut such a starry figure that he was known at
home as *Der Kaiser* – 'The Emperor'. Selling the idea of a World
Cup in the desert to a man of this stature was not, on the face of
it, going to be an easy task. But Bin Hammam knew that
Beckenbauer had a soft spot for Qatar that he could exploit.

The Emperor of German football had added to his roll call of
triumphs when he led his country's successful bid to host the
2006 FIFA World Cup. Qatar had been a supporter of his

campaign and, crucially, Bin Hammam had helped to round up the bloc of four Asian votes which propelled the German bid to victory. Now, he wanted a return on his investment.

Bin Hammam had invited Beckenbauer to Doha to visit the Emir at the Diwan Palace, to remind him of his debt to Qatar. The German football legend would be accompanied by his close associate, Fedor Radmann, a roving sports consultant who had played a key role in the German World Cup campaign. Radmann was a schmoozer, a smooth-talker in four languages, a man who lurked in the fancy hotels where collars were loosened and gossip flowed freely. He was a lobbyist in the politics of world football, and there was always a hefty fee for his 'priceless' knowledge and intelligence. Anyone who knew anything about the politics of the international game knew that if you wanted to get to *Der Kaiser*, then you went through Radmann. It was vital to get him on board.

But there was a complication. Radmann's exorbitant consultancy fees had already been paid by one of Qatar's biggest rivals: the Australian bid. Its chairman, Frank Lowy, had hired the lobbyist and his business partner Andreas Abold to produce its official World Cup bid book at a princely cost of A$11.2 million. The arrangement had been negotiated by none other than Peter Hargitay, the Sepp Blatter confidant who had written to Bin Hammam the previous year scoffing at Qatar's chances. England had sacked him early in its campaign but you couldn't keep a man like Hargitay down and he was now being paid about $850,000 by the Australians for his wise counsel.

Bin Hammam had a few things to straighten out in his own relationship with Australia before he got down to business. Until recently, the country's football association had been part of the Oceania Confederation which loosely covered the far-flung islands in their corner of the Pacific. But under Lowy, who owns the Westfield shopping empire, they had developed major ambitions. They didn't want their national side to be playing only New

Zealand or whatever teams the South Pacific islands could muster in Oceania. They wanted proper competition, which is why they applied to become part of Bin Hammam's Asian confederation.

Bin Hammam had been delighted to help because Australia expanded his power base, and he did everything he could to make them welcome when they joined the Asian football family in 2006. In the process, he had become close to Lowy, and the two men had spent much time schmoozing in the garden hotels of Kuala Lumpur. They had a lot in common. Lowy, a Slovakian refugee then in his late seventies, was a truly self-made man, and Bin Hammam respected that. So when he declared he wanted to bring the World Cup to Australia, his new Qatari friend was initially supportive.

Lowy announced his ambition before Bin Hammam knew that his own country was going to enter the running, and he had advised Lowy to hire the best team of lobbyists money could buy: Hargitay and his friends Abold and Radmann. Abold had been instrumental in securing the German World Cup alongside Beckenbauer and Radmann as the bid's strategic consultant and he was a trusted member of *Der Kaiser*'s inner circle. If he and Radmann were on board, Beckenbauer's vote would be in the bag, or so the reasoning went, and with such an influential backer on the Exco other votes would be sure to follow. Bin Hammam's advice had not stopped there: he had also advised his Australian friends that the best way to win support for their World Cup bid was to target football officials across Africa and Asia to lay down a bedrock of support across two continents – just as he would later do for his own country.

The whole business had become acutely embarrassing when Bin Hammam had realised his Emir wanted the World Cup too. There was no question as to where his loyalty must lie. Lowy had always told Bin Hammam that his country felt secure in bidding for the World Cup because they could rely on the AFC president's support, but that was no longer the case. When the secret got out and Qatar's intention to bid was becoming known, Bin Hammam had to come clean with Lowy and tell him that he would have to support his home country. The billionaire had been furious to lose Bin Hammam's support, but he was still counting on Radmann and Abold to deliver Beckenbauer's vote.

Now, Bin Hammam wanted to interfere with that too. He might not be able to persuade Beckenbauer to vote for Qatar in the first round if Radmann and Abold were in the pay of Australia. But if Australia was knocked out in the early rounds, how would Beckenbauer vote then? If Bin Hammam and the Emir could remind *Der Kaiser* of the debt he owed them for their help in delivering the German World Cup, perhaps his vote could be won in the crucial later rounds which would ultimately decide the victor.

So it was that Beckenbauer and Radmann touched down in Doha on a hot afternoon in late October 2009, and climbed into the air-conditioned limousine which took them to their suites in the five-star Sheraton Hotel on the Corniche. They were treated to all the finest hospitality Bin Hammam could offer and, first thing the next morning, they were driven with the Qatari football grandee a few hundred metres along the West Bay to the Diwan Palace to meet the Emir.

The German football legend and his lobbyist would remember the visit for years to come, dining out on their surreal meeting with the ruler of the world's richest country. Bin Hammam walked tall as he graciously ushered the two men through the grand marble corridors of the palace and into an anteroom outside the Emir's private chamber. But when they were invited to enter, he dropped back. Sheikh Hamad was all charm in his gold-trimmed dishdasha when he greeted Beckenbauer and Radmann. But Bin Hammam seemed to cower in the corner, stooping with his neck bowed and his two hands clasped over the back of his head in reverence. The European visitors were nonplussed. This man was not just a leader of world football; he was a multi-billionaire, a captain of industry, and a royal counsellor. Why was he crouching in the corner like the lowliest serf? Beckenbauer and Radmann would tell their friends when they flew home that they had realised then more than ever before just how absolute was Sheikh Hamad's power. Bin Hammam was entirely in his thrall. It was no wonder the other royal courtiers called him The Slave.

The Emir duly reminded Beckenbauer of the support his country had given to the German 2006 World Cup campaign, and how Bin Hammam had helped secure the Exco votes he had needed to win. The conversation was awkward. Beckenbauer was a World Cup winner, and he knew what it took to play football at that level. He and Radmann tried to reason with the Emir. The heat was too severe, they told him. It just wasn't possible to play football in those conditions. They respectfully urged him to think again. Why not have another go at the Olympics? But leave the World Cup alone. The Emir was implacable. He wanted the World Cup in Doha. Nothing else would do. And he expected Beckenbauer and Radmann to help him get it.

So now Beckenbauer was in a quandary, and when he went back to Germany he talked anxiously to friends about his dilemma. Australia was expecting his vote and it would be bad form to back out of the assurances his associates had given to Lowy. But he was an honourable man, and the weight of the gratitude he owed to Qatar bore down heavily on his shoulders. Bringing the World Cup to Germany in 2006 had been one of the crowning glories of his career, and Bin Hammam had helped him by rounding up those crucial Asian votes. Could he turn his back on his friends in Doha after all they had done?

Bin Hammam continued to invite a procession of key FIFA voters to enjoy his legendary hospitality in Doha as 2009 drew to a close, at the same time as getting to know the young men whom the Emir had put in charge of Qatar's official bid committee. He invited the Spanish voter Ángel María Villar Llona to meet 'Qatari higher ranking peoples' in November, and the Brazilian voter Ricardo Teixeira was flown in on the Qatari's private jet with his wife and daughter the same month. Teixeira dined privately with Bin Hammam on the evening of 13 November, and the whole family were taken to watch a friendly match played between Brazil and England in Doha's 30°C November heat at the Khalifa International Stadium the following day. Bin Hammam's aides emailed Teixeira's full itinerary to Hassan Al-Thawadi, the new chief executive of the Qatar 2022 committee. It was important to let him know when a big fish was on the hook.

While Bin Hammam attended discreetly to his friends inside FIFA, Al-Thawadi was assembling his team to mount Qatar's official campaign. His new second in command was his surly older sibling, Ali Al-Thawadi, who was about as unlike his brother as it was possible to be. Where Hassan was tall, smart and slim, Ali was short, sluggish and round. Hassan was extensively travelled and most comfortable in a well-cut lounge suit, but his brother liked his home comforts in Doha and he favoured the traditional dishdasha over all that tight Western tailoring. He was gruff and charmless, lacking his younger brother's polish, but he was loyal and Hassan looked after him. So Ali Al-Thawadi was brought in to be deputy chief executive of Qatar's official bid committee. He was kept in the background, without appearing at the press conferences or in the official photographs of the bid team. Instead, he ambled along doing his younger brother's bidding behind the scenes, and sometimes getting on with things the squeaky-clean public faces of the bid team didn't want to think too much about.

Ali Al-Thawadi had met Bin Hammam when he visited Kuala Lumpur as a 'special guest' of the AFC in September, accompanied by Khalid Al Kubaisi, the bid committee's new director of finance, and Nasser Al-Khater, its slick new communications director. The relationship between the older Al-Thawadi brother and Bin Hammam was key, and it was important that the two men became well acquainted. Ali was to be the principal point of contact between the bid committee and Bin Hammam in the coming months, as Qatar's man inside FIFA brought his African campaign to fruition. A plan had been hatched to host a third junket for Africa's top football officials, in Doha rather than Kuala Lumpur, and this time the official Qatar bid committee would be picking up the bill. Perhaps that was one of the things Hassan would rather not know too much about, but Ali was there to take care of it.

Ali was back at Bin Hammam's side on 7 November and this time Hassan was there too when the brothers joined the AFC president at the Asian Champions League final in Tokyo. With them was Mohammed Awada, another conduit between the bid team and Bin Hammam. Awada had been the AFC president's PR man until he went to work for the official Qatar bid committee as a back-room spin doctor. The two men remained close, so it was nice to be reunited in Tokyo, and catch up on the latest developments in promoting the country's bid.

Despite all the excitement of a tense match, in which South Korea's Pohang Steelers beat the Saudi team Al-Ittihad 2-1, Ali and Bin Hammam had other things to discuss. They were busy planning their Doha junket for the African officials. The day after the final, the bid's deputy chief executive emailed Najeeb Chirakal in the Qatari billionaire's private office asking him to provide daily updates on which CAF officials had accepted the invitation.

Bin Hammam needed to maintain a decent distance from the bid team, mindful as he was of the need to keep his covert activities separate from their public-facing campaign. But that didn't mean he couldn't give them the benefit of his wisdom behind the scenes. He had four decades of experience under his belt in football administration, and these young pretenders had no idea how the game really worked. Sheikh Mohammed, Hassan Al-Thawadi and their staff were on a steep learning curve, and they looked up to Bin Hammam. He spent many hours advising them on how to sell the country's official bid to the world.

One way of getting noticed was to sponsor big events where the bid could plaster its branding over every surface, make speeches promoting the Qatar 2022 campaign and send its ambassadors out to work the room and whisper in ears. Where better to start than with the AFC's own annual awards dinner? The bid pledged $100,000 to bankroll the flashy AFC event in Kuala Lumpur on 24 November, and the entire committee attended the gala led by their royal figurehead Sheikh Mohammed.

Hassan Al-Thawadi took the opportunity to hold a press conference before the dinner announcing that the Saudi player Sami Al Jaber had signed up as an official ambassador for the bid, and the Middle Eastern football star adorned Qatar's table that evening. The room was packed with influential Asian football officials, many of whom were growing accustomed to enjoying Qatari hospitality and patronage by now.

There was Rahif Alameh, the president of the Lebanese FA, who received an unexplained payment of $100,000 into his personal bank account wired by staff at Kemco earlier that summer. Also present was Mari Martinez, the president of the Philippines FA, who had money transferred into his wife's bank account from one of the Kemco slush funds in July. And then there was Ganbold Buyannemekh, president of the Mongolia FA, whose daughter's university education was being funded by Bin Hammam. It was all part of the service. The only thing he asked in return was loyalty. That evening, the guests were treated to a sparkling display of traditional dance and acrobatics as they tucked into the banquet, this time courtesy of Qatar's official World Cup bid committee rather than their usual benefactor, Bin Hammam.

Afterwards, when the invoice for the Qatar bid's sponsorship was paid to accounts staff at the AFC, the director of finance Amelia Gan fired off a wry email to a colleague. 'I'm pleased to inform that we received USD99,9953 from Qatar today,' she wrote. 'I will collect the shortage of USD47 from President. hahahah.'

By the end of the year, the draw for the South Africa World Cup was fast approaching, and Bin Hammam's focus on Africa had rubbed off on the young leaders of Qatar's official bid committee. Hassan Al-Thawadi had decided to make his own fledgling attempt to win hearts and minds across the continent with the power of his chequebook. The bid's chief executive favoured a subtler approach than the cash handouts, junkets and slush-fund bungs that had worked so well for his experienced mentor.

Rather than going to the continent's football officials directly, he had decided to make overtures to a single man whom he thought had the power to unite all of Africa behind him. So it was that Al-Thawadi contacted Desmond Tutu, the first black archbishop of Cape Town and Nobel peace prize winner, beloved and revered for his social-rights campaigning and vigorous opposition to apartheid. Tutu had lent his weight to South Africa's successful bid to host the 2010 World Cup, and Al-Thawadi hoped he could be persuaded to do the same for Qatar. The dynamic young bid chief got in touch offering a donation of $100,000 in exchange for Tutu's support. By the autumn he thought they had a deal. Al-Thawadi wrote to Tutu in October saying: 'How grateful we are for your kind support and your acceptance to be an Ambassador for the Qatar 2022 Bid.' His letter concluded: 'In deep gratitude for your kind support, it will be the Qatar 2022 Bid's great pleasure to make a donation of $100,000 to be divided, as you suggested, between your two chosen humanitarian charities.'

The money was to go to the Tygerberg Children's Hospital in Cape Town and the Desmond Tutu HIV Foundation. But while the hospital received its $50,000 donation a month after Al-Thawadi's letter, the money that had been promised to Tutu's own HIV foundation was not immediately forthcoming. A fortnight after the Tygerberg hospital had cashed its cheque from Qatar, Al-Thawadi received a nasty shock. The Australia 2022 bid wheeled out their new ambassador on the eve of the World Cup draw in Cape Town, and it was none other than Archbishop Tutu wearing the yellow shirt of the country's national team, the Socceroos. The Nobel laureate met Australia's bid chief Lowy at the Tygerberg Hospital and promised the billionaire his unstinting support. Qatar had been outbid. Its Australia rivals had donated a million South African Rand ($130,000) to Tygerberg in exchange for Tutu's backing.

It was a humiliating moment for Qatar's official bid committee, and Bin Hammam might have been forgiven for wondering what the youngsters were playing at as he watched from the wings. Donations to charity and overtures to archbishops were all well and good, but that wasn't how a World Cup vote was won. Yes, Tutu was well respected across Africa, but did Al-Thawadi really think the continent's football officials were going to vote with their hearts? Football administration was a hard-headed game. The young tyros had a lot to learn about the way the sport really worked at the top if they thought charity would get them anywhere.

While Al-Thawadi was dilly-dallying with Tutu on the eve of the Cape Town draw, Bin Hammam had been busy doing deals with a real member of African football royalty. He had met Kalusha Bwalya – the former Zambian footballing superstar known as 'King Kalu' to his countrymen – at the end of October to find out what he could do to win the influential official's loyalty. The strapping Zambian was one of the continent's all-time greatest players, having been named African Footballer of the Year in 1988 and shortlisted for FIFA World Player in 1996. Now he was running his country's football association.

Bwalya had built up his powerbase as a member of FIFA's

football committee, chaired by the UEFA president Michel Platini, and he sat alongside Africa's four voters as a member of CAF's powerful executive committee. This was a man with real influence, and Bin Hammam wanted to have him on side. After the meeting in October, Bwalya wrote to the AFC boss thanking him for his time and reminding him of his obligations. 'As per our conversation, please Mr President if you could assist me with about 50 thousand Dollars for my Football Association and personal expenditures,' his email said. The Zambian FA chief said he hoped to repay the money one day, and provided his bank details.* On 2 December, the day after Tutu's humiliating defection to Australia, Najeeb Chirakal emailed Bwayla a bank transfer slip showing that $50,000 had been paid into his personal bank account from one of the slush funds operated by Kemco. That was how you did business in world football.

As the Kemco cash was winging its way into Bwalya's account, Bin Hammam was sipping mint tea at 30,000 feet on his private jet en route to Cape Town. His bagmen Amadou Diallo and Mohammed Meshadi as well as his AFC office director Jenny Be all flew in as part of his entourage, and Najeeb Chirakal arranged for them to pick up $10,000 from his FIFA account as spending money for the trip. The group stayed at the five-star Westin Grand Hotel, with panoramic views of Table Mountain and the emerald waters of the adjoining bay.

The leaders of Qatar's bid committee were also in South Africa. They knew this was a big moment, and they had opened their coffers accordingly. The bid had bought up a major presence at the SoccerEx conference in Johannesburg where the great and the good of world football congregated days before the draw ceremony. They had shelled out for display stands boasting flashy interactive videos and handed out Arabic coffee, promotional

---

* When questioned about the payment, Bwalya said: 'I don't vote for World Cup. It's FIFA executive who vote.'

paperweights and Qatar 2022 t-shirts. Sepp Blatter toured the vast halls of the Sandton Conference Centre flanked by his CIA-style security detail in their suits and shades, with the press pack swarming after him whichever way he turned.

All the bidding countries were in the scrum at SoccerEx, trying to collar the FIFA president and key members of his Exco for one-to-one meetings and photo opportunities, but Qatar and Russia had spent by far the most money on showcasing their bids on the conference floor. Sheikh Mohammed was in town, with a whirlwind media programme to get through. The bid's communications team had put together a list of friendly journalists for him to speak to. The briefing document he was handed explained that they had: 'Identified accredited media that, by virtue of their geographical reach and status, may be read/viewed/listened to by certain FIFA ExCo members – for example list includes key Brazilian, Nigerian, and German media that could help reach Teixeira, Adamu and Beckenbauer.'

When the SoccerEx conference stands came down, football's global boss class jetted across to Cape Town for the spectacular show that had been laid on to mark the official World Cup draw. The streets outside the Cape Town International Convention Centre were a riot of colour with live music and parades as thousands gathered to watch the ceremony on giant screens. The event was beamed around the planet to an audience of 150 million people in 200 countries as the South African President Jacob Zuma joined Blatter on stage to welcome the world at the start of the 90-minute live broadcast. Nelson Mandela, the country's former president and hero of the struggle against apartheid, delivered a pre-recorded message about football's power 'to inspire and unite'. He said: 'The people of Africa learned the lessons of patience and endurance in their long struggles for freedom. May the rewards brought by the FIFA World Cup prove that the long wait for its arrival on African soil has been worth it.'

Inside the auditorium, a privileged elite of 3,000 dignitaries and journalists sat to watch the ceremony at first hand. The audience was dotted with some of the world's most dazzling football celebrities; from David Beckham and Franz Beckenbauer to Michel Platini and Roger Milla. The apartheid-beating Nobel laureates F.W. de Klerk and, of course, Archbishop Tutu, looked on. Charlize Theron, the Oscar-winning South African actress, partnered with FIFA's secretary general Jérôme Valcke to announce the 32 teams who would take part in the 2010 finals. It was the perfect showcase of football's global star-power, six months before the World Cup kick off.

Qatar's own World Cup hopes suffered a couple of setbacks during the festivities surrounding the draw in Cape Town. First, Reynald Temarii, the FIFA Exco member from Oceania, announced that he would be voting for the Australian 2022 bid. This was natural enough, since the country had been part of Oceania until only three years before, but coupled with Tutu's defection days earlier and the signing of the A-list Australian actress Nicole Kidman as an ambassador, Qatar's rival bid seemed to be gathering unwanted momentum.

Then Franz Beckenbauer made matters worse by saying publicly that Australia's bid was 'perfect' and had a great chance of victory. Bin Hammam knew that Beckenbauer had to stay outwardly loyal to the bid that had hired Radmann and Abold, but such a high-profile show of support for a rival from one of the greatest footballers of all time was a blow to Qatar that he could do without. Still, he had to remain focused. His fixer Amadou Diallo was at his side throughout the draw, and the two men were already planning the next phase of their own campaign.

It was nearly time for Bin Hammam to bring his African brothers home to Doha for an all-expenses paid junket which he hoped would be a decisive moment in Qatar's World Cup quest. Diallo had been drawing up the list of guests to target. This time it would not just be the presidents of national football associations who Bin Hammam invited to enjoy his famously lavish hospitality. The moment had come to target Africa's voters directly.

Issa Hayatou, the president of CAF, was flown into Doha straight after the draw in Cape Town, with the Nigerian voter Amos Adamu and Jacques Anouma from the Ivory Coast following a fortnight later. Bin Hammam's men Chirakal and Diallo worked together to arrange for the three voters and 35 African football association presidents to fly in first-class and stay at the pyramid-shaped Sheraton Hotel on the shores of the Persian Gulf at intervals throughout December.

It was a busy time for the official Qatar 2022 team as they prepared to submit their signed bidding agreement on 11 December. But Ali Al-Thawadi presided anxiously over the arrangements for the junket – repeatedly asking Chirakal to send him the latest list of delegates who were expected, wanting to know the details of the programme Bin Hammam had arranged for them and instructing him to forward the invoices for all the flights and hotel rooms to the bid for payment. 'Please forward me the final list of CAF delegation arrival and departure. The full cost of their flight expenses and accommodation. The full program that has been arranged for them in their visit in Qatar,' he wrote in one email on 16 December. He wrote again at the end of the month: 'Please provide us with the invoices regarding the African FA's visit last week from the accommodation and the travelling expenses in order to not delay those payments.'

The junket was a turning point, because Bin Hammam was going to lay his cards on the table and ask the officials outright to pledge their support to his country's bid. From the humblest football association president of the most minor African country, through the members of the powerful CAF executive committee right up to the FIFA voters themselves, he wanted to be assured that Qatar had their backing. Bin Hammam wanted to ensure that every man who visited left Doha feeling a debt of gratitude that they would remember when the World Cup vote neared in a year's time. And he knew how to make men grateful.

Both Hayatou and Adamu already had reason to be thankful to Bin Hammam, having seen payments of $400,000 channelled to their national federations at the start of that same month from the FIFA Goal Programme football development funds which he and his committee controlled. The money was earmarked to renovate their association headquarters into spanking new offices fit for FIFA royalty. Anouma was not left out of the Goal Programme spending spree: the Ivory Coast federation had already received $400,000 that summer, and was granted another $400,000 the following year.*

Founding the Goal Programme had been a stroke of genius by Blatter a year after Bin Hammam had helped him get elected in 1998. It was both a laudable use of FIFA's cash and a sure-fire way of shoring up support among the world football electorate. As a reward for his loyalty, the president had given his Qatari friend the job of chairing the Goal Bureau which controlled its coffers. In the years that followed, the scheme had dished out major grants to fund more than 500 football development projects from artificial pitches to technical centres in 193 of FIFA's member associations. Bin Hammam had pulled the purse strings for Blatter for more than a decade, and now he had an agenda of his own. If the Qatari intended to curry favour with the three African voters for his country's World Cup bid by dishing out football development cash to their federations, no one was going to stop him. Those sorts of conflicts of interest were allowed to flourish unchecked inside FIFA.

* Hayatou and Anouma said there was nothing wrong with their federations accepting Goal Programme funds and denied that their votes were influenced improperly in any way.

Anouma was delighted with his visit to Doha, and enjoyed a generous welcome from Qatar's Emir as well as from his host and fellow Exco member. Days after he returned from Doha, the secretary general of his FA wrote to say Bin Hammam's 'very good friend' Anouma had asked him to prepare a proposal to 'push very hard the bid of Qatar'.

Anouma followed up with his own email: 'After my recent stay in Doha at your invitation, I would like to express all my thanks and gratitude for the fraternal welcome you reserved for my wife and I and members of our federation. I want to tell you how much I appreciate your availability and your attention vis-a-vis African federations hereof. It is no doubt that the Doha meeting will contribute to tighten the bonds of friendship and brotherhood between, first, the African federations and your confederation, and secondly, between yourself and leaders of African football.' He went on: 'I would like to assure you of my desire to ensure that the discussions we had together during this stay translate into concrete action. I would ask you to convey to His Highness the Emir of Qatar, my sincere thanks and expression of my deep respect.' Quite what Anouma had to be grateful for was not made explicit, but it was clear that the Emir's kindness had made quite an impression.

Bin Hammam had used the Doha junket that December to hold a series of private meetings with the delegates at which he lobbied them to throw their support behind Qatar's bid. At the same time, some of the guests had been offered handsome payments from the Kemco slush funds.* David Fani, the president of the Botswana FA, emailed Bin Hammam afterwards to say how impressed he had been by Qatar's preparations for the 2022 bid. 'I have no doubt that your country will be ready for the 2022 FIFA World Cup and,

---

* There is no evidence in the FIFA Files that the official Qatar 2022 committee knew about the payments Bin Hammam was making to football officials to win support for the bid.

even without a vote, I pledge my support to you in this respect. If there is anything that I can do, no matter how small, to assist your course, I would be happy to oblige,' he wrote. 'I will write to you in the New Year concerning assistance to Botswana Football Association as per our discussion of 21st December 2009.'

John Muinjo, president of the Namibian FA, also emailed Bin Hammam to express his enthusiasm for the Qatar bid – at a price. 'Kindly take note that Namibia Football Association will always be behind you in its unequivocal support at all times,' he wrote. 'Dear President, allow me to sign off by humbly requesting you for the 2022 Bid Committee to consider as we discussed the legacy of putting up an artificial turf in the densely populated area of the North of Namibia which will positively score you points in the final analysis as you embark upon the mammoth task of securing the bid for vibrant Qatar in 2022 ... We would want to be assisted with a once off financial assistance to the tune of U$50-000 for the 2010 season to run our second division leagues that went crippled by the prevailing global economic melt down.' Bin Hammam responded personally: 'I really appreciate your kind support to Qatar Bid for 2022 World Cup ... As far as the request made by Namibia Football Association, I will see that it will be delivered as soon as possible.'*

The junket had been a runaway success. Just as Bin Hammam had hoped, it marked a turning point. Days after the last of the delegates returned from Doha on 7 January 2010, CAF announced that it had struck a deal worth $1.8 million for the official Qatar 2022 bid to sponsor its congress in Angola at the end of the month. The money would be paid into the confederation's bank accounts, which were ultimately controlled by its president, Hayatou.

---

* John Muinjo said his federation had been in need of funds but denied that the money was ever paid.

His secretary general Mustapha Fahmy emailed all the other bids after the deal was done to tell them that they had been effectively gagged by Qatar. 'Kindly note that CAF has signed an exclusive sponsorship agreement with Qatar 2022 for the CAF Congress 2010, which as a consequence means that no other bidding nations for the FIFA World Cup will be allowed to make any presentations at the Congress ... However, your delegation and representatives will be allowed to attend as "observers", but without the possibility to organise press conferences, distribute any promotional material or erect stands to that effect within the venue and its vicinity on that day.' Bin Hammam's African campaign had come to fruition. CAF belonged to Qatar.

Six

Cocktails, Conspiracy and a Million-dollar Dinner

The djembe were drumming and the atmosphere was fraught. It was January 2010 and a big year for African football with the continent's first World Cup just months away. But as the continent's best national teams descended on Angola for the Africa Cup of Nations, the celebratory mood was cut down by a crackle of machine-gun fire. A bus carrying the Togolese team had been peppered with bullets by terrorists as it crossed the border into the Angolan province of Cabinda ahead of the first game. The driver and an assistant coach died instantly and members of the team were rushed to hospital suffering from life-threatening gunshot wounds.

Togo called on the leaders of the Confederation of African Football to cancel the tournament, but it went ahead without them, nonetheless, as did the grubby deals of football politics. The final weekend of the Cup of Nations was when the CAF congress of 53 federations met to hammer out their business. Many of Mohamed bin Hammam's well-paid African friends were flying into Luanda, the coastal capital of Angola, with its palm-fringed beaches buffeted by Atlantic waves. The city, like

Doha, had thrust up quickly following an oil boom in the years after the country's bloody civil war, but it remained a grim place for millions of its inhabitants. The Luandan slums stank of bad drains and exhaust fumes from the city's gridlocked streets. The poor lived cheek by jowl in the cramped bairros with no running water or electricity, scavenging for scraps from the privileged few who hoarded the riches of the country's black gold rush.

These were not matters that needed to concern the CAF delegates. Their congress was being held in the spacious Talatona Convention Hotel on the city's southern fringe. The rainbow-coloured structure was the only five-star hotel in Luanda and was surrounded by open space, a stark contrast to the foetid over-crowding of the city outside its garden borders. Inside this haven of crisp linen and tall marble corridors were four FIFA Exco members – Issa Hayatou, Amos Adamu, Jacques Anouma and the new boy on the block, Egypt's Hany Abo Rida, who had been elected the previous year. Around them were scores of African football officials who might influence their votes in the ballot later that year to decide the host of the World Cup. Many were staying in the hotel's luxurious villas, a short walk through the abundant gardens for a morning dip in the pool. Over breakfasts of fruit and creamy cassava porridge, the delegates could see huddles of men in white dishdashas. Everyone knew why they were there. Those men from the Middle East were paying for the whole jamboree. It was nice to have such good friends.

News of the Qatar 2022 team's involvement in the CAF congress had shattered the respectful peace that had so far existed between the rival bidders. The bombshell was dropped by CAF's secretary general Mustapha Fahmy two days before the bullets had ripped through the Togolese coach. Qatar had quietly paid $1.8 million to sponsor the CAF congress and they wanted their money's worth. The other bid teams were livid when Fahmy informed them that they would be banned from promoting their World Cup campaigns. CAF had nailed its colours to the mast: the Qatar 2022 bid's advertising was plastered across the hotel and its logo was on almost every scrap of paper including the menus and invitations to Saturday evening's gala dinner – itself paid for by the men from the Gulf, naturally.

Qatar was the only bid allowed to take up the time of the African federation delegates with a slideshow presentation extolling the virtues of a Doha World Cup. As for the other bids, they had to sit on their hands as mere 'observers'. They were furious. The Swiss-Hungarian lobbyist Peter Hargitay was especially piqued after learning that the Australian bid he was working for had been excluded. He rang around the other countries to try to coordinate a complaint to FIFA, but it was to no avail. The bidding rules were not robust enough to prevent Qatar buying up the delegates' undivided attention in this way – as long as no CAF officials got a personal cut of the cash.

At the podium in the hotel's conference room, the Qatar bid's chief executive Hassan Al-Thawadi was in confident mood, displaying none of the doubts about his country's chances that had privately troubled Bin Hammam since the beginning. The script for his presentation had been written down for him and he had rehearsed carefully; by now he had the patter off by heart. The pitch went as follows: Qatar would present a 'very, very strong bid' which would be its gift to the entire region. People from Egypt, the Emirates or Kuwait had previously been unable to attend a World Cup. This would be their chance. Those from outside the Middle East would have an opportunity to see and experience a different culture when they visited Qatar. FIFA was a wonderful organisation that could bring the world together. Qatar had already hosted the Asian Games in 2006, and the 2022 World Cup would be a further catalyst for the development of football in the region. Al-Thawadi called on FIFA to repeat its historic decision in awarding Africa its first World Cup and hand the 2022 finals to the Middle East. He said Qatar shared Africa's ambition to harness 'the power of football as a vehicle for hope and understanding'.

Perhaps some of the delegates were listening and perhaps they weren't. Some looked anxiously at their watches wondering whether there would be time for a quick cocktail on a poolside sun lounger before daylight turned to dusk. And more importantly, where was their friend Amadou Diallo? Their fellow African *bonhomme* who paid for all the drinks was not in sight that day. He was fixing the side meetings in the enviable suite of the man who mattered most to the Africans: Bin Hammam. The rumours had been spreading. He was offering more cash to his friends in Africa and there were no strings attached. It was safest to pay the money into your personal bank account – that way it was in the right hands.

Al-Thawadi soldiered on through his carefully thought-out catchwords, which were illustrated with Powerpoint slide projections showing artists' depictions of the world-class facilities Qatar promised to build. The Gulf state was developing unique 'environmentally friendly' futuristic cooling technologies that would make the game playable in even the hottest weather. Air cooling systems had already been installed at the Khalifa International Stadium in Doha, and the bid was looking at ways to introduce those innovations to training grounds and fan zones too. He showed two video presentations, one of which showcased England's friendly match with Brazil at the stadium the previous November. It was possible to host major international games in Qatar – albeit in late autumn.

Yes, Qatar was a small country, but a geographically compact bid was a virtue, Al-Thawadi confidently stated. Small was good. Why? Because it meant that teams and fans would not have to worry about travelling or making hotel reservations in different cities hundreds of miles apart as they would in Australia or the US. Qatar had enough space for everybody out in the desert; enough to build a whole new city to accommodate the World Cup. The new metropolis of Lusail would be located 23km outside Doha, beyond the West Bay lagoon, and it would be a pleasureland of marinas, island resorts, an entertainment district, luxury shopping and leisure facilities (including two golf courses). There would even be an all-giraffe zoo. Why not? But the jewel in the city's crown would be the new Lusail Iconic Stadium, with a capacity of 90,000, which would host the opening and final matches of the 2022 FIFA World Cup. This sort of no-holds-barred innovation was what made Qatar special. The country was 'the epitome of a global village', Al-Thawadi said.

The Qatar bid had recently commissioned a socio-economic impact study by the UK chartered accountants firm Grant Thornton, which calculated that $11.6 billion would be injected into the nation's economy if the country were named the host of the 2022 World Cup: $6.7 billion from construction work; $2.1 billion from the tournament itself; and $2.7 billion from tourism. That was the true value of the prized tournament. Al-Thawadi acknowledged that Qatar was in a good financial position to provide a well-funded World Cup, insisting that the bid's real purpose was to further the development of his country and region. 'Qatar is a small nation with a big heart and huge ambition and it carries the hopes and dreams of millions of people across the Middle East,' he said. Then, to round off his presentation, he unveiled the Cameroonian football legend Roger Milla as the latest handsomely paid ambassador for the Qatar bid team, joining other heroes such as Gabriel Batistuta and Ronald de Boer on its star-studded roster.

The delegates applauded. It was time to get back to their

friends and family by the pool. As Al-Thawadi stepped down from the podium, he was ushered away by a woman in a smart dark-blue shirt suit and long raven hair. Phaedra Al-Majid was the bid's international media officer; she had prepared answers in advance to possible questions from journalists which might be posed to her chief executive after his congress speech. If asked about the sensitive matter of Bin Hammam's role in the World Cup campaign, Al-Thawadi was instructed to say no more than: 'Mohamed bin Hammam is a supporter of the bid in his role as a Qatari citizen, there is no doubt about that.' That was an under-statement, and Al-Thawadi knew it. However, Al-Majid's role in the Luanda conference was to acquire far more significance than her work as a press officer. She would end up making headlines around the world herself.

Al-Majid had joined the Qatar 2022 bid team in May 2009 as a specialist in communications work. She was a single parent of joint Iraqi and American nationality who had recently split up with her Qatari husband and was looking after her two sons, one of whom was severely autistic, on her own in an apartment in Doha. Quick-talking and combative, she often found herself in conflict with her Qatari male bid team colleagues in a culture where women were expected to take a subordinate role. She was, however, very useful to the bid. She had been heavily involved in organising the trip to Luanda, and had helped write Al-Thawadi's presentation. She was also fluent in French and was therefore called upon to translate when the bid met African members of the executive committee who did not speak English or Arabic as their first language.

Al-Majid attended a series of such meetings at the Talatona Hotel suites during the CAF congress in Luanda, and she would one day claim to have been shocked by what occurred at the congress. Two years later, Al-Majid was to become the first whistleblower to come forward and raise concerns about corruption in Qatar's World Cup bid. She would say that, at meetings in the hotel with the CAF president, Issa Hayatou, the Nigerian Amos Adamu and the Ivory Coast voter Jacques Anouma, Qatar had offered the eye-watering sums of $1.5 million each in exchange for their votes. The money would go to their football associations, she said, but there would be no questions asked about how it was used. 'It was said in such a way that "we are giving it to you",' she recalled. 'It was going to their Federation, basically if they took it into their pocket, then we don't give a jack.'

Al-Majid would eventually make her allegations in an interview with *The Sunday Times*, and her claims were published in a submission of evidence sent to a committee of MPs in the House of Commons. They caused a storm of controversy which momentarily threatened to engulf the 2022 bid. Its leaders denied her claims absolutely, as did Hayatou, Adamu and Anouma, but Al-Majid's testimony would leave a lingering stain on Qatar's World Cup dream.* However, the storm was a long time coming. For now, all was peaceful in Luanda where the CAF delegates were lapping up the hospitality of their friends from the Middle East.

The family of Amos Adamu were particularly enjoying the congress and the riveting football at the Africa Cup of Nations. They had cheered in the stands as their Nigerian team had battled through to the semi-finals and ended up in third place with a 1-0 win over Algeria. The small, stocky figure of Adamu was accompanied throughout the congress by his favourite son, the 26-year-old playboy Samson. While Adamu senior was taciturn

---

* Al-Majid would later retract her claims in a sworn statement, before saying she had been pressured into doing so by legal threats from Qatar 2022 and reasserting the allegations.

to the point of being monosyllabic, his son was a gregarious communicator with all the sheen of the best private education that his father's expanding fortune could buy.

Adamu had three sons who participated in the family's businesses. Phillips, his eldest from his first marriage, was a dry cleaner who also dabbled in sport; his second son, Ezekiel, was the manager of his father's thousand-seat events centre, one of Lagos's most profitable venues with the unlikely title Balmoral Hall. The tall, good-looking Samson was trying to get his foot in the door of the football business and was casting around for new money-making opportunities. He had been privately educated in Lagos and then sent away to study at the American University in Paris after a brief and unsuccessful stint in the Nigerian army.

A few months before the congress, Samson had graduated from the Université de Neuchâtel in Switzerland with a FIFA masters degree in sports administration. The bill for his degree had been taken care of by FIFA, who gave scholarships to five African students each year as a way of encouraging the sport's growth in the developing world. Along with his dry-cleaner brother Phillips, he had set up a company called Kinetic Sport Management with a share capital of £4,000 just three months before the Luanda trip. The company was registered at his father's high-walled villa in a wealthy suburb of Abuja, the Nigerian capital.

His company was largely dormant, but in the foyer at the Talatona Hotel he had met a very nice man in a flowing white robe who seemed keen to help get his business off the ground. It was none other than Ali Al-Thawadi, the deputy chief executive of the Qatar bid committee. The two men hit it off over strong black coffee, and hammered out a plan. Qatar 2022 wanted to sponsor a gala dinner to celebrate famous former African football players on the eve of the World Cup in South Africa that June. It would be called the Legends' Dinner and it was their way of demonstrating Qatar's continuing support for African football in the wake of the Luanda congress.

Ali seemed like a very kind man and a pleasure to do business with. He wanted Samson to be the organiser of the dinner, and he didn't ask any awkward questions about his inexperience in the world of commerce or the fact that Samson had never managed such an event before. After all, his FIFA Exco father knew how to throw dinners for hundreds of people – Adamu had been doing it for years in the family's Balmoral Hall events centre. Ali was surprisingly matter-of-fact about the details. He didn't need to see complicated costings for the event, there was going to be plenty of room in the budget. Qatar 2022 proposed to pay Samson the round sum of $1 million to put on the dinner. It was a very generous business proposal to the son of one of the Exco voters the bid needed to woo.

Standing majestically in the West Bay marina area of Doha is a glinting cigarette lighter of a building, 30 storeys and 125 metres high. The curved mirrored surface of the Qatar Olympic Tower concealed a hive of activity within. The 2022 bid team had their offices there, as did Mohamed bin Hammam. It was where the billionaire's life was organised by Najeeb Chirakal, his loyal and ever-affable personal assistant. If one of his master's entourage wanted a flight booked, they went to Najeeb. When somebody was paid off by Bin Hammam's slush fund, the payment slips would go to Najeeb. When the Qatar bid needed personal details of the FIFA Exco members or their wives, Najeeb would be their man. Indeed, Chirakal was so close to the Qatar 2022 bid committee that in January 2010, shortly before the Luanda congress, they had given him an employment contract to work for them part-time. He was to continue to run Bin Hammam's private office and at the same time provide 'international relations' services to the bid committee. The arrangement was kept under wraps. There was to be no public link between Bin Hammam and the team officially leading Qatar's World Cup campaign.

Chirakal was also Amadou Diallo's main point of contact for Bin Hammam. The Guinean was now working full-time for his Qatari boss to muster support for the World Cup bid. He would bellow the greeting 'Barakallah Feek!' – 'May the blessings of Allah be upon you!' – to his Indian friend when he phoned the Olympic Tower to arrange logistics for his various trips. Immediately before heading off to Luanda for the African congress, Diallo had been dispatched on another mission for the boss. As a fluent French speaker he was the ideal man to make overtures to the Netherlands–Belgium campaign for the 2018 World Cup and gather intelligence.

He took the train from his Paris home to meet the dreadlocked former French football player Christian Karembeu, who was employed as a special advisor to the Low Countries bid. On the way back, he dashed off a report for Chirakal to pass on to Bin Hammam. He said that the Dutch and Belgians had discussed deals with two of executive committee voters: Jacques Anouma and Reynald Temarii. Anouma was no surprise to Diallo. He wrote: 'The Belgians have confirmed that which I knew already: The Belgians have offered Jacques Anouma a collaboration within the scope of security and training. For example it is expected that the first module of training for the referees and coaches will be from the 31-01 to 5-02 [31 January to 5 February 2010] in Abidjan ... Oceania: The Belgians have proposed to Temarii through Louis Michel, former commissioner for Development at the European Union, a collaboration in the development, as Temarii has high political ambitions.'

The 2018 bid had also offered Diallo a sweetener in the form of a success fee if he helped use his contacts in Africa. But Diallo had to ask the boss first. He enquired: 'In the personal case of Diallo: the Belgians have proposed to me with Karembeu a premium in case of victory but I have said to them that I must ask your permission!!! What do you say?'*

Diallo had plenty of time to discuss his side-deal with the boss as they would be meeting in Luanda. Chirakal made the arrangements as usual and Diallo flew out to the Angolan capital to mingle with his African brethren and arrange meetings with Bin Hammam ahead of his boss's arrival four days later. Bin Hammam was still attending to important business in Doha. His guest on 25 January was one of the giants of African football, the great Liberian striker George Weah. The one-time World Player of the Year had plied his trade in the top tiers of French, Italian and English football, and was now dabbling in the game's politics.

The meeting with Weah went well. Later that day, Weah emailed Chirakal to confirm his agreement with Bin Hammam and offer his bank details: 'I write because after meeting with the President, he told me to pass on my contact and bank details information to you urgently.' No sooner had the email arrived at Olympic Tower than another one came in from one of Weah's associates, Eugene Nagbe, a prominent Liberian politician. 'George has repeatedly spoken of his support for our future plans in world football and we all look forward to your ascendency,' he wrote, adding that 'conservatively, an amount of about USD 50,000 will be needed ... to lock the election down' for Liberia's football federation chief, the 'Iron Lady' Izetta Wesley. 'Please be assured Mr President, that this is just a step in the bigger scheme of things to come. George have lined up most of the other former stars and the federations in Africa and South America so that when we are ready, your victory will be assured,' Nagbe added. The next month $50,000 was paid into Weah's personal bank account by one of Bin Hammam's slush funds, ostensibly for his 'school fees'.

---

* The Netherlands–Belgium bid denied offering any improper deals to voters.

For Bin Hammam, the Luanda conference was a chance to build on the friendships which had been forged during the two junkets in Kuala Lumpur and Doha. There was a hectic schedule of meetings ahead of him at the Talatona Conference Hotel. It was a busy week. Knocking on the door to Bin Hammam's suite were such familiar figures as John Muinjo, the Namibian FA boss, Seedy Kinteh of Gambia, and Ahmad Darw, the president of the Madagascar football association. Over tea and biscuits the chatter was convivial, and if the guests were a little obsequious, Bin Hammam was used to people fawning over him. The football officials had been impressed by Hassan Al-Thawadi's Powerpoint presentation. They were delighted to learn that Bin Hammam was doing so much for their continent and, coincidentally, they had heard that he might be in a position to help them out financially. American dollars would be fine, and they were happy to supply their bank details.

The delegates were quick to email Bin Hammam to remind him of his promises after the meetings in Luanda. Muinjo was first. 'Your delegation and their presentations left a lasting impression on the African continent,' wrote the Namibian. 'I have also congratulated the Bid 2022 Ceo, Mr Hassan Al-Thawadi afterwards through e-mail correspondences. Mr President, I am drafting these few lines as a follow up to our discussion with regard to the financial assistance please.'*

Seedy Kinteh was in dire straits again and needed cash to pay for his federation's annual congress. Chirakal sent him a remittance slip showing that a transfer of $10,000 had been made to his personal bank account from Bin Hammam's daughter Aisha. Ahmad Darw informed Chirakal that Bin Hammam had 'promised to give me a help' with his own re-election as president of the Madagascar FA. Asked by Chirakal how he would like the

* John Muinjo denied that he ever received the money.

money paid, he provided two options: 'by bank swift or I can take it in Paris with … Diallo.' Arrangements were made for the bagman to meet Darw in Paris in March to hand over the cash.

By the time Bin Hammam and his henchmen, Diallo and Meshadi, were in the limousine picking its way back through Luanda's traffic jams on the return to the airport, they had every reason to pat themselves on the back. Angola had been the icing on the cake after 18 months of hard graft. He was confident that he had the four African votes in the bag.

Seven

A Crimefighter in Cowboy Boots Comes to Zurich

The classy district of Ikoya, with its bustling designer shops and cocktail nightlife, is the most affluent area of Lagos, Nigeria's most populous city. It is crammed with high-rise buildings and luxury apartments with starting prices of $1 million, affordable only to the country's ruling elite or oil industry expatriates on expenses. Ikoya is Africa's most expensive patch of real estate. Within its boundaries is the more sedate and extremely exclusive Park View Estate, with easy access to the golf course and country club that serve as a reminder of the city's colonial past. This was the second home of Amos Adamu, the Nigerian FIFA executive committee member, when he wasn't in the capital, Abuja. His wasn't just an apartment in Park View – he had a mansion built in the style of a Spanish villa with pink roof tiles and white-rendered walls, standing in one acre of gardens. And, as if all this wasn't enough of a symbol of wealth and status, the villa's address left no doubt about the eminence of its main resident: Number One, Dr Amos Adamu Close.

The Adamu clan had barely enough time to unpack their suitcases from the trip to Angola before an email popped up in

Samson's inbox. It was from Ali Al-Thawadi, the man in the robe Samson had met in Luanda, using his official Qatar 2022 email address. 'It was a great pleasure meeting you and I hope you had a safe journey home,' fawned the campaign's deputy chief. 'I would like to congratulate you on the fantastic event held by CAF, which I thoroughly enjoyed.' That was generous of Al-Thawadi, given that his own bid had paid for the whole shebang, to the tune of $1.8 million. Next, he cut short the pleasantries and got down to business. 'Can you provide me with the full name and address of your personal company in order for me to get the contract and scope of work prepared between the two parties. I look forward to hearing from you as soon as possible.' Al-Thawadi had been as good as his word. One million dollars was coming Samson's way.

Samson acted quickly on his side of the bargain. He did not want such a large amount of cash to be paid through his Nigerian company, which was registered at his father's other home in the capital, Abuja. So he got on the phone to Daniel Magerle, a partner at the law firm of Magerle Jenal Stieger in the medieval Swiss city of Winterthur, and asked him to set up a company there. The fledgling entrepreneur may have been an ingénu in the world of business, but he was smart enough to know that a wire transaction to Switzerland might get less clogged up with red tape than if it went directly to his own country. International transfers of that size to Nigeria tended to set alarm bells ringing in banks' anti-money-laundering divisions. Samson had just returned from Switzerland with his FIFA masters degree, and he trusted the Swiss to handle his big payday with their usual discretion.

Magerle took up the negotiations with Ali Al-Thawadi the following day. 'Dear Sir, I am contacting you on behalf of Samson Adamu,' he wrote in an email. 'I am representing and legally advising Samson and the association regarding the African Legend [*sic*] dinner. On behalf of Mr Adamu, I inform you that the name of the association is "Kinetic Sports Association", an association under Swiss law.'

The Qatar bid was eager to get on with the deal. Within days, a contract had been drawn up by their lawyer, Romi Nayef, and sent to Samson on 10 February 2010. Entitled 'Legends of African Football – Gala Dinner – Sponsorship', it set out Qatar's offer of 'One Million United States Dollars' for the sponsorship rights for the dinner, which was to be held in Johannesburg on 10 June 2010 along with a three-day workshop for African journalists earlier the same month. The agreement was to be made between the newly created Kinetic Sports Association in Switzerland and a 'private institution' in Qatar 'which is bidding to host the 2022 FIFA World Cup ... and wishes to acquire certain exclusive rights in connection with the events in order to promote its bid to host the competition'. The bid team was clearly unrepentant about locking out their rivals in Angola: all the other 'competitor associations' were to be banned from marketing at the dinner under the contract.

The signatories on behalf of the bid committee were Hassan Al-Thawadi, its sharp chief executive, and its chairman Sheikh Mohammed, the son of the Emir. This was a dangerous move by the young leaders of Qatar's official bid. Samson was the son of one of the 24 FIFA voters they were trying to influence, and he stood to make a gigantic profit on this deal. The costings for the event, when they were eventually calculated, added up to no more than $220,000, but he was going to be paid $1 million. FIFA's rules forbade bidding countries from offering the voters or their relatives 'any monetary gift' or 'any kind of personal advantage that could give even the impression of exerting influence, or conflict of interest, whether directly or indirectly, in connection with the bidding process'. But Samson was going to walk away from his deal with Qatar with a cool profit of $780,000, just for organising a dinner. It was a breach of the rules on a massive scale, and the official Qatar bid team had always been so careful to keep their hands clean until now. What possessed Sheikh Mohammed and Al-Thawadi to put their names to such a contract? Had their success in Luanda gone to their heads?

Samson's next step was to get the elders of African football on-side. He flew to Lubumbashi, in the Democratic Republic of the Congo, on 20 February to present his vision for the gala dinner celebrating the continent's football legends to the Confederation of African Football executive committee who were meeting that day. In an email to Ali Al-Thawadi two days later, he enthused that the members had assured him of their 'total support and willingness to grace the occasion'. He went on: 'CAF's support is good in that it adds more credibility and prestige to our event.'

Back in Switzerland, his lawyer was compiling the paperwork for Samson's new association and arranging a bank account to receive the payment. 'The relationship to Switzerland would probably add a lot of additional credibility to the project,' Magerle assured his client. Then the lawyer encountered a snag. UBS had refused to open an account for the new association, he explained to Samson, because: 'Swiss banks are very sensitive these days and international pressure has increased on certain matters. I had to mention the nationalities of the persons involved. Nigeria is on the list of sensitive countries I am afraid. I would have to provide a whole list of documents and declarations to open the account.' It was just as Samson had feared, but the canny Magerle quickly found a solution. He could ask Qatar to pay the cash into the client account of his own law firm.

A meeting was arranged with Ali Al-Thawadi and a delegation from the Qatar bid at the five-star Intercontinental Hotel in London on Thursday 4 March. Samson would take his lawyer, and the deal would be sealed.

*

For Bin Hammam, Angola had been a great success. His ground-work over the past 18 months had paid off handsomely and he was encouraged by the messages of support for the Qatar bid which flooded into his inbox from his African brothers and sisters. There were still ten critical months to go before the secret ballot which would decide the hosts of the 2018 and 2022 tournaments, and his job was far from complete. It was time to step up his charm offensive a gear with the executive committee members whose votes he needed to win.

His private jet would be invaluable over the next few months. From Angola, Bin Hammam jetted in to Zurich to attend a finance committee meeting, sending FIFA a $16,342 bill for his expenses on the visit. Then he was back on the plane again the next day for lunch with Michel Platini at UEFA's modern university campus-style headquarters in Nyon, France on 3 February. The UEFA president's staff had scheduled a group lunch, but Bin Hammam insisted on a private session with Platini. Even his trusted bagman Mohammed Meshadi was left outside as the two grandees sauntered into a small corporate dining room, where the food was the nearest thing to Michelin-standard that a staff canteen can be. It took just a little over an hour for Bin Hammam to make his compelling pitch for Qatar to host the World Cup, and impress on Platini that the Gulf state and his home country, France, could enjoy excellent relations. The two men gave each other a comradely hug, then Bin Hammam was back in his car heading for the airport.

He was in a hurry because he had another important dinner lined up that evening back in Zurich at 7pm sharp. A giant Mercedes eased to a halt outside the foyer of the Baur au Lac Hotel and out stepped a man who looked as if he owned the place. It was Fedor Radmann, the debonair lobbyist who had accompanied the executive committee voter Franz Beckenbauer to Doha for the meeting with the Emir the previous October.

Radmann had the appearance of a minor European royal straight off the yacht. His white hair was carefully coiffed, and a pink silk handkerchief flopped out of the breast pocket of an elegantly tailored dark suit that neatly disguised the expanding girth of a man in his late middle age. He paused briefly to exchange pleasantries with the concierge before heading off to the place where he did much of his business: the Pavillon restaurant in FIFA's favourite hotel.

There, among the ever so delicately arranged sprays of out-of-season lilies and purple orchids, was his old friend Mohamed, looking equally urbane in his figure-hugging black Nehru jacket as he sipped his sparkling mineral water. The two men had a lot to talk about and they got straight down to it after Radmann summoned the waiter and ordered himself an aperitif. Radmann was, of course, working for the Australians along with Andreas Abold and Bin Hammam's old friend Peter Hargitay, so there was always the chance of picking up intelligence on what Qatar's rivals were up to. More importantly, Bin Hammam wanted to keep reminding Radmann and Beckenbauer of their debt his country, which had done so much to help Germany win the contest to host the 2006 World Cup. When, as Bin Hammam anticipated, the Australian bid was eliminated in the early rounds of the 2022 ballot, he expected Beckenbauer to vote for Qatar.

The billionaire couldn't linger in Zurich: he had to rush back to Doha to greet another very important guest. He was hosting Reynald Temarii, the executive committee voter from Tahiti, and he intended to make sure he was given the best in Arabian hospitality. Temarii was travelling with the secretary general of his Oceania confederation, Tai Nicholas, but he had a lunch scheduled with just himself, Bin Hammam and members of the Qatar 2022 bid. He also insisted that he should have some further private time with his Exco colleague.

These were encouraging signs. Temarii had publicly pledged

his vote to Australia during the World Cup draw in Cape Town the previous December, but just like Beckenbauer there was every reason to target his vote in the later rounds, assuming the Australians crashed out early. So Bin Hammam gave Temarii the full royal blue carpet treatment. The Oceania voter was chauffeured to the striking white Diwan Palace overlooking the West Bay to see the Emir on 9 February. As was customary, Bin Hammam sought a corner of the vast state reception room and stood with his head bowed while Temarii was presented to His Highness. Humbled by the experience, the Pacific islander wished the bid well. Another good sign.

Bin Hammam had to keep moving. Two days later, he was climbing the steps of his jet again. His first stop-off was Bangkok where he and Meshadi were welcomed by their friend and fellow intriguer Worawi Makudi, the FIFA Exco member from Thailand. Makudi was Bin Hammam's long-time ally in FIFA and it was natural that the squat Thai colleague was a fully signed-up supporter of the Qatar 2022 bid. Bin Hammam touched down in Bangkok to scoop up Makudi and then it was up in the air again, bound this time for the most heavily populated city in the world: Tokyo. There the two men renewed their acquaintance with Junji Ogura, Japan's respectfully quiet and gentle executive committee member. The entire official Qatar bid committee were also in town for the East Asian Championship. It was another chance to promote their campaign and appeal to Asia's four voters.

Still the punishing schedule did not let up. Soon Bin Hammam was once again burning aviation fuel as he sped to the South Korean capital, Seoul, where he, Makudi and Meshadi met one of the city's richest residents, Dr Chung Mong-joon, the final member of the Asian Exco quartet. That night they all dined in style in a revolving restaurant at the top of the landmark Seoul Tower, perched on Mount Namsan. The next day, Chung took

Bin Hammam to meet the country's premier, Lee Myung-bak, at the Blue House, an imposing presidential pavilion with a traditional Korean blue-tiled roof in the shadow of Bugaksan mountain. After his meeting with the president, Bin Hammam published a blog post on the Asian Football Confederation website extolling the unifying potential of the South Korean bid. 'What impressed me during the meeting was the Korean President's vision for football and his noble dream that it would bring peace to the two Koreas. No wonder, Korea's bid for the 2022 FIFA World Cup has his full and unqualified support,' he said.

The dinner with Chung was ahead of the two-day AFC congress, which was being held in Seoul that year. All four Asian bids were in the room, and it was important that Bin Hammam kept everyone happy. At a congress press conference on 17 February, he issued a rallying cry to FIFA, in his capacity as AFC president, to award the rights to host the 2022 World Cup to one of the bidding countries from Asia. He took the opportunity to speak publicly for the first time about his own country's bid, telling journalists: 'There are so many advantages if Qatar gets to host the World Cup . . . All the group matches can be played in venues which are within reasonable distance of each other . . . Secondly, Qatar will be representing the wishes and hopes of the Middle East.' With Ogura at his side during the speech, and Chung watching in the wings, he still had to maintain the appearance that the AFC president was neutral, so he was diplomatic: praising Qatar's rivals just as warmly. He would be equally happy if Japan or South Korea won, he fibbed. They had wonderful bids. Bin Hammam didn't have much to say about the Australian contenders, but then they didn't having a representative on the executive committee whose votes he wanted to win. His message, though, was clear. What he really wanted as AFC president was to see the World Cup come to Asia. It didn't matter where.

It was his next move that came as the really big surprise. Bin Hammam told the delegates that 'the time has come' for Asia to put up a candidate to challenge Sepp Blatter in the next FIFA presidential election. 'We would like to see an Asian as the president of FIFA,' he told the news conference. 'I believe that the time has come for an Asian to come forward for this position. And there is more than one potential candidate available from Asia to lead world football. When we have that person, I hope the whole of Asia will unite behind him.' The media seized on his words and widely speculated that Bin Hammam himself was preparing to enter the presidential race in the election the following year, though he played down that suggestion. All he wanted was to see an Asian at the top of FIFA, and he would swing his support behind any candidate from the region, he insisted.

The AFC president then did something even more overtly seditious. He told the *Guardian* newspaper that he and 'colleagues' on the executive committee planned to call for FIFA presidents to be restricted to serving two terms, just as Blatter had promised him back in 2002. This looked like a clear attack on the FIFA president as he neared the end of his third term. It wouldn't cut off Blatter's legs in the next election, because Bin Hammam's proposal would come into force later, but it was a clear statement about his suitability to rule over world football indefinitely. The president was quick to hit back. He called an impromptu press conference in Zurich to declare his determination to secure a fourth term. 'Now it is obvious there will be candidates for the FIFA presidency in 2011 – a candidate from Asia,' he said. 'I have not changed my position. I am still here, and I hope to still be here in 2011. I have not now finished my mission, and if the Congress will decide so, I will be at their disposal.'

Such a public spat with the FIFA president less than a year before the World Cup vote looked like a kamikaze move, and the lobbyists backing Qatar's rivals sniggered behind their hands. Bin Hammam had really overreached himself now. Blatter would be furious. The truth was that Bin Hammam wasn't so sure he could count on Blatter any more, and this was a good way of hedging his bets. Relations between the two men had been strained in recent months, and they had clashed at the previous meeting of the FIFA executive committee on South Africa's Robben Island. Blatter's support for Qatar seemed to be wavering, and the word was out that the decade-old alliance between Bin Hammam and the FIFA president was beginning to crumble. So Bin Hammam had to do something bold to turn things around.

Issuing such threats to Blatter's presidency from within his Asian power-base had two virtues. First, it addressed Bin Hammam's top priority of the moment: shoring up regional loyalties, which he hoped would ensure that Ogura and Chung transferred their votes to Qatar once the Japanese and South Korean bids crashed out in the early rounds of voting, as he intended they should. The gentle-spirited Ogura was easily pliable, but Chung was a tougher nut to crack. He and Bin Hammam had a long history as sworn adversaries which needed to be remedied. The AFC president's carefully worded statements in Seoul were the start of an ingenious strategy he had devised to win the South Korean's loyalty. Chung had his own well-known designs on the FIFA presidency, and this threat to mount an Asian candidate to topple Blatter was a sop to him. The assault on presidential term limits had been devised during private talks between the two men ahead of the AFC congress, and the plot continued by email in the months that followed.

The second virtue of Bin Hammam's show of muscle in Seoul was its potential to make Blatter rethink his recent frosty treatment of the Qataris. When it came to it, he believed all the FIFA president really cared about was clinging on to power, so if Bin Hammam had any leverage over the old campaigner it was the threat of toppling him from his gilded perch. If Blatter was backed into a corner, he could go one of two ways. He could either try to undermine his rival by destroying Qatar's bid, or he could attempt to ward off a presidential coup by backing the Gulf state in order to regain Bin Hammam's loyalty. The public challenge the Qatari had issued in Seoul was a gamble. Would it pay off?

You didn't mess with a man like Sepp Blatter and get away unscathed. A week after Bin Hammam threw down the gauntlet in Seoul, he received a nasty surprise. A round-robin email arrived from the president, casually informing members of the Exco that FIFA was saddling up a new ethics committee to police the bidding race for the 2018 and 2022 World Cups. Qatar's $1.8 million payment to sponsor the CAF congress had stirred up a hornet's nest of tensions between the rival bidders, and by February 2010 the tumult had still not died down. Rumours were swirling – no doubt fomented by Qatar's opponents – that other payments had been made directly to football officials.

Blatter's email announced that FIFA had finally appointed a new chairman of its ethics committee, filling a position that had been vacant since the departure the previous year of the last incumbent, Lord Coe, to head the organising committee of the London Olympics. The ethics body had been rudderless when the first complaints about the Angola congress sponsorship had been made to FIFA in January, but now something had spurred Blatter into action. The new chairman was Claudio Sulser, a 54-year-old former international football player turned lawyer, part of the Swiss clique that Blatter felt he could rely on. The president wrote: 'It is high time that the Ethics Committee took up its duties once again. Therefore, I would like to convene a meeting of the committee to address, in particular, the important matter of the bidding procedure for the 2018/2022 FIFA World Cups.'

Why was Blatter doing this? What could be gained from airing such dirty linen? Bin Hammam looked at the letter again. Did the ethics committee really have jurisdiction over the bids for the World Cup? It certainly never had before, but it was a relatively new body and the scope of its powers had yet to be tested. He was not going to take this without a fight. So he instructed Chirakal to send the letter on to the AFC's lawyers for a legal opinion. 'President referring the attached letter to you and would like you to verify if Ethics Committee is appropriate body to address the World Cup Bidding procedure,' Chirakal wrote in an email to Nguyen thi My Dung in the legal department. Nguyen's response confirmed Bin Hammam's fears. The ethics committee only acted in cases of misconduct or undignified behaviour by officials, which included 'discrimination, ineligibility to be official, conflict of interests, confidentiality, accepting gifts, bribery'. Bin Hammam could see this was a dark cloud on the horizon and Blatter had to be squared off.

Bin Hammam had always had mixed feelings about the FIFA ethics committee. World football's governing body had first introduced an ethics code in 2004 and then, at a meeting in Munich on the eve of the German World Cup two years later, congress had accepted the formation of a committee to enforce the new rules. It had been a laughably toothless body, as Bin Hammam knew full well: he had been one of its initial members. It had no investigative powers and was limited to reviewing the evidence put before it in the form of a written complaint.

Its first and only high-profile case had been four years earlier against Jack Warner, the notoriously rapacious Trinidad and Tobago executive committee member. Warner was alleged to have sold tickets for the German World Cup on the black market through one of his own businesses, Simpaul Travel, when they should have been distributed among members of the Caribbean football associations.

At a meeting to assess the case in Zurich, Bin Hammam was one of the ethics committee members who expressed disapproval of Warner's activities. 'What was unethical about the matter was that the company belonged to Mr Warner. As a FIFA vice-president, he should not be selling tickets for the World Cup,' Bin Hammam told the committee. Warner was found to have committed three ethics breaches, including a failure to declare his interest in Simpaul. Infractions of that sort were deemed so serious that the penalty stipulated by the code was 'eligibility for . . . removal from office'. But when the ethics committee's report on the case went to the Exco, they couldn't quite bring themselves to kick out one of their own. Instead, Warner's company was meekly requested to donate $1 million to charity. It was never clear whether it did so, and Warner kept his position.

However, Bin Hammam could see that the newly configured ethics committee might soon have teeth. FIFA had just appointed an investigator for the first time, as its 'security chief'. He was from the world outside complaisant Switzerland, where crimes like bribery were punishable by imprisonment. Chris Eaton cut an incongruous figure in jeans and cowboy boots as he strolled into the smoked-glass corridors of FIFA's Zurich headquarters to start his new job in April 2010. A balding 58-year-old Australian, with a greying handlebar moustache, Eaton seemed to be a genuine crime-fighter. He had been head-hunted from Interpol to improve FIFA's reputation by cleaning up international football and the federation's executives had great expectations of their new man. If the sleepy ethics committee – staffed by elderly judges and football administrators – was not fit for purpose in the modern era of global sport, Eaton had decades of domestic and international policing experience. Here was someone who could lead serious investigations into corrupt officials and match-fixers, and supply the ethics committee with hard evidence on which to act.

The chance to work at FIFA was a golden opportunity for the investigator who started his career as a police constable in the Melbourne seaside suburb of St Kilda. He had risen up the ranks as an agent in the Australian federal police, and served two stints as the national secretary of his country's police federation, before joining Interpol at its headquarters in Lyon, France. FIFA was offering him the chance to earn some serious money for the first time in his career. He told friends it was a 'very well-paid' job which would allow him to buy a new home for his retirement in seven years' time.

He had been recruited by Jérôme Valcke, the FIFA secretary general, on the recommendation of their mutual friend Louis Freeh, the former FBI director who ran the Washington-based private investigations company Freeh Group. Eaton had been promised a budget and a team to run proactive investigations. In an email he described his new job as advising Valcke and FIFA on 'issues impacting or potentially impacting on the World Cup and related events and in protecting the reputation of FIFA with respect to allegations of malpractice'. Bin Hammam did not like the way things were going.

The new ethics committee first meeting was scheduled for 15 March, but Bin Hammam had no time to waste worrying. He was notching up the air miles again that day, this time to Belgium, with Meshadi and his ever-loyal AFC office director Jenny Be in tow. It was a chance to meet up and discuss tactics with the executive committee voter Michel D'Hooghe in the more convivial surroundings of his home country, and further the entente with the Low Countries bid which had developed following Diallo's visit two months before.

The Belgians pulled out all the stops for Bin Hammam and his entourage in the manner he had so often done for his Exco colleagues. Accompanied by D'Hooghe and several members of the

Netherlands–Belgium bid, he was driven through Brussels to meet the Prime Minister Yves Leterme and then given a tour of the Palais de la Nation, the home of the Belgian parliament. He was then taken north of the city to the Chateau de Laeken, following in the footsteps of Napoleon as he crossed the threshold of the royal palace. Dressed in a sleek black suit and shirt with an orange silk tie, Bin Hammam was introduced to His Majesty the King Albert II of the Belgians, who was keen to impress on his guests the readiness of his people to host a World Cup. While very honoured to be in such exalted company, Bin Hammam was equally pleased to have successfully cemented a strong relationship with one of the other bidding countries. Afterwards, his hosts sent him a framed picture of his audience with the King to add to the impressive wall of celebrity photographs in the hall of his Doha home.

In return, Bin Hammam invited the leaders of the Dutch–Belgian bid to the draw for the 2011 Asian Cup in Doha on 23 April. The event was turning into a great opportunity to showcase his country's World Cup credentials. He had already sent out an invitation to another bid team he was cultivating: the Russians. Alexei Sorokin, the bid chief executive, and Vyacheslav Koloskov, their former executive committee member, were flown in to the Gulf state on a private jet for a five-day visit. Alas, the new Exco member and bid chairman Vitaly Mutko was unavailable to travel, but his underlings sent him a rapturous report of the hospitality they had received. The Qatar Football Association which was officially in charge of the country's bid was offering all-expenses-paid trips to the event for some of Bin Hammam's African friends, such as Fadoul Hussein of Djibouti and Said Mahmud Nur of Somalia.

The Qatar FA was also generously picking up the flight, hotel and meal bills for another key Exco voter, Hany Abo Rida. The Egyptian had fast become a close ally of Bin Hammam's since his election to football's ruling committee in 2009. Abo Rida had the appearance of a minor North African dictator in his light suits, outsized black shades and close-cropped hair. Having risen from relative obscurity in Egyptian football, his new power at FIFA had made him useful to the ruler of his country, the bloodthirsty President Hosni Mubarak, and Abo Rida was enjoying increased status at home. Football had that kind of exalting effect. The shrewd Egyptian could see that Bin Hammam was a powerful man to cosy up to, and he had given his new ally a cast-iron assurance of his vote for Qatar in the secret World Cup ballot that December. So he received a particularly warm welcome when he touched down in Doha that April.

The most special guest of all at the Asian Cup draw had received his invitation directly from the Diwan Palace and would be spending several days in Doha. Bin Hammam was notified the week before Sepp Blatter's arrival in a short letter which read: 'Dear President, I am very pleased to inform you that I will pay a courtesy visit to the Qatar Football Association and the Amir of Qatar's family next Tuesday, 20 April 2010 ... Looking forward to seeing you soon.' Bin Hammam knew that the old fox could never resist a request from the Emir, and this was the chance to rebuild bridges. He instructed Chirakal to make arrangements to receive Blatter and make sure he had the best room in the Sheraton Hotel. Bin Hammam himself went to the airport to meet the FIFA president off his private jet, and the pair were photographed together on the airstrip. Relations between the two men had become increasingly fraught since that dinner with the Emir two years earlier, when Blatter had suggested the World Cup should come to Qatar, and Bin Hammam wanted to know where he stood now. This was an opportunity to test the president's shifting allegiances.

The immediate crisis dissipated just as the dust whipped up in a sandstorm falls to earth when the wind subsides. Blatter was once again his disarming charming self – impeccably polite to his hosts. Bin Hammam did not mince his words during his talks with Blatter, and the FIFA president would later describe his Qatari friend as having been 'aggressive' during their encounters. But his candour had the desired effect, as did the gracious hospitality from the Emir. At the end of his visit, the FIFA president was a fully signed-up supporter of Qatar's World Cup dream once more. And he didn't just give pat reassurances in private: he decided to go on record and tell the globe how wonderful it would be to see the tournament take place in the desert country.

At a news conference in Doha, flanked by the president of the Qatar FA, Sheikh Hamad bin Khalifa bin Ahmed Al Thani, he declared: 'The Arab world deserves to host the World Cup. We are now nearing the end of the bidding process for the World Cups in 2018 and 2022 and Qatar is the only country bidding from the Middle East. I was an advocate of the FIFA rotation policy. It was important to bring the World Cup to North America and Africa. Now I strongly feel that the World Cup should come to Qatar. I'm a regular visitor to Qatar and every time I land there, I am impressed by all the development.' The FIFA president said he was certain that Qatar had the organisational abilities to host the tournament and dismissed suggestions that the country's low ranking in world football would have any bearing on its bid. 'What matters are the guarantees the bidding country has to offer and on that count I have no doubt that Qatar will put on the table all that is needed to host the event,' he enthused.

It was exactly what Bin Hammam and the Emir wanted to hear, but Blatter's pronouncement caused consternation among the other countries bidding for the 2022 tournament. The Australian press reported that the A$43 million their own bid had so far spent on its campaign had 'gone up in smoke' and there was speculation in America that the US bid was dead in the water. Qatar had gone from being a rank outsider to being the country to beat. No one could claim the tiny Gulf state was not a serious and viable contender now. The FIFA president had said so.

Bin Hammam was delighted. He wrote to Blatter after he returned to Zurich in May rhapsodising that it had been wonderful to have the FIFA president back in his 'home Qatar', adding: 'It was really very pleasant moments to my heart that we exchanged brotherhood discussions.' Blatter was duly rewarded. Later that summer, Bin Hammam neutralised the threat he had issued at the AFC congress in Seoul. 'Let me be very clear, I will not run against Sepp Blatter: I will be backing him to remain in office for a new mandate. He is my very good friend,' he told journalists. The presidential powerplay had paid off handsomely, and all was well again.

Keeping the African voters sweet remained a priority for Bin Hammam as the official Qatar 2022 committee prepared to unveil the bid book containing its bold plan for a desert World Cup to FIFA in May. A fortnight after Blatter's visit, on 7 May, Bin Hammam headed down to Abidjan, the home of Jacques Anouma, the Ivory Coast executive committee voter who had pledged to 'push hard' for a Qatar World Cup following the Doha junkets. He was there to preside over the inauguration ceremony for the Ivory Coast's third FIFA Goal Bureau project to improve the facilities of a football training centre at Bingerville, an eastern suburb of the Ivorian capital.

The Goal Programme had long been mired in allegations that Blatter had used the development cash to buy African support for his presidency in successive elections and, as the president's placeman heading its committee, Bin Hammam understood its power to peddle soft influence only too well. In the two years before the

World Cup ballot, three of the Exco voters' home country associations – Nigeria, Cameroon and the Ivory Coast – were recipients of Goal generosity. Anouma's football association had already received two tranches of $400,000 from FIFA to build this National Technical Centre in Bingerville, a city where children still died from starvation and poverty was commonplace. This third project was funded by another $400,000 from FIFA to improve the dormitory facilities and build a new gym at the centre. Indeed, Anouma's pet scheme would receive a further $400,000 for an unprecedented fourth Goal project a month before the ballot. The record was seen as a badge of pride for Anouma.

A large crowd had gathered from far and wide on the centre's football pitch for the event. There were the usual town bigwigs and two government ministers. But the guest list had been arranged by Amadou Diallo and as a result football officials from no fewer than 17 African countries had flown in to the Ivory Coast – including Amos Adamu. Diallo had also brought in Christian Karembeu, his ally from the Netherlands–Belgium bid who had himself been lobbying Anouma. Karembeu was pictured showing off his skills, juggling a football for the photographers. The ceremony started with Bin Hammam cutting a ribbon and unveiling a foundation stone. Then Anouma launched into a long speech expressing his appreciation and thanking almost everyone present on the pitch by name. There was only a fleeting mention of the 'Qatar delegation', but any savvy observer would have deduced that the men from the Gulf state were the most significant guests.

The members of the Qatar 2022 bid committee stayed out of shot of the many photographs that were published after the event. The bid committee's attendance had been organised by Diallo, and Bin Hammam's staff had hired their private jet for the trip – later sending the $105,000 bill for the plane to the bid. Alongside Bin Hammam on the jet to the Ivory Coast were the four leading figures in the bid: Hassan Al-Thawadi, the chief executive; Ali Al-Thawadi, his deputy; Hamoud Al Subaey, director of government affairs; and Sheikh Sultan bin Abdulrahman Al-Thani, director of international relations. The bid committee liked to keep its distance from Bin Hammam publicly, determinedly maintaining that he was not associated with their campaign, but this was too good an opportunity to miss. By making their presence felt at the ceremony in Bingerville that day, the official Qatar bid team could piggyback on the goodwill Bin Hammam had secured by dishing out the Goal Programme cash to the Ivory Coast. This was the sort of advantage that came from having a powerful point-man inside FIFA: the perfect chance to rub shoulders with the African voters and remind them of Qatar's generosity to their continent as they prepared to unveil the details of its bid proposal.

The ceremony in Bingerville had coincided with another happy event: Bin Hammam's 61st birthday on 8 May. When he returned to Doha he found his inbox full, as usual, with gushing emails wishing him many happy returns. Flattered, Bin Hammam sent a global email to all his acolytes in the AFC thanking them for their kind messages, but one correspondent deserved special attention. He replied by letter to Fedor Radmann expressing his gratitude to the German fixer and his 'lovely' wife Michaela for remembering him on his 'special day'.

Chirakal was busy chartering a jet to fly 14 members of Qatar's bid committee to Zurich to hand over their 20-chapter bid book on 13 May, but there was another important matter to attend to before they took off. It was time for Bin Hammam to top up the coffers of that familiar rascal, Jack Warner. He'd known Jack for more years than he cared to recall. They had pressed shoulders in the premium seats at some of the world's best stadiums; they had swapped stories at some of the world's most tedious FIFA congresses; they had sparred on committees; and in happier times they had plotted long into the night to make sure their patron Blatter retained the presidency.

Jack was a live-wire, a coiled spring, as funny as he was outrageous: a useful friend but a dangerous opponent. Bin Hammam had seized a chance to quell this unpredictable bundle of energy in 2006 with his righteous outburst about Jack's black-market ticket business in the ethics committee meeting. It should have proved fatal, but the man who styled himself by email as 'd'survivor' had brushed off the attack by calling in favours from his executive committee friends and walked away as ever with his head held high. There was no doubt: Jack Warner remained a force to be reckoned with. Bin Hammam therefore had done everything he could to repair the damage to their friendship, including opening his chequebook wide. It had worked, and Warner now called him 'my only brother in football'.

The Qatari had taken Warner to China back in 2008, flattering his ego by calling on his expertise as a 'consultant' to the Vision Asia project and paying for his flights, hotels and chauffeur-driven limousines all the way. The pair were accompanied on their junket by the wily old lobbyist Peter Hargitay, and the group narrowly escaped disaster when the Sichuan earthquake struck the Chengdu Shuangliu International Airport – just moments after their private jet took off from its runway. The calamity provided a useful cover for Bin Hammam to spoon a bit more honey into Jack's teapot. He wired Warner $250,000 that year as a goodwill gesture, ostensibly to cover 'losses' he had sustained to his personal property in the earthquake they had escaped. Now the great survivor was back for more.

Warner was a player. As the president of CONCACAF he held sway over the confederation's three Exco votes, including his own. As we have seen, FIFA's rules forbade any associate of a bid committee from giving voters any benefit which might appear to influence them in the bidding process. But there was no other way of keeping Jack happy and this was an important moment, with Qatar on the cusp of unveiling its bid book to the world. On 12 May, the day before the delegation flew to Zurich to hand over the document to Blatter, Najeeb Chirakal wrote to Amelia Gan and Jenny Be at the AFC to tell them Bin Hammam wanted the details of the bank account 'where you have last made a transfer to Jack Warner'. Be responded attaching a document containing the CONCACAF bank details, explaining 'this was the account we made the transfers to'. The money would be paid through one of the Kemco slush funds and even FIFA's crack new investigator Chris Eaton would find it difficult to get to the bottom of one transaction among millions from an electrical company in a country as secretive as Qatar. So Chirakal ordered the Kemco clerks to pay the CONCACAF account which Warner controlled a further $200,000.

Two days later, Sheikh Mohammed and Hassan Al-Thawadi touched down in Zurich with 12 of their colleagues on a jet chartered for them by Chirakal in his capacity as a bid employee. They were chauffeured to FIFA headquarters, where they met Sepp Blatter and Jérôme Valcke to present their bid book. The tome revealed for the first time the full details of what the first World Cup in the Middle East would entail. It set out plans for 12 proposed stadiums, and promised that Qatar 2022 would be a carbon-neutral World Cup, using eco-friendly technologies and state-of-the-art cooling systems for stadiums, fan zones and training grounds. Spectators, players and officials would enjoy comfortable open-air conditions not above 27°C, the bid book promised. Qatar's transportation system would be revolutionised with a new Doha International Airport and the new Qatar Metro high-speed rail network linking all 12 stadiums.

That day, Sheikh Mohammed released a statement saying:

'The submission of our bid book today in Zurich is a historic moment for Qatar and its people. Today I am here not only on behalf of the Government of Qatar and all those involved in the game of football; I am here to represent the dream of each and every single boy and young girl of Qatar, to express and share with you the passion of our athletes and our fans who have supported our Bid from the very beginning, to manifest the desire of every family in our region who has shared our ambitions and hopes to bring the World Cup to the Qatari people. A World Cup in Qatar will be a New World Cup, bringing people and different cultures together in the name of football. Our bid book sends a clear message: Qatar is ready.'

The bid team flew home the following day, on the jet chartered by Chirakal. Four days later, the fat sum of $200,000 plopped into Jack Warner's CONCACAF bank account. The ever-efficient Chirakal sent a confirmation email back to Bin Hammam on 18 May 2010 enclosing a facsimile of the payment slip to Warner, with the note: 'Dear President, please find attached the document for your information.' Bin Hammam's loyal aide would one day come to regret leaving a paper trail like that. While Bin Hammam was not officially associated with the bid, keeping the taint of his corrupt payments away from its leaders, Chirakal had signed an employment contract with Qatar 2022 earlier that year. Warner was one of the 24 voters who would be sent the bid book Qatar had just submitted to FIFA and asked to assess its merits ahead of the secret ballot that December. Now he would also have Bin Hammam's $200,000 payment weighing on his mind – and it had been facilitated by an employee of Qatar's official 2022 bid.

Qatar had suffered a few knocks since the controversy over its sponsorship of the Angola congress, but now it was time for fortune to favour the brave once more. While Bin Hammam was mulling over his payment to Warner, a major controversy had broken out which completely distracted the world's media from Qatar's behaviour. The England bid had imploded in spectacular fashion. It was a very English farce that would never have happened in Qatar. The World Cup was due to start in South Africa the following month, and the ballot for 2018 and 2022 was less than six months away. Lord David Maxim Triesman, the 66-year-old FA chairman who was leading the English bid, had met a younger woman for coffee in a London café a couple of weeks earlier. The woman, a 37-year-old civil servant named Melissa Jacobs, had dined with Triesman several times and the pair had exchanged some mildly flirtatious texts.

On this occasion, she had decided to record their conversation covertly and hand the tapes to a national newspaper whose photographer was waiting outside the café with a long lens. Over coffee Triesman, formerly a junior government minister, entertained Jacobs with gossip he had picked up while travelling the world promoting England's bid. Soon after the meeting, Triesman heard the stomach-churning news that the *Mail on Sunday* newspaper was planning to publish his indiscreet comments to the world. Despite the FA's eleventh-hour attempt to halt publication of the story with a court injunction, it became front-page news and Triesman was forced to fall on his sword immediately. The headline read: 'FA Chief: Spain in bid to bribe World Cup referees.'

In the tape recording, Lord Triesman had told Jacobs: 'There's some evidence that the Spanish football authorities are trying to identify the referees ... and pay them.' He continued with an overly optimistic view of England's chances. 'I think the Africans we are doing very well with. I think we're doing kind of well with some of the Asians. Probably doing well with Central and North America,' he said.

Bin Hammam knew the African and Asian voters well, and there wasn't a prayer of them voting for England. The chances of the self-styled home of fair play and moral rectitude securing the backing of men like Jack Warner and his North American cronies were even more laughable. His Lordship had continued by saying: 'My assumption is that the Latin Americans, although they've not said so, will vote for Spain.' He was right about that, and Bin Hammam was factoring the Latin voting bloc into his strategy. Then Triesman had returned to his extraordinary allegation about a Spanish plot to rig the upcoming World Cup in South Africa through bribery. 'If Spain drop out, because Spain are looking for help from the Russians to help bribe the referees in the World Cup, their votes may then switch to Russia.' This whole idea seemed preposterous to Bin Hammam. Spain were the best team in the world: why would they need to bribe referees? Lord Triesman later admitted he had merely been passing on tittle-tattle he had learnt from unnamed journalists.

The whole affair was acutely embarrassing for the stuffed shirts who ran English football, and Bin Hammam soon received a grovelling letter from Sir David Richards, the vice-chairman of the FA. 'Dear president, on behalf of The FA I would like to sincerely apologise for any embarrassment which has been caused to FIFA and the national associations due to alleged comments attributed to Lord Triesman on Sunday in an English newspaper,' the letter began. 'In my capacity as Vice Chairman of the The FA I wanted to notify you personally that Lord Triesman has resigned as both Chairman of The FA and Chairman of England's FIFA World Cup Bid Board. Clearly, the newspaper reports are highly embarrassing and I want to make clear to you and everyone at FIFA that the comments allegedly made by Lord Triesman do not in any way reflect or represent the personal, private or official views of the FA, England's FIFA World Cup Bid Board or myself.'

Bin Hammam replied graciously. 'I really appreciate your taking the time to explain the situation to me,' he wrote.

'Wishing you all the best and looking forward to seeing you in the future.'

This was too delicious. The England bid was finished. Its Exco member Geoff Thompson was rushed in to lead the bid as Triesman's replacement, but that was all they needed. Thompson was universally disliked by the members of the bid, who said they felt his promotion of the country's campaign had been decidedly lacklustre because he had been piqued at having been initially overlooked for the job as chair. Senior figures on England's bid board complained privately that Thompson was 'a terribly self-serving man' who was doing 'nothing to help us'. One was even heard dismissing England's voter as being 'just a blazer – a small-minded man from Chesterfield'. And now they were stuck with him. It was all very amusing to Bin Hammam.

What's more, Spain were furious, Russia were incandescent and the members of the FIFA executive committee roundly deplored Lord Triesman's indiscretions. While the FIFA family fulminated in the 48 hours after the story broke, Bin Hammam's $200,000 bung slipped unnoticed into Warner's bank account. The FIFA ethics committee, which had been asked by Blatter to keep an eye on the bidding process, launched an immediate investigation into Triesman's claims, politely asking the Spanish and Russians whether they were paying bribes. Following their inevitable denials, the new ethics chair Sulser promptly declared that there was no evidence, and all was forgotten. This was the sleepy ethics committee Bin Hammam knew so well. They had not even involved their new investigator, but Bin Hammam was keeping a wary eye on Chris Eaton nonetheless. The cowboy-booted corruption fighter remained a potential threat.

The South African World Cup was now on the horizon and, on 28 May, an email arrived in Bin Hammam's inbox inviting him to a black-tie event on the eve of the tournament at the Vodaworld centre in Midrand, Johannesburg. The message was from Samson Adamu with a haplessly glaring error in the opening line. 'Dear Sir,' the 26-year-old wrote. 'As the distinguished President of UEFA, Kinetic Sports Management requests the honour of your presence at the first ever African Legends dinner. The African Football Legends dinner is an exclusive event to honour the continent's football heroes.' There was no reference to the Qatar 2022 bid as official sponsors. What had happened?

After the scheduled meeting in London with the Qatar bid in March, Samson had steamed ahead with the preparations for the dinner. He had sub-contracted organisation duties to a South African sports events company called Champion Tours, which quickly calculated that the dinner would cost a maximum of $220,000. The event was to go ahead on 8 July, two days earlier than originally planned. The organisers had been driven to distraction by the lack of coordination from Samson. No running order or table plan was put in place, and the young entrepreneur did not arrive at the venue until two hours before the event was due to start. At the last moment, he announced that an additional 30 places had to be included for extra guests, further instructing the organisers to hire eight hostesses and have special costumes made for them to wear. A seamstress was brought in the evening before the event and made to work through the night to get the outfits ready.

On the evening of the dinner, Samson seemed less than self-assured as he stood to address the candlelit ballroom packed with the great and the good of African football. Admittedly, he was looking sharp in his well-cut black suit and a crisp white dress shirt, but he spoke haltingly as he welcomed the 300 eminent guests. At the tables were leading figures from the world of football including David Dein, the ex-Arsenal chairman, and Lennart Johansson, the former UEFA president. The members of the CAF executive committee kept their promise to 'grace' the event with their presence, as did around six FIFA Exco members. There were 20 famous former African footballers, including Bin Hammam's friend Kalusha Bwalya, the former Zambian winger, and Jomo Somo, the former South African midfielder, who had been flown business class into Johannesburg to be honoured at the dinner.

The guests were welcomed by Issa Hayatou, the CAF president, and Kirsten Nematandani, the president of the South African FA. Samson had every reason to feel on edge. It was the first time he had ever organised an event on anything close to this scale. To add to the pressure, his father Amos Adamu was watching closely from a nearby table in full Nigerian costume as his son assured the glittering crowd that his company had 'no commercial affiliates' and was driven by one pure goal: 'To celebrate with you the achievement of our past football heroes.'

As the guests sipped champagne, enjoyed live African music and their three-course dinner, they may not have stopped to wonder where their young host had found the funds to provide them with such a lavish evening of free entertainment. Mysteriously, Qatar did not make any attempt to promote itself as a sponsor and left no trace of its involvement with the dinner. An early guest list drawn up by Samson showed that a table of eight was initially reserved for Qatar 2022, but nobody from the bid team actually attended the event on the night. Something had spooked the bid in the months since they first sent Samson the contract. Perhaps it was a hangover from the row over the sponsorship of the Angola congress, or the fact that the reformed FIFA ethics committee – with a serious investigator at its disposal – were now actively looking into the bidding process. The official Qatar bid team would say, when questioned later, that they had backed out of the deal after belatedly considering the 'relevant FIFA rules'.

So who did pay for the dinner? Samson's company, with its share capital of just £4,000, could never have afforded it, especially as the tickets were free and there was no visible sponsor.

Samson's lawyer, Magerle, said the meeting with the Qatar bid officials in London had never gone ahead because the deal had fallen through for reasons which were unknown to him. He had aborted the plan to set up a Swiss association and did not know how the dinner was financed, but assumed his client had found some other source of ready money.

A prominent African journalist had been approached by Amos Adamu in March to ask for help identifying legendary footballers to honour at his son's dinner. The journalist said he was later told by Samson that the event was being paid for by 'friends in Qatar'. Was this so? If so, which Qatari individual or organisation had picked up the tab dropped by the 2022 bid? Samson also brought in a friend called Nadia Mihindou to help him with arrangements for the dinner. She believed the event was being paid for with 'private funds' arranged by Samson, but would not say exactly where the money had come from. When told that her friend had been all set to receive $1 million from backers in the Gulf state, she responded incredulously. 'If that dinner had cost a million dollars, I think I would have known about it.'

The funding of the African Legends Dinner would remain shrouded in mystery. It was not so much a whodunit as a whopaidit. Two years later, when *The Sunday Times* published documents exposing Qatar's $1 million offer to the son of a voter to host the event, Samson's little deal with the Qatar bid would spark the biggest internal ethics investigation FIFA has ever undertaken. But the puzzle remains unsolved.

Eight

My Enemy's Enemy

South Africa was braced. The greatest sporting show on earth was about to arrive in Johannesburg, and the whole world was watching. The red-and-gold mosaic cauldron of the Soccer City stadium, built specially for the event, stood empty in an expectant hush as the vuvuzela sellers unloaded their crates on the streets outside. Troops of drummers, dancers and musicians practised their performances for the opening ceremony, while at training camps around the country the world's football superstars were limbering up for the greatest challenge of their careers.

It was this single month every four years that gave FIFA its true power and purpose: four heady weeks in which the entire planet would be whipped into transports of patriotic fervour and united by the universal language of the glorious game. That pass; that move; that tackle; that save; the painted faces chanting in the crowd; the short roar of delight spiked by instant dismay as the ball hurtles goalwards but glances off the post. The agony and the ecstasy of football. There could only be one winner because there was only one World Cup. Now it had arrived in Africa.

Mohamed bin Hammam knew just how critical this moment was for his own campaign. It would bring together the 24 members on FIFA's executive committee six months ahead of the secret ballot to decide the hosts of the 2018 and 2022 tournaments. All nine bidding countries would be there, jostling fiercely to win their votes. The official Qatar 2022 bid committee was paying Najeeb Chirakal to handle all the logistics of their own stay in South Africa, while at the same time he co-ordinated Bin Hammam's movements during the trip. The committee would be there in force, led by Sheikh Mohammed, to press the flesh and promote their campaign at all the glittering events going on around the tournament. While Qatar's figureheads shone brightly in the public eye, Bin Hammam would be executing big plans of his own in the backstage shadows.

The Qatari football grandee and his entourage flew into Johannesburg days ahead of the kick-off on 11 June. He was accompanied, as he so often was, by Jenny Be and the trusty Mohammed Meshadi. Even Chirakal came along for this trip. Bin Hammam's bespectacled lieutenant was a home bird who was rarely spotted outside Doha, but the chance to see the world's greatest tournament was too good to miss even for him. The three aides were good friends, and they made a merry party. Be joked that her male companions looked like Asia's answer to Men in Black as they reclined on the jet's cream leather seats in their black suits and dark glasses. The two men had formed a firm smokers' friendship over many leisurely cigarette breaks outside the AFC building in Kuala Lumpur, and they chatted easily. Be was fond of Najeeb and just as starry-eyed as all the AFC women were about Meshadi, who swanned around with his sunglasses hooked raffishly into the unbuttoned collar of his shirt.

The white winter sun shone brightly as the jet touched down in Johannesburg, but June is one of South Africa's coolest months, with evening temperatures of around 6°C, and the party were unused to the chill. One of Bin Hammam's first acts before the tournament began was to visit the city's branch of Loro Piana, his favourite luxury Italian clothes store, and shell out $3,072 on a cashmere overcoat to keep the cold at bay. It was small change for a billionaire, but he stuck it on his AFC expense account anyway. The four of them checked into the palazzo-style Michelangelo Hotel in the wealthy 'white flight' district of Sandton, where all of football's head honchos would be staying in the best suites while the tournament was in town. Schmoozers like Fedor Radmann and Peter Hargitay would be waiting under the soaring glass ceiling of the vast lobby atrium to buy them drinks and whisper in their ears at the bar.

Amadou Diallo wasn't travelling in Bin Hammam's immediate entourage, but of course the Qatari billionaire had paid for his African bagman to fly in for the continent's first World Cup. He had stipulated that Diallo be placed in the 'African delegates' hotel' and gave instructions to send on the bill for all the guests he entertained there during his stay. Diallo had plenty to keep him busy. It had been a few months since the continent's football bosses last had their coffers replenished in Angola, and the requests began rolling in thick and fast before he had even had time to unpack.

The opening ceremony on 11 June was a spellbinding display of African culture. It began with a five-plane flypast over the 94,000 capacity Soccer City stadium, built to look like a giant African calabash cooking pot, followed by a flamboyant procession of drummers and dancers, who performed a welcome song introducing the ten cities around the country where the tournament would be played. A giant wicker dung beetle dribbled the Jabulani – the official match ball of the 2010 tournament – around the stadium before performers created an aerial map of the continent and then the world out of swathes of streaming cloth. Hundreds of dancers swirled around a vast, smoking calabash in the centre and musicians and artists from the other African finalists – Algeria, Cameroon, Ghana, Ivory Coast, and Nigeria – all had their chance to perform alongside the locals. At the climax, R

Kelly sang the ceremony's showpiece song, 'Sign of a Victory', backed by the Soweto Spiritual Singers to a rhapsodic crowd.

In the stadium, Archbishop Tutu and President Zuma were joined by illustrious guests including the United Nations secretary general Ban Ki-moon, Prince Albert of Monaco and the vice-president of the United States, Joe Biden. The display was beamed around the world to hundreds of millions of viewers in more than 200 countries. And then came the kick-off of the first match, drawn 1-1 between South Africa and Mexico, and the tournament was underway.

Africa's first World Cup was a global sensation: the most-watched TV event in history. It was as if the axis of the earth had tilted so that the whole planet spun around Soccer City for those four weeks. But inside, the stadium was strangely empty. It was the same at many of the 64 games at the ten World Cup stadiums across South Africa: the stands were scarred by areas of empty seats. FIFA's critics said football's avaricious governing body had priced local fans out, charging exorbitant ticket fees in a country where 10 million people were still living in extreme poverty. The organisation insisted that the tournament was sold out, and blamed foreigners who had bought tickets and then hadn't bothered to travel for the thousands of vacant places. It was a shame if the people of South Africa couldn't afford to watch the tournament that had cost their country 40 billion rand ($3.55 billion) to stage, but it didn't matter much to world football's top brass. They were busy sipping champagne inside the stadiums' VIP enclosures, and being paid handsomely for the privilege.

The World Cup was a jamboree like no other for FIFA's rulers. The Exco were the luckiest men on earth. Millions of football fans around the world would give their eye teeth to watch just one World Cup match from the terraces, but these 24 men had gold-plated tickets to all the games they cared to grace with their presence. It was a privilege beyond riches, but FIFA's beneficence towards its own did not stop there. On top of the $100,000 annual honorarium they all received for the handful of committee meetings they were expected to attend in Zurich, every man would trouser a further $200,000 that year as a 'World Cup bonus'. Just for showing up. That was before they had even sent in their expense forms for the $700 allowance they raked in for each day they spent watching the world's best-loved tournament – on top of the first-class flights and five-star hotel suites which all came free as a perk of the job. Yes, life was sweet in FIFA's boss class.

Everyone who was anyone in world football was in South Africa. Here came the clip of Chris Eaton's cowboy boots: the swaggering new investigator had been brought in to co-ordinate the security for the tournament alongside Johannesburg's deputy chief of police, Andre Pruis. And there was Jérôme Valcke, stalking through the Michelangelo Hotel in his navy FIFA blazer and his light-blue shirt, with his usually curly hair cropped close to his scalp. This was the secretary general's big moment. Valcke had played a major role in the organisation of this tournament, overseeing all the preparations, cajoling the local organising committee into action when they fell behind schedule, and leaping to the defence of the host country when the English media criticised South Africa's shaky infrastructure and high crime-rate. 'It's sad that every morning you wake up and there are articles saying people should not fly to South Africa, that it's a dangerous country . . . that FIFA made the wrong decision to go to South Africa,' Valcke had protested at the start of the year. 'It's insane. It's definitely completely wrong.'

The criticism had not looked so insane back in December, when the England team visited its base camp at the Royal Bafokeng Sports Campus in Rustenburg and there were cries of consternation from officials at the parlous state of the training pitches. But Valcke had saved the day, persuading the Exco to sign off an increase in South Africa's organisational grant from $282 million to $349 million to help get the team training camps into shape. FIFA's $3.5 billion income from the tournament would more than cover it. South Africa was expecting a big payday for its efforts, too – it had been predicted that the tournament would add as much as 0.5 per cent to the country's GDP that year, a large chunk of which would come in tourism revenues from the hundreds of thousands of foreign visitors expected to flock to the country.

Alas, it wasn't to be. The 2010 World Cup was a commercial flop for the host country, attracting only 300,000 extra visitors over the whole year. That was far fewer than had been expected, meaning every extra tourist the tournament had attracted came with a price tag of $13,000.* But for FIFA the World Cup was as much of a cash bonanza as always, and South Africa's economic disappointments were yet to emerge. Now, everything was looking perfect, and Valcke was receiving pats on the back all round.

No one was more cock-a-hoop about the South African World Cup than Blatter. The FIFA president had promised to bring the tournament to Africa during his very first election campaign back in 1998, and it had taken until now to deliver. Although he had publicly supported the South African campaign for the 2006 World Cup, he had secretly voted for Germany, for pragmatic reasons, when it came to the ballot in July 2000. A tournament in Europe's economic powerhouse was sure to bring in maximum revenue, and South Africa would have been too high a risk coming straight after the financial uncertainty of the forthcoming 2002 finals in South Korea and Japan. All would have been fine had his treacherous secretary general Michel Zen-Ruffinen not gone on to reveal Blatter's double dealing to the world. It had

---

* The government spend of approximately $3.55 billion was topped up with FIFA's grant of $349 million, bringing the total cost of the tournament to around $3.9 billion.

been a serious blow to the president's credibility in his African heartland, but finally he had come good and his image as the continent's benefactor was restored.

Once the tournament was in full swing, the lobbying and back-room wheeler-dealing by the nine countries in the running to host the 2018 and 2022 World Cups could begin in earnest. The Michelangelo was to be Bin Hammam's centre of operations during his stay in South Africa, and he had two particularly big meetings coming up.

Sunlight streamed through the atrium's vast glass roof as Bin Hammam ushered his guest, a smiling Englishwoman, to the breakfast table. The World Cup was now well underway, but the two figures entering the splendour of the Michelangelo's breakfast room were not thinking about the day's big games. They both had their sights set on the tournaments of the future. The Qatari's companion was Clare Kenny Tipton, a glamorous international strategy advisor to the England 2018 bid, and she had been dispatched to breakfast with a mission. She was there to use all her cut-glass British charm to win Bin Hammam's vote and to roll out the red carpet by offering him an audience with Prince William and David Beckham. Bin Hammam was gracious, but he had his eye on a far bigger prize in exchange for his World Cup ballot than just a handshake with the world's most famous footballer and the heir to the British throne. He, of course, had his own mission that morning.

Bin Hammam knew Kenny Tipton well. She had worked for him at the AFC in Kuala Lumpur until two years before as his director of marketing, media and communications. The pair had crossed swords several times during her tenure at the AFC. Kenny Tipton had baulked at Bin Hammam's dictatorial style. She was part of the contingent who called him a pedant; a serious sports administrator who resented the way he micromanaged her work.

She had refused to pander to his ego by calling him 'Your Excellency' or 'Mr President', instead addressing him plainly as 'Mohamed'. Perhaps she was insubordinate, but Bin Hammam liked this sparky English brunette in her typical pearls and white blouse, with her black jacket nipped in smartly at the waist. She had substance. She had style. He knew a good thing when he saw it. Kenny Tipton was there to trade on that regard. She had been hired by the England 2018 bid for her connections in Asia, and she was hoping to come away from breakfast with her old boss's vote in the bag. So after exchanging the usual pleasantries over coffee and pastries, she cut to the chase. 'Will you vote for England to host the 2018 World Cup?'

Bin Hammam's response caught Kenny Tipton completely off guard. 'You know in my heart I would want to vote for England,' he told her smoothly. 'But I would only vote for the country in Europe that brings me the most votes for Qatar. My job is to win the World Cup for Qatar. As a Qatari, I have to, for my country.' Therefore Bin Hammam wanted to know something from Kenny Tipton. If he voted for England 2018, how many executive committee members could England persuade to support Qatar 2022 in return? It boiled down to one question: 'How many votes does England have from Europe?'

Kenny Tipton had no answer. Her bid had been lobbying frantically to win the support of European Exco members, but nothing was in the bag. They knew that Michel Platini, the French president of UEFA, was a crucial ally to win and they had done all they could to woo him, but so far he had given them no reason to expect his support. The team weren't even sure they could count on the vote of their own surly Exco member, Geoff Thompson, who remained lukewarm towards the campaign even now he was its chairman. England had nothing to offer. After the breakfast, Kenny Tipton got in touch with the leaders of England's bid to tell them Bin Hammam was prepared to trade his own vote with whichever country in the 2018 race could muster the most votes in Europe for Qatar's 2022 bid.

Bin Hammam's offer became a topic of hot discussion among members of the England bid team after Kenny Tipton described her breakfast meeting to her colleagues. They all agreed that the proposal was improper: it was the sort of vote-rigging collusion between bidding countries that was strictly outlawed by the rules of the contest. But from that point on, it became clear to them that this was how the race was going to be decided. They reasoned that Bin Hammam was not confident that he had any European votes in his pocket by that stage in the contest, so he was relying on striking a deal with one of the 2018 nations to bring them in.

Kenny Tipton and her colleagues were right. Bin Hammam was casting around for an alliance. He wanted to know which of the European bids for the 2018 tournament could offer him the most votes for Qatar. In return, he would pledge his own vote and those of his closest allies to whichever 2018 bid made him the best offer. He felt confident that his loyal backers Hany Abo Rida of Egypt and Worawi Makudi of Thailand would go along with him and back the 2018 bid he chose. It was clear from the meeting with Kenny Tipton that England would be no good to him, but he had high hopes for the other bidders. The beauty of the secret ballot was that he could strike as many deals for his vote as he pleased, and no one would be any the wiser.

Diallo had reported back an interesting conversation with the Netherlands–Belgium bid earlier that year, in which the bagman said the Low Countries were working hard to secure the votes of Jacques Anouma and Reynald Temarii, and claimed they would give him a success fee if he helped them win. Bin Hammam had already travelled to Belgium and been received in fine style. Perhaps there was an opening there, but he did not believe that the Belgians would have much luck with their two quarries.

Temarii was planning to vote for England, who had signed a new memorandum of understanding to send development funds to his Oceania confederation, and the feeble Low Countries bid wasn't likely to change his mind. In any event, neither bid would be able to trade his 2022 vote because it was pledged to Australia. And Anouma was well known to be in the pocket of the Russia 2018 campaign, so the Low Countries weren't going to have much luck in their attempts to woo him. Plus, Bin Hammam was counting on the Ivory Coast voter already. There wasn't much to be gained from an alliance with Netherlands–Belgium.

Far more interesting to Bin Hammam were the other two European bids. Behind the scenes, he had been working hard to build links with the Russia 2018 team, and he had lavished the official bid committee with his finest hospitality when they visited Doha in April. Russia and Qatar were the world's two biggest gas exporting countries, and they had plenty of common interests to explore in order to cement an alliance. Platini and Beckenbauer were thought to be in the Russian camp, and the votes of those two football superstars would carry enormous weight. Bin Hammam was also mulling an approach to Spain's voter, Ángel María Villar Llona. The Spaniard was known to have the three South American voters tied in to a vote pact to back the Iberian bid – as Lord Triesman had just blabbed so ill-advisedly to that honeytrap. If Bin Hammam could offer a bundle of votes to Spain–Portugal's 2018 bid, and Villar Llona would agree in return to throw the four Latin voters behind Qatar 2022, then both countries would have a strong bloc of support in the opening round.

Collusion deals weren't the only way Qatar's secret World Cup fixer was hoping to win votes in Europe. He was still working hard on winning Franz Beckenbauer's vote in the later rounds once Australia had crashed out and, like the England bid, he knew that Platini could be key to securing the support

of the UEFA contingent. Qatar was mulling some big investments in France that it would discuss later with the president,
Nicolas Sarkozy, who was close to Platini. But in the meantime, it was as well for the country's World Cup bid to do all it
could to convince the French football legend of the merits of
its campaign. So Bin Hammam cornered Platini in South
Africa and asked if he would be willing to grant the official
Qatar bid committee an audience at UEFA headquarters in
Nyon later that year so they could give him a private presentation. The UEFA president was happy to oblige, and a meeting
was arranged for that October. It was a big opportunity for
Qatar's young bid officials to make an impression on a giant of
world football.

Bin Hammam's little party of three aides were having the time of
their lives on their master's coat-tails in South Africa. They piled
into the stands to watch the best games – with Be sandwiched
between Meshadi and Chirakal – and afterwards they dined out
together and watched live late-night musical performances in the
Michelangelo. Between matches and official duties in
Johannesburg, the two men would be seen hovering outside the
Michelangelo Tower smoking in Nelson Mandela Square –
Chirakal in his comfortable chinos and baggy black jacket;
Meshadi as smart as ever in a fitted black suit and lavender shirt.
When Jenny Be came by she joked that they were 'male models
looking for jobs', and Meshadi threw her a grin.

The three flew between the tournament's nine cities on Bin
Hammam's private jet, snapping aerial photographs out of the
window. Be's South Africa photo album was full of pictures of
the group, between shots of the sun going down over the sea in
Port Elizabeth, the morning haze around Cape Town's Table
Mountain and the Johannesburg skyline from her high hotel bal-
cony in the Michelangelo Tower. In one picture, Meshadi and

Chirakal slouched smiling with their arms around each other's shoulders in the Soccer City stadium. In another, Meshadi hung fondly over the back of Be's restaurant chair, grinning as she leaned in close with a mojito in front of her on the table. Be had written the caption: 'When we are all still sober.' The friends rarely had such fun.

While the trio enjoyed themselves, Amadou Diallo was hard at work on Bin Hammam's African brotherhood. It was the bagman's job to fix the deals over drinks in the hotel, and then the baton would be passed to Chirakal to make the necessary transactions. During the stay, the secretary general of the Somalia FA, Abdiqani Said Arab, emailed Chirakal his bank details. Sure enough, $100,000 was paid to the federation from Bin Hammam's daughter's account. Another $50,000 was paid to the Niger FA from the same account and Aboubacar Bruno Bangoura of Guinea was sent €10,000 in Paris – both at Diallo's request. Bin Hammam's loyal champion, Fadoul Hussein of Djibouti, asked him to foot the bill for his wife and children to spend Ramadan in Doha, and Chirakal was duly instructed to book them a suite in the luxury Ezdan Hotel overlooking the Persian Gulf. This time all the charges were to be settled by the Qatar FA, rather than Bin Hammam. The month after the family returned from their holiday, Hussein would email his Qatari benefactor: 'I think we have very good chance for to win the organisation WORLD CUP 2022 IN CHALLAH.' Diallo had done sterling work in Africa again.

Bin Hammam himself bought 60 tickets to key games costing around $5,000 and had them delivered to the hotel suite of the CAF president, Issa Hayatou, during the tournament.* He was confident of Africa's support for his country's World Cup bid, but

* Hayatou denies receiving the tickets and says he had access to as many World Cup matches as he wanted as a FIFA Exco member and didn't need any extra seats from Bin Hammam.

you could never be too certain, and why miss a chance to make a powerful man grateful? It was necessary to maintain his largesse to keep the pot boiling in Africa, but Bin Hammam's real focus was elsewhere at this crucial stage in his campaign. He needed to lock down the three voters from Asia.

The World Cup was reaching its close and the crowds were flocking back to Johannesburg ahead of the final between Spain and the Netherlands, to take place at Soccer City. FIFA's pampered officials were enjoying the last round of galas and glitzy parties before the whole hoopla packed up for another four years and they drifted back to their home countries. Tonight, six days before the final, the soaring strains of the famous South Korean soprano Sumi Jo floated out on the night air as Mohamed bin Hammam stepped onto the lantern-lit veranda of the Johannesburg Country Club. The Qatari football grandee moved among the illustrious guests milling around on lawns which sloped gently towards the lake in the twilight of the warm July evening. His companion that night was every bit as refined: Bin Hammam was there as the special guest of a new and powerful ally, the South Korean FIFA voter Dr Chung Mong-joon.

The two men had become all but inseparable during the 2010 World Cup in South Africa. They had travelled together between matches on Bin Hammam's private jet, shared the astonishing luxury of FIFA's VIP hospitality suites during key matches and dined together in the faux-Renaissance splendour of the Michelangelo. The entente with the South Korean voter was the cornerstone of Bin Hammam's strategy to lock down the support Qatar needed in Asia.

Chung was a haughty, handsome man with neat silvery side-parting and a proud countenance. He was no more overawed than Bin Hammam by the wealth flaunted around them at the Country Club that evening. As the majority shareholder in the car giant Hyundai, he was just as well acquainted as his new Qatari friend with the power of money. Bin Hammam's cheque-book would never have got him anywhere with a man as rich as Chung, but he had executed a more sophisticated plan to win the Hyundai scion's loyalty. It had taken a masterful feat of diplo-macy, largesse and political patronage to get to where they were tonight. No casual observer watching the two men chatting con-spiratorially on the lawns would have guessed that these had been sworn enemies only a year before.

Track back to spring 2009 and the two football bosses were locked in a bitter war of words which threatened to drive a wedge through the heart of Asian football. Chung was sup-porting a mutinous Bahraini plot to topple Bin Hammam from his position on the FIFA executive committee, and the Qatari was fighting tooth and nail to ward off the attack. Bin Hammam was being challenged for the West Asian seat that he had held unopposed for 14 years by Sheikh Salman bin Ebrahim al-Khalifa, the wealthy president of the Bahrain Football Association, and the contest would be decided at an election during the AFC's congress in Kuala Lumpur that May. The elections for the seats allocated to Asia on FIFA's executive committee took place separately from the ballot to elect the AFC's own ruling officials, so Bin Hammam would not have to stand for re-election as president of his confederation until January 2011, even if he had lost his position at the FIFA. But limping on like that was unthinkable, and he had vowed pub-licly to stand aside as AFC president if he was deposed from the FIFA Exco. Bin Hammam was nothing if not a proud man, and that sort of failure would not be an option. He was deter-mined to win at all costs.

The Qatari had paid his old friend Peter Hargitay to conduct covert surveillance on Chung, whom he suspected of bankrolling Sheikh Salman's campaign. He was also using the services of

Manilal Fernando, a corpulent Sri Lankan hustler and long-standing ally employed as FIFA's South Asian development officer, to fix votes in his favour. By the end of March, Bin Hammam had received intelligence alleging that Chung's associates were offering bribes of up to $200,000 to Asian national football associations to back Sheikh Salman, and he decided the time was right to strike. Live on Australian television, he accused the South Korean of attempting to buy votes to unseat him.

The AFC president's extraordinary broadside against a fellow executive committee member prompted an investigation by the usually sleepy FIFA ethics committee. It was met with outraged denials from Chung, and the South Koreans launched a counter-attack by lodging their own ethics complaint about bizarre remarks Bin Hammam had made on television implying that he wanted to cut Chung's head off.

Hargitay swung into gear, whispering in the ear of tame reporters to ensure that his paymaster's allegations got as much attention as possible and pouring scorn on the South Korean complaint. He boasted he had enlisted a patsy journalist he kept in his pocket to write a story which was sent out on the international newswires in mid-April, reporting that FIFA was investigating allegations that Bin Hammam's rivals were paying bribes to try to unseat him. Hargitay sent the story to Bin Hammam, with the note: 'Dear brother ... Below please find a wire service story ... it took me the better part of today to satisfy lawyers and other lunatics to let the story run ... They had to add some Salman quotes for legal reasons (objectivity, etc) but have beautifully managed (with my insistence and input) to ridicule the Korean "complaint".' That was the sort of masterful media manipulation that made Hargitay's services worth every bit of his hefty bill.

But Blatter was furious. The FIFA family did not air its dirty linen in public. Its inner machinations were kept hidden from public view. That was how it survived. A furious row had now erupted between Chung and Bin Hammam, and it was damaging the image of world football. 'Chung and myself have never enjoyed a good relationship ... This man knows nothing about football,' Bin Hammam briefed journalists acidly. He claimed Chung was paying to have him unseated to clear the path for his bid for the FIFA presidency. The South Korean went even further, accusing his Qatari nemesis of 'acting like a head of a crime organisation' as president of AFC and 'suffering from mental problems'. 'I am afraid that Mr Hammam may be a sick person who needs to be at a hospital rather than at FIFA,' he told gobsmacked journalists.

Blatter could take no more. The FIFA president issued an unusually sternly worded statement calling the warring candidates to play fair. 'Football is a universal sport based on the fundamental principles of discipline and respect for opponents,' it began, seraphically. 'These values must be applied not only on the field of play, but also in the administration and governance of football, particularly in the area of sports politics. And of course, this includes elections to the governing bodies of football.'

The two squabbling opponents were duly chastened and the public slanging match abated somewhat, but Bin Hammam had no intention of playing fair. Hargitay was hard at work digging up intelligence ahead of the AFC congress. 'Below please find a first input re S-Korean delegation with initial descriptions of the assignment, private mobile numbers, arrival dates,' he had written in a report sent to Bin Hammam on 29 April 2009. 'Photographs are of course also available of the key people. The next report will provide further information about their detailed plans, what those plans are, who they are seeing or planning to see, where and what offers will be made and to whom.'

Meanwhile, Fernando was busy drumming up the votes Bin Hammam needed to defeat the Bahraini challenger, and his own electioneering methods were far from straightforward. The fixer sent Bin Hammam one report guaranteeing the votes of 12 AFC countries, adding: 'I am sure of Pakistan and Afghanistan because I sent a mobile phone and both photographed the ballot paper inside the booth and showed it to me.' The Sri Lankan fixer also received a payment of $23,000 from one of Bin Hammam's slush funds as reimbursement for a cash gift he had given to Alberto Colaco, the general secretary of the Indian Football Association, after winning a guarantee of his support.

The coup fizzled out in short order with the help of Fernando and Hargitay. Bin Hammam won the election comfortably at the AFC congress in May 2009. He needn't have been so worried. Few were surprised when FIFA's ethics committee cleared all concerned of wrongdoing: that was the way of handling spats in the FIFA family, and no real evidence had emerged to support the startling allegations against Chung. With his presidency once again secure, Bin Hammam could now return to his main focus: Qatar's bid for the 2022 World Cup. Suddenly, attacking one of the 24 FIFA voters live on television didn't seem like it had been such a good idea.

Bin Hammam needed to take remedial action to restore his support base in Asia, and fast. When it came to the football bosses who ran the continent's national associations, there was often an easy way of patching up fractured loyalties or rewarding longstanding friendships. Hammam made payments totalling $1.7 million to football officials and their federations across Asia from secret slush funds operated by his private company, Kemco, including his daughter's bank account, in the period before and directly after the December 2010 World Cup vote, and his own re-election as AFC president the following month.

The core targets of his World Cup strategy, however, were his three fellow Asians on the Exco: Chung, Worawi Makudi of Thailand, and Junji Ogura of Japan. Bin Hammam could count on the unfailing loyalty of Makudi, but Chung and Ogura presented a knottier problem because both South Korea and Japan were also in the race for 2022. In Chung's case, the rivalry was now not just patriotic, but personal. But Bin Hammam reckoned that if he could be brought around, the pliable Ogura would follow. There was no hope of persuading the two men not to back their own countries at the outset, but no one was expecting South Korea or Japan to make it through the first rounds of voting anyway. What he wanted was to persuade them to swing their votes behind Qatar once their own countries had crashed out. If they agreed, then the entire Asian voting bloc would belong to Qatar in the final rounds that would decide the result. This was the end game Bin Hammam had in sight, but first he had to find a way to bury the hatchet with Chung.

The Qatari billionaire knew well what motivated his old South Korean foe, because it was a trait he shared. Chung was driven by his thirst for power. You couldn't buy this man's support for any amount of cash, but if you could offer him a leg up the ladder he might just consider it priceless. Everyone knew that Chung wanted more than anything to become FIFA president. Bin Hammam was the man credited with getting Blatter elected, and if he could hold out the hope that he might play kingmaker to Chung as well, that could just be enough to secure his loyalty.

So there was a marked change of tack in Bin Hammam's attitude towards the South Korean as summer turned to autumn in 2009. The charm offensive was to start here. In October, when Jenny Be arranged for Chung to travel to Kuala Lumpur on AFC business, she made a special effort to upgrade the South Korean's room at the five-star Shangri-La Hotel to a top suite and ensure he was given a dedicated car. The two rivals breakfasted together in the hotel's Lemon Garden restaurant on the morning of 24 November, and the meeting marked a turning point. From that occasion onwards, whenever Chung visited Kuala Lumpur, he was to be given the type of lavish hospitality that Bin Hammam reserved for his closest friends and allies. Be later instructed staff in the AFC's logistics department: 'Please ALWAYS accord Dr Chung the presidential suite. This is a standing instruction.' And then: 'Following my earlier email, please also ensure that the car for Dr Chung is Hyundai (highest range model) or if that is not available, then a Mercedes 300 or 500 model (newest model). This is also a standing instruction.' The extra cost was all to be charged to Bin Hammam's presidential account at the AFC.

The hospitality was reciprocal. The two men's assistants were soon arranging for Bin Hammam to travel to South Korea in February 2010 to be hosted by Chung at the five-star Grand Hyatt Hotel with its dazzling views of Seoul's futuristic cityscape. After Bin Hammam met the South Korean president, Lee Myung-bak, he gushed on his blog that the visit to the Blue House had been set up by 'none other than my good friend and comrade-in-arms Dr Chung Mong-joon'. It was over dinner on that trip that the two men cemented their alliance. They agreed to undermine Blatter by jointly proposing a change in FIFA statutes to ban presidents for standing for more than two terms, and Bin Hammam announced the move days later at the AFC congress in Seoul. His very public promise to throw his support behind an Asian candidate at the next election for FIFA president was a message to Chung. He later sent the South Korean a letter he had drafted to Valcke proposing the presidential term limit 'as discussed in Seoul'. The proposal never came to pass, but Bin Hammam had given his new ally a clear statement of intent. If Chung wanted to be president, he needed Bin Hammam on side.

The FIFA presidency was the main prize, but first both men needed to survive the next AFC election, which would be a few weeks after the World Cup vote, in January 2011. This was when Chung's position as Asia's FIFA vice-president would be up for

grabs, as would Bin Hammam's presidency of the Asian confederation. Bin Hammam swore he would do all he could in the
run-up to the vote to help Chung get re-elected. In so doing, he
intended to establish a vital claim on Chung's loyalty that would
pave the way for a World Cup vote-swapping pact which would
sweep Qatar to victory in the ballot the month before.

Bin Hammam gave Chung the use of his trusted electoral fixer,
Manilal Fernando, whose gerrymandering had helped him win
successive elections to his own West Asian Exco seat and scup-
pered the attempted coup the previous year. The Sri Lankan set to
work lobbying voters to back Chung for FIFA vice-president and
Bin Hammam for AFC president. He was also seeking a seat on
FIFA's Exco for himself. 'I have just returned from Dubai, where
I had a meeting with my group,' the fixer would write in an email
to Chung later that year. 'All these countries agreed to support Mr
Bin Hammam for president, you for FIFA vice-president and
myself for FIFA Exco member. Already Sri Lanka, India, Bhutan,
Nepal and Tajikistan have signed your nomination. In addition
Afghanistan, Bangladesh, Maldives, Usbekistan [*sic*] and Pakistan
will send your nominations directly to the AFC to Mr Bin
Hammam. Mr Bin Hammam is campaigning very hard for
you ... You are in a strong position with Mr Hammam, myself
and Warawi [Makudi] all supporting you ... Like I worked for
Hammam last time I will work for him and you this time, do not
worry we are winning.'

The Sri Lankan sought large rewards for the countries whose
support he locked down.* Like Amadou Diallo, he had an official role with the Goal Programme, the FIFA fund for football
development in poor countries chaired by Bin Hammam. He
sent the Qatari a list of countries in his group which were to be

---

* There is no suggestion – or evidence – that Dr Chung was aware of the illicit payments by Manilal Fernando in support of his election.

given payments under the programme of $400,000 each. They were Pakistan, Afghanistan, Nepal, Bhutan, Kyrgyzstan, Uzbekistan and Sri Lanka. Fernando wanted Bin Hammam to use his position to obtain approval for the payments from the Goal Bureau. He was also keen that another source of football development money was generously lavished on key voters, writing to Bin Hammam in the summer to recommend loosening the purse strings of the AFC's own Aid 27 budget. 'Until elections are over we must see that all funds due from Aid [27] to countries are paid without making it difficult for them with too many questions asked,' he suggested.

Bin Hammam continued to shower Asian football bosses with direct payments from the network of slush funds operated by Kemco. Asatulloev Zarifjon, president of the Tajikistan football federation, received $50,000 in June 2010. The next month, Fernando's ally, Nidal Hadid of the Jordan FA, received $50,000 into his personal bank account from the account of Bin Hammam's daughter, Aisha. Another loyal ally of Fernando was handsomely rewarded for supporting Bin Hammam. Ganesh Thapa, president of the Nepalese FA, was paid a total of £115,000 from two separate Kemco accounts in the spring and summer of 2010.*

Chung and Bin Hammam kept talking behind the scenes after their meeting in Seoul and by the time of the South African World Cup, the Qatari was ready to bring Ogura into the circle of trust. It fell to Chung to set up a meeting in Johannesburg. The South Korean emailed Ogura, Bin Hammam and Makudi, inviting them to a summit over a lavish meal at the Michelangelo Hotel. Bin Hammam would later bill the AFC $3,482 for a 'dinner with Exco members'.

---

* Ganesh Thapa claimed the money was paid as part of a business arrangement he had with Kemco.

It ought to have been a tense gathering – with the most senior officials of three rival bidding countries in one room representing interests which, on the face of it, were diametrically opposed. But Bin Hammam's pacific approach would soon relieve the tension. His proposal was simple: he was just asking the men around the table to remember their loyalty to Mother Asia when they went to the ballot box in December. He was a Qatari, he told them, so he was duty-bound to vote for Qatar, and he understood that they felt the same about their own countries. They were all patriots, and rightly so, but the Asian football family must stick together. He was simply asking Chung and Ogura to promise that they would transfer their votes to another Asian bid if their home countries failed to survive the early voting rounds of the World Cup ballot that December, as he would also do if Qatar dropped out.

Bin Hammam was secretly confident that he had enough votes in his pocket for his country to storm through the early rounds. His covert campaign had already stacked the deck heavily in Qatar's favour, but to reach an absolute majority in the final stages he needed to know that Chung and Ogura would ultimately support Qatar once their own bids had been eliminated. Even if Ogura backed South Korea initially once Japan crashed out, the pact would compel him to transfer his vote to the only Asian contender left standing – Qatar – in the end. It was a neat solution to a knotty problem and, encouragingly, his fellow Asian voters seemed amenable.

After the dinner, Bin Hammam continued his courting of Chung. The South Korean shared Bin Hammam's private jet between World Cup matches, and was invited to enjoy VIP hospitality alongside the Qatari crown prince, Sheikh Tamim bin Hamad bin Khalifa Al Thani, at a game in Cape Town. By the end of the tournament, the pair were close friends. On 2 July, Chung emailed Bin Hammam a friendly message: 'There will be the quarter-final between Uruguay and Ghana in Soccer City today. I would like to go with you and watch the game together. On the way, we can talk about various topics of mutual interest.'

Days later, the Qatari was delighted to receive another invitation from Chung to an 'evening of music' at the Johannesburg Country Club hosted by Dr Lee Hong-Koo, the former prime minister of Korea, on 5 July. The invitation promised: 'The event will feature various entertainers including world-renowned soprano Ms Sumi Jo. I sincerely hope that you can attend this event as it would give us the opportunity to shift gears into a more relaxing mode to celebrate together the first World Cup in Africa.' As he and his new ally strolled the lawns by the lake in the dusky evening light, Bin Hammam could congratulate himself in a masterful feat of diplomacy. In just a year, he had gone from being Chung's worst enemy to his close friend.

Six days later, on 11 July, the World Cup came to its spectacular end. Be, Chirakal and Meshadi huddled in the stands at Soccer City, braced against the cold as darkness descended and the floodlights were dimmed. A squadron of Gripens from the South African Airforce roared over the stadium and hundreds of dancers and musicians exploded onto the field to form the shape of a giant vuvuzela. Be snapped photographs of the firework display that marked the closing ceremony, and the three were on their feet with the rest of the crowd as South Africa's Ladysmith Black Mambazo belted out their famous 'Weather Song'.

Then came the nail-biting final, in which Spain defeated the Netherlands 1-0 with a goal from Andrés Iniesta four minutes from the end of extra time, lifting the trophy in a blaze of golden confetti. It was a bitterly cold night, and Chirakal wore a knitted hat and warmed his hands in his pockets, while Meshadi pulled his thick wool coat about him and threw his grey scarf over his shoulder. Be sat wedged between her two friends in her blue jumper and black coat, her face lighting up with excitement for all that she felt she was freezing. 'It was so cold, we almost fell asleep during the game (hypothermia) … ah, that would be totally embarassing,' she wrote to friends. And now it was all over. The first African World Cup had been a sensation.

Now Bin Hammam had opened up to his fellow voters in Asia about his loyalty to Qatar, he no longer felt the need to maintain the public pretence that he was impartial as the president of the AFC. After he returned from Johannesburg, it was not long before his jet was firing up again to carry him to Singapore for the SoccerEx football convention. There, for the first time, he publicly declared his support for his country – with a nod to the deal he offered his fellow Asian voters. 'I have one vote … and frankly speaking I will vote for Qatar, but if Qatar is not in the running I will vote for another Asian country,' he told journalists. There was not a snowball's chance in hell that Qatar would not be in the running if he had anything to do with it, but this was the premise of the pact he had proposed. So successfully had Bin Hammam kept his covert campaign for his country's bid under wraps, that the announcement caused quite a stir. Reuters reported that 'Qatar's bid to host the 2022 World Cup received a huge boost on Wednesday when Asian Football Confederation President Mohamed Bin Hammam threw his weight behind his country's campaign.' Hassan Al-Thawadi thanked him warmly for so generously lending his backing.

When Asia's four Exco members were together again in Kuala Lumpur in August for a meeting of the AFC's own ruling committee, the foundations of their vote-swapping pact were recorded in the formal minutes. 'We have four Asian nations bidding and three are represented in the FIFA executive committee,' Bin Hammam told the assembled officials. 'I, Dr Chung, Mr Ogura will be supporting our respective nations, Qatar, Korea Republic and Japan. But we should promise each other that if any of our bid loses, then the support will be switched to the other bidders not only by voting but also by campaigning for each other. I think this is the one thing we owe to our continent.'

This was not something to be discussed too publicly, because the Asian voters were entering a grey area of the rules. FIFA banned member associations and bid committees from striking 'any kind of agreement with any other member association or bid committee as regards to the behaviour during the bidding process [which] may influence the bidding process'. But private agreements between the Exco members of bidding countries were impossible to police and in effect fell outside the regulations. That was the beauty of a secret ballot – no one need ever know.

The ploy worked – both Chung and Ogura pledged their loyalty to their fellow Asian bids if their own countries dropped out. Presenting the Japanese bid to the Asian Football Confederation the same month, Ogura said: 'The AFC President has made it clear that he will support Qatar. While I will surely vote for Japan, Dr Chung must be on his own country's side… but no matter what, what is most important for the Asian football family is seeing the World Cup back on Asian soil.'

Bin Hammam had the final votes of his two Asian rivals in the bag. Added to his own and that of his ally Makudi, all four of the continent's votes would now belong to Qatar in the final rounds that really mattered. The Thai voter had demonstrated extraordinary loyalty to Bin Hammam and he had pledged his unstinting support to Qatar 2022. There was also the hope that Makudi would allow his Qatari friend to trade his 2018 vote too as he cast around for an alliance with one of the European countries in the running for the earlier tournament. Makudi was a true friend indeed, and it was about time that Bin Hammam gave something back to the man from Bangkok. That was the next item on the agenda.

Nine

Who Is Sim Hong Chye?

The walls of the attic hideout were plastered floor-to-ceiling with scraps of paper scrawled with a muddle of names, dates and figures in multi-coloured felt-tip pen. The journalists joked that the room they had come to call 'the bunker' looked as if it had been inhabited by a crazed prisoner who had covered his cell in demented scribble over years in solitary confinement. It was 2am. The pubs had long since turned out and the town outside was still. Gentle rain fizzled at the windows. The servers hummed. Otherwise, all was silent as Calvert and Blake hunched over their computer screens, scanning through document after document, panning for gold. The bins were brimming over with discarded ready-meal packets and their desks were cluttered with jumbled papers, coffee mugs and crumpled Red Bull cans. On the table nearby were the abandoned cartons of the Indian takeaway they had devoured a few hours earlier. Summer had come early, and in the rising heat their increasingly foetid environment brought back memories of university, pulling all-nighters in the offices of their student newspapers.

The journalists had been hard at work mining the cache of documents they were now calling 'The FIFA Files' for two months. In that time, they had built up an astonishing picture of Bin Hammam's multi-million-dollar campaign of bribery, logging details of each of the payments he made to officials across Africa and Asia from his Kemco slush-funds and the bundles of cash he handed out to visitors on his junkets. They had goggled at the size of the two bungs he had paid directly to the shameless shake-down merchant Jack Warner, Trinidad's voter on the executive committee, in the run-up to the World Cup ballot. The Qatari's attempts to woo Franz Beckenbauer and Reynald Temarii away from voting for Australia were a source of fascination, as was the masterful powerplay he had pulled off to win the loyalty of Chung Mong-joon. Reading through the documents, the journalists were increasingly amazed that Bin Hammam's role in Qatar's World Cup victory had been kept so successfully out of the public eye. How had he managed to maintain the pretence of neutrality until announcing his intention to vote for Qatar at SoccerEx in July 2010, when he had really been campaigning vigorously for the country for two years by that point?

When Calvert and Blake had first set up camp in this attic, they had wondered how far all this work would really get them. Allegations of corruption had swirled around Qatar's World Cup bid for years, but no one had ever been able to make anything stick. At the beginning, they had not been sure they were going to find any evidence strong enough to really prove that the bidding process had been corrupted. Two months on, they had no such concerns. The scribblings all over the walls, coupled with the monster spreadsheets they were compiling, documented their haul of damning facts. But after two months of reading Bin Hammam's correspondence, they had also come to feel a strange sense of familiarity with this distant Qatari billionaire and his loyal aides.

His activities were unquestionably corrupt, but it was hard not to warm to Bin Hammam for his graciousness, dignity and – ironically – his generosity. He fed the dozens of men who turned up at his house every night. He paid for the medical bills of ailing football officials in foreign lands, or he bankrolled their children's education. And the aides he kept close adored him. Najeeb Chirakal was a man they couldn't fail to feel fond of when they read the unstinting patience and courtesy with which he conducted his master's affairs, and the gossipy chatter of the messages between the trusted trio of women at the AFC often had the journalists in fits of giggles. It was a strange thing, to inhabit a man's world like this. They had come to imagine they really knew the characters whose activities they were unravelling.

The journalists were feeling a lot of pressure. Their newsdesk back in London had been as patient as they could ever have expected in allowing them to disappear for months like this, but their editor had told them in no uncertain terms that their story must be ready by the start of the 2014 World Cup in Brazil that summer. That meant they had until 1 June to finish trawling the millions of documents, pull all their voluminous evidence together and distil it, somehow, into a succinct series of coherent articles fit for print. It was early May, so they had less than a month to finish the job. At the start of the project, they had allowed themselves breaks at the weekend to catch the train back to London and snatch a day or two with their families and friends, but that sort of time off was a luxury they could no longer afford. Weekends had been cancelled and now work continued far past midnight each evening. They had each worn every item of clothing they had brought with them dozens of times, and they were both in need of a haircut. But then hiding in an attic for several months was never going to be glamorous.

The source had become a trusted friend by this stage in the investigation, and the mutual wariness that had persisted for the first few weeks had dissipated. He was often abroad but when he

was in the UK he popped in from time to time, kindly bringing
rations of fruit, bags of crisps or sushi boxes, and had generously
installed a mini-fridge to keep their energy drinks cool when
summer arrived early. He was somewhat baffled by the journalists' mania for their story – their willingness to put their entire
lives on hold and devote themselves so single-mindedly to this
peculiar task. He observed the two increasingly bedraggled characters in the attic, their impenetrable in-jokes, strange Fleet
Street slang and occasional squabbling, with perplexed amusement. But he'd grown oddly fond of them, and the feeling was
mutual. Now that the reporters had been separated from everyone they knew except each other for two months, the source was
always a welcome sight when he popped in to remind them that
an outside world existed beyond those four walls. Otherwise, the
only people they saw were the receptionists in their nearby hotel
when they slipped out at 7am or came back pink-eyed and
woozy from hours fixed to their computers in the early hours of
the morning.

Calvert and Blake had devised a system to sift through their
unconquerable mound of material as efficiently as they possibly
could, without overlapping. They kept a growing spreadsheet of
keywords – the names of major players, companies, places or
organisations – and divided them up each morning to make sure
there was no crossover in the searches they ran across the vast
database that day. Tonight, Calvert was wading through the hundreds of results thrown up by his searches for the lobbyists
associated with the German voter Franz Beckenbauer – Fedor
Radmann and Andreas Abold. They made fascinating reading,
and he had barely looked up from his screen since discarding his
empty carton of Chicken Korai and scoffing the last scraps of
naan bread several hours before. Meanwhile, Blake was burrow-
ing into an intriguing seam of documents which seemed to relate
to some sort of gas deal involving Bin Hammam and a man

called Sim Hong Chye. And suddenly, it was all beginning to fall into place.

'Oh my God, Jonathan,' she exclaimed. 'You have to come and look at this!' There was silence. When Calvert was deep in concentration, it often took several attempts to rouse him, and Blake was not famed for her patience. 'Jonathan? Jonathan! Look at this!'

'Hmm?' he said dreamily, without looking up. Blake sprang out of her chair, exasperated, and crossed the room. He lifted his eyes from the screen and met her gaze blearily. 'What's up?'

'I've found a whole chain of emails which show that Bin Hammam set up top-level bilateral gas talks between Qatar and Thailand for Worawi Makudi,' she said, standing over her colleague with her hand on her hip. 'I thought you might be interested?' Calvert looked quizzical.

'Really?'

'Come and look!'

Calvert shuffled across the room on his wheelie chair and parked himself in front of his colleague's computer. He looked shattered. She leaned over his shoulder and pointed at the name Sim Hong Chye in the address line of an email on the screen.

'Look. Bin Hammam is arranging for this guy to go and see Qatar's deputy prime minister, who's in charge of energy, to talk about a massive gas deal between Qatar and Thailand. It's worth tens, hundreds of millions. Maybe billions.'

'But who is he?' Calvert asked. 'I don't recognise the name. What's he got to do with football?'

'I was confused too, but he usually goes by an alias. This is Joe Sim, Worawi Makudi's chief advisor at the Thai FA. The guy who owns all the casinos.' Calvert raised an eyebrow.

'So, Bin Hammam's setting up gas talks for an associate of a major voter.' He peered at the screen. 'And it's August 2010, so just months before the World Cup vote.' He wrinkled his nose.

'It's very smelly. But how do we know what went on in that meeting? For all we know nothing was agreed.' Calvert had a maddening, but often crucial, habit of zoning straight in on the single gap in a piece of information, without missing a beat. But Blake was prepared.

'Something *was* agreed. The emails show they're talking about the sale of liquefied natural gas from Qatar to Thailand. I've just checked it out, and at the time Thailand was planning to buy millions of gallons of the stuff, but they were trying to drive Qatar down on the price. And the Qataris agreed – the deal was done, after this meeting.' Calvert was tugging his bottom lip and nodding slowly. Then he gave half a smile.

'Okay. You're right. That is big.'

They agreed it was too late to delve into this now – they needed to come back to it with fresh eyes. It was time to drive back to their hotel and knock themselves out with a few single malts at the bar before sloping back to their rooms and crashing out. They had never slept so deeply as they did during those strange months.

The next morning, the journalists were back at their screens bright and early, dividing up all the keywords they could think of associated with the deal. There was 'Brian Teo', a Singaporean businessman from the gas instruments company 'Alco', who accompanied Sim to meetings with two Qataris in charge of the country's energy sector, 'Abdulla bin Hamad Al-Attiyah' and 'Abdul Aziz bin Ahmad Al Malki'. Then there was 'Qatargas', the company selling the gas, and 'PTT', the Thai state energy company which wanted to buy it at a lower price. Through their searches, they pieced the deal together. It was suddenly clear that the Qatari plot to buy the World Cup had not just consisted of the bungs Bin Hammam had paid to football officials to drum up a groundswell of support across Africa and Asia, and the direct deals they could see he was doing with the voters on the FIFA

Exco. There was a third tier to the strategy: Bin Hammam had apparently arranged for Qatar to use its vast mineral muscle to court FIFA voters through major geopolitical trade deals. The story had just got much bigger.

Ten

The Casino King, the Thai Voter and the Gas Deal

In the south-eastern corner of Thailand, the seabed was being dredged and a small army of workers were beavering away on the shoreline slotting together a giant Meccano set. Cranes heaved huge steel pipes onto a long jetty snaking over the water to a thin strip of reclaimed land where powerful pumps and storage tanks were being assembled. The new terminal in the port of Map Ta Phut would be the first of its kind in the region, and Thailand was very proud of the cutting-edge technology it was introducing to secure its energy supply for the future.

The terminal was being built at a cost of $880 million to perform a single task: to receive and recondense liquefied natural gas (LNG). In order to transport the largest possible quantities, the gas is cooled and compressed until it becomes a dense liquid, that is then shipped around the world in the holds of enormous supertankers. Map Ta Phut was designed to accommodate these giant vessels, offering a deep harbour and the necessary maze of pipes to bring their precious cargo on shore. Once there, the fluid would be reheated into its original gaseous state to be despatched as much-needed fuel to power Thailand's burgeoning economy.

This industrial landscape could not have been further removed from the playful pursuit of international football but, from more than 3,000 miles away, Mohamed bin Hammam had his sights set on the new port at Map Ta Phut. It would have an important role to play in his relationship with one of the key voters who would decide whether Qatar was to host the 2022 World Cup.

The supplier of the fuel for the Thai terminal would, of course, be Qatar. While the Gulf state did not have a monopoly in the global export of natural gas, it was the world's leading producer. It had the stuff in abundance, and the prices it set for hydrocarbon resources could make or break a fragile democracy like Thailand. In the summer of 2010, Thailand also had something that Qatar wanted badly: the vote of Worawi Makudi, its FIFA executive committee member. Bin Hammam didn't know much about gas, but he knew how to spot an opportunity to make a deal and reward a loyal ally.

It was a sweltering Sunday evening in Doha in mid-August 2010, and a secret cabal of guests were checking into the Sheraton Hotel on the West Bay waterfront. They had flown in from Egypt, Nigeria and Thailand at short notice for a summit. Each was greeted warmly at the hotel's reception and placed on Bin Hammam's charge account. The billionaire was taking care of everything, including the mini-bar. 'Their charges at hotel for Room, Meals, Laundry and all extras will be settled on our account,' Najeeb Chirakal had informed the hotel in an email shortly before the arrivals. The first to make his way past the lobby's indoor palm trees was the short, round figure of Amos Adamu, dressed for the heat in his white African boubou robe.

The Nigerian FIFA executive committee member had his wife, Muna Alabwaina, at his side, watching as a porter piled their collection of straining suitcases onto a trolley. Bin Hammam had also picked up the bill for Mr and Mrs Adamu's business-class air

tickets from Lagos to the tune of £4,500 return. The Adamus
were followed by a robust, balding man in a camel-coloured suit
and shades. It was the Egyptian voter Hany Abo Rida, with his
own wife on his arm. They had also been treated to first-class
flights from Cairo, setting Bin Hammam back £2,500 for their
tickets. As the two couples made themselves comfortable in their
executive suites and enjoyed a refreshing drink on their balconies
overlooking the Persian Gulf, a third member of the cabal came
strolling through the hotel's revolving glass door and past the
atrium water feature. It was the squat Thai voter Makudi, flanked
by two unfamiliar figures.

There should have been a fourth executive committee member
checking in to the hotel with the others that night. Jacques
Anouma had accepted Bin Hammam's invitation to attend the
secret meeting, but he had been forced to pull out at the last
minute under orders from his close associate, the country's bloodthirsty premier Laurent Gbagbo. The presidential elections were
looming in the Ivory Coast and Gbagbo had asked Anouma to be
at his side as he toured the country during the celebrations for the
50th anniversary of independence. You didn't say no to a man like
Gbagbo, who had a nasty habit of sending out death squads to
terrify and murder those who displeased him. So Anouma had
been forced to disappoint his friend Bin Hammam. That was a
pity, because with less than four months to go before the big vote,
the intention had been to bring together four of the staunchest
supporters of Bin Hammam's World Cup campaign for the
summit in the hotel that night.

Adamu, Anouma and Abo Rida were big advocates of Qatar
2022 on the back of Bin Hammam's efforts in Africa, and
Makudi was his most trusted side-kick in Asia. Of all of them, the
Thai and Egyptian were by far his most steadfast allies. These two
were so loyal that they were widely said to have entrusted their
2018 votes to Bin Hammam, so that he could bundle them up to

trade with the European bidder who could offer Qatar the most votes in return. Even without Anouma, there would be plenty for the four Exco members to discuss over dinner that evening.

The other two guests on Bin Hammam's charge account at the hotel that night were the unfamiliar men who had strode into reception alongside Makudi. Their Qatari host believed in hierarchy, so he had instructed Chirakal to book these two lesser mortals into single rooms rather than the plush suites he bestowed upon his friends from the ranks of FIFA royalty. They were, nonetheless, essential. Makudi's two companions were in town at Bin Hammam's invitation to discuss a massive gas deal, whether or not the other men from the Exco knew it.

The first of the pair was Makudi's right-hand man, the caddish Sim Hong Chye – known throughout Asia as Joe Sim, the 'Casino King'. Sim was a self-styled venture capitalist from Singapore who had been given the title of chief advisor to the Thai FA. He was not an obvious choice to give counsel on football matters – and even less so about gas. He was more at home with roulette, blackjack and poker, having earned his nickname running a string of gambling dens in Sri Lanka before fleeing the country during a police crack-down on such establishments. Sim had gone on to become a wheeler-dealer businessman, drumming up investments in various dubious consortiums, proposing leisure complexes and golf courses which often didn't quite come to fruition. Now that his main business was football, he would impress potential clients by speed-dialling his acquaintance Sir Alex Ferguson, the manager of Manchester United, on his mobile phone. With him was a fellow Singaporean called Thian Sang Teo, though he went by the name of Brian. Teo's obscure company, Alco, in Singapore sold monitoring equipment to the oil and gas industries but, like Sim, he was new to the world of bilateral trade negotiations.

Bin Hammam had made special arrangements for this pair to

meet one of the most powerful men in the country. The next morning, they would be taken to see Abdullah bin Hamad Al-Attiyah – Qatar's deputy prime minister, energy minister and chairman of the state-owned Qatargas company. This firm was the commercial entity that made Qatar the biggest LNG exporter in the world, and consequently one of the chief sources of the small nation's unrivalled per-capita wealth. It boasted on its website that 'For the Qatari people and Qatari society, [Qatargas] has had a very positive impact on our lives, prosperity and well-being. It affects our economy and the development of our country.' Perhaps it was a bit of a risk to send two complete novices in to meet so lofty a figure, but whatever others might think of him, Makudi trusted Sim more than anyone. The Casino King was therefore the ideal person to represent Bin Hammam's friend's best interests at the talks the following morning.

The next day Sim and Teo were up early to be chauffeured to the diplomatic district of Doha. The car pulled up outside a vertiginous mirrored building, shaped like a blade to slice through the prevailing Gulf winds. The 52-storey Navigation Tower was home to both the Ministry of Energy and Industry and Qatargas – the twin fountainheads of the Gulf state's torrential wealth. The businessmen were whooshed straight up to the top floor to meet the man credited by many as the architect of Qatar's economic success.

Abdulla bin Hamad Al-Attiyah had pure white hair set against a flawless bronzed complexion which looked buffed by years of exposure to the abrasive desert breeze. At the age of 58, even his lofty title of deputy prime minister failed to convey the true power and influence he had accrued. When Sheikh Hamad had seized control of the country from his father in 1995, Al-Attiyah had already been at the helm of Qatar's energy policy for more than a decade and he was a wise counsellor. He had formerly led

OPEC, the all-powerful oil and petroleum trading bloc, and he was a kindred spirit who shared the Emir's reforming instincts. So after the coup he was unleashed to make the most of Qatar's hydrocarbon resources, and he became a trusted friend of Qatar's ruler. Prosperity quickly followed, but Al-Attiyah kept driving forward with the goal of making his country the world's biggest supplier of liquefied natural gas. Having achieved that dream, and by some margin, the energy industry was his fiefdom, both at home and abroad: he sat at the head of the international Gas Exporting Countries Forum which controlled the global trade of natural gas. This was a man who could save Thailand billions of dollars at the wave of a hand, if he so chose.

Al-Attiyah could have been forgiven for thinking that the two men who were ushered into his office on 16 August 2010 – the 'Casino King' and sidekick – were a touch out of their depth, but he was as effortlessly polite and gregarious as ever. They were there to discuss a gas deal between Qatar and Thailand and, by meeting them, he was told he was doing a great service to relations between the two countries in the world of football. Perhaps the connection between energy and sport wasn't immediately obvious – Al-Attiyah wasn't a great football fan and he didn't involve himself much in his country's ambitions on that score. But everyone knew how much this business mattered to his old friend the Emir. He was happy to help.

Thailand at that time had found itself in a bit of a bind. Its own modest natural gas production capacity wasn't enough to keep pace with the country's rapid economic expansion, and the government had laid down plans to secure its energy supply by beginning to import the fuel in the liquefied form. In January 2008, the Thai state energy company PTT announced plans to build the Map Ta Phut port to make the importation of liquefied natural gas possible for the first time. Qatar had quickly emerged as the obvious supplier. Qatargas signed a heads of agreement with PTT in February 2008 to provide one million tons of LNG a year at a fixed price for a decade once the terminal was completed.

Ten months after the agreement was signed with Qatar, the Thai state energy company had reached for its chequebook and struck a sponsorship deal with the Thai FA amounting to $2.2 million over three years. The latest payment of $750,000 had been made in March 2010, and Makudi was named as the 'beneficiary representative' of the Thai FA when the money was signed over. By then, the construction of the Map Ta Phut terminal was well underway, but alarm bells had started to ring. PTT had firmed up the deal to buy its gas in bulk from Qatar at a fixed price over ten years by signing a memorandum of understanding, but the price of the commodity had plummeted by almost half on the international market since the initial agreement was signed. The favourable price they had shaken hands on in 2008 looked like a terrible deal for Thailand by 2010. It would be much cheaper, as things stood, for PTT to take its chances and buy gas piecemeal on the rapidly fluctuating spot-market than to stick to the arrangement with Qatar. But that approach would be riddled with uncertainty. PTT wanted to buy its gas cheap, but it also wanted to ensure the security of the country's energy supply over the next decade.

In May 2010, an executive from PTT had broken ranks and briefed journalists that its ten-year agreement with Qatar would lock the company into prices 20 per cent above the current market value. This was clearly a catastrophe. It would mean paying billions of dollars extra over a decade if Map Ta Phut was to move to full capacity as intended. The company sought advice from the Thai government and announced that it would have to buy its initial consignments of gas for the terminal on the open market.

As the world's biggest exporter of LNG by a vast margin, Qatar remained the obvious supplier. Thailand was effectively asking the Gulf country to forget the original ten-year deal, and start selling it shipments at the rock-bottom spot price when Map Ta Phut opened in less than a year's time. It also desperately needed the certainty of a new long-term arrangement with the Gulf state, and that was what the country's envoys were trying to pressure the men from Qatar into accepting. But importing gas simply didn't work like that: either you signed up for the long haul, stuck to the agreed price and shielded yourself from the vagaries of the market, or you took the risk on fluctuating costs. Thailand was trying to have its cake and eat it. Why should Qatar yield to such petulant demands?

When Sim met with Al-Attiyah, there were therefore two inter-linking issues preoccupying Qatar and Thailand. Would Qatar be willing to start selling its gas to PTT at the cheaper spot market price to help get Map Ta Phut up and running? And were the country's rulers prepared to countenance a new long-term deal at a lower fixed price than had been previously agreed? Neither move looked much in Qatar's interests. It might have been a tough sell in normal circumstances.

But the meeting Bin Hammam had set up for Makudi's lieu-tenant went well. Ten days later, Sim sent Al-Attiyah an email, copying in Bin Hammam and Makudi. He confirmed that an 'LNG sale' had been agreed and that the meeting with Al-Attiyah had done wonders for football relations between Qatar and Thailand. Sim was effusive. 'Your Excellency,' he began. 'It was a great honour for me to have an audience with Your Excellency on 16th Aug 2010. My team, sincerely, would like to thank Your Royal Highness for all your kind supports in promoting the bilat-eral co-operations in soccer developments and activities between the Qatari FA and Thai FA. With Your Excellency granted per-mission, I will liaise with the CEO of Qatargas Operation Company Limited for a meeting to conduct all the follow up actions on the LNG sale. Your Excellency, I have the honour to remain Yours humbly, Joe Sim Chairman of Venture Group.' The chief executive he was referring to was Sheikh Khalid bin Khalifa bin Jassim Al Thani, the young royal who had taken the helm of Qatargas. He was another very powerful ally for the Casino King and his sidekick to make on Thailand's behalf.

Sim followed up with a fawning email to Sheikh Khalid himself, again copying in Bin Hammam and Makudi. He wrote: 'Your Excellency. His Excellency Deputy Premier, Abdulla Bin Hamad Al-Attiya, has directed me to liaise with Your Excellency on the LNG sale. Your Excellency has mentioned next week would be a good time to meet. Please let me know the time and venue for the meeting. Kindly grant me the permission for a meeting for me to discuss follow up actions with Your Excellency and co-coordinating staff appointed by Your Excellency. Your Excellency I have the honour to remain Yours humbly Joe Sim.'

That was four months ahead of the ballot for the 2022 World Cup. Bin Hammam had ushered the right-hand man of one of the crucial voters into negotiations about a major gas deal at the highest levels of the Qatari government. It would benefit Makudi's country and the company that was paying millions of dollars to his football association. Although the Qatar 2022 bid were not involved, FIFA's rules expressly forbade its associates from providing benefits to voters: 'The Member Association and the Bid Committee shall refrain, and shall ensure that each entity and individual associated or affiliated with it shall refrain, providing to FIFA, to any member of the FIFA Executive Committee ... or any of their respective relatives, companions, guests or nominees ... any kind of personal advantage that could give even the impression of exerting influence, or conflict of interest, either directly or indirectly, in connection with the Bidding Process, such as at the beginning of a collaboration, whether with private persons, a company or any authorities ...

and . . . any benefit, opportunity, promise, remuneration or service to any such individuals, in connection with the Bidding Process.'

A week later, in early September 2010, Sim and Teo were back in Doha and their bills at the Sheraton were, inevitably, once again being footed by Bin Hammam. Chirakal had also arranged the two men's visas at the request of Makudi. They had a second appointment at the Navigation Tower, but this time the encounter was on a different floor. They were escorted to a noon meeting with Sheikh Khalid in his palatial offices overlooking the West Bay. In the weeks and months that followed, Sim was to become closer to Bin Hammam, travelling alongside the billionaire on a tour of Cambodia and Myanmar. He returned to Doha a couple of times alongside Makudi – and again both trips were arranged by Chirakal. The new bilateral 'cooperation' between the Thai and Qatar FAs that had been under discussion at the meeting with Al-Attiyah received no publicity whatsoever. News of the gas deal also went dark. There were no public announcements from PTT or the Thai government except for an acknowledgement in December that they were still in talks with Qatargas.

However, a few months after the World Cup ballot, the completed Map Ta Phut terminal sprang into action. It was daybreak on a cloudy morning in May and the workers were running through last-minute drills as five blue and white tug boats buzzed around the harbour in readiness. Out at sea, a gargantuan dark steel prow was carving a path through the turquoise waters. The *Golar Viking* was a vessel the length of three football pitches and there could be no doubt about its cargo: the initials LNG were emblazoned on its side in white letters, ten metres high. It took four hours for the tugs to manoeuvre the unwieldy supertanker into position at the end of the terminal's brand new jetty when it docked on 31 May 2011. It would remain fixed in this position for eight days disgorging the 60,000-tonne shipment that

Qatargas had sold to Thailand at the rock-bottom spot price, exactly as PTT had requested. The tanker began its journey two weeks earlier from the port of Ras Laffan, 50 miles north of Doha – the hub through which Qatar supplied LNG to the world. At full capacity Ras Laffan could berth six supertankers the size of the *Golar Viking*, making Map Ta Phut's single terminal puny by comparison. But the shipment from Qatar was a big deal for Thailand. It was the terminal's first ever consignment of gas.

The man Sim had met to discuss the 'LNG sale' a matter of months earlier, Sheikh Khalid, was delighted to have been such assistance to Thailand. It was to be the first of several 'commissioning cargos' supplied by his company which would make Map Ta Phut fully operational. Announcing the 'historic' event on the Qatargas website, the Sheikh radiated pride: 'Qatari LNG continues to have a key role to play in helping governments around the world improve the diversity of their energy supplies. We are pleased with this development which will help to meet the growing request for energy in the Kingdom of Thailand.' He added, with reference to PTT, 'This delivery will further strengthen the relationship between both companies over the long-term.'

In turn Wichai Pornkeratiwat, an executive vice-president of PTT, was similarly joyous at the new relationship. 'We are very grateful to have Qatargas deliver the first LNG cargo to Map Ta Phut terminal, Thailand, which can be considered as the first LNG receiving terminal in South-East Asia. The success of commissioning of Map Ta Phut LNG receiving terminal is a significant milestone that will lead us to the successful commencement of terminal operations in July 2011,' he said.

It was the beginning of a beautiful friendship. The first shipment was only a taster. It was followed by a further 27 deliveries of LNG to Map Ta Phut over the next three and a half years. Three months after the first consignment arrived, Makudi was made a trade representative on behalf of the Thai government, with a brief that covered the discussions with Qatar over a new long-term deal to supply oil and gas. The deal was extended to cover not one decade but two, and Qatar gave Thailand exactly what it wanted. It set aside the original agreement from 2008 and allowed PTT to buy from its huge stockpiles of gas at the lowest market prices, with all the security of a 20-year guaranteed supply. The exact price that Thailand agreed to pay under the new long-term deal, signed in December 2012, was to remain a closely guarded secret, but it was a saving worth hundreds of millions, if not billions, of dollars for the Thai government and the FA's sponsor, PTT. The power of football knew no limit.*

* In a statement, PTT denied 'that Mr Worawi Makudi, Thailand Football Association President, is involved with the LNG trade deal between PTT PLC and Qatar Liquefied Gas Company Limited (Qatargas) in exchange of supporting Mr Mohamned [sic] bin Hammam, the Qatari Football Chief, to be selected as President of FIFA and Qatar to host the FIFA World Cup in 2022.' Makudi said: 'The story of oil/gas concession for me is not a true story.'

Eleven

Spies, Siberia and the Psychic Octopus

At the zanily colourful headquarters of England's 2018 bid inside Wembley Stadium, two shiny-suited sports supremos were hunched over a table pushing 24 plastic counters around a makeshift gaming board. It was autumn 2010 and the bid's squirrelly chief executive, Andy Anson, was spending many hours like this with his chief of staff, Simon Greenberg. The pair were anxiously trying to fathom the way the votes were going to fall in the secret ballot that December.

Anson, the former commercial director of Manchester United, was a no-nonsense Lancastrian businessman who was lost in FIFA's Machiavellian world, but Greenberg was an operator. The former spin doctor for Chelsea FC spoke fast, with a faint cockney twang and all the loose geniality of an East-End wheeler dealer. He had learned his street smarts working alongside Chelsea's billionaire owner Roman Abramovich, and he knew how the game was played. He had been brought in to try to haul England's too-gentlemanly bid through the mucky field of football politics to victory.

The World Cup gaming board he and Anson were poring over

was his pride and joy. Sellotaped to the top of each counter was a photograph of a FIFA voter, and the two men slid them into clusters on sections ruled off in marker pen to represent every country in the race to host the World Cup. They played out each of the rounds of the ballot over and over again, imagining all the possible ways the men on the executive committee could shift their votes between bids as the least popular countries tumbled out of the contest one by one. But this was an increasingly forlorn pastime. England's bid leaders were coming to accept that they were staring down the barrel of serious humiliation.

Anson and Greenberg had just received a devastating report on the bidding race from an elite security firm with close links to Britain's secret foreign intelligence service, MI6. If the old spooks at Hakluyt & Company were correct – and they almost always were – England was in line to get a maximum of three votes, and probably only two. For the country that invented football, such a total wipe-out in the contest to host the game's ultimate tournament was a sickening prospect.

They knew their bid was the best by far, on paper. They had done everything they could and they could not understand where it had gone wrong. England's football infrastructure was unrivalled and there was no country in the world where the public worshiped the game more fervently than they did here. All the stars had come out for the England bid: it had the enthusiastic backing of the heir to the throne, Prince William, and was adorned by the world's most famous footballer, David Beckham, as its vice-president.

That was before Greenberg had earned his spurs as the bid's new chief of staff by pulling off the biggest PR coup of all with the signing Paul the Octopus as an official ambassador for England. The psychic cephalopod had become famous during the South Africa World Cup by correctly predicting the results of all seven of Germany's matches and calling Spain's victory in the final by eating mussels out of boxes decorated with the flags of the winning teams. 'Pulpo Paul' lived in a German Aquarium, but when Greenberg discovered he had been born at the Sealife Centre in the British seaside town of Weymouth, the shrewd spin doctor was determined to claim the creature for the England bid at any price.

The 'Octopus Oracle' had proved an unruly signing – refusing over many attempts to pluck his chosen mussel out of the box marked with England's flag, despite Greenberg's spirited attempts to entice him. In the end, it was decided that Paul had 'retired' from picking winning teams. The mystic mollusc was unveiled to the world amid fanfare as a 'proud Englishman' who was backing his country patriotically – mussel or no mussel – in a promotional video in August 2010. Greenberg had hoped hiring talent like that would transform England's fortunes. So how had it all gone so badly wrong?

The bid had been spying on its rivals and the voters on the FIFA Exco since the start of the World Cup race, trying to get the measure of the competition and the men who would determine the victors. Intelligence flooded into Wembley from a network of private security firms, former MI6 officers and British embassies around the world, and the Hakluyt report was the latest dispatch to land on Anson's desk. The operation had been one of Lord Coe's expert suggestions, in his role as an advisory board member. The London Olympics chief had taken Anson to one side soon after his appointment as chief executive, slapped him heartily on the back and told him he needed to have eyes and ears on all the other bidders from the moment the starting gun was fired. England should establish an extensive intelligence network to build up a database of what Coe called 'campaigning information', seen only by a trusted inner sanctum within the bid. It was the only way to stay ahead of the race.

Anson had listened carefully. As a first step, a consortium of sponsors and associates of the England 2018 bid had hired a

Mayfair-based agency with close links to the British secret services to conduct surveillance on the eight other bidding nations in 2009. The agency was contracted for two years and filed regular dispatches on what its operatives found. Hakluyt would be brought in later, in mid-2010, to put the competition under its own brand of penetrating scrutiny. In addition, Anson and his senior colleagues were in close contact with the British government, and drew information on the campaigning activities of England's rivals and the voters they were pursuing from foreign embassies. The team was also gathering its own inside intelligence, collating and triangulating rumours gleaned from within the bidding circuit by its officials, consultants and advisors. The material England gathered was all funnelled into a central database stored in an encrypted file on the bid's internal server, accessible only to the handful of officials in Anson's inner circle.*

With each new dispatch, Anson and his men had come to see with increasing clarity that the technical merits of their impressive World Cup offering weren't worth the glossy paper the bid brochure was printed on. This contest wasn't about which country had the best stadiums and team training facilities, or which would put on the most joyous jamboree for the fans. In the end, it wasn't really about choosing the right place to hold the world's most beloved sporting tournament at all. It all seemed to shake down to which of the bidders could offer the biggest boost to the fortunes of FIFA's voters. The whole contest was awash with dirty money. There were allegations of direct bribes, astonishing gifts, and even massive state-level trade deals being used to sweeten the men on the Exco. Even if a handful of them voted in good faith,

* The details of the intelligence gathered by the England 2018 bid in this chapter are drawn from a submission of evidence from *The Sunday Times* which was published by the House of Commons Culture, Media and Sport committee in November 2014 http://data.parliament.uk/writtenevidence/committeeevidence.svc/evidencedocument/culture-media-and-sport-committee/the-2022-world-cup-bidding-process/written/15880.html.

a decisive majority of FIFA's rulers would cast their ballots on the next two World Cup hosts on the basis of personal, not professional interests. It was, Anson and Greenberg agreed, a 'Wild West of a bidding process'.

Anson and his team had appreciated early in the campaign that they would have to loosen both their purse strings and their buttoned-up British morals if they wanted to be serious contenders in this grubby process. They weren't prepared to break any rules, but they knew they would have to find ways to satisfy the greed of certain men on the Exco if they were to have any hope of winning support for their bid.

England's lobbying efforts had centred in particular on Jack Warner, the Trinidadian president of CONCACAF, who was thought to control the votes of the confederation's other two Exco members, Chuck Blazer and Rafael Salguero, as well as his own. Anson was no fool. He knew what sort of man Warner was, describing him privately as a 'rogue and a vagabond', but CONCACAF's three voters had backed England's last World Cup bid, after the FA agreed to fund football development in the Caribbean, and it seemed essential to win this triple-vote bloc again. So when Warner began to blitz England's bid officials with constant demands for payments, gifts and favours, they struggled to toe the line between keeping him happy and stumbling over FIFA's rules. While they rebuffed Warner's most outrageous demands with as much charm as they could muster, England's officials did agree early in their campaign to foot the bill for a training camp for Trinidad's Under-20 team in Britain, and helped arrange a part-time job for one of his associates in London.

Warner enjoyed dangling the prospect of his vote in front of the bid's over-eager executives and then slapping them down when they got above themselves. After giving the impression that he was backing England early on, he had rounded on them publicly in October 2009, accusing Anson and his team of 'creeping along' in their campaign when they should be 'galloping' and saying: 'I want to disabuse anybody of the view that CONCA-CAF is in the FA's corner.' He was momentarily pacified when England bestowed a £230 handbag by the luxury British designer Mulberry upon his wife – but events took a turn for the worse when the BBC caught wind of the gift.

The bid had bought 24 of the handbags and intended to hand them out to the wives and girlfriends of all of FIFA's voters when they visited England during the campaign. Little acts of generosity like this were *de rigueur* in world football, and the handbags were comfortably within the limits set by FIFA's rules, but the appearance that England's bid was offering inducements to World Cup voters caused a storm in the ever-irascible British media. Warner was used to creaming off millions of dollars at a time from his football confederation without hearing a peep out of anyone, and he was furious to have been exposed to such stinging criticism for the sake of a paltry present. The CONCACAF president sent his wife's handbag back to England's bid team, ranting in a widely leaked letter to its then chairman Lord Triesman that the gift had become 'a symbol of derision, betrayal and embarrassment' for him and his wife. It was a disaster.

England just weren't cut out for this sort of thing – their attempts to play FIFA at its own game always seemed to backfire. They had scrambled to pacify Warner, paying £35,000 into the CONCACAF accounts he controlled to sponsor a dinner for officials from the Caribbean Football Union (CFU) the following February. The man from Trinidad was initially mollified, saying on the eve of the event: 'It is costing the FA about thirty-five thousand pounds, but I think that is money well spent as it allows them to speak to all thirty-two countries from the CFU. It also means I will be able to get the collective view of my membership about who they think should host the World Cup when the time comes for me to decide who I should vote for.' This move would later blow up in England's face too: when it came to the attention of FIFA's investigators years later, the bid would come in for harsh criticism for paying a voter to put on a dinner in the Caribbean.

Still, after all their efforts to woo Warner, England had hoped they had CONCACAF's three votes in the bag. They were counting on the vote of Reynald Temarii, too, after renewing a generous memorandum of understanding to provide football development assistance to his Oceania confederation. Issa Hayatou had promised to vote for England to pay back a long debt of gratitude for the FA's support for his presidential campaign back in 2002. And now that they had made Geoff Thompson their chairman after Lord Triesman's downfall, they hoped they could rely on Britain's own curmudgeonly Exco member to vote patriotically. So if all went to plan, England had been expecting to snag at least six votes at the outset. It would be enough to propel them comfortably through the first rounds, and then they would be sure to pick up more support as other countries dropped out. It had seemed like a solid strategy. That was until the Hakluyt report had poured icy water on all their aspirations.

England's intelligence-gathering efforts were largely preoccupied with the bid's most fearsome rival – Russia 2018 – and Anson's team believed their own campaign of espionage was being matched with equally Cold War-style tactics by their rivals in Moscow. The officials heard that the Kremlin had installed a special surveillance unit in London to spy on their activities, so they paid private security companies to sweep their Wembley offices regularly for bugs. Their fears were so pronounced that they enlisted the help of MI6 to set up surveillance countermeasures when they met FIFA voters. Government security officials went ahead to sweep the rooms for Russian bugs, and issued the bid's envoys with lead boxes to protect their phones during meetings. It was known that Moscow had the technology to hack into their phones and turn them into microphones so they could eavesdrop remotely.

The information trickling in about Russia's campaign had not given Anson and Greenberg cause for serious concern until the spring of 2010. Until then, Russia's bid had drifted along under the lacklustre leadership of the country's Exco member Vitaley Mutko, but a few months into the year of the ballot, operatives inside Russia began to raise the alarm that Vladimir Putin had seized control and the operation was being 'cranked up'. The then Russian prime minister was an ice-hockey nut with no love for football, and he had shown virtually zero interest in his country's World Cup hopes until this point. But the reports suggested that Putin had suddenly woken up to the prospect of a humiliating defeat on the world stage, and had sprung into action. The operatives in Russia said the prime minister had sworn: 'I can't lose the World Cup. I can't watch it happen. I've got to do something about it,' and had 'dragged in all sorts of capabilities' to turn the bid around. Sources said Putin had summoned a select group of oligarchs to the Kremlin and tasked them with doing whatever was necessary to ensure victory for Russia, including striking 'deniable' deals with voters. If true, this was terrible news for England.

The reports coming back from Moscow now contained the alarming suggestion that Fedor Radmann and Andreas Abold were in the pay of the Russians. England's intelligence database already contained unproven suggestions that the two fixers had touted themselves as consultants to various countries, offering to write their official bid books for a vastly inflated fee of millions of dollars and promising to deliver their friend Franz Beckenbauer's vote in return.* Anson and his colleagues had disliked Radmann

---

* Radmann and Abold both denied that they had offered to deliver Beckenbauer's vote in exchange for their consultancy fees, and said he had not received any portion of the money they were paid by any bid.

ever since the lobbyist sidled up to them at a bidding convention and told them: 'You English haven't got a chance, you ... aren't going to play the game.'

That was after the England bid had sent Radmann's ally Peter Hargitay packing with a flea in his ear for suggesting ways of sweetening the men on the Exco, which had offended the English sense of fair play. It was no skin off England's nose when Radmann and Abold had gone to work for the Australia 2022 bid* with Hargitay, but the news that they were allegedly now in the rival Russian camp was a serious blow. The dispatches suggested that Radmann 'controlled Beckenbauer's actions' and that the German football legend was now 'completely in on the Russian bid'.† So, if the intelligence was correct, *Der Kaiser*'s vote belonged to Moscow.

Next came the astonishing claim that another key European voter, the UEFA president Michel Platini, had been given a priceless painting by Pablo Picasso from the Russians, plundered from the country's state collection in the vaults of the State Hermitage Museum or the Kremlin archives. The painting was said by sources in Moscow to have been given to Platini by Viacheslav Koloskov, a former Russian executive committee member who was working for the 2018 bid. Platini would strenuously deny ever having received any painting from Koloskov‡ and no proof emerged to support the claims that such an extraordinary gift had been made.

But then a second Exco voter, Michel D'Hooghe of Belgium, confirmed over dinner with England's bid officials that he had been given a painting by Koloskov. The operatives in Moscow

---

* Australia categorically deny attempting to procure Franz Beckenbauer's vote by hiring Fedor Radmann and Andreas Abold.
† Franz Beckenbauer has always denied that his World Cup vote was improperly influenced in any way.
‡ Platini described the allegation as a 'ridiculous rumour' which was 'totally fictitious'.

had sent back reports that Koloskov had given D'Hooghe a valuable landscape painting believed to be from the Russian state collection, in exchange for his World Cup support. When the Belgian voter met Anson and a small group of other senior bid officials over dinner, he told them casually that: 'My friend Koloskov gave me this very nice painting which is on the landing' – though he would insist later, when questioned, that the landscape was 'ugly' and he had left it in the attic because it was of no value.

None of the intelligence pouring into England's central database could be proven, but if the hired spies were barking up the right tree, Russia had made significant inroads with three major voters. More worryingly, England's bid chiefs feared that the men in Moscow had snagged the invaluable backing of the most powerful voter of them all – Sepp Blatter. The FIFA president had been courted by Roman Abramovich – one of the oligarchs alleged to have been tasked by Putin with using his wealth and status in world football to bring the 2018 World Cup to Russia.

The owner of Chelsea FC had swept into the contest during the World Cup in South Africa, and England's bid officials had watched queasily as the powerful billionaire glad-handed the voters. Rumours, which were never substantiated, began to circulate that he was offering FIFA's men the use of his private jet. Then, after the bidder's fair in Johannesburg ahead of the tournament's kick-off, one of the bid's executives had spotted Abramovich ushering Blatter upstairs to a private meeting, and his heart sank. The men on England's bid team knew from Greenberg just how potent an enemy Abramovich could be. The official who saw the oligarch disappearing upstairs with the FIFA president gloomily told his colleagues the news at the bar, adding: 'We don't do that, so we are fucked.' From that point on, all the intelligence suggested that the FIFA president was 'working very closely' with Putin and was 'absolutely committed' to the Russian bid. Beckenbauer, Platini and D'Hooghe were bad enough, but if Blatter was in Putin's pocket, England was in serious trouble.

Hakluyt had been called in on the advice of wealthy figures on the bid board, when the manoeuvres of the Russian bid were starting to make England really jumpy in mid-2010. There was no classier private intelligence outfit in the world than this secretive agency, with its plush offices nestled between the grand embassies in Mayfair's diplomatic quarter. Hakluyt had studied the activities of all 24 FIFA voters, and come to the conclusion that most of the men England were relying on had no intention of voting for its bid in the secret ballot – whatever they might have promised. The whole contest had been rigged top to bottom by bribery and skulduggery. However many hours Anson and Greenberg spent anxiously shuffling the pieces around on their strategy board, they knew they could never compete with the kind of financial muscle the Russians were allegedly throwing around. It was just as England's spirits plummeted to this all-time low that things suddenly got much worse. With the bidding process reaching its final stages, a new and dreadful spectre emerged on the horizon. Mohamed bin Hammam was prowling Europe on the hunt for an alliance, and now the financial monster that was Qatar loomed menacingly over the contest for the 2018 World Cup.

England's efforts at espionage had been largely concerned with its direct rivals in the 2018 race, but its operatives around the world had kept a watching brief on the 2022 contest as well. Reports that Qatar was using its vast oil and gas wealth to buy up FIFA's voters flowed into Wembley thick and fast, and there was a section of England's intelligence database devoted entirely to the small Gulf state. The Hakluyt report had identified payments made by a Qatari sovereign wealth fund into real-estate companies owned by Worawi Makudi which were developing holiday resorts in Thailand, and the intelligence suggested 'that was how they bought his vote'. Michel Platini was reportedly under intense political pressure from the then French president, Nicolas Sarkozy, to vote for Qatar in exchange for big commercial investments in France. Then there were claims that the Cypriot voter Marios Lefkaritis was in line for a £27 million land deal from the Qatar investment authority.* This was all fascinating tittle-tattle, but it was unproven and, as long as Qatar's activities were confined to the 2022 race, it didn't make a material difference for England.

That had all changed when news surfaced that Qatar was forming a deadly alliance with Spain–Portugal 2018 which threatened to blow England's bid out of the water. The rumours that Bin Hammam had sealed a pact with the Spanish voter Ángel María Villar Llona began to circulate as the summer of 2010 drew to a close. The deal was said to be simple. The Qatari had pledged his own vote, and those of his Exco allies Hany Abo Rida and Worawi Makudi, to the Iberian bid. In return, Villar Llona had reportedly promised Qatar his own vote and those of the three South Americans on the Exco – Ricardo Teixeira of Brazil, Julio Grondona of Argentina and the president of the continent's Conmebol confederation, Nicolas Leoz of Paraguay. If this was true, it was a devastating blow to the England bid team. The deal would guarantee Spain–Portugal seven votes in the first round, and Hakluyt had told England they would be lucky to expect just three. It could knock them out of the contest in one fell swoop.

*A piece of land understood to have been owned by the Lefkaritis family was sold to the Qatar Investment Authority for £27 million the year after the World Cup vote. England's intelligence suggested the amount Qatar paid far exceeded the true value of the land. Lefkaritis has strongly denied 'any suggestion that my vote for 2022 was influenced in any way whatsoever by any commercial consideration'. He added: 'As far as the transaction mentioned ... is concerned, please be informed that all related information is fully transparent and available for inspection through the District Land Registry in Cyprus, the Registrar of Companies in Cyprus and the Cyprus authorities in general.'

There was no denying that the rumours had the awful ring of plausibility. England's bid leaders had known that Bin Hammam was pursuing a collusion deal with one of the 2018 bidders since his breakfast with Clare Kenny Tipton in South Africa. The official line was, of course, that Qatar's Exco member was not working on behalf of his country's World Cup bid, but everyone in the England camp knew that was nonsense. They frequently saw Bin Hammam at Hassan Al-Thawadi's side on the campaign trail, and he had told Anson proudly that he was 'a soldier in my country's army' when they discussed the World Cup contest earlier that year in Kuala Lumpur. England's worst fears were eventually confirmed when one of the bid's officials met Makudi to ask for his backing and the Thai Exco member responded regretfully that his 2018 vote was no longer his own. The official reported back that Makudi told him: 'I am with Bin Hammam and he has told me to vote for Spain–Portugal.'

At the same time, England's spy network was lighting up with rumours about how Qatar was allegedly sewing up relationships with the South Americans who came as part of Villar Llona's bloc. The unproven suggestion logged in the database was that the Gulf state was offering 'government-to-government deals' to the voters' countries in exchange for their support. One big allegation was that Qatar had agreed to underwrite the losses of the Argentine Football Association after a botched rights deal in order to win favour with Grondona. The *Wall Street Journal* would later report that Qatar had paid the astonishing figure of $78.4 million to bail out the country's FA in order to secure Grondona's vote – a claim which was hotly denied by all parties. Another was that Qatar had agreed to meet any deficit on the cost of the infrastructure spending on the Brazil World Cup to secure the support of the country's voter, Teixeira, who has also denied any wrongdoing. It was impossible to prove that votes were being bought, but there was no doubt that the Gulf state was investing in South

America. In June 2010, Qatar Airways had launched heavily sub-sidised daily services to Brazil and Argentina. The Qatar FA planned to host a friendly match between the two countries in Doha that same year, which would generate big payments to both football federations.

The corridors of FIFA were abuzz with speculation about how Qatar was locking down the Latin vote, but no one knew the story of how Bin Hammam and Villar Llona had forged their alliance in a string of secret talks in the late summer and early autumn of 2010. These liaisons, arranged by Najeeb Chirakal, were coupled with attempts by the Qatari to woo the men in South America who came as part of the package with Villar Llona, and were intriguingly tied up with Bin Hammam's final meetings ahead of the ballot with Africa's most powerful FIFA voter. At the start of August, Bin Hammam had begun speaking on the telephone with the Spanish voter's son, Gorka Villar, a young sports lawyer destined to become the legal director of the South American football confederation, Conmebol.* Days after first speaking to Gorka, Bin Hammam emailed a letter to Villar Llona senior, the contents of which were later deleted by his staff. At the end of the month, Villar Llona wrote back, gushingly welcoming an 'ambitious' coaching deal that had apparently been proposed between Spain and Qatar.

Meanwhile, Bin Hammam was scheduling a meeting with South America's most powerful football chief. The president of Conmebol, the lordly Paraguayan Exco member Nicolas Leoz, was one of the four voters who came as part of the Latin package. Two days after first speaking to Gorka Villar, Bin Hammam wrote cordially to Leoz reminding him of a conversation they had had in South Africa and offering to visit him in his country's

* Gorka Villar became the legal director of Conmebol in 2011 and was appointed its general director in 2014. There is no suggestion that he was involved in any wrong-doing.

capital, Asuncion, between 17 and 20 August. Leoz responded warmly: 'It was a pleasure seeing you in the World Cup as well, I have enjoyed very much each moment of it. It's so good news that you are coming to Paraguay!'

Bin Hammam let Leoz know that he would be travelling to Asuncion with his voting ally Hany Abo Rida in tow. The Egyptian was in Doha for the secret gas summit with Makudi and Joe Sim directly beforehand, and he would accompany Bin Hammam on the long flight across Africa and the South Atlantic to South America. Mohammed Meshadi was also scheduled to come along for the trip. Leoz invited the group to fly to Porto Alegre in Brazil to join him for a match in the South American Cup, and then share his private jet back to Asuncion where Conmebol has its headquarters. The Paraguayan football chief was in bountiful spirits, and offered to pick up the whole party's hotel tab at the city's five-star Sheraton. Bin Hammam and Abo Rida were to have the best suites, as befitted FIFA royalty, while the lowlier Meshadi was booked into a single room.

The party was on track for a wonderful trip to the tropics, and then – suddenly – Bin Hammam pulled out. The night before the group were supposed to set off for Porto Alegre, Chirakal emailed Leoz's aide. 'You are aware that he has regretfully cancelled his trip to Paraguay and Brazil. I write to extend my gratitude and appreciation for your friendship and all kind assistance and help offered in facilitating Mr Bin Hammam's trip.' It was unlike Bin Hammam to renege on his arrangements – especially with the Exco voters he was working so hard to win favour with. But Leoz needn't feel snubbed. His FIFA colleague may have stepped back, but a far more powerful Qatari was coming to Asuncion instead.

The Emiri jet touched down in the Paraguayan capital on 18 August, and Sheikh Hamad stepped out onto the airstrip in the gold-trimmed finery of his royal bisht cape. The ruler of the world's richest country had flown in to coordinate an investment in a planned gas pipeline running through Paraguay, Uruguay and Bolivia. It was one of the biggest trade deals in Paraguay's history. The Emir's cavalcade carried him into the heart of Asuncion and up the manicured garden drive of Palacio de los López, the marble fortress which served as the seat of government, where he met the country's president, Fernando Lugo. Sources would later whisper that the Emir had also met Leoz secretly during his visit,* and unproven claims abounded that the trip had been designed to secure his World Cup vote. But Bin Hammam's mysteriously aborted visit to Paraguay, scheduled for the same day, never came to light – until now.

The Qatari football boss was busy at the end of August arranging a trip with his country's official bid committee to see the CAF president, Issa Hayatou, in Cameroon. The bid team flew to Yaounde with Bin Hammam on the Emir's jet, accompanied by the ever-faithful Meshadi. The party met Hayatou on 3 September, and gave the overlord of African football a private presentation on Qatar's bid. It went well, and another meeting was quickly scheduled with the CAF president – this time in Cairo. Bin Hammam got on the phone to Gorka Villar soon after they returned, on 11 September, and it was agreed that his father ought to be in the room too. 'Mr Ángel Maria Villar asked Mr Bin Hammam if he can join the meeting in Cairo, so please check with President [Hayatou] if he agree this,' Chirakal enquired of the CAF president's aides in an email.

No objection was raised, so Villar Llona was flown into Cairo with his close aide Eduard Dervishaj to join Bin Hammam and Meshadi in the meeting with Hayatou. The Spanish voter – a former star player for his national team – was lobbying passionately to drum up as many votes as he could for the Iberian bid as

* *France Football* magazine reported that Sheikh Hamad had met Nicolas Leoz secretly to discuss the World Cup on the visit to Asuncion.

the contest reached its fevered conclusion, and he knew how much sway Bin Hammam had in Africa. The chance to get in on the Qatari's private meeting with Hayatou was a golden opportunity to fly the flag for the Spain–Portugal cause. Two weeks later, Bin Hammam invited Villa Llona to Doha for further discussions. He was so keen to see his Spanish ally that he chartered a plane at a cost of tens of thousands of dollars to make sure Villar Llona could get to Doha and then fly on to another meeting in Belarus the next day.

By September, the deal between Qatar and Spain was an open secret within FIFA. Everyone was talking about it. If it could be proved, it was an outright breach of FIFA's rules and both bids could be thrown out of the contest. But England's bid leaders despaired: they could see no way of exposing a private pact between two men about the way they would vote in a secret ballot. Then, while all the countries in the race were fretting about the implications of a deal between Villar Llona and Bin Hammam, England received news that an even more frightening alliance was being formed. If their network of spies was to be believed, Qatar had teamed up with Russia to create a double-headed bidding behemoth that could not be beaten.

The men hired to spy for England in Moscow had sent intelligence back to Wembley that Russia and Qatar had traded votes through a massive bilateral deal that gave the Gulf state access to vast untapped gas reserves in Siberia. The spies said an 'extremely well-placed source' had told them the gas deal was 'significantly related to the World Cup'. Their hypothesis was that Bin Hammam had agreed to back Spain–Portugal in order to reel in the Latin voting bloc in the full knowledge that the Iberian bid wouldn't survive through to the final rounds of voting. They said Bin Hammam's real intention was to back Russia in the crucial final stages of the ballot that would decide on the next World Cup hosts.

The fresh intelligence about collusion between the Russian and Qatari bids centred on a visit to Doha in April 2010 by Igor Sechin, Russia's deputy prime minister and the country's most powerful oil magnate. Sechin was there to discuss a big joint venture between Qatar and Russia to develop gas fields in the Arctic wastes of the Yamal Peninsula. England's intelligence operatives reported strong suspicions that there were also 'other items on the agenda, of which the World Cup was one'. Was it a coincidence that in the same month Sechin had visited Doha for intergovernmental talks, the Russia 2018 bid delegation had also been in Qatar visiting Bin Hammam to discuss the World Cup contest? In a letter to the Qatari the next month, the Russian FIFA Exco member Vitaly Mutko had written: 'I was told about the friendliest and most candid discussion which you had with my bid colleagues. I am happy that leaders of our countries enjoy very good relations.' Bin Hammam had immediately forwarded Mutko's letter by email to the bid chief Hassan al-Thawadi.

Shortly after the visit to Doha by Sechin and the Russian 2018 bid team, Qatar and Russia announced that the Gulf state would join efforts to extract gas from the Yamal Peninsula. The Emir was anxiously preparing for a future when Qatar's energy riches would run dry, and this deal allowed access to the untapped reserves in Siberia's boundless gas fields – the biggest on the planet, running to trillions of cubic metres. It worked well for Russia too: extracting gas from this ferociously hostile stretch of the Arctic was an enormously expensive endeavour, so the world's richest country was the perfect partner. Qatar had the cash; Russia had the limitless supply of gas. It was a perfect match.

The joint venture was announced by Russia's energy minister and his Qatari counterpart, Abdullah bin Hamad Al-Attiyah, the week after Sechin's visit. Al-Attiyah was the same energy broker who oversaw the sale of liquid natural gas to Thailand for Makudi's henchman Joe Sim at Bin Hammam's behest in

August. England caught wind of the alleged collusion deal between Qatar and Russia in the months after the Yamal venture was announced. Then, weeks before the World Cup ballot, the Emir visited the Kremlin to shake hands on the deal and the warning lights in the Moscow intelligence network started flashing red.

Sheikh Hamad flew to Russia to see Vladimir Putin and the then president Dmitry Medvedev on 2 November. It was an official state visit with much fanfare and cordial public pronouncements on both sides. What the world didn't know was that Bin Hammam had flown in to Moscow for his own meeting at the Kremlin days before, on 30 October.

In an open letter to the Emir before the state visit, Medvedev wrote: 'Russian–Qatari relations are showing steady growth and have become more dynamic and unquestionably more mutually advantageous of late.' The Emir replied: 'We are also interested in developing economic co-operation between Qatar and the Russian Federation. I have already had interesting meetings on this subject yesterday and today, including with the prime minister [Vladimir Putin], and with Gazprom CEO [Alexey] Miller.'

When Bin Hammam had visited Moscow on his private jet days before, with Abo Rida loyally in tow, he had Gazprom on his mind. Qatar's football boss had been invited by Russia's Exco member and World Cup bid chairman, Mutko, to discuss 'bilateral relations' in sport with Putin. A briefing note prepared by his private staff before the visit advised him: 'Most of the bid committee are former Gazprom officials. Gazprom is the largest extractor of natural gas in the world and the largest Russian company.'

The England bid had only the scantest information about the Yamal deal in its database: nowhere near enough to get close to proving that it was linked to a vote-swapping pact between Qatar and Russia. But the claim from its well-placed sources inside Moscow that the two countries had traded blocs of votes was a fearsome prospect for England. Qatar was known to have solid backing across Asia and Africa. Russia was believed to have powerful allies in Franz Beckenbauer, Michel Platini, Michel D'Hooghe, Jacques Anouma and Sepp Blatter. If they teamed up, they would bulldoze every other bid.

England's bid leaders sat at their chequered gaming board with their heads in their hands. They were defeated. Anson was determined to press on through to the ballot, but Greenberg knew the game was up. Chelsea's old spin doctor was already hunting for new jobs as the vote approached at the end of the year.

Bin Hammam was cock-a-hoop. The campaign to bring the World Cup to Doha which had once seemed so hopeless was now powering towards victory. By autumn 2010, the Qatari had the four African voters in his pocket, his powerplay in Asia had worked like a charm, and his quest for a collusion deal had paid off handsomely. The deal with Spain alone would bring him a further four votes, and the alliance he had forged with Mutko promised still more. But Bin Hammam was not one to rest on his laurels, even with victory within reach. He was keen to reinforce the good work he had already done in Europe by reaching out again to continent's most powerful figure – Michel Platini.

Bin Hammam had been working hard to win Platini's vote, and he had made the Frenchman promise to allow the official Qatar bid committee to visit him in Nyon when the two men had met during the World Cup in South Africa. In the months afterwards, Chirakal had diligently followed up on the agreement and made sure all the arrangements were fixed. All the leading lights of Qatar's official bid committee flew to Nyon in October, two months before the World Cup ballot, to give the UEFA president a private presentation. Bin Hammam had originally been scheduled to lead the delegation, but he was called away on other engagements at the last moment, leaving Hassan Al-Thawadi at the helm.

Qatar's bid team gave a slick display at the formal meeting, but the real inroads were made the night before, when Platini dined privately at Geneva's Tsé-Fung Chinese restaurant with Qatar's crown prince, Sheikh Tamim bin Khalifa Al Thani. The heir to the throne had kept a low profile in Qatar's World Cup campaign until now, allowing his little brother Sheikh Mohammed to revel in the limelight. But with the vote fast approaching, it was time for Qatar to roll out the heavyweights. After the private dinner with Platini, Sheikh Tamim had travelled to Zurich for a meeting with Blatter which had been arranged in a phone call between Bin Hammam and the FIFA president.

A month later, with just ten days to go before the ballot, Sheikh Tamim returned to Europe for his most important meeting. The president of France, Nicolas Sarkozy, had invited him to dine in the classical splendour of the Elysée Palace in Paris. The other guest at the lunch was Sebastien Bazin, an executive representing the investment fund which owned the then struggling French football club, Paris Saint-Germain (PSG). It was Sarkozy's favourite club and it was haemorrhaging an estimated €20 million a year. Its executives had been courting Qatar for months looking for investment to bail it out. A third guest had entered the grand corridors of the palace with some apprehension, not quite knowing quite why the president had summoned him. Michel Platini was ushered into the room and did a double-take. He had not expected to be reintroduced to the heir to the Qatar throne so soon after their recent dinner.

The discussion that lunchtime remained secret until years after the World Cup vote when the magazine *France Football* reported that Sheikh Tamim had proposed that Qatar would buy PSG, and create a new TV sports channel in France to compete with

Canal Plus, an outlet that Sarkozy despised. At the same time, Sarkozy used the gathering to put Platini under intense pressure to vote for Qatar.* Indeed, the Gulf state's sovereign investment fund would pay €50 million to buy PSG the year after the World Cup vote, and the Qatari-owned Al-Jazeera went on to create a French sports channel called beIN Sport and paid €150 million for the rights to screen French football until 2016.

Platini had been won over and Bin Hammam could congratulate himself on laying the foundations for another major coup. His country's once feeble World Cup bid had become an unstoppable force.

---

* Platini has acknowledged that he came under pressure to vote for Qatar from the French president, but denies strongly that commercial considerations played any part.

Twelve

Sex, Lies and Videotape

A tiny secret camera had been carefully positioned on the smoked glass table of the hotel room, pointed directly at Michel Zen-Ruffinen. The former FIFA secretary general had continued to work in football as a lawyer since his well-publicised falling out with Sepp Blatter eight years earlier, and was now advising some lobbyists backing the American bid on the contest to host the World Cup. He had been promised a £230,000 consultancy fee and had been working his football contacts as hard as he could in return. Zen-Ruffinen had renewed his acquaintance with Mohamed bin Hammam's fixer Amadou Diallo in Cairo the previous month and had been in phone contact with him for several weeks.

A tall man in crisp blue shirt and dark tie, Zen-Ruffinen had greyed a little around the edges since his FIFA days. His brows furrowed as he delivered some bad news to the lobbyists in the privacy of his London hotel room on the morning of 13 October 2010. The hidden camera recorded every word: 'There is an alliance Qatar [and] Spain, and there are seven votes committed to Qatar right now, but committed, committed which is probably impossible to turn ... and that's a real alliance. It's bound, tacked with a nice gift ribbon and that's really problematic. This is the most problematic thing. I was informed about it last week. And this is not just a rumour, that's a fact.'

Five days later, a copy of the video containing Zen-Ruffinen's comments was handed to a FIFA official at Heathrow airport. The official boarded the first flight to Zurich and delivered the package by hand to the desk of the ethics committee secretary in the headquarters of world football's governing body. That day Jérôme Valcke, Zen-Ruffinen's successor as secretary general, summoned the man with the handlebar moustache and cowboy boots into his office. FIFA's new investigator, Chris Eaton, was to be tasked with looking into Zen-Ruffinen's allegations about Qatar's collusion with the Spain–Portugal bid. Bin Hammam's covert deal with the Iberians had been unmasked. This was serious: there were just over six weeks left before the secret World Cup ballot and Eaton was threatening to dismantle a key pillar of his strategy.

It was to be a bloody week for FIFA. *The Sunday Times* Insight team had gone undercover after receiving insider tip-offs about corruption in the World Cup bidding process, and Zen-Ruffinen was one of nine FIFA figures who they had secretly recorded during their investigation. Posing as lobbyists working in support of the US 2022 campaign, Jonathan Calvert and a former colleague had spent four months going round the bidding circuit finding out what it would take to win the ballot.

The first instalment of their investigation had appeared in the newspaper that weekend under the banner headline 'World Cup Votes for Sale', and it had thrown the competition into chaos. FIFA had demanded the newspaper's evidence and the Insight team was pleased that their findings were being taken seriously by world football's governing body, so Calvert was happy to hand over the package of tapes to the official at the airport on 18 October 2010. It contained multiple allegations of bungs, bribes and requests for payment, implicating FIFA executive committee members in a seismic scandal that shook world football's governing body to the core.

Two executive committee members, Amos Adamu and Reynald Temarii, were instantly placed under provisional suspension and it now appeared highly unlikely that they would participate in the 2 December ballot. Adamu had been caught on camera agreeing to sell his vote for the 2018 tournament, and it was a disaster for Bin Hammam to lose the Nigerian Exco member whose vote he was counting on. Temarii had been recorded asking an undercover reporter seeking his vote for NZ$3 million (US$2.3 million) for a sports academy.

A further four of the FIFA executive committee's former officials were relieved from their football duties, pending the ethics committee's investigation. Their colleagues on the Exco fumed at the insolence of the English media and were aghast that FIFA had pandered to them by taking such a brutal action against their friends. But there was no choice. FIFA had the film in their possession and the world's media were bearing down like never before. Questions were being asked about whether the World Cup ballot should now be postponed. The boil needed to be lanced post-haste.

It was bad enough for Bin Hammam to have lost a key voter in Adamu, and for the bidding process to be exposed to such scrutiny in the full glare of the world's media, but that was not the worst of it. Eaton's investigation into the collusion deal with Spain was the most awful consequence of the bomb *The Sunday Times* had dropped. This sort of meddling was exactly what Bin Hammam had feared when Blatter announced the ethics committee was going to be overseeing the bidding process. Bin Hammam had previously asked his lawyers whether there was any way to challenge the unnecessary interference of FIFA's sleepy ethics men, but he had been told there was nothing he could do to stand in their way. Eaton's intervention was the last straw. This was the first time that FIFA had enlisted a proactive sleuth to police the bids. Could they really do this? There certainly wasn't anything in the statutes about using the services of an investigator to carry out the work of the ethics committee. Where would Eaton's investigation lead? What else might he find out?

For FIFA's new investigator, this was the first big opportunity to cut his teeth on some serious work. Eaton instantly recognised the developing scandal as a great chance to build his empire. 'This is the time for me to push a good security structure for FIFA,' he said in an email to a friend. 'My attitude is that we have one big shot here to get it right operationally and politically,' he wrote later to another associate. 'This combination of incidents will force FIFA to create an internal capability they never really thought they would need. So we will take that positive out of it if nothing else.'

Valcke wanted Eaton to report directly to him on the collusion allegations, independently of the ethics committee which already had its hands full dealing with the other evidence contained in the package the newspaper had supplied. Football's favourite spin doctor Peter Hargitay was also on the case, emailing Valcke with a story from the *Daily Telegraph*, once the news of the investigation had been officially announced that evening. 'In case there are further similar pieces, I send them to you.' Hargitay kindly offered to his friend 'cher Jérôme'.

Eaton had his work cut out for him with Qatar – the official bid committee was not going to accept his interference without a fight. Immediately after receiving a dossier of the allegations in the secret tapes from *The Sunday Times*, Hassan Al-Thawadi had written a furious letter to FIFA demanding that the ethics committee exonerate his bid. The letter from the Qatar bid chief executive was indignant. 'We are writing to you to inform you of allegations presented to us by *The Sunday Times*,' he wrote. 'The

Insight Editor, requested our comments on 14 October 2010, as he is legally obliged to do so. The accusations he presented are completely unfounded, including allegations of collusion and bribery, all of which are completely false.'

Al-Thawadi was particularly stung that the newspaper had quoted FIFA's rules at Qatar in its letter. He continued: 'The article also makes reference to the Bid registration rules. Based on FIFA's instructions, we understand that this document, along with all bid documents, is strictly confidential. We question how *The Sunday Times* was able to obtain a copy of it. We are outraged. As we're sure you can appreciate, these allegations not only damage our bid to host the 2022 World Cup, but they also disparage the honor of the State of Qatar. The bid has always adhered to the highest ethical standards, in line with the State of Qatar's policies. We are conducting our own investigation into these matters, and strongly urge the FIFA Ethics Committee to also look into them.'

On the same day, Al-Thawadi sent a separate message to Bin Hammam's personal email account attaching a copy of FIFA's bidding rules on collusion and gifts to football officials. His email did not say why he felt the need to refresh his countryman's memory about such illicit practices when Bin Hammam, a former member of the ethics committee, already knew they were strictly prohibited.

Eaton got down to business straight away, firing off identical letters to the Qatar and Iberian bids. He addressed the first letter to Ali Al-Thawadi, the Qatar bid's deputy chief executive: 'Greetings to you,' he wrote. 'My name is Chris Eaton and I am the Security Adviser to FIFA. Secretary General Valcke has directed me to investigate the recent media reports of collusion between your Committee and the bidding Committees of Portugal/Spain. My purpose in writing to you is firstly to introduce both myself and my role in investigating this media report, and secondly to ask you whether you and your Committee will cooperate with my investigation. Should you agree to cooperate with the investigation, and as a first step, can you advise as soon as possible of the name and contact details of the person in your Committee who will be my point of contact and with whom I will initiate my inquiries.'

A couple of hours later he sent both bids a further message to say: 'To be clear my investigation under the direction of SG Valcke, is independent of and additional to the ongoing investigation of the FIFA Ethics Committee.' The Iberian bid responded immediately offering full cooperation, but Doha remained silent.

Eaton had been with FIFA for just six months but he realised he would have to tip-toe gingerly through a minefield of internal political agendas – especially if he was to use the investigation to cement his position in the organisation. One of his security team, an Englishman named Terry Steans, wrote to warn him that any investigation into Qatar was sensitive because Bin Hammam was said to have funded Sepp Blatter's election campaigns. 'It means you treading carefully if Hammam is that close to the President,' wrote Steans, an outwardly gentle teddy-bear of a man with a sharp grasp of football politics who often took the role of Eaton's *consiglieri*. 'I appreciate this heads up mate,' Eaton responded. 'I am pretty well aware of how close Blatter is to Bin Hammam. I'll take it into account in my approach, but that's all.' Eaton was already of the view that Qatar was colluding with Spain, but he knew it would be hard to prove. 'From what I can see there is nothing solid yet on the collusion, but on the balance of probabilities, it happened,' he wrote to Steans. 'I am working from that premise.'

The package containing the evidence from *The Sunday Times* had been copied and distributed to Eaton and his team. In his small office in FIFA headquarters, Eaton placed a disc into his computer, swung his boots up on the table and sat back to watch the footage. There was hours of it. The reporters had posed as lobbyists representing a consortium supporting the American bid and they had initially met a series of former FIFA officials who were offering their services as consultants advising on how to secure votes. Their tapes were to be quite an education about the darker side of FIFA for its new security advisor.

The scene in the first tape was a table elegantly set with an array of glasses. Into shot came a bald man, dark-eyed in his late thirties, wearing an open-necked blue shirt and black jacket. The accompanying notes from the newspaper indicated that this was Michel Bacchini, who had been employed as FIFA's director of competitions for eight years and was now running his own football consultancy. The footage had been filmed in August at a Michelin-starred restaurant on the banks of Lake Zurich, a five-minute drive down the hill from Bacchini's home. The athletic Swiss consultant had represented Indonesia's short-lived bid for 2022 and had clearly been doing his homework. He knew an awful lot about the bidding process, which he was confidently imparting to his two lunch companions.

Bacchini's advice to the fake American lobbyists was that votes would come with strings attached and that often meant paying money, alas. The way to win votes was to encourage big corporations to offer FIFA executive committee members business deals that would generate income for them. This had to be done at arm's length. He advised his lunch companions that the voters would have 'somebody doing their job for them' who would cut a side deal on their behalf. 'And when it comes to the worst, he doesn't know anything, you know, you can't trace anything because it's somewhere in an account which is not him, in the beginning,' he said. Warming to his theme, he said he knew 'how to get to' one member of the committee who he alleged had become wealthy as a result of his dealings with the successful German bid for the 2006 World Cup. That man's vote would cost 'easily' $1 million. But such approaches would come at a price. 'I can reach out easily to several [FIFA Exco] members myself. But you have to consider I take a big risk and if I take a big risk, this would be significantly more expensive. I need to cover my risk,' he said.

In preparation for the lunch, Bacchini had been thinking about how to make sure an Exco member could be made to honour a pledge of support. He had learnt much from his bitter experience working for the Moroccan bid as a consultant in the run-up to the May 2004 ballot for the 2010 World Cup, eventually won by South Africa. He claimed his Moroccan colleagues had paid Jack Warner upfront for his vote, but the Trinidadian executive committee member had double-crossed them. 'They were paying him and at the end when they were voting here in Zurich, you know, he was making a big scene, he was running out of the hotel complaining that somebody was cheating. He was the guy who cheated, he was making a big scenario out of it. I know a hundred hundred per cent that he was voting for the South Africans and pretended to vote for the Moroccans. ... I always say you never have to pay any money upfront.' His proposed solution was to place the money in an escrow, from which it would be released only once the American bid had been successful.

Even to a seasoned investigator such as Eaton, the frank discussion of such illicit practices must have been surprising. And there was worse to come. The main threat to the American bid, Bacchini contended, came from Bin Hammam and Qatar, 'because of the money'. 'I know that Bin Hammam is working on 2022 – for Qatar,' he said. As the cameras rolled, Bacchini set out his understanding of where Qatar's bid was. He had been making phone calls and was confident that Bin Hammam had the support of the

Africans – Jacques Anouma, Amos Adamu and Issa Hayatou. He was unsure about Hany Abo Rida, because he was unfamiliar with this newcomer to the executive committee. Worawi Makudi was a certain voter for Qatar. 'He's a Bin Hammam guy, you have to know he's Bin Hammam,' said Bacchini. 'He is in this position because of him, he backs him and so on. He would only change his opinion if the top guy comes, which is only one guy, the [FIFA] president, or he gets a really good deal.'

Bacchini believed Bin Hammam was also wooing Chung Mong-joon. He continued: 'And I know Bin Hammam is clever enough, he knows that a guy like Chung, he's not giving his vote for the first vote or the second-round votes, because if Korea stays in, he would always vote for Korea. Once it's out, then we need to get his vote. So that's where you win.' Chung was not someone whose vote could be bought because 'he is just straight', but the way to appeal to him was with 'power, politics'. Bacchini was absolutely sure the three South American voters were backing Spain for 2018 – which apparently confirmed at least half of the story about the collusion deal with the Qatar. There was a possible lead for Eaton.

Reynald Temarii was almost certainly voting for Australia, and Bacchini thought Qatar would struggle with the European voters. 'The Europeans don't want to have Bin Hammam having the World Cup in Qatar. But he tries,' he said. Bin Hammam was a dangerous foe. Bacchini warned his two new friends that the Americans would have to have deep pockets 'because the Qataris are, hey I mean Qataris, they don't care, they pay you ten million'.

Eaton could see that Bacchini had no direct evidence that Bin Hammam was offering payments to the voters, but he was a seasoned insider in world football and his comments were worth bearing in mind. It was time to flick on to the next recording. A bulky figure with a voluminous grey jacket and mottled skin filled the screen, almost blotting out what appeared to be the interior of

a hotel bar behind him. It was Ismail Bhamjee, who had been a
FIFA executive committee member for eight years before he was
forced to resign over a ticketing scandal four years earlier.
Bhamjee was popular and well known in world football, and he
remained an honorary member of CAF.

Aged 66, Bhamjee was a grandee who had been to every World
Cup since 1966. But experience had clearly not brought him discretion. Was it really necessary for him to confide in the two
lobbyists he was meeting for the first time that FIFA had paid his
$150,000 a year salary, plus expenses, into a London bank account
so that he could dodge tax in his home country, Botswana? It was
to get worse. Bhamjee was apparently sipping only water, not alco-
hol, but he was becoming increasingly loose-lipped.

Like Bacchini, he told a story about Warner receiving a bung to
support Morocco in 2004. 'I know they gave, they gave, Jack
Warner personally a lot of money for the CONCACAF. But
please, this is confidential . . . he got, I think, a million-plus something dollars.' Bhamjee had been there as an Exco member with
a vote. Warner wasn't the only one allegedly taking bribes. He
named three close colleagues from the executive committee
whom he claimed had been given cash to vote for Morocco. He
believed the amount paid was $250,000 per head. Now he was
instructing the lobbyists to do the same if they wished to win over
the African voters. 'We speak to them and say, "You guarantee us
your vote" . . . We tell them: "Look, we give you two hundred
thousand dollars and if we win the bid, we'll add on another two
hundred thousand dollars".'

The old hand confided that he was pessimistic about Qatar's
chances of bringing the World Cup to Doha, although he said it
with a heavy heart because he was 'close' to Bin Hammam. 'I
doubt most people will go for it because it's too hot. And
although they've said they have closed roofs, air-conditioners, it
would be very difficult. But I didn't want to say anything now,

because Bin Hammam is a friend of mine.' Loyalty did not, however, stop him from being even more indiscreet about the activities of his friend's country. Bhamjee had been told that the Africans would receive payments from Qatar for their 2022 vote. 'Anything from a quarter to half a million dollars ... This is separate from the football,' he said, and it was to be money for their own personal use.* Bhamjee was later to send a £100,000 invoice to the lobbyists for his advice that evening.

The recordings continued to roll on. Eaton called up a video which had been filmed in a high-ceilinged salon in Paris where another current official was touting his services as a World Cup consultant for £300,000. This was the moustachioed Slim Aloulou, the 68-year-old chairman of the FIFA disputes resolution committee, who has been around FIFA for 30 years and had spent 16 years on the executive committee before being made an honorary member in 2004.

The lobbyists enquired as to how World Cup votes had been acquired in the past, and what was a reasonable offer to make. 'What I can tell you is that a little while ago, these things were really not common, unlike what is said,' Aloulou replied. 'Unfortunately, I hear that this kind of practice is spreading more and more. About amounts, I can't frankly tell you, but these amounts must be quite high. It's not for peanuts. I can make inquiries and try to figure that out.' The lobbyists said they were thinking of paying $800,000 per vote for football projects and Aloulou agreed that the figure was in the right ball-park, but thought they would need to up it to 'around a million dollars'. He explained: 'Yes, yes! Per member. I think, but the cost might be even higher than I think. I believe it could be around that level. You know, people invest much more than that to get the World Cup.'

---

* This allegation was published by the House of Commons Culture, Media and Sport Committee in May 2011.

Doha: then and now

In the 1950s, when Mohamed bin Hammam was a boy, Doha, the capital of Qatar, was a quiet town on the Persian Gulf. But with the development of the oil industry, it was transformed into a glittering modern city.

Mohamed bin Hammam, the chairman of the Qatar Football Association, Sheikh Hamad, and Sepp Blatter pose for the cameras at the Aspire Academy in February 2008. Later that day, Blatter would suggest to the Emir bringing the World Cup to Qatar.

Mohammed Meshadi, Jenny Be and Najeeb Chirakal, three of Bin Hammam's most loyal aides, at the South Africa World Cup.

Michelle Chai, the assistant general secretary at the AFC, was another key figure in the Bin Hammam camp.

Bin Hammam's daughter Aisha – many of the secretive payments made by Bin Hammam went through bank accounts in her name.

Bin Hammam was rarely seen publicly with members of the Qatar 2022 bid team, as officially he was supposed to be neutral. Here he is with Hassan Al-Thawadi, the bid's chief executive, in July 2010.

Harold Mayne-Nicholls shakes hands with Sheikh Mohammed ahead of his inspection of the Qatari facilities in September 2010. His report would make devastating reading, but the Exco would ignore his recommendations.

Lionel Messi celebrates the only goal of the match in a friendly against Brazil in November 2010, just ahead of the World Cup vote.

Jérôme Valcke, secretary general of FIFA, greets Sheikha Mozah as she arrives in Zurich to help make the final pitch for Qatar. Her speech to the Exco impressed all who heard it.

Chuck Blazer sits next to Bin Hammam as Blatter reveals the winning World Cup bids – he was horrified to see the names the Qatari ticked off in his notebook during the voting.

Peter Hargitay, the Swiss-Hungarian lobbyist, pictured here with Jack Warner, knew exactly how to operate in FIFA's world, but even his wiles weren't enough to secure the World Cup for Australia.

Michel Platini and Issa Hayatou, two key members of the Exco, share a joke while watching the Club World Cup in Abu Dhabi in December 2010.

Blatter reveals the news that astonished the world: Qatar had won the rights to host the 2022 World Cup.

Almost unnoticed, Bin Hammam congratulates the Emir after the announcement had been made. He had achieved everything he had set out to do.

Celebrations in Qatar after the World Cup bidding victory was announced. The Emir had finally got his 'big cake'.

Blatter and Vladimir Putin together in Moscow as preparations get under way for the 2018 World Cup in Russia.

Bin Hammam and Jack Warner together in Port of Spain in May 2011, as the Qatari tried to ensure the support of CONCACAF for his bid to overthrow Blatter as FIFA president.

Arriving at FIFA's Zurich headquarters in May 2011 to try to save his
career following allegations of bribery in Port of Spain, Bin Hammam
finds himself outmanoeuvred.

Chris Eaton lectures on
'Ethics and Integrity in
Sport' in New Delhi.
The Australian had
joined FIFA in 2010
as its security chief,
but was recruited by
Qatar to set up the
International Centre for
Sport Security in Doha.

Michael Garcia (left)
and Hans-Joachim
Eckert of the FIFA
ethics committee shake
hands, but when a
summary of his report
on corruption in the
World Cup bidding
race was published by
Eckert, Garcia publicly
disowned it and
resigned.

Then there was a series of six phone calls on a crackly line to Mali with Amadou Diakite, another former FIFA Exco member, who now served on the referees' committee. Diakite was also offering his services as a consultant and claimed to be in constant contact with African Exco members – although it wasn't clear from the recordings whether he was acting through an intermediary. Qatar, according to Diakite, was already in pole position. 'I think that Qatar could be favourite for 2022. This is the impression I got,' he said. This was because the Gulf state had offered each of the African members huge sums of money to finance unspecified 'projects' in their home countries. 'I think it's about one million dollars to one point two million dollars of projects they are going to realise . . . they proposed that to the four African voters this year for projects they are going to do in their country,' he said. The FIFA official then agreed to find out whether the Africans could be turned away from Qatar and persuaded to vote for America if the consortium purportedly supporting the bid offered more money. He advised that it would be normal to make a financial offer ahead of the ballot and the voters would collect the cash once the bid was successful.*

The former Exco members were seemingly queuing up to spill the committee's secrets. There was now a cheerfully chubby Polynesian hogging the screen. Eaton glanced down to his notes. This one had been recorded in a hotel near the airport in Auckland, New Zealand. It was Ahongalu Fusimalohi, the former FIFA executive committee member who had been ousted when Reynald Temarii took his Oceania seat three years earlier. He was keen as mustard to work with the lobbyists and share his wisdom on how to secure votes.

For Fusimalohi, vote-buying was not in itself wrong, but there

---

*This allegation was published by the House of Commons Culture, Media and Sport Committee in May 2011.

was a practical trade-off between the size of the financial reward and the risk if someone found out. As an executive committee member six years previously, he had been offered an unsatisfactory bribe for his vote by the Moroccans, he claimed. 'They were trying to buy me cheap, but my selling price would have been a full retirement, and in shame, if I was to ever get caught, so I said sorry,' he said. The amount was a substantial sum, $150,000 or more, but that was not enough. He continued: 'And they'd put it in a separate bank account and I said, "Bullshit, if I get caught I mean that's a waste of my whole career. I'm not going to buy into this small-time petty cash money."' His advice for the current campaign, however, was to pay a direct bung into the account of his successor, Temarii. 'You've got twenty-four members making that decision,' he continued. 'It's only corrupt if you get caught – these people will go all over the world ... to get it at any price. It's sad but it's true.'

Assessing the strengths of the various bids, Fusimalohi said England stood little chance because they were too careful to abide by the rules. 'England have got every reason why they should host the World Cup ... but they don't strike the deals,' he said. He thought Qatar would struggle, too. 'It is a dream that won't come true for Bin Hammam. He is really going against Blatter, because it's part of the challenge to overthrow him next year. If Chung Mong-joon does not stand, then Bin Hammam will stand.' The winner of the contest to host the World Cup would have to offer financial assistance to the voters or their countries, he said. One of the fake lobbyists asked whether there might be difficulties if FIFA found out. 'Oh yes,' Fusimalohi replied. 'It's going to be a big problem. It has to be strictly confidential ... The eleventh commandment of the CIA is just never get caught.'

It must have been an illuminating few hours for Eaton, discovering the seamy underside of his shiny new employer. Here were four former members of world football's ruling committee – plus an ex-FIFA employee who had previously worked on World Cup bids – all saying the same thing. In order to win a contest to host the World Cup, you had to bribe some of the voters. The men clearly believed this had happened in the past, yet apparently none of them had reported these practices to the authorities. Moreover, they were now secretly advising these fake lobbyists that cash payments were the route to success in the current contest.

On the face of it, there were certainly sufficient allegations to investigate the Exco's dealings with the Moroccan bid. But would Blatter and Valcke really want him to go about prising open a can of worms which was well past its sell-by date? Especially as the claims seemed to implicate the apparently untouchable Jack Warner. Eaton had also learnt that the relationship between Bin Hammam and Blatter needed to be handled with care. And what was Bin Hammam conniving at now? Was there any truth in the claims that Qatar had been offering inducements to the voters, as Bhamjee and Diakite had let slip? Should these allegations be part of a wider probe into Qatar, or should that poisoned chalice be left to the ethics committee?

It was time for Eaton to turn to the tape of the primary source for the collusion allegations, Zen-Ruffinen. There was a substantial amount of footage of the 51-year-old Swiss lawyer to wade through. He had been filmed at lunch in Geneva, at breakfast in Cairo and finally in his hotel room in London. This was Blatter's protégé who had worked his way to the very top of FIFA's bureaucracy before ill-advisedly attempting patricide by going public with a dossier pinning concerns about financial irregularities within the sports body on the president.

Blatter could not tolerate such a betrayal: 'The executive committee will deal with our Mr Clean,' he had tersely told a Swiss newspaper, before Zen-Ruffinen was forced to step down. Yet here was 'Mr Clean' rearing his unwelcome head again, only now he was getting grubby by advising these phony lobbyists on how to buy votes, just as the others had done. Although Zen-Ruffinen morally disagreed with vote rigging, he said this was how it worked: for a fee, he would find out what the members wanted and make the right introductions.

The first video showed Zen-Ruffinen at a table in the chintzy brasserie of the five-star Hotel d'Angleterre on the shores of Lake Geneva. FIFA's ex-secretary general gave a withering assessment of the men who would vote in the World Cup ballot. It would have been amusing if his allegations weren't so serious. Inevitably, he started with the notorious Jack Warner, who he described as 'the biggest gangster you will find on earth'. Zen-Ruffinen alleged that Warner had profited handsomely from previous World Cup bids and would expect his palms to be lavishly greased once again. 'I can imagine that the total of what he would receive in money and in other advantages would be as a minimum half a million,' he said.

Ricardo Teixeira, the Brazilian Exco member, was also allegedly open to offers.* 'Teixeira, it's money. We can go to Rio and talk with him on a terrace, no problem. Openly, openly,' he said. A third member of the executive committee, he suggested, would have his head turned by 'ladies and not with money'. A fourth was compromised because a video tape was in circulation which showed him having sex with a prostitute in a hotel room. A fifth, Amos Adamu, would want something for his vote: 'The guy from Nigeria [Adamu] was also on the list as being okay to accept,' said Zen-Ruffinen. And a sixth was 'a nice guy', but Zen-Ruffinen alleged that his vote was all about money and he was the 'member who is asking for the most, I can tell you'. Zen-Ruffinen did not know how much it would cost, but he promised 'I can sort it out.'

Fast forward to September 2010 and there was Zen-Ruffinen again, a few weeks later, sharing breakfast with the lobbyists in the gardens of Cairo's luxury Marriott Hotel on the banks of the Nile.

* Teixeira has always denied that his World Cup vote was ever improperly influenced.

This was where the whole of the CAF executive committee was staying in preparation for a crucial meeting to make their final decision on which bid the continent's four FIFA voters would back in the World Cup ballots. Hayatou, Adamu and Anouma were in town, although Abo Rida was not with them because he was standing for political office in Egypt.

Zen-Ruffinen had travelled there with the fake lobbyists to get among the voters. Over coffee and croissants, they discussed rumours that Bin Hammam's fixer Amadou Diallo had sealed the votes of the four African members for Qatar. Zen-Ruffinen knew Diallo well and had been with him in the garden of that very hotel only the previous evening. He described Diallo as 'a small guy from Guinea' who had worked his way up through the federations and knew everything about football. 'This is the kind of person who you never see officially somewhere but he will be everywhere,' he added enigmatically. 'He is definitely the right person to talk to because he is the world champion of lobbying.'

The camera was now jerkily entering a wood-panelled room. It was the office of the president at CAF headquarters in Cairo. The stooped frame of Issa Hayatou was sitting uneasily in a small chair at the centre of the picture wearing a spotlessly white boubou. He leant across to his coffee table and prodded a large carved wooden statue of a British lion to show that its tail was dropping off. The sculpture was falling apart just like the England bid which had presented it to him a year earlier. The side of Zen-Ruffinen's head popped in and out of the picture as he spoke to Hayatou in French and then translated for the two fake lobbyists.

The CAF president was explaining why it was important for bidding countries to have the backing of federations across Africa if they wanted the continent's four votes. The federations had been prohibited from discussing the ballot until the South African World Cup was over, and a special meeting of the CAF executive committee had been convened for 22 September when the continent's position would be discussed for the first time. 'He says the CAF statutes give him the right to centralise the African vote if there is a reason for people to do so,' interpreted Zen-Ruffinen. Hayatou said he might not enforce the rule but he was certainly going to attempt to "harmonise' the four votes in line with the CAF executive's wishes. The lobbyists asked what they could do to help influence the decision. There was chatter in French before Zen-Ruffinen came back. 'OK, so to answer your specific question, I mean, there are discussions in that respect but the [CAF] Executive Committee will decide what kind of support will be requested from the bidders. If this is [in the] interest of Africa. For example, financing football projects somewhere.'

There was more video from the same hotel in Cairo that evening and that name Diallo kept coming up again and again. Zen-Ruffinen was having a drink in the garden with the man from Guinea, but he was reluctant to meet the lobbyists. So Zen-Ruffinen suggested that they take a stroll and 'accidentally' bump into him in order that he could briefly introduce them. This was the chance for Eaton to see the face of the mysterious fixer on his computer screen. Diallo shunned the limelight and there were no photographs of him on the internet. Very little was known about him publicly, except that he had worked for Bin Hammam on FIFA's Goal Bureau. Eaton followed the camera as it made its way through the Marriott Hotel's ornate Islamic arches into the dimly lamp-lit garden. It continued past the giant cylindrical topiary bushes to a small outside bar area, then stopped. Zen-Ruffinen's voice was loud and clear. 'Hello, how are you? This is Diallo,' he said. For a split second Diallo's face appeared in the corner of the screen. But it was too quick and the film was too grainy in the evening gloom. No matter how many times Eaton rewound it, it was impossible to get a proper view.

Later, Zen-Ruffinen reported back that Diallo had agreed to help the Americans. 'He said that once he has the reactions, and provided they are all, let's say, in principle ready to accept something, then we would have to define how to proceed,' he told them. He claimed there were many people working behind the scenes in the same way as the lobbyists: 'The key is that everybody knows how it works but nobody should have the proof that this has been worked like that.' A series of telephone calls followed about Diallo's progress. The negotiations went slowly because Diallo had become suspicious after learning that the lobbyists were speaking to the voters themselves. In one of his last recorded conversations, Zen-Ruffinen was heard to say that an unnamed figure from Qatar was claiming to have secured several votes. 'If he says "secured", it means that half of them have been bought,' he said.

It had become a drama of many parts. The sub-plot in the Cairo garden on the banks of the Nile had brought together Bin Hammam's elusive fixer, the reporters pretending to be lobbyists and FIFA's 'Mr Clean', who had once again allowed himself to be mired in his former employers' compost heap. So where was Bin Hammam as these events unfolded? He had been there too, but one step ahead of everyone else, as usual – leaving no trace of his visit for Eaton to find. On 15 September, the day before the lobbyists taped Hayatou at CAF's headquarters, Bin Hammam and Meshadi were in the very same office. Fresh from sealing the collusion deal with Spain, the Qataris had brought their new ally, Ángel María Villar Llona, to meet the chief of African football. But there were no tape recorders running in this secret meeting, so FIFA's investigator remained blissfully unaware that it had taken place.

Of course, Diallo's flirtation with the Americans had not been what it seemed. He only ever had one master, Bin Hammam, who had been in the background pulling the strings in Cairo on the night that the Guinean fixer was first approached by Zen-Ruffinen. If the Americans wished to give away their strategy and leave all the approaches to the African voters to Diallo, more fool them. It worked perfectly for the greater purpose: a Qatar World

Cup. Diallo would dutifully report back any intelligence to the boss. However, there was one bloated fly in the ointment in the hotel garden that very same evening: the clumsy and avaricious Amos Adamu.

The week of the Nigerian voter's spectacular downfall in October, Bin Hammam had been away in China on AFC business. It caught him by surprise. Everything had been going so perfectly until *The Sunday Times* sent the letter to FIFA setting out the explosive collusion allegations and giving details of their encounter with Adamu.

As was his lofty habit, the man with the pink Park View mansion had been late for his appointment with lobbyists in the same Cairo hotel on the evening of 15 September. When he arrived, he took them out into the garden and found a quiet place behind the topiary. It was a swift exchange as the basic terms of the deal had already been discussed at an earlier meeting in London the previous month.

At the time, the USA was bidding for both the 2018 and 2022 tournaments. Adamu agreed to give his 2018 vote to the Americans and in return he would accept a payment of $400,000 before the ballot and $400,000 afterwards. The money was ostensibly to pay for artificial football pitches in Nigeria, but Adamu wanted it paid into his personal bank account rather than to his football federation. He believed he had been careful as he talked through the illicit deal. To give the transaction the cloak of respectability, he made it clear that money should not be seen 'as a precondition for voting'. However, this was exactly what the deal was. Adamu was also happy to pledge that he would give his second-round vote to the USA for 2022, but he could not give his first. 'I've already given my word to some other bid,' he said. He later admitted that the 'other bid' was Qatar.

When the recording of the encounter arrived at FIFA headquarters on 19 October, Adamu was suspended immediately. He wrote to FIFA protesting his innocence, forwarding the letter to Bin Hammam, but the Qatari knew Adamu was finished, and that meant he was one vote down. It was a real blow to the solid core of support he had built so carefully in Africa. Everything had been going so beautifully, but now it seemed all his hopes were in jeopardy.

Bin Hammam was entering the eye of the storm when he travelled to Zurich for the biannual summit of the executive committee on Friday 29 October. The meeting of FIFA's rulers was sure to be a volatile affair. The old guard, led by Grondona, were spitting mad that the Exco's honour had been so impugned and questioned why Blatter had not adopted the usual strategy of retreating to the ramparts and refusing to entertain these outrageous allegations. Bin Hammam would join in the condemnation, because he needed his colleagues' support for a more important matter. Eaton's investigation into collusion was still ongoing and it was scheduled to be discussed during the executive committee meeting. That would mean Bin Hammam and his new ally Villar Llona would be put on the spot. They would have to deny categorically that any deal had taken place.

Ahead of the meeting, Chirakal emailed FIFA's finance office to say that Bin Hammam's chauffeur would be dropping by as usual to pick up $20,000 in cash. When the committee met in its Dr Strangelove-style underground bunker, the two empty seats of Adamu and Temarii further inflamed tempers. Bin Hammam sat apart from Villar Llona to avoid the appearance of being too close in this of all meetings. Several of their colleagues were between them, including the bulky figure of Chuck Blazer. The members had a brief discussion about the collusion allegations but this was swiftly passed over. The Exco was more angry about the messenger than the message. Valcke pacified the men, assuring them that there was no concrete evidence of collusion, even though Eaton had only been on the case for ten days and had not even spoken to the Qatar bid.

Villar Llona could not contain his delight that the secretary general was so dismissive of the allegations. When the discussion moved on to another topic, the triumphant Spaniard scribbled a note which read 'Congratulations, vamos a ganar'. He folded up the scrap of paper and handed it to his nearest colleague, requesting that he pass it down the line to Bin Hammam. Maybe Villar Llona had forgotten that the man bulging out of the chair next to his Qatari ally, Blazer, spoke fluent Spanish. Bin Hammam was bemused by the note when it reached him, and leant across to Blazer to ask him to translate. The American reached for his reading glasses, and scanned the scrap of paper. Then he looked up with a raised eyebrow. 'It says "Congratulations, we are going to win,"' he drawled. Bin Hammam winced. His neighbour, after all, was supporting the rival United States 2022 bid. As soon as the meeting wound up, Blazer ambled up to a friendly reporter at the Associated Press and blabbed about what he had read. 'I don't think it was the time or place. I think Mohamed was slightly embarrassed,' he whispered. 'It's the type of thing that shouldn't have happened but nothing more than that.'

When the story broke, the world read it as confirmation that the deal between Qatar and Spain was back on, if there had ever been any doubt. It was yet another cock-up, but Bin Hammam had no time to stop and reflect on the damage. Straight after the meeting, he and Hany Abo Rida boarded the private jet that would carry them to Moscow for their meeting at the Kremlin.

Eaton was carrying on regardless. Even as the executive committee was discussing the collusion deal, he was in his office on the floor above emailing Ali Al-Thawadi, who had not responded to any correspondence since his investigation had started. He was bristling with frustration as he typed. 'I do not seem to have a response from you or your Committee to my emails (copied below),' he wrote. 'As I am sure you are aware, the Ethics Committee enquiry is ongoing. While for the present there is no need for me to speak directly with you or your representatives, my independent investigation is also ongoing.'

Eaton added that he would be in Doha from the following Monday for a few days as a delegate at the Interpol general assembly, which was being held in the city. It was the perfect opportunity for the Qataris to meet him and answer the collusion allegations. But there were other things in store for FIFA's investigator when he got to Doha: the trip was to be the beginning of a glittering new opportunity. While attending the general assembly, Eaton was invited to meet Sheikh Abdullah bin Nasser Bin Khalifa Al Thani, a member of the ruling family and Qatar's interior minister, who was destined to become the prime minister.

Sheikh Abdullah was keen to discuss his idea of setting up an international centre for sports security in Doha to investigate serious integrity issues – such as corruption in the bidding process for the hosting of sporting tournaments. 'At the meeting Sheikh Abdullah raised the possibility of Qatar developing an International Centre for Sports Security,' Eaton recalled later in an email to a friend. He was receptive to the idea. 'I said to him at the time that not only was this an interesting proposal generally, but that should Qatar win the bid for 2022, that on behalf of FIFA I would do my best to promote the concept widely. A specific Academy dedicated to Sports Security professionals is crucial at this time in my opinion.'

Such a centre would surely require a top-notch sports investigator who, since it was Qatar, would have a multi-million-pound budget at their disposal. When the plan got up and running, that was where Eaton would come in. It was a curious coincidence that Sheikh Abdullah had sought to sound out FIFA's investigator about the venture at the very time he was investigating the

Qatar bid. Furthermore, Eaton also had a friendly *tête-à-tête* with Hassan Al-Thawadi at the Four Seasons Hotel while he was in Doha. It was good to have cordial relations with the men from the Gulf state, even if they were refusing to cooperate with his inquiry, and it was to pay off handsomely a year later when Eaton would land a big new job in Doha.*

Days after returning from Qatar, his investigation into Bin Hammam's deal with Villar Llona was quietly shelved. The Qatar bid committee did eventually respond to FIFA about the collusion allegation. It wrote to complain that FIFA had overstepped its own rules by bringing in Eaton when the matter should have been dealt with by its ethics committee alone. Claudio Sulser, the ethics committee chairman, announced a week later that FIFA was closing its file on collusion. 'We didn't find sufficient grounds to reach the conclusion there was any collusion, therefore we didn't move forward on that case,' said Sulser. 'Obviously, it's harder to prove collusion even though doubts may always arise.' FIFA had reverted to type. It scapegoated a few individuals, and then shut the door on any further investigation into the wider allegations from the video. The consultants who had been caught being so indiscreet on camera were given suspensions, mostly for breaking the rules by talking out of turn about things they had no business discussing with strangers. The World Cup ballot would have to go ahead with only 22 voters, because Adamu and Temarii were banned from football after being caught discussing the sale of their votes. The goalposts had been shifted and Bin Hammam would have to adapt.

---

* Eaton denies that the prospect of employment had arisen during his November 2010 visit to Qatar.

Thirteen

Only God Knows What You Do for the Brothers

The World Cup ballot was now just two weeks away, and it was time for one last jamboree before the fate of Qatar's 2022 bid was sealed. The more modern members of Doha's high society had donned their finest designer outfits, the traditionalists were in their richest robes, and all were heading to the Al-Khalifa Stadium in their Porsches and Baby Bentleys for a thriller. Qatar was hosting a football match between two great teams: Brazil and Argentina. It was a contest that would have graced any final of the World Cup and that was the whole point.

The friendly match was the glittering centrepiece of a week-long sports conference to extol the virtues of bringing the globe's most prestigious tournament to the Gulf state in 12 years' time. Journalists from all round the world had been invited to view the spectacle on the temperate winter evening of 17 November. Mohamed bin Hammam captured the mood of cheerful optimism as he penned an open letter to the official figureheads of his country's World Cup campaign ahead of the event, even slipping in a reference to the king of pop. 'You are a phenomenon deserving to be respected and supported. You are about to write history,' he raved. 'You are, as Michael Jackson sang, the WORLD. You are so close. You can do it!'

Bin Hammam was eagerly awaiting the chance to see such gods of the game performing on his home soil. But the events on the field were of secondary importance. The match was an opportunity to offer his supporters one last big junket before the ballot. Amadou Diallo had been given the role as 'coordinator' of the guest list, which, of course, meant it was well attended.

More than 20 presidents of African football federations were flown in to Doha at Bin Hammam's expense and put up in the Ritz Carlton alongside a similar number of Asian federation heads. Among them was Colonel Djibrilla Hima Hamidou, president of the Niger FA, who had enjoyed Bin Hammam's hospitality at the South African World Cup and afterwards had been very thankful to Diallo for arranging $50,000 to be paid to his federation from the billionaire's slush fund account at Kemco. He checked in at the Ritz alongside Ganesh Thapa, president of the Nepal FA, who had received £100,000 for 'business promotion' from the same slush fund a couple of months earlier.

As ever, with such a large group of people there were logistical problems which, inevitably, fell on the ever-patient Najeeb Chirakal to sort out. Hassan Bility, the Liberian president, was affronted when his wife was asked to hand over her credit card on check-in at the Ritz. 'Please note that my wife [was] requested to make payment for the Hotel Today before being allowed to enter the hotel. Pls follow it up and handle them for me,' he ordered Chirakal.

Most of the guests were as thankful as ever for their Qatari friend's generosity. None could have been more delighted than Fadoul Houssein, the president of the Djibouti football association who had previously solicited $30,000 for the medical treatment of his general secretary. He was so moved he felt only full capitals could express the depth of his gratitude. 'DEAR

BROTHER ONLY PRESIDENT GOD KNOWS WHAT YOU DO FOR BROTHERS … STILL CONTINUE TO PRAY TO WIN THE ORGANIZATION OF OUR WORLD CUP 2022 WORLD … WE ARE ALWAYS BESIDE YOU AND PERSONALLY I AM RECOGNIZING OUR FRATERNITY AND I ALREADY SEE THE LIGHT OF THE WORLD CUP ON THE BEAUTIFUL CITY OF THE WORLD DOHA.'

Ganbold Buyannemekh, president of the Mongolia football federation whose daughter's university education was being bankrolled by Bin Hammam, was just as supportive, telling his friend he was 'confident Qatar deserves to be a winner in the coming bid for FIFA World Cup 2022'.

While the junket was a great way to reward Bin Hammam's 'brothers in football', the event also had the even greater virtue of cementing Qatar's relationships with the two voters from Brazil and Argentina. The match had been arranged three months earlier in late August, when Bin Hammam had been stitching up the collusion deal with Spain that had since caused such jitters in the bidding race. Despite all the turbulence of the last month, he had survived unscathed with the three Latin voters in the bag – among them Brazil's Ricardo Teixeira and Argentina's Julio Grondona. He had extended an invitation to the two men to be his guests in Doha for the fixture and also invited the third member of the voting bloc, Nicolas Leoz of Paraguay.

'Dear friend,' he wrote to Leoz on 4 November. 'On 17th November Qatar will be hosting a Friendly Match between two giant teams of your continent Brazil vs Argentina. It is my personal desire to invite you to witness this match in my home town. I hope that you will be able to spare some time to visit my country for that purpose. I would like to extend my cordial invitation also to your lovely wife. Our friend Mr Ricardo Teixeira will be arriving on 14th November via Paris and I waiting confirmation from our friend Mr Grondona. Please honour my invitation to visit my country.'

There would be a big pay-day for the Brazilian and Argentinian federations for their role in the match, which was organised by the Qatar FA in conjunction with the country's official 2022 bid committee. Exactly how much the two federations were paid, and by whom, was kept carefully under wraps. The Qatar Football Association submitted accounts to the AFC stating that it had taken $534,000 in gate receipts from the game, and that there were no other revenues. But the match was being privately sponsored by a conglomerate owned by a super-rich Qatari that channelled payments to Grondona and Teixeira's associations for fielding their national teams. The name Al Saad & Sons Group was emblazoned on all the official boards inside the stadium. This Qatari construction and engineering company was poised to swoop on the multi-billion-dollar infrastructure contracts if the country's bid was successful.

It was owned by one Ghanim bin Saad al-Saad, who was also the managing director of Qatari Diar, the Emir's global property investment firm, and a director of the country's sovereign wealth fund. There were only a handful of men in Qatar who were closer to the Emir than Saad al-Saad. His company made sure Grondona's Argentine federation was well paid for sending its team to Doha and also made a $10 million investment in a fund called Global Eleven which had a contract to organise and promote the exhibition matches played by Teixeira's Brazilian team.

The match itself was a cagey affair between two teams of expensive superstars who were reluctant to overcommit themselves in case they angered their clubs by picking up an injury in a meaningless mid-season friendly. It was settled by a single goal from the world's best player, Lionel Messi, who dribbled diagonally through the heart of the Brazilian defence before using his incredible balance to cut the ball back across the outstretched goalkeeper, and into the opposite corner of the net. The full capacity crowd of 40,000 cheered and revelled in the celebratory atmosphere.

The vibrant event was a refreshing break from the hard work on the campaign trail and it encapsulated all Bin Hammam's hopes for the future of football in Qatar. But just as he allowed himself to relax and enjoy himself, he was winded by yet another body blow.

FIFA released its evaluation report assessing the suitability of all nine bidders to stage a World Cup on 17 November, the day of the big match, and Qatar was singled out as the country with the highest risk of operational failure. The report by FIFA's team of technical assessors made Bin Hammam wince. It was a complete demolition of his country's plans.

The technical delegation had been led by Harold Mayne-Nicholls, the former head of the Chilean football association, and Doha was the last stop on their round-the-world tour two months earlier. The visit had been a disaster. The team had tried to arrange the trip for August, but the Qatar bid had stood in their way, telling them this was not possible because of Ramadan. The month-long Islamic fasting period had not prevented Bin Hammam carrying on with business in Doha – the secret summit which led to the gas deal with Thailand had taken place that August and it would certainly not have been wise to have FIFA's inspectors in town at the same time. Mayne-Nicholls was suspicious that the Qataris were using Ramadan as a cover because they did not want his team to experience the extreme heat at the height of the summer, and the distrust coloured his view of their bid from the outset.

When he arrived in September, however, FIFA's top inspector could not deny that he found his hosts very hospitable and

charming. The rotund figure of Ali Al-Thawadi had been desig-
nated to shadow Mayne-Nicholls on the three-day tour of Doha,
and the two men got on well in the back of their chauffeured car
as they drove between the key sites where the proposed tournament would be held. Mayne-Nicholls joked that his guide had
eaten all the puddings for his younger brother, the bid's slender
chief executive Hassan, and Ali giggled obligingly.

The team were taken to see the American University, the
Islamic Museum, the Aspire sports academy and the Qatar
Foundation, and were given a boat trip around the bay. The
Qataris were doing their best with what few cultural attractions
they had, but Mayne-Nicholls took note that there was not much
to do or see in Doha. He also observed that a Qatar World Cup
would be crammed into the most geographically compact area
since the tournament was held in Uruguay, 80 years before.

More than anything else, FIFA's top technical inspector was
deeply concerned about the climate. When he was being driven
to a football match during the trip, the Chilean decided to break
free of his handlers and walk to the game as a fan might do. Even
in mid-September the street thermometer signs were reading 38
or 39°C and the sun was beating down. Mayne-Nicholls was a fit
man who still played football at the age of 49, but he was sweat-
ing profusely by the time he reached the stadium. He was
convinced the heat was unsuitable for such a major football tournament and remained sceptical about the bid's bold claims for
futuristic air-cooling technology which could supposedly refrig-
erate a whole football ground using only the power of the sun.
The inspectors were shown a solar-cooled five-a-side pitch, but
this was a fraction of the size of a stadium.

On the final night of the visit, the inspection team was escorted
to an old colonial building where they were greeted by the Emir,
his elegant wife Sheikha Mozah and their two sons. The inspection team were on their best behaviour – it was an honour to be

invited to a family dinner with the royals of the world's richest country. A long table was set with a sumptuous array of dishes and glasses of chilled water, and the guests were invited to help themselves. The Emir was a gregarious host who could barely contain his enthusiasm as he rhapsodised about his love of football. Mayne-Nicholls was taken by his obvious passion for the game: Qatar's ruler and his sons talked about nothing else for the whole dinner, while Sheikha Mozah listened patiently. There had been an awkward moment when Sheikh Hamad regaled the men from FIFA with a story about how his wife's repeated interruptions during a World Cup qualifier had meant he missed the deciding goal against Qatar. He turned laughingly to Sheikha Mozah.

'Do you remember, dear?' There was a silence as his wife's countenance froze.

'I do not remember that,' she said icily.

'You do!' he insisted. 'You remember, you kept interrupting me!' She recovered her poise with a tight smile. 'It must have been your other wife,' she said. The Emir grinned sheepishly.

'Oh, you're right, it was!' and the conversation moved on.

Eventually the Chilean plucked up the courage to ask why the Emir was so determined to bring the World Cup to Qatar, despite all the obvious logistical problems. The answer was simple: 'I want the tournament to be here in my home,' he was told. Mayne-Nicholls nervously ventured that it might be prudent to pursue a more realistic ambition: perhaps Qatar could hold a smaller club tournament instead. 'No! I want the big cake,' Sheikh Hamad had boomed.

Mayne-Nicholls might have liked his Qatari hosts, but that wasn't sufficient to alter his view. His detailed evaluation, published a few hours before the game between Brazil and Argentina, was damning of the Emir's ambitions and offered few crumbs of comfort for the Qatar 2022 bid team. The bid's plans were deemed to represent a 'high' operational risk, mainly because the country was too small, the infrastructure would have to be built from scratch and the climate was too forbidding. 'The fact that ten out of the twelve stadiums are located within a 25–30 kilometre radius could represent an operational and logistical challenge,' Mayne-Nicholls wrote. 'Any delay in the completion of the transport projects could impact FIFA's tournament operations. Moreover, it appears to be difficult to test a transport concept prior to the event under conditions comparable to the World Cup.'

Most damningly of all, Mayne-Nicholls added: 'The fact that the competition is planned in June-July, the two hottest months of the year in this region, has to be considered as a potential health risk for players, officials, the FIFA family and spectators, and requires precautions to be taken.' Of the other bids, England had been Mayne-Nicholls' number one choice to hold the World Cup and it was given a 'low-risk' rating. Russia came out second worst overall, receiving criticism for its shoddy airports and poor transport system which was inadequate for a tournament spread across such a large country. Qatar, though, was the only country FIFA's inspectors had deemed a high risk. They had come out the worst by far of the nine bidders.

The Qatar team was crestfallen. They had done everything they could to make the world 'Expect Amazing', in the words of their enthusiastically ungrammatical bid slogan, but they had clearly not convinced the inspectors. Bin Hammam tried to bolster their confidence with a public statement expressing his faith in the bid's revolutionary cooling technology. 'The temperature inside the stadiums in July and August will be 25–26 degrees which is actually a perfect climate to play football,' he said. 'In some other countries people complain about the cold. In South Africa we had one of the best World Cups but the temperature was zero, which was not ideal.'

Just as Bin Hammam thought things couldn't get any worse, another bomb dropped on Qatar's bid. The ink had barely dried on FIFA's devastating technical report before a second awkward document was commissioned. This one would remain a closely guarded secret for the eyes of the executive committee only.

Jérôme Valcke had decided to order an assessment of the risks posed by a terror attack in each of the bidding countries. He had asked André Pruis, the deputy commissioner of the Johannesburg police force, who had worked with Eaton on security during the South Africa World Cup, to produce the risk assessment. The brief was for Pruis to 'work alone and discreetly' to 'urgently review and report on each bidding nation ... in terms of their structural vulnerabilities to co-ordinated or simultaneous multi-site terrorist attacks'. FIFA memos said the work was necessary because of the 'extremely high global profile of a FIFA World Cup and the potential gravity to the attending public, players, officials and FIFA generally from terrorist attacks during this competition'. Pruis accepted the job despite his reservations about the tight deadline he had been given for such an important piece of work.

His finished report was based on the mass of information which had been downloaded onto a secure 'extranet', detailing all the bidding countries' plans and proposals. The results threatened to be catastrophic for Qatar. Pruis singled out the Gulf state as the only country where there was a 'high risk' of a 'major incident' shutting the tournament down. He identified the main danger as Qatar's close 'proximity to countries with an ... Al Qaida presence' alongside its plans to cram millions of fans and players into a small area mainly based around Doha. Transport-wise, he was concerned about the planned high-speed rail link connecting Qatar to other countries in the Middle East and any threat at Doha's new international airport, because it served as the only major international gateway to Qatar.

The risk assessment was particularly wounding because it dec-
imated one of the bid's chief selling points: the concept of a
compact tournament with stadiums, players and fans all close
together. This would cause chaos and overcrowding in the event
of a major incident, Pruis warned. He wrote: 'The fact that ten of
the 12 stadia are located in a 25–30 km radius will not only create
an overlapping of certain security zones but will also cause major
crowd management and traffic problems before and after
matches. Any incident in a security zone around a stadium may
immediately create a spillover to one or more of the other stadia.
Such a situation may create immense security challenges if ...
matches are played in close proximity to one another. The fact
that the majority of rooms for accommodation will be concen-
trated in properties not far from each other will cause an over
concentration of fans in shopping malls, restaurants and local
markets or souks. Such a situation will have a negative impact on
the utilisation of a sector security system since even the deploy-
ment of CCTV – and other technological systems – may be
hampered by an overloading of visuals and data.'

There were too many opportunities for terrorists to paralyse
the tournament, he argued. 'The proposal for a single competi-
tion-related event venue, the Doha Convention Centre, also does
not make sense from a security perspective. A single incident can
neutralise all event operations as well as event-related services.
The proposed Team Base Camp Village approach poses a threat
to teams since teams will be accommodated in two villages each
containing 16 clusters of luxury housing – up to 16 teams could
live and train in each village. Although strict access control may
be implemented the possibility of stand-off attacks should be kept
in mind. Although the high speed rail network which will con-
nect Qatar to various countries in the Middle East before 2020
will provide excellent opportunities for fans in the region to
attend the event, it will also create an opportunity for terrorist

movements in the area. The fact that the new Doha International Airport will serve as the main gateway to Qatar during the FIFA World Cup may create not only logistical but also security challenges during the event. Any major incident – aircraft crash or terrorist attack – may lead to the closing of the airport with severe consequences for the event.'

The security expert concluded: 'In view of the risks related to the proposed centralised approach Qatar is allocated a risk rating of high. I am of the view that it would be very difficult to deal with a major incident in such an environment without having to cancel the event.' Qatar stood out. Seven other bidding countries, including England, were deemed to be a low risk and the next worst was Russia which was moderate.

Qatar's fragile World Cup dream had already withstood a series of crushing body blows in the last weeks before the ballot, but this one had the appearance of a *coup de grâce*. The report was due to be handed over to the men on the Exco on the eve of the vote in Zurich at the start of December. However self-interested FIFA's rulers might be, even they might think twice before casting their ballots for Qatar once they read this chilling document. Surely no one would vote for a World Cup which would put the lives of millions of fans and players at risk. Or would they?

It ought to have been fatal, but Bin Hammam knew his colleagues well. Some of the Exco might well read the technical evaluation and the terror report and be alarmed by the harsh appraisal of Qatar, but others would leave the documents unopened gathering dust on their shelves. What really mattered was protecting the deals he had done with the men on the Exco. That was where he had to focus all his efforts in the final fortnight before the secret ballot.

Fourteen

In Every Crisis, an Opportunity

The collusion scandal, the loss of two voters and the devastating official assessments of Qatar's bid had made it a calamitous autumn for Mohamed bin Hammam's World Cup campaign. He was determined to salvage something from the wreckage. The loss of Amos Adamu was an infuriating setback after the months he had spent coaxing the Nigerian to pledge his vote to Qatar, but blessedly there were other countries smarting from the suspensions caused by the undercover investigation by *The Sunday Times*, too.

Qatar's rival, Australia, was also in disarray after being deprived of its one bed-rock vote: the Oceania president Reynald Temarii. The genial South Sea islander had resisted all Bin Hammam's attempts at courtship and had eventually been formally mandated by his confederation to back Australia in the first round, and the newspaper's revelations had made clear his intention to choose the USA second. Therefore, Temarii's one-year suspension on 18 November had deprived two of Qatar's main rivals of a key supporter. At least it was a score draw. But then Bin Hammam heard word that Oceania's officials were lining up a replacement to vote in Temarii's place, and he resolved to do everything in his considerable power to stop them.

Temarii's difficulties had begun two months earlier, in late September, when he received a visit from Jonathan Calvert posing as a lobbyist for the USA bid. It was a Friday morning and a blanket of grey cloud was smothering the sun outside the Oceania president's office in Auckland. Dressed in grey slacks and an open-collar blue shirt, the Tahitian had relaxed back into a brown leather armchair as he listened to the visitor who had flown across the world from London. The 'lobbyist' explained that he was representing a consortium of companies who were willing to provide cash to finance football projects in the Oceania region if Temarii gave his vote to America.

Temarii had leaned forward to give his analysis of how the ballot would unfold. He was candid: he would be voting for Australia in the first round, as he had stated publicly, but the antipodean bid would not survive the initial rounds and the real 'battle' would be between Qatar and the USA. In other words, his second preference would be the choice that really mattered. He then returned to the offer made by the lobbyist. 'Talking about your proposal, for sure, it's interesting,' he said. 'For me I just tell you that when the people come to see me I usually say: "Okay, what will be the impact of your bid in my region?" If there is something concrete on the table, then it's interesting to discuss. If not, forget it.'

He went on: 'So right now we have a special project, here, in this area.' His fingers circled the air to indicate that he was talking about the buildings and football pitches around his office. 'We need to improve the academy, we need to extend with the rooms, with the boardrooms. We need to have an artificial pitch. The English FA have already sent us someone to work on it. He leaves tonight. He came here to give us some idea of the cost.'

England had signed a memorandum of understanding with
Oceania to assist with football development in the region, and its
officials were there to cost-out the improvements Temarii wanted.
They reported that the work would require someone to pay
NZ$3 million (US$2.3 million), and Temarii thought that might
be a project which could be financed by Calvert's fake consortium. 'Yes, this kind of thing I am keen to discuss, because this
technical centre is the one which will accommodate all of our referees, best players, coaches, teams of the Pacific,' he said. Other
bid committees had offered to finance the project, but Temarii
would not be drawn on who they were: 'I cannot tell you, but
there is two bid committees who offer us huge ...' The sum he
was alluding to was much more than the NZ$3 million. 'I cannot
talk to you about that, but for me this is a basic approach when
I talk with someone who wish to get my vote.'

Any deal would have to be ratified by the Oceania executive
committee. There was then a pause in the conversation as Temarii
looked to Tai Nicholas, his general secretary, who had been sitting
quietly as the FIFA Exco member talked. Nicholas wished to
clarify 'just for the regulations' that the cash offers to the confederation were not 'formally linked' to the voting. 'We are asking
the bid teams to talk about "If you win, what would you provide
Oceania as a region?"' he said.

The prompt reminded Temarii to say that his vote was 'not
about the money', but his subsequent comments suggested
otherwise. He was voting for Australia because its government
had given the Pacific region almost $1 billion for infrastructure
projects and education initiatives to improve living standards in
the impoverished islands. He owed a debt of gratitude to the
Australian taxpayers. Since the Oceania football confederation
was dependent on cash from FIFA for 95 per cent of its revenue,
it needed to base its decision on which World Cup hosts would
maximise television revenues for the sports body. Temarii had

been given a private briefing by 'FIFA directors' who had told him that the most profitable outcome would be a European World Cup in 2018 and the USA in 2022, which would pave the way for the growing economic giant China to make a bid for the 2026 tournament. 'Then we feel we would have the guarantee of revenues for the next twenty years,' he said.

But did the Australians give Oceania any money for football, the lobbyist enquired? His answer was illuminating. 'They do,' Temarii responded, 'but it is peanuts if I compare with the proposals that are coming from the other bidders. It's nothing, nothing. With some bidders we are talking about ten to twelve million US dollars.' He added: 'But I will not vote for this bidder that proposes twelve million.' Was that bidder Qatar? the reporter wanted to know. 'No, I can't tell you,' he replied.

The lobbyist asked whether he could tell his consortium that Temarii would definitely pledge his second vote to the US if it funded his academy project. There was a flicker of discomfort across Temarii's features. 'I cannot say that, because then we will have to face an ethics committee,' he said. But he asked the lobbyist to inform the consortium that it 'made sense' for the World Cup to go to America for three reasons. The first was the TV revenue that would be generated: 'Only for that reason we should vote for the States, whether you give us the money or not.' The second was that he admired Sunil Gulati, the leader of the US bid, as a man of integrity who might be propelled onto the FIFA executive committee if his country was successful. 'And then the third reason why we could vote for the States,' he said, 'is because this kind of support coming from a private company would be useful, helpful for us.'

Temarii then asked whether his academy project could be financed before the vote, and offered to fly to America in mid-October to discuss it with the consortium. 'I will tell them, it makes sense for the States, and then it is up to them to decide if they want to assist us or not.' The financial assistance could not be directly linked to his vote but he understood that it was a delicate matter. He asked for future communication to be over the phone and not written down.

There was one mystery remaining. Which bidders had offered $10-12 million to Oceania for Temarii's vote? Temarii voluntarily returned to the subject near the end of the meeting. 'I can tell you that there is a huge proposal. Two, two, huge proposals,' he said. The money was to 'build academies, here and in the region,' and he elaborated: 'They made the proposal in South Africa, so I have to meet them in October, November. They then come to Tahiti, my home country.'

At that time, arrangements were already underway to welcome Qatar's delegation to Pape'ete, the Tahitian capital. Three weeks earlier, Tai Nicholas had sent an email to Bin Hammam's assistant Najeeb Chirakal. 'Hi Najeeb, I hope this email finds you well. We have moved offices and I cannot locate the business cards for His Excellency Sheikh Mohammed bin Hamad bin Khalifa Al Thani and Hassan Al-Thawadi. I need the email addresses of these two so that the OFC President can invite them and the Qatar Bid team to Tahiti in November. Kind Regards, Tai.'

The Qatar delegation was coming to Tahiti in exactly the same period when Temarii was expecting to be visited by bidders he said had made him a 'huge' offer. How many other contenders was he meeting in those last crucial weeks before the big ballot? What were the Qataris there to discuss? There were certainly grounds for FIFA's ethics committee to investigate the alleged offers further when they received the package of tapes from *The Sunday Times*. But their inquiry concluded without ever getting to the bottom of Temarii's claims about the mystery bidders who were coming to see him.

*

The ethics committee had deemed that Temarii was not guilty of accepting bribes. But they threw the book at him anyway, because he had been disloyal in spilling the secrets of the World Cup ballot, and had broken some other 'general' unspecified rules. Like so many decisions taken by world football's taciturn governing body, the reasoning of the committee remained hidden from public view. Not even the Tahitian himself was informed as to how exactly he had broken the rules. The suspension was devastating for Temarii when it was confirmed on 18 November. He was angry to be punished by his friends in Zurich, but not nearly so furious in public as his firebrand Paris-based lawyer Géraldine Lesieur, who vented her gallic rage against *The Sunday Times*, calling its journalists 'crooks' and 'fabricators'. Lesieur was in no doubt that her client had been shabbily treated and would be making an appeal against his suspension to the Court of Arbitration for Sport in Lausanne. However, this was to cause a big headache for his Oceania confederation.

Oceania did its best to punch above its weight in world football. It was made up of only ten Pacific islands, plus New Zealand, and its national teams were inconsequential on the football field, especially since Australia had departed to join Bin Hammam's Asian confederation. The single vote in the World Cup ballot therefore meant an awful lot to the confederation as it was one of the few privileges that gave it leverage within corridors of football power. Oceania's executives had not lost hope that one of their members could participate in the ballot, even with Temarii blacklisted. They moved quickly to install David Chung as acting president – a Malaysian who had emigrated to the south Pacific as a young man with a logging company and had found his true calling as a football administrator. The man Oceania was putting forward to replace Temarii as a FIFA vice-president represented Papua New Guinea – an island with the dubious distinction of fielding the joint-worst national side in the world.

With David Chung at the helm, Oceania approached FIFA to beg for him to be allowed to replace Temarii on the executive committee in time for the ballot. FIFA would oblige only if Temarii resigned his seat and dropped his appeal against the suspension. There was only one solution for Oceania: Temarii had to be persuaded to abandon the appeal for the good of his confederation and step down to make way for Chung. This was a tormenting decision for Temarii, who was at home in Tahiti as the events were unfolding. Should he sacrifice the hope of an appeal which might restore his reputation and his job, or should he bow out now as his colleagues wished? Having lost his FIFA salary, how would he even afford to fight the appeal? He couldn't do it alone. But Temarii would soon find out he had a very powerful friend in Doha.

Bin Hammam had sent Temarii a message of support within minutes of the 'World Cup votes for sale' story being published in October. 'Dear friend,' he wrote. 'Hope this mail finds you in good health and spirits. Having heard the news of *Sunday Times* I would like to extend to you my full confidence and support. Rest be assured that you have a brother in Qatar. Best regards, Mohamed.' As Temarii agonised about his predicament on 21 November, three days after his suspension, he clicked reply to Bin Hammam's email. 'Dear Mohammed,' he wrote, 'Could you please give me your mobile phone to call you? Bests regards, Reynald.' Bin Hammam was on the phone to his Tahitian friend within a couple of hours. The next day, he spoke to Temarii again with his office door firmly closed. His staff had observed that he was in a temper that morning and they listened out anxiously to try to deduce what was wrong.

'His mood already off now,' one of the AFC secretaries said to Jenny Be in a message.

'Let's be careful today and make sure we do our best to smooth things around,' Be replied. 'Don't want to make him more angry or stress.'

Bin Hammam arranged to meet Temarii in Kuala Lumpur that weekend for a proper face-to-face discussion. This would be a chance for the billionaire to restore the beleaguered official's battered spirits with some especially pampering hospitality. He sent out instructions to his staff that Temarii and his companion Lara Farahei were to be treated as the 'president's VVIP [very very important] guests'. They were to be flown first-class to Malaysia on 25 November and the $19,975 bill for the flights would be paid from his daughter Aisha's slush-fund account at Kemco. The reason stated for the payment was simply 'business promotion'. When they arrived, a chauffeur-driven car was to be put their disposal for the entire trip which, along with their club suite at the Mandarin Oriental Hotel, would be paid for by Bin Hammam. No expense was to be spared to make Temarii and his companion feel welcome.

The meeting between Bin Hammam and Temarii took place in private the following day. The Qatari could see his guest was in a tight spot, and he knew how to exploit a weakness. The billionaire used all his powers of persuasion to push the Tahitian to resist the pressure to step down and instead press ahead with his appeal. If Temarii stuck to his guns, all his legal costs would be covered by Kemco. It was a tempting offer for the man from the Pacific. He was no fool, and he could see that Bin Hammam was manipulating the ballot in favour of Qatar, but he treasured his position at FIFA's top table too greatly to wave away this offer of the resources he needed to fight. Still, he would face a bloody battle with his colleagues in Oceania if he refused to stand aside and deprived them of their vote. The meeting with Bin Hammam gave him much to consider.

Meanwhile, the aides at the AFC were worrying about how to dress up Temarii's visit in public. Michelle Chai asked Jenny Be what she should say about why he had come, if she was asked for a statement by the media.

'It's OK, just courtesy call,' Be replied.

'I received my good friend, President of the Oceania Football Confederation and FIFA Executive Committee member, Mr Reynald Temarii at the AFC house ... and we spoke about how FIFA kicked him out,' Chai joked. 'One liner is like leaving someone hanging. Because if people read, due to the fact it is Temarii, of course next question is ...So?? What you discuss.'

'Hahahhaa. Football in general?' was Be's suggestion.

'I thought,' said Chai. 'But even then ... the guy is suspended. Never mind la. Just leave one liner. Safest one I supposed.'

'If the guy is suspended he cannot have friends?' asked Be.

'Can have friends, but what's the point to discuss football? 'Cause he's supposed to be suspended for one year from football ... the "what we discuss" bit is a bit of a headache.' Be thought it was safest to let the boss handle that question.

'Hahahaha – let him finish that,' she advised.

Originally it had been planned that Temarii would stay in Kuala Lumpur for two days, but he had to cut short his trip and take the 9.30pm flight to Auckland on the Friday night because Oceania's executive committee had called an emergency meeting to discuss his fate the following day. The World Cup ballot was now just five days away. The meeting resulted in bad news for Temarii, as his colleagues decided that he must be replaced by David Chung. To soften the blow, they offered to delay Oceania's next congress until December 2011 so that the deposed president could apply for re-election once he had served his full suspension. In a statement issued after the meeting, Oceania said its 'committee believes it has the right to appoint a replacement FIFA vice-president for the remainder of the term. An enquiry has been made to FIFA to seek further clarification on this.' Chung was told to get on a flight to Zurich in the expectation that FIFA would allow him to take part in the ballot on 2 December.

Temarii was wobbling under the pressure that weekend and was considering tendering his resignation if FIFA would only tell him what confidentiality rules he had broken. His fiery French lawyer, however, was not so lily-livered. 'He gives up his rights and sacrifices himself, or he sticks by his guns and that will be held against him that the OFC did not vote,' Lesieur fumed in a press interview. 'If he is obliged to [waive his appeal], then it will be true blackmail.'

On the Monday morning Temarii sent a doleful email to Bin Hammam. 'Dear Mohammed, can you call me,' he wrote simply. He wanted to arrange a telephone call between his Qatari friend and his lawyer. By now, the other bids were descending on Zurich and the world's media were confidently predicting that there would be 23 votes in the ballot, with David Chung stepping in for Temarii. Andy Anson, the chief executive of the England bid, was delighted as Oceania was widely expected to favour his country in the 2018 ballot. Frank Lowy, the leader of the Australian bid, was similarly confident. 'I understand that Oceania is going to get a vote,' Lowy briefed reporters from his hotel in the Swiss city, 'I understand that FIFA will accept the person that is representing Oceania. It requires Temarii not to lodge an appeal.'

Bin Hammam was trying urgently to get hold of Lesieur to find out what was happening with Temarii but, before they talked, she sent him the email he had been dreading. 'Dear Sir, Reynald Temarii yesterday took the decision to step down. I have requested him to delay his decision by 24 hours ... I would like your help to convince Reynald not to give in to the pressure. Yesterday I already tried to get you to join on your mobile. I propose to you that I will call you at 19h Kuala Lumpur time (12h from Parisian time), knowing that there remains very little time before Reynald makes his decision,' she wrote in French.

Bin Hammam managed to work his magic. Later that afternoon Lesieur released a statement to the media saying that Temarii had now decided that he would not stand down. Temarii was quoted saying: 'Despite pressures and issues at stake for the OFC, I decided not to waive this fundamental right to restore my honour, dignity and integrity following the calumnious accusations I suffered from *The Sunday Times.*'

The announcement was heavily criticised in Oceania and Australia, with one media outlet accusing Temarii of sabotaging the antipodean bid. But there would have been uproar and mutiny if the other countries in the World Cup race had known what had really taken place at the meeting in Kuala Lumpur a week earlier. Bin Hammam had cut a deal to bankroll Temarii's legal fees explicitly to keep Oceania out of the ballot. The billionaire was to pay €365,540 to Temarii in the next five months. It wasn't just Lesieur's bills he was covering: the Qatari also paid off Temarii's €4,000 fine for his breaches of FIFA's ethics code, picked up his travel expenses, and footed the bill for the services of a company called JCB Consulting International, which was carrying out private detective work on his behalf.

The payments, including the legal fees, were all channelled through the Swiss-based JCB Consulting. The first message to Bin Hammam from the company's director said: 'Per Mr Temarii's request, please find attached the current provisional budget for Mr Temarii's defense and the bank account details of my company following the signing of an administrative and financial management agreement between us.' It set out Temarii's expenses dating back to October and included €260,000 in fees for Lesieur. JCB also took its cut of €30,000. Kemco paid JCB Consulting €200,000 in February 2011, using Bin Hammam's daughter Aisha's account. A second payment of €105,000 was made in April 2011 from a $1 million slush fund operated by one of his closest business associates.

It was a small price to pay to level the pitch again after the set-backs Qatar had suffered. By slamming the FIFA boardroom door in David Chung's face, Bin Hammam had effectively nulli-fied the damage caused by the loss of Amos Adamu. Qatar had lost a voter, but so had two of its biggest rivals. Now the secret ballot he had been anticipating for so long was almost upon him, and his country's World Cup bid was back on track.

Fifteen

Who Watches?

A clattering on the street outside jolted Calvert out of his immersion in the strange saga of Reynald Temarii. He leaned forward and pressed his eye to a tiny gap in the plastic sheeting covering the window. The full moon cast long pockets of impenetrable shadow across the street, and the scene was still. Then a discarded drink can rattled along the kerb in a puff of breeze, and Calvert's shoulders loosened. The journalists had been warned a couple of days before that someone might have been hired to keep watch on the office, and it was easy for paranoia to take grip after months holed up in the attic. But now something was shifting in the blackened doorway opposite. Was that a human shape, crouching in the shadows? He told himself not to be ridiculous. It was sure to be a fox, scavenging in the bin bags outside the chip shop. This was like being five years old again, and scared of the dark.

Calvert and Blake were dealing with a massive leak of confidential data on an unprecedented scale, and the nightmare was that powerful figures in world football might rumble their source. Earlier that week, the whistleblower had taken a call from a friend in the security industry who had picked up rumours that a private contract had been put out to spy on him. It was not clear who might be watching, or why, but if it was true then he could have been followed to this very building, and the source would be blown if the journalists were spotted here too and identified.

They were now taking even greater precautions to keep their whereabouts under wraps. The windows were blacked out with strips of opaque plastic behind the thick blinds, and the weary reporters slipped in and out of the building's back exit under cover of darkness each night, and crept back in at dawn with their hoods up and their heads down. The source was equally cautious, regularly having the computer system they were using scanned for unwanted intrusion. Since the telephone tip-off a few days before, there had been no real signs that anyone was spying. But that could change at any moment.

Calvert drew away from the window and flopped back in his chair, tipping his head back and pressing the balls of his hands into his tired eyes. It was past midnight again and the journalists were still trawling the documents under the attic's harsh fluorescent lighting. There were just two weeks to go before their deadline to deliver the story, on the eve of the Brazil World Cup, and the pressure was bearing down on them heavily. He tapped his password back into his computer and shifted closer to the screen. Both he and Blake had become fascinated by the lengths Mohamed bin Hammam had gone to in order to knock out Oceania's World Cup votes, and they had spent many hours piecing together the timeline of the secret talks leading up to Temarii's refusal to resign, and the payments that followed. Blake had moved on now to unravel a string of bribes Bin Hammam had paid to football officials in Asia, but something about the deal with Temarii was still niggling at Calvert, and he was flicking again through the lawyers' bills the Qatari had paid to keep the Tahitian voter fighting.

The odd thing was that Temarii's lawyer, Géraldine Lesieur,

had been paid through a separate company called JCB Consulting, which had also creamed off a cut of Bin Hammam's funds. There was no clue in the files as to what role this shadowy company had played, but something about those initials rang a bell deep in the recesses of Calvert's memory. He pulled up his Google search page and tapped in the company name. Then, he let out a small yelp.

Blake spun round: 'Christ! What is it?'

'Sorry! But ... Wow! This is spooky.' Her colleague's face was pale in the harsh light. Blake began to cross the room towards him, concerned.

'Hey, are you okay? What have you found?' Calvert had turned back to his computer and was peering closely at his screen. She rested her hands on the top of his chair back and leaned in to look at what had rattled him.

'Jean Charles Brisard,' he replied, pointing at an image of a blond, elfin-featured man with pale-blue eyes gazing coolly out of his Google search results. 'That's the private detective who was hired to spy on me years ago, after we did the "World Cup votes for sale" story.'

'Huh. Looks like butter wouldn't melt,' said Blake. 'What about him?'

'No, he was nasty,' said Calvert. 'He came up with a whole smear campaign.' He had pulled up an invoice on screen and was pointing to the name JCB Consulting.

'This is his company,' he said, seeing Blake's eyes widen. 'He was working for Mohamed bin Hammam all along.'

Jean Charles Brisard had first come to Calvert's attention three years before in 2011 when he had been exposed as the private detective who ran 'Project Airtime', an attempt to discredit members of the Insight team following their undercover investigation into the World Cup race. The Frenchman was a private investigator of some renown: he had been given the National Order of Merit by Nicolas Sarkozy in 2008 for his work on the financing of terrorist networks. He now ran his JCB Consulting security and intelligence company from an office in the Swiss town of Préverenges on the shores of Lake Geneva and, in the weeks after *The Sunday Times* broke its undercover story, Brisard had been hired on Temarii's behalf to try to dig up some dirt that could be used to smear the journalists and restore his reputation.

Brisard had uncovered their home addresses, family information, foreign travel records, and details of previous investigative work, including other identities they had adopted for old undercover operations. 'He tracked down where I lived; researched my family; and tried to draw some sinister conclusion from a planning application my builder had made for an extension to my loft,' Calvert explained indignantly to Blake. 'And he managed to blag my hotel bill from the trip to Auckland when I met Temarii.'

Brisard was a formidable operator, but this time he had been unaccountably clumsy, and had somehow allowed his error-strewn Project Airtime report to fall into the hands of a freelance journalist who was friendly with the Insight team. The 24-page dossier which had been shown to Calvert was a strange muddle of inaccuracies and distortions. Dates, addresses and a supposed company directorship were wrong. Calvert had been accused of using a false name in official correspondence, based on a planning application which had actually been submitted and signed not by him but by the family's builder. The report also falsely suggested that Parliament had previously accused him of withholding evidence from an official inquiry. In fact, the unfounded allegation had come from the lawyer of a disgraced peer who had been exposed by Insight for fiddling his expenses. In short, Project Airtime had been a shambles.

The Sunday Times had published a story in June 2011 revealing that Brisard had been employed to do his grubby work by

Temarii and his lawyer, and pointing out all the errors in his report. Lesieur rejoined that the investigator's efforts had demonstrated the newspaper had 'tried to manipulate FIFA's procedures with incomplete information'. This was based on Brisard's *pièce de résistance* – a detailed analysis of a 17-page transcript of the undercover meeting with Temarii in which he counted '153 errors or omissions, including significant changes in the meaning of several sentences' and cited this as evidence that the newspaper had tried to mislead FIFA. That charge had clearly struck a chord with Claudio Sulser, who ran FIFA's ethics committee. When he formally suspended Temarii, Sulser pandered to the furious executive committee members by telling the world's press that *The Sunday Times* had twisted the facts. 'What I cannot tolerate is the fact that they changed the sentences,' he fumed.

Blake knew this was one of Calvert's bugbears. The newspaper used an outside agency to produce transcripts of its undercover tapes, which were always in a messy state when they came into the office. But all the quotes that appeared in the newspaper would be checked over and again so that they were 100 per cent accurate. FIFA had wanted the transcripts and tapes the day after publication, so Calvert had sent an accompanying letter explaining that 'in cases where we have provided transcripts, they are for your guidance only as they are working transcripts. This means they may have words or phrases that are slightly wrong. The quotes used in the newspaper, however, are entirely accurate as they are checked many times over.' In any case, FIFA had the tapes, so there was no doubt about what had been said in the meetings. But Brisard had been clutching at straws, and he was happy to use anything he could find to cast doubt on the story which had brought Temarii into disgrace.

All that had since dissolved into the soft fog of distant memory, until now. The discovery that Mohamed bin Hammam had been Brisard's true paymaster was chilling. Calvert and Blake had almost come to feel they knew 'Big Mo' or 'Bin Bung', as they affectionately called him. They had no doubt that his activities in the lead up to the World Cup vote were nefarious, but they could see he was driven by genuine patriotism and passion for football and somehow couldn't help but feel his heart was in the right place, even if his ethics weren't. This strange discovery, intersecting his world unexpectedly with their own, suddenly threw a new, disturbing light on the man they had spent the past months studying. The irony of the situation was not lost on them. But Brisard had been in the business of smearing the Insight journalists for cash, rather than pursuing the truth. And if Bin Hammam had hired a man like that to spy on Calvert before, it suddenly seemed all the more likely that the same thing could happen again.

'This is weird,' said Blake, pulling her baggy hoody tighter and wrapping her arms around herself. 'It's sort of given me the creeps. Shall we get out of here?'

'Yes, let's call it a night,' said Calvert.

The reporters shut down their machines, scooped up the day's empty coffee mugs and made their way down the narrow attic stairs. They dumped the washing up by the sink in the small downstairs kitchen, swept the latest ready-meal wrappers into the brimming bin, shut off all the lights and set the alarm. Then they pulled up their hoods, crept down the back fire escape and slipped off into the dark. The leaves whispered faintly in the soft breeze behind the high garden walls on either side of the back alley as they hurried towards the car park where Blake left her battered VW Polo. As they rounded the corner into the usually deserted lot, they spotted two sparkling sports cars parked side by side in the far corner.

'Ooh, I think that's a Lamborghini,' said Calvert. Abruptly, the headlights flashed on, catching the journalists momentarily in their beam. The car shot out of the bay and screeched towards the exit, cornering fast into the road and speeding off into the night.

'Woah! What was all that?' said Blake. 'Get in the car, quick.' They jogged towards the Polo and jumped in, locking the doors and pulling on their seatbelts as Blake switched on the ignition and began reversing out of the space. Calvert was peering out of the window.

'I think there's someone in the other car,' he said. She looked over. Sure enough, there was a figure at the wheel, sitting still in the pitch darkness without any inner lights on. The clock on Blake's dashboard read 3am. Was he looking their way? She hit the accelerator.

Once they were out on the road heading back towards their hotel, Blake slowed to a regular speed and relaxed back into the driver's seat. Her heart was beating fast.

'What was that about? What was he doing just *sitting* there in the dark at three am? Why did that other car shoot off like that?'

'I don't know, is the honest answer,' said Calvert. 'Could have been a drug deal I guess, but a pretty high level one with cars like that.'

'Ahh, yes. A drug deal makes sense.' She blew out her cheeks. 'God, I'm really jumpy. I think I need sleep.'

'What you need is a drink,' said Calvert. Blake chuckled.

'How well you know me.' Then her eyes flicked up to the rear-view mirror and flared. A black car was speeding up behind them, its headlights on full beam. Blake's mother was forever fretting that she was going to get 'bumped off' one of these days, if she kept writing stories antagonising rich and powerful people. When told not to be silly, she had a habit of cocking her head with a knowing look and saying things like: 'Car crashes *do happen* late at night with no witnesses, you know.' Suddenly those words were flashing through Blake's deliriously tired mind as she watched the gleaming black Mercedes racing up at the rear. Now it was hard on her tailgate, veering from side to side.

'What's this guy doing, trying to run us off the road?' Her voice had come out at a strangely squeaky pitch. Calvert glanced over and rolled his eyes.

'Heids, you're doing eighteen miles an hour and hugging both lanes. You're right – you do need sleep.'

Ten minutes later, the Polo rolled into the hotel car park. The journalists stumbled sleepily through the lobby, waved at the all-night barman who had come to know them well, and headed downstairs to their rooms looking out over the gardens. Blake flipped the lights off and threw herself onto the bed fully clothed. She lay there in the dark with her eyes closed, the image of Jean Charles Brisard's blue-eyed stare floating in her mind, beginning to sink into a half-dreaming haze of names, faces and imagined places far away.

The phone let out a shrill ring. Blake jolted upright, staring at the handset. It was 3.30am. Who was calling at this hour? She picked up tentatively.

'Hello?'

'Madam, this is Sam from the bar upstairs. I've taken the liberty of preparing you two gin martinis. You both looked like you could use a drink.' Blake rubbed her eyes, and smiled.

'Are they dirty?'

'Yes madam, with olives.'

'We'll be right up.' She knew Calvert would never say no to a dirty martini, whatever the hour.

The pair headed back upstairs and spent an hour sipping their deliciously briny drinks, wondering what was going to happen when their story finally broke. After all these months in hiding, there were just two weeks to go until they would have to let the genie out of the bottle and reveal the extraordinary secrets they had found in the attic. How would the world react?

Sixteen

A Fine Lesson in Machiavellian Expertise

In the last few days of 2010, Zurich was in an excited state of expectancy. Europe's wealthiest city was preparing to surpass itself by proffering the most comfortingly expensive luxuries that a plastic expense card could buy. The champagne crates were piled high, the fridges were bursting with truffles and foie gras, and the great chefs were dreaming up irresistible epicurean feasts to entice, delight and financially deplete their customers. Every decent hotel room was already taken, every taxi was making itself available, and the red light district along Langstrasse was expecting business to be brisk. The 'FIFA family' was coming to town in numbers that had not been seen for many years. There would be heads of state, prime ministers, billionaires, actors, models, fixers, public relations teams, football officials, journalists, TV crews and pundits, and an abundance of current and former players. This was a towering event which the world would be watching: the ballot to host not one but two World Cups.

The Qatar 2022 bid had booked early for the momentous event. Six months before, Mohamed bin Hammam's uncomplaining assistant Najeeb Chirakal had been ordered to find three presidential suites, six executive suites and 54 deluxe rooms for the whole fortnight before the ballot. They were to be put up in the best hotels: the Baur au Lac, the Dolder Grand and the Savoy. The bill Chirakal passed on to Hassan Al-Thawadi for the entire stay was $960,000, including $150,000 for limousines.

Bin Hammam had flown in to join them in the Baur au Lac on the Monday, three days ahead of the vote, and was accompanied by his two right-hand men, Mohammed Meshadi and Amadou Diallo. There were butterflies in his stomach. This would be his moment of crowning glory or snivelling shame. Bin Hammam had paid the cash, done the maths and prayed that it would be the former.

If previously he had been a closet supporter of his country's bid by force of necessity, he was now well and truly out and proud. Indeed, Sheikh Mohammed, the young royal chairman of Qatar 2022, had eulogised about the pivotal role he had played in the campaign in an interview a month before. 'When it comes to executive committee members, we don't really get involved in what happens inside the committee, because FIFA is very strict,' he said. 'But outside the executive committee and within the bid itself, Mohamed bin Hammam has been a very good mentor to us. He's been very helpful in advising us how to go about with our messaging and can have the biggest impact. He's always been advising us and always been by our side. He's definitely our biggest asset in the bid.'

Bin Hammam was now taking up the cudgels on behalf of Qatar like never before. Stung by a whispering campaign against his country's bid in the wake of the collusion scandal and FIFA's withering technical assessment, he kicked the week off by issuing an open letter on his website rallying the 'sons, colleagues and friends of the Qatar bid' to take no heed of the naysayers: 'I did warn you that your noble cause to host the World Cup 2022 will face some unethical resistance . . . You should expect more of this hidden war against your bid.'

As usual, the British media were daring to rain on FIFA's parade. The news story dominating the airwaves came from a BBC *Panorama* documentary by the irrepressible journalist Andrew Jennings. It was aired with impudent timing on the Monday evening before the vote and its ripples would continue to be felt throughout the week. With his unkempt white hair and Cumbria-casuals dress sense, Jennings may not have looked like FIFA's most ferocious adversary, but the men who ran world football's governing body loathed and feared him. They tried to ban him from their media events but he cocked a snook at them every time – once even unbuttoning his shirt during a press conference to reveal a t-shirt saying 'FUCK FIFA'.

Jennings had a wicked sense of humour, but he also happened to be a first-class journalist who was born to stick his microphone in the faces of the rich and powerful, keeping a straight face while asking the most excruciatingly pointed questions. It was Jennings who had picked apart FIFA's ISL scandal layer by layer and, after years of patience, his contacts had finally come good with a piece of paper which showed exactly who had taken the bungs. His programme revealed that three of the voters – Ricardo Teixeira, Nicolas Leoz and Issa Hayatou* – had received kickbacks in the nineties from ISL and a fourth, Jack Warner, was involved in attempting to sell World Cup tickets to touts. The FIFA executive committee were incandescent.

They were still fuming when they gathered together in their boardroom at FIFA headquarters on Wednesday morning, the eve of the vote. Sepp Blatter knew how to placate them. The South African World Cup had been a tremendous success financially and as a result they were to receive a $200,000 bonus on top of their $100,000-a-year salary. But the money meant nothing to Bin

---

*All three denied wrongdoing. Hayatou said the payment was for CAF. Leoz said he had given it to a school eight years after receiving it.

Hammam and his mood darkened as two guests were ushered before the executive committee.

The first was Andre Pruis, the South African police chief, who was there to deliver his terrorism assessment on the bids. His report was, of course, damning of Qatar's security plans and Bin Hammam sat with an implacably serious face as the police chief singled out the Gulf state as the highest risk of all the bidders. Were any of his colleagues taking any notice? The faces around the room looked bored. He hoped they would ignore the warning.

Next up was Harold Mayne-Nicholls, the man who had been funded by FIFA to travel the world assessing the bids with his technical team to produce the definitive account of the strengths and weaknesses of the bids. He was proud of the thoroughness and independence of his work, and expected the executive committee to give his report some sober consideration before they made up their minds. But he was to leave disillusioned. The Chilean spoke for half an hour, but he felt as though he might as well have been talking to the wall when he singled out Qatar as the worst bid. The executive committee sat in silence and Mayne-Nicholls formed the impression that many of them had not even bothered to read his report.

Towards the end of his presentation, he grew tired of listening to the sound of his own voice and asked the Exco if they had any questions. The room froze, before one voice gently enquired about the hospitality Mayne-Nicholls had enjoyed on his tour of the bidding countries. 'Did they all treat you well?' That was the only thing the Exco wanted to know. The technical inspector packed up his files and left the room, wondering what his months of work had all been for. He was now convinced that the Exco's decision would not be based on which country was best equipped to hold a World Cup. They clearly had other agendas.

By the afternoon it was time for the five 2022 bids to unveil their expensively made videos and deliver their final presentations to the executive committee. The photographers shivering outside on the FIFA hilltop came to life as a fleet of limousines drew into world football's headquarters. The Qatari royal family had arrived. Sepp Blatter stepped up to the podium at 4pm to announce the distinguished guests who would present the Gulf bid to the Exco and the assembled media: the Emir, his wife Sheikha Mozah, the chairman of the bid Sheikh Mohammed, and the president of the Qatar FA Sheikh Hamad bin Khalifa bin Ahmed Al Thani. 'They are all the same family,' Blatter said with a smile. 'It is now up to you to present your bid and try to convince the executive committee, I wish you well.'

Sheikh Mohammed took the stage first, and appealed in fluent French to the Exco to back his country. But it was the final speaker, his mother, who captured everyone's attention. Sheikha Mozah looked like a finely sculptured mannequin in her tightly tailored burgundy silk dress, the national colour of Qatar. 'Mr Blatter, members of the executive committee, I would like to ask you a question. When? When do you think is the right time for the World Cup to come to the Middle East?' she began.

Not a hair was out of place; not a mannerism ill-judged. Her delivery was slow and winsome: 'Based on my feelings not just as a mother of my own children but as a mother for an entire generation of youth across the Middle East, for us football is not just a game. It is a sport for our time, anytime. In 2022, more than half of the population of the region will be under twenty-five and the World Cup here will have a different impact here than anywhere in the world. You can help us realise this elusive dream. You can help the youth of the region accomplish a lot.'

It was a masterpiece of controlled elegance which Michel Platini was later to claim was the thing that had won him over. She ended with the same question: 'When? When do you think is the right time for this,' – she motioned around the room – 'to come to the Middle East? Ladies and gentlemen, the time has come. The time is now.'

It was a measure of her performance that she managed to eclipse two of the world's greatest communicators. On next was a video with President Barack Obama rooting for the US bid, followed swiftly by a real-life former American president on the stage: it was Bill Clinton, a man renowned for the head-spinning power of his personal magnetism in any given room. The Americans had also rolled out Morgan Freeman, but even Hollywood's most distinguished voice failed to move the FIFA audience. The commentators found the Americans insincere, perhaps because football was not a game the country's luminaries had ever really played or watched.

The Australians had pitched in earlier with their own world-renowned beauty, the supermodel Elle Macpherson. As one antipodean blogger quipped, 'Who needs bungs when we've got The Body?' South Korea argued that a World Cup would help bring peace to their divided peninsula, although it wasn't clear that North Korea had officially signed up to that idea. Japan outlined a futuristic vision for the tournament, promising to deck out 400 grounds around the globe with giant Sony 3-D flatscreens to give hundreds of millions of fans the opportunity of watching. But Sheikha Mozah had stolen the show. Bin Hammam sat back in his auditorium chair and relaxed. The butterflies had subsided. He had completed his groundwork with what felt like a million air miles and more illicit payments than he cared to recall, and now his country's beloved first family had given the campaign the last lick of royal gloss it needed to sparkle on the night.

The four European bids for 2018 would be given their opportunity to make their final pitches the next morning before the ballot at 1pm, but Bin Hammam could sleep easily that night in the knowledge that everything was going to plan. He had been out for dinner with the whole Exco that evening and there was frenetic activity afterwards when the group spilled out into the bars and lobby of the Baur au Lac. The fixers and bid teams were buttonholing the Exco members hoping for a scrap of new information or the chance to make a last pitch that might seal their vote.

The England bid had developed something of a Blitz spirit. Even if their cause was hopeless, they were going to fight to the bitter end. Maybe, just maybe, they could snatch victory from the jaws of defeat as the London 2012 Olympics team had done when they pipped the French five years earlier. The British prime minister David Cameron had flown out to Zurich earlier in the week, popped home briefly to attend questions in the House of Commons, and was now back again. Exco members would be given a gentle tap on the shoulder before being escorted to a suite upstairs at the Baur au Lac where they were greeted by Cameron and Prince William. FIFA's rulers lapped up the attention from a prime minister and an heir to the throne, and several made all the right noises about supporting England. It would have been rude not to. The premier and the prince weren't to know that, in this murky world, a promised vote wasn't worth the ballot paper it was not yet written on.

In the same suite, Andy Anson, the England bid chief, and his sidekick Simon Greenberg were still shuffling around the counters on their improvised gaming board, trying to work out how the ballot would finally play out. There were a mind-boggling number of permutations but, even if the handful of votes they had been promised came good, hardly any of them worked out well for England. Greenberg's heart was no longer in it. He had read the Hakluyt intelligence report warning that his country was likely to get only two votes, and he had long since told his colleagues they had all been 'royally fucked'.

England had never been popular with the FIFA executive committee, and the recent intrusions by the British media had merely provided the men on the Exco with a justification for their inclination to cold-shoulder the country's bid. The England 2018 team publicly attacked the BBC for airing *Panorama* in the week of the ballot, but it left them in no-man's land: they were always going to be losers, and now they had conceded the moral high ground as well.

In the quiet of the night, once the whisky glasses had been drained and the hotel bars had emptied, many of the bid teams were already reflecting on what might have been. Five out of the nine understood that it was all over. Japan had given up the ghost on a victory long ago. Its Exco member Junji Ogura had struck a reciprocal vote-swapping deal with Belgium's Michel D'Hooghe, but his country would be lucky to progress beyond those two votes. The Netherlands–Belgium bid had always been an outsider and its cycling-friendly green bid was now peddling furiously to avoid being humiliated in the first round. Australia had lost Reynald Temarii and could now count on only Franz Beckenbauer's support. Sepp Blatter was promising to back them, but they knew his word of honour held about as much water as a didgeridoo. Chung Mong-joon was still doing deals, but it was all about damage limitation for the South Korean. All that mattered now was to muster a respectable number votes to keep his political ambitions at home alive and if that meant offering his support to more than one country, then so be it.

There was a small glimmer of hope for England when the country's own voter Geoff Thompson finally came good and announced he had made a deal to exchange votes with Chung. The deal had looked golden when the South Korean had even promised his vote to Cameron and Prince William. But then, on the morning of the ballot, a senior member of the England bid team had spied him at breakfast with the Russian voter Vitaly Mutko in the Baur au Lac. He watched as the two men retreated to a discreet table and chatted for a while, before standing up and shaking hands decisively. 'He's just fucked us!' the England official reported to colleagues. 'He's going to vote for Russia!'

So as the winter sun came up over a bitterly cold snow-fringed

Lake Zurich, there were only four bids with real reason for optimism on the day of the ballot. The Americans were quietly confident because Blatter had said he was backing them. They were a commercial powerhouse which would generate more billions in television revenues than any of their rivals. Spain knew it could rely on the solid seven votes from the collusion deal with Qatar and that was a great platform to build on.

The Russians were gaining momentum at just the right moment. The country's prime minister, Vladimir Putin, had decided against attending the ballot, but had issued a statement twisting the knife in a tender wound for England: their media. 'Recently, we have been saddened to see an overt campaign unleashed against members of the FIFA executive committee, who are being smeared and compromised,' Putin lamented. 'I see this as unfair competition in the run-up to the vote to choose the host of the World Cup.' He added: 'I should refrain from attending out of respect ... for members of the FIFA executive committee, in order to give them an opportunity to make an unbiased decision calmly and without any outside pressure.' The England bid had picked up intelligence that he and the FIFA president were jointly lobbying Exco members to back the Russians over the phone and the Kremlin-supporting *Izvestia* newspaper was reporting that 'Blatter is our ally'.

And then, of course, there was Qatar. Bin Hammam's plan had been perfectly executed and barring a last-minute disaster, the Emir would have his 'big cake' at last.

Snow was swirling around the FIFA hilltop when the 22 voters filed into the snoozily warm boardroom at 2pm on 2 December 2010. The door was shut firmly behind them and blackout blinds were pulled down. In front of them were a notary and an observer from the KPMG accountancy firm who had been tasked with making sure that the ballot for the two World Cups was fair and proper. This was the moment that Bin Hammam had been working towards for two years. He could hardly wait for the voting to start, but he would have to be patient for a few minutes because the ballot for 2018 was first.

It was hardly a surprise that the first act of the FIFA executive committee was to kill off the England bid. The birthplace of football and home of the Premier League received only two votes, just as Hakluyt predicted, and they were out. Issa Hayatou had kept his word and voted for England in return for the FA's support for his presidential bid back in 2002. The second vote was Thompson's, who would honour his promise to vote for South Korea in the 2022 race, but Chung had double-crossed him and gave his ballot to Russia. When he was angrily confronted over the betrayal later by an English official, the South Korean would reply serenely: 'That's football.'

The last-minute lobbying for Russia by Putin and Blatter had clearly paid dividends, as its bid stormed straight into the lead in the opening round, with nine votes. Moscow had been relying upon Vitaly Mutko, Chung, Franz Beckenbauer, Jack Warner, Chuck Blazer, Jacques Anouma and Blatter in the first round, and it looked as if they had all come good. They were followed closely by Spain who had exactly the seven votes guaranteed by their collusion pact with Bin Hammam. The Netherlands–Belgium bid defied expectation and survived the opening round, notching up four votes. D'Hooghe had made a vote-swapping deal with Ogura, which accounted for two of those, but the identity of the other two remained a mystery.

The ballot then went to a second round, when a clear winner emerged. The margin between Spain and Russia had been tight enough to make it tough to call which way the votes had shifted. The victor would be announced in a ceremony that afternoon, but the nervous 2018 bidders would have to wait until the 2022 ballot had run its course first.

Now it was Bin Hammam's big moment. He opened his notebook and glanced down at the names of the members he hoped would have voted for Qatar by the final round, ready to tick them off as the ballot progressed. There were the seven voters from the Iberian collusion pact – him and Spain's Ángel María Villar Llona, then his own supporters Worawi Makudi and Hany Abu Rida and the three Latin voters the Spaniard had brought to the table, Julio Grondona, Nicholas Leoz and Ricardo Texeira. Then there was Michel Platini, who had promised the French president Nicolas Sarkozy he would vote for Qatar, as well as the other two remaining Africans Issa Hayatou and Jacques Anoua, and his well-paid brother Jack Warner. These were his core supporters.

He hoped very much that the 'bilateral relations' he and Vitaly Mutko had been discussing between Russia and Qatar would bring him another vote, and he had done his best to remind Franz Beckenbauer of the debt of gratitude he owed Qatar after the German World Cup, so he hoped *Der Kaiser* would switch over his support once Australia was out. He wondered whether his efforts to woo Michel D'Hooghe of Belgium would bear fruit. One certainty lay in his pact with the Asian voters, Junji Ogura and Chung, who he knew would transfer their votes to Qatar once Japan and South Korea crashed out.

The voters handed in their ballots, and the notary sifted through them before announcing the results. Qatar had stormed straight to the head of the pack with 11 votes – exactly half the total and just one short of instant victory. Bin Hammam's heart swelled with joy. It would be almost impossible not to win from here. The Iberian pact had held good with seven votes and he also ticked the names of Platini, Anouma and Hayatou on his list. After chewing contemplatively on his pencil for a moment, he also checked off Warner. South Korea were second with four, including votes from Mutko and the guileless Thompson. Both the USA and Japan polled just three votes each and Australia were knocked out with a paltry one. Later, Blatter and Beckenbauer would both tell the Australians that this solitary vote had been theirs.

Now Australia were out, Bin Hammam was hoping for Beckenbauer's vote and he put a tick next to *Der Kaiser*'s name. That would hand Qatar victory. But when the second-round results were announced, his heart sank. Rather than gaining the one extra vote it needed to win, Qatar had lost ground and dropped down to ten. Which of his colleagues had abandoned him? Still, he remained well ahead. The USA and South Korea progressed to five each, and Japan dropped out. Qatar gained Ogura in the third round and went back up to 11 – once again just a tantalising single vote from the 12 needed to reach a majority. Just as he hoped, South Korea dropped out after being pipped narrowly by the US, who now had six votes. That meant Chung's vote belonged to him.

It was nearly time for the fourth round, and Bin Hammam was staring down at his notebook again. He added a tick next to Chung's name, alongside marks against Abo Rida, Anouma, Beckenbauer, Grondona, Hayatou, Leoz, Ogura, Makudi, Mutko, Platini, Teixeira, Villar Llona and Warner. He was so close to victory, but the disappearing vote after the first round continued to perplex him. Qatar's tally stood at 11, but there were 14 names now ticked off on his list, not including his own, which meant three of the supporters he had been counting on had not behaved as he had hoped. What if more of Qatar's voters dropped away in the final round?

In his state of nervous excitement, the Qatari hadn't stopped to think that he was sitting next to Chuck Blazer, who was representing the last rival still in the ballot, America. Blazer could not resist glancing over Bin Hammam's shoulder to get a peek of what he was up to, and one of the names on the list made his blood run cold with fury: Jack Warner. The president of CONCACAF *had* to vote for the USA. So why had Bin Hammam ticked his name? It was a moment that was to shatter the once inseparable friendship between Blazer and Warner forever. The US bid leader, Sunil Gulati, would never speak to the man from Trinidad again. It was such a little error by Bin Hammam, allowing the CON-CACAF general secretary to read his list over his shoulder. It was just a momentary lapse in concentration as he got caught up in the big moment he had been working towards for two long years. And yet the consequences of that split-second misjudgement would haunt him for the rest of his life.

Bin Hammam crossed the box next to Qatar on his ballot paper for the fourth time and handed it in. He scrutinised the faces of his colleagues as they made their marks. The papers were counted, and then it was all over. The Exco were informed that a winner had emerged, and the victor would be named at a ceremony to follow. Barring an implausible collapse in the final round, Bin Hammam knew Qatar must have triumphed, but he wouldn't quite believe it till he heard Blatter say it. The names of the winners were printed on two cards and placed in white envelopes which were sealed with red wax. The notary, with the observer in tow, then took them by car to the Messe conference centre where the world's media and all the bid teams were waiting anxiously in the auditorium.

The heat of the television lights were burning onto an empty podium waiting for Blatter to step up onto the stage at 4pm and reveal the results of the election. It was a room adorned with princes, prime ministers and presidents. The Emir's family waited patiently three rows back on the left side of the vast room, with Bill Clinton and the sparrow-faced Gulati directly in front of them. The Russians were on the right flank alongside the England bid, who were already looking stony faced. All along the front row were the real overlords of the occasion, the FIFA executive committee. Bin Hammam looked relaxed as he leaned back in his chair but Mohammed Meshadi, many rows behind, was so nervous he had almost not been able to bring himself to attend. 'That bugger didn't dare go to the conference centre for the announcement,' Bin Hammam's assistant Jenny Be would later tell Michelle Chai. 'I had to drag him there.'

With half an hour to go, Al Jazeera was already reporting that Qatar had won, but the sage football journalists in the media centre were dismissing the reports as speculation. Surely, even FIFA's wonky executive committee wouldn't choose such a preposterous candidate? Blatter was now up on the stage and had placed the golden World Cup trophy on the podium next to him. He was keeping the suspense with one of his long, meandering speeches about how FIFA represented a billion people who were involved 'directly' or 'indirectly' through their families in football – a reminder to the heads of state in the room that Blatter's fiefdom was bigger than theirs. He was still waffling about football teaching 'fair play', 'discipline' and giving 'hope to the humanity', when a tweet from Dmitry Chernyshenko, the chief executive of the Winter Olympic Games in Sochi, started doing the rounds in the press centre. 'Yesss! We are the champions! Hooray!!!!' he had tweeted. And sure enough, a few moments later, Blatter pulled the winner's name card out of the 2018 envelope and announced that Russia had indeed triumphed, with 13 votes.

After the Russian speeches and back-slapping, the auditorium hushed again. Bin Hammam scanned the line of executive committee members along the front row. Had they stayed true in the final round? He was quietly confident, but nothing was ever certain in the shifting quicksands of football politics. By now, Blatter had torn open the envelope and was fiddling inside to make sure he pulled out the card with the winning name on the correct side. 'The winner,' he began, 'to organise the FIFA two twenty-two

World Cup is ...,' and he momentarily flashed the name on the card to the world's television audience before proclaiming: 'Qatar!'

The royal family erupted in cheers, leaping to their feet and throwing their arms in the air. The young Sheikh Mohammed thrust up a punch of delight before being rugby tackled from behind in a jubilant hug by his brother Sheikh Tamim, the country's future ruler. Their father, the Emir, was clapping vigorously, his face a picture of delight. At last, he had his big cake. Seeing his sons overcome with rapture, he strode across and wrapped his huge arms around the young Sheikh Mohammed, almost squeezing all the air out of the slender youth. The Emir spun round and was about to kiss his wife when he saw someone else standing there, waiting patiently.

It was Bin Hammam. He had sidled quietly up to the third row amid the uproar, and was keeping a discreet distance from the royal celebrations. In the past, he had stood head bowed in the presence of his mighty ruler, but today he was a national hero and the Emir reached across without thinking to give the architect of Qatar's victory a warm and thankful hug. Next, Bin Hammam stepped up to Sheikh Mohammed and kissed him on the cheek. He marvelled internally at what he had achieved. Qatar had won with 14 votes to eight – trouncing its final rival, the USA. The weight of anxiety he had borne on his shoulders for more than two years had lifted and he could at last relax into the happy certainty that he had made his country, and his ruler, proud. The World Cup was coming to the desert and he, Mohamed, had made it happen.

In the row below Bill Clinton was smiling and shaking hands, but his companion Gulati now looked more like an angry bird than a sparrow, as he glowered across the room at Warner. Qatar's royal family poured onto the stage and Bin Hammam was mobbed as he returned to his seat by passing members of the bid team following the royals into the limelight. An emotional Sheikh Mohammed was at the microphone. 'Thank you for believing in change,' he said breathlessly. 'Thank you for believing in expanding the game, thank you for giving Qatar a chance, and we will not let you down! You will be proud of us, you will be proud of the Middle East and I will promise you this!' The tiny Gulf state had done the impossible. Out in the streets of Doha, cars were hooting their horns and flags were being unfurled in the streets. Was the World Cup really coming to Qatar? Nobody could quite believe it.

After the stage had emptied and the crowd had spilled outside into the freezing evening, Chris Eaton had been left in the hall with a few members of his security team. They were checking the empty room to make sure nothing had been left behind. At the podium, Eaton came across the wax sealed envelope and the card with Qatar's name on it, and his eyes lit up. He took a quick look from side to side, then slid the card under his jacket.

Bin Hammam had taken a back seat in Zurich, allowing the royals to glory in his achievement, but his friends throughout world football knew he was the true architect of Qatar's triumph. He was flooded with emails of congratulation and gratitude from the football bosses whose support he had secured over the past two years. Some could barely wait for the celebrations to subside before queuing up for their rewards.

The day after the vote, Seedy Kinteh emailed: 'On behalf of the Gambia Football Family and indeed on my own Humble self to warmly congratulate you for winning the FIFA Award to host the World Cup in 2022 in your beautiful country Qatar.' He followed up with a message to Bin Hammam's assistant a few days later. 'I write to find out about the progress of my appeal concerning the Vehicle. I have already got in my possession a colosal sum of ten thousand Us Dollars ... and any assistance will be of immense value to me.' Kinteh said he needed the car to travel to football projects in the Gambian countryside.

Nicholas Musonye, the general secretary of the Council of East and Central Africa Football Associations (CECAFA), wrote to Bin Hammam: 'This is a glorious moment to all of us in our zone and we congratulate you for the hard work and all the efforts you put in this bid. Your many years of hard work have been rewarded and you will go down in history books for what you have achieved for Asia and the people of Qatar.' Two days later, he forwarded CECAFA's bank details to accompany a request for $200,000 to fund a tournament in Tanzania and the money was paid.*

Tidiani Median Niambele, president of the Mali federation, extended his congratulations to Qatar 'and especially you personally' for winning the World Cup ballot. Bin Hammam replied: 'I take this opportunity to extend my gratitude and appreciation for your support and I am confident that with your continued support Qatar can stage an amazing and ever greatest World Cup in 2022.' And then Gu Jian Ming, president of the Chengdu FA wrote to say: 'Allow me to express my congratulations on Qatar's success in the bid to host the 2022 Football World Cup, which I believe cannot be separated from the great efforts you have made.'

In public, Bin Hammam took little credit for Qatar's stunning achievement, but he felt it was safe to do so with his African friends who had helped out with his campaign. When Izetta Wesley, the head of the Liberian football federation got in touch to say 'Dear Brother . . . Congratulation for winning your World Cup Bid,' Bin Hammam wrote back acknowledging both his own role and his debt to his African supporters. 'Thank you very much for your kind greetings,' he wrote. 'I would not have succeeded if not for the support from friends and believers like you.'

---

* Nicholas Musonye said the sponsorship was legitimate and was unrelated to the World Cup vote.

No one was more overawed by what Bin Hammam had done than his son, Hamad. The day after the victory was announced, the student sent his father a heartfelt letter. 'Dear Dad, Yesterday was the best day of my life,' he wrote. 'It was better than any college acceptance letter, any official school reward and any job or internship offer. If I was an actor and I won an Oscar, it still wouldn't be the best feeling; no moment like yesterday's announcement made me happier. And I've always been proud of you, and I thought that it wasn't possible to be proud of you more. But I was wrong. I'm not even more proud, I'm honored. I'm the luckiest person in the world to be your son. I am so lucky that sometimes people say, "You look like Mohamed bin Hammam," or, "You have his eyes." I would be lucky to be, not half the man you are, but quarter of the man you are. And I wish I could leave a legacy in our country as strong as yours.

'You're a trendsetter and, most importantly, you helped make history for our people and for our family. Your efforts to get us the world cup finally put mom, you, myself and my brothers and sisters on the map; it put the citizens of Qatar on the map. And, I think it is safe for me to say that I speak on behalf of all Qataris when I say that without you, and, of course, His Highness the Emir Sheikh Hamad bin Khalifa Al Thani, his outspoken first lady Sheikha Moza bint Nasser Al Misned – perhaps one of the most incredible women and most influential persons I would love to meet – and His Excellency Sheikh Mohammed bin Hamad Al Thani, a remarkable man, and, of course, the entire Qatar 2022 Bid Team. This can't be happened without you, we appreciate your efforts.

'And to speak for myself, I love you, and you are my idol. I may not want to be involved in the field of sports by the time I finish college, but I would love to be the reflection of you. One day, I will speak French, Spanish, German and Hebrew for you so I can show people that I was raised in golden, open-minded arms. Just like you showed the world, I will show Qatar that I, too, can be of great significance. And I will owe it all to you. Love you always, Hamad bin Mohammed.'

To Hamad's surprise, his letter was later emailed back to him by Najeeb Chirakal with an instruction to edit it and resend it to his father. Hamad was told that it was unseemly to have claimed such a big share of the victory for the Bin Hammam tribe. He must alter his words to give more prominence to the role played by the royal family and official Qatar bid committee, and mention his father's contribution only as a secondary factor at the end. Once the letter was re-sent, Hamad was told, it was going to be published on the AFC website. He glumly agreed to do as he had been asked.

The next morning, on 6 December, the letter caused a stir among the assistants in Bin Hammam's offices at the AFC.

'Check out P's blog,' Jenny Be messaged Michelle Chai. 'He is right about growing up in the golden open arms ... more like golden, diamond studded arms.'

Chai was tickled. 'Hahahahahaha. But son is right ... world cup was his doing ... people can say what they want about the bid but he did it.'

'Yes, he did it.'

'I think he is proud too,' Chai added.

'He should be,' responded Be. 'That's why he published the letter.' After a pause, she ventured: 'I kinda pity the son.'

'Why ah?'

'Coz he has to write to his father to tell him how he feels,' wrote Be. 'No time even when they are in the same city.' Later, she told her friend: 'Bugger, I have more than 500 emails in my inbox to clear, all congratulating our boss. They started to contact me when they couldn't get to the boss. Yesterday I had to switch my phone off to get some sleep.'

'Wah ... euphoria not died yet,' said Chai. 'When you think

about it, this must be his biggest legacy,' she went on. 'I mean dreams of millions and millions of people.'

'Yes,' Be agreed. 'Coz he may not be there in 2022 but this is something he contributed to his country and to Asia.'

'I hope the Qatari people and the QFA people and the bid team realises it as well,' said Chai. 'Realises and don't forget.'

'Yeah, and he said that they do, so am happy for that,' Be said.

'Sometimes people forget too easily,' Chai cautioned.

'Yeah, especially when you have those who don't blink an eye before they take others' credits,' said Be, suddenly incensed at the prospect.

'Yeap,' said Chai.

'Let him enjoy his moments,' Be said firmly. 'He is a hero.'

For all the hundreds of congratulatory messages that had flooded in from Bin Hammam's supporters, no praise was quite so sweet as that of an adversary. Qatar's triumph had humiliated Peter Hargitay, the master PR guru and lobbyist who had warned Bin Hammam two years earlier the Gulf state didn't stand a chance. Now the boot was on the other foot. All Hargitay's machinations on behalf of the Australian bid had managed to produce just one supporter. Since Hargitay had helped the Australians part with tens of millions of dollars on their campaign, that measly return for their investment was a contender for the most expensive single vote in history. Hargitay had waited four weeks until New Year's Eve before sending a long email to Bin Hammam. His message bristled with bitterness, but Hargitay could not conceal his admiration for the masterful way Bin Hammam had manoeuvred behind the scenes.

'I have reflected upon the – many good – times I spent in your company over the years, and the remarkable changes of your varying positions,' he wrote. 'I recall the one afternoon we spent talking for several hours in the lobby of the Mandarin. And I admit that some of the changes in your positions left me stupe-fied, while others were clear: you have always forged alliances where the expected outcome would justify the choices you make. And of course you have always harvested, as you should, when the time to do so was opportune. Clearly, this philosophy – not a new one by any means – has generated the kinds of results you have wanted, and you must be pleased with that. And I com-mend you for your remarkable achievements, which, in the context of Qatar, are plain spectacular.

'I, for one, can only observe and acknowledge the stupefying achievements I witnessed by your hands, mind and spirit. When we first met, years ago, there was one Mohamed bin Hammam who was soft-spoken, discreet and by no means prepared to chal-lenge this, that or the other. Not openly, nor quietly for much of the time. Today, the Mohamed that is, has become a leader who goes the route of many leaders.

'Your strategic "savoir faire" and, more so, the tactical savvy that won your country the World Cup bid is spectacular. There can only be admiration for the way you handled the mine-field of changing loyalties. But your modus operandi, based on years of experience, combined with intimate knowledge of the players on the chess set of group dynamics, and your ability to offer what others could not, was a fine lesson in Machiavellian expertise, combined with cultural history – both of which combined, gen-erated the results you wanted to achieve. Accept my respectful congratulations for that. Well done, remarkably executed, utterly accomplished . . . As always, your Peter.'

Seventeen

No Pause on the Path of Treason

The air of elation was still palpable on the streets of Doha as the leaders of world football swept in at the start of January 2011. The city had burst into a state of jubilation when Qatar's victory in the World Cup race was announced – with every street, souk and square packed with revelling crowds waving the national flag, singing and tooting pink vuvuzelas in a blizzard of glittering confetti. Now, a month later, Doha was gearing up to show the football world what it was made of as FIFA's gilded elite swarmed into town for the Asian Football Confederation's annual congress ahead of the long-awaited Asian Cup. The giant clock counting down to the Asian tournament on the Corniche had nearly reached zero and now the cheering crowds were out in force again. They lined the streets to greet the trophy that had been flown into Doha and handed ceremoniously to Mohamed bin Hammam that morning, and was now being was held aloft on an open-topped bus tour of the city.

The president of Asian football was basking in the glory of the crowning achievement of his life, but he could not afford to pause. The World Cup that his country had won the rights to host was still 11 years away, and anything could happen in the intervening years. It was essential that he held on to his ruling position within FIFA so that he could continue to guard Qatar's interests. Bin Hammam had promised back in August that, rather than running for the FIFA presidency this June, he would back Sepp Blatter to remain in office and stand for re-election as head of the AFC instead. With the World Cup safely in the bag, hanging on to the presidency of his confederation was his main focus as the election at the congress on 6 January neared. The urgency of shoring up his position felt increasingly pressing because Blatter's latest manoeuvres had started to raise his hackles.

The FIFA president, who had once seemed so supportive of Qatar's World Cup dream, appeared to have been severely discomfited by the country's improbable victory. Bin Hammam had shown the extent of his power within world football by persuading FIFA's rulers to send their prized tournament to the desert, and now his advisors were warning that Blatter was on the warpath. The sly old fox had been glad to assure the Emir of his support for an apparently impossible project, so the reasoning went, but Qatar's eventual victory had caught him completely off guard.

Blatter was an arch pragmatist who could see better than anyone that the tournament in the Gulf was going to be a commercial, popular and sporting flop for FIFA. He wouldn't like that prospect one bit, but what would stick in his craw more than anything was the fact that Bin Hammam had managed to pull off the impossible stunt right under his nose and, in the end, without his support. If his old Qatari ally was capable of this, he was capable of anything. One close advisor warned Bin Hammam that he may have 'provoked a death penalty by collecting those fourteen votes'. From now on, his counsellors cautioned, the president would make it his sole mission 'to destroy Mohamed bin Hammam'.*

---

* These quotes and interpretations are based on extensive conversations with confidential sources within Mohamed bin Hammam's inner circle of aides and advisors.

The first real sign of trouble came four days before the AFC congress, when Blatter announced unilaterally that he would set up an anti-corruption committee to police world football's governing body. The 'World Cup votes for sale' story in *The Sunday Times* continued to cast a long shadow over the bidding contest. Blatter had told the Swiss newspaper *SonntagsZeitung* that the independent committee, which he seemed to have dreamed up on his own over Christmas, would consist of seven to nine members 'not only from sport but from politics, finance, business and culture'. He said it would 'strengthen our credibility and give us a new image in terms of transparency,' adding: 'I will take care of it personally, to ensure there is no corruption at FIFA.'

Bin Hammam was horrified. What was the president thinking? It was bad enough that he had given the ethics committee oversight of the bidding process and brought in that meddlesome investigator Chris Eaton to stick his nose into everyone else's business. How dare he announce that he was going to bring in another bunch of strangers to police the running of world football, without even mentioning it to his executive committee in advance, let alone consulting them? Several of FIFA's rulers were seriously agitated by Blatter's shock manoeuvre, but no one was more incensed than Bin Hammam.

The Qatari fired a first return salvo on the eve of the AFC congress, saying tersely in a public interview that: 'Some of FIFA's acts I do not approve of or agree with.' He went on: 'I am a member of the FIFA executive committee and we never discussed this idea inside the executive committee – I read about it in the media. I don't appreciate that tomorrow we go to a meeting of FIFA and we find already that a committee has been formed, that members have been appointed and the code, or whatever, has been decided ... If we are serious, there has to be a serious discussion within the executive committee first.' Never had Bin Hammam spoken such stern words about his master's deeds in public. He was livid. Blatter was jeopardising everything he had worked so hard to achieve. When asked if he thought the time had come for a change at the highest level of FIFA, he replied darkly: 'A change is a demand for an improvement really. I cannot be one hundred per cent frank with you, but I think FIFA needs lot of improvement.'

The following morning, Bin Hammam strode into the AFC congress resplendent in a gold-trimmed bisht cape over his ordinary dishdasha. This was a statement. Bishts are the preserve of the loftiest dignitaries in Qatari society, and it was rare to see Bin Hammam in anything grander than his traditional white robe and keffiyeh. Things had changed now he was the man who had achieved the Emir's dearest wish. He was a national hero in Qatar, and he wanted his friends in world football to know it. When the delegates settled into their chairs, Bin Hammam took the podium to open the congress, addressing the assembly. Speaking slowly and deliberately, he issued a *cri de coeur* to his supporters across the continent. 'While Asia has not yet taken over the world, the rumblings of Asia can now be felt,' he declared. 'We strongly believe that the future is Asia and we are working very hard towards the future. We must push our limits and challenge the status quo.'

Then it was Blatter's turn. The 74-year-old bounded up to the lectern to dismiss any suggestion that his beloved FIFA was in need of change, and swat away the scandal which had claimed two members of its executive committee before the World Cup vote. The enemies of world football would be crushed and the leaders of the glorious game would be restored to the respect they deserved, he promised. 'In 2010 we had some milestones in the history of football, starting with the first World Cup on the African continent, and what a success,' the president stated. 'And then the decision of FIFA's executive committee to go to new destinations in 2018 and 2022.' His eyes narrowed, and he lowered his tone confidentially. 'All these successes have created a lot of envy and jealousy in our world because you cannot satisfy everybody,' he said.

Then Blatter loosened his shoulders and adopted a more avuncular manner. He wanted to quell any fears that such malicious slurs on the reputation of the global game would stick. FIFA's children needn't worry: the family was invincible. 'The success story of FIFA can continue because we are in a comfortable situation, despite the criticism given to FIFA,' the president assured the delegates. He was resolute. 'We have the power and the instruments to go against any attacks that are made.'

When it was time for the election, the Asian delegates filed up to the ballot box and slotted in their voting slips while the room hummed with idle chatter. No one was surprised when the announcement came that the man who had just won the right to host the World Cup in Asia had been re-elected unopposed as president. More good news followed quickly when Bin Hammam's friend and fixer Manilal Fernando rolled to victory, winning a seat at FIFA's top table for the first time.

But then came a bitter shock. Dr Chung Mong-joon was defeated. The South Korean had been toppled from his treasured perch as Asia's FIFA vice-president, despite Fernando's enthusiastic efforts to turn the ballot in his favour. Chung had been slain by Prince Ali bin Al-Hussein of Jordan, an avowed Blatterite whose campaign had benefited from the firm backing of the FIFA president. He became the youngest member of the Exco at just 35. The news sparked celebrations among the Arab delegations at the congress, while Chung stood stiffly and stalked out of the hall, his face set in a blank stare.

Bin Hammam rose to shake Prince Ali's hand and congratulated him, concealing his disappointment beneath a cool smile. He had worked hard to assist Chung's AFC re-election campaign after securing his pledge to back Qatar's World Cup bid when South Korea fell out of the ballot. As a point of personal honour, he hated to have let his new ally down. He would have to find a way of making it up to Chung, he thought, as he watched the back of his friend's silvered head retreating through the crowds amid the Arab celebrations.

Chung's defeat was a major boost for Blatter: instantly extinguishing the threat of the South Korean's challenge to the FIFA presidency. Now Chung had been unseated from world football's ruling committee, he no longer had a hope of making a successful run for the top job. What's more, Prince Ali's backers immediately repaid Blatter for his support, pledging their loyalty in the presidential election that June. 'I can confirm that the twenty-five people who voted for Prince Ali today will vote for President Blatter at the FIFA congress because Blatter deserves to continue as FIFA president,' said Sheikh Ahmad Ali Fahad Al Sabah, the head of the Kuwaiti FA. Bin Hammam scowled.

Blatter was in ebullient spirits when the Asian Cup began the next day, bouncing into Khalifa International Stadium in his gold buttoned blazer ready to cause more mischief before the first match had even kicked off. The FIFA president took it upon himself to announce, apropos of nothing, that the Qatar World Cup would have to be held in the winter in order to protect players from the summer heat. 'I expect it will be held in the winter,' he opined at a press conference before the match. 'When you play football, you have to protect the main people: the players.' Then he dropped in an ominous reminder that FIFA maintained the right to move the goalposts at any moment before 2022. 'Do not forget there is still eleven years to go, and although we have the basic conditions of their bid for a June and July World Cup, the FIFA executive committee is entitled to change anything that was in the bid,' he said. Perhaps the renewed promise of uncontested power was making Blatter giddy. Or did he have a more sinister endgame in in mind?

The suggestion that the tournament might be moved caused pandemonium. Shifting the World Cup to winter threatened chaos for European football, which some said would be disrupted for at least three seasons, bringing sponsorship and broadcast deals into jeopardy. Qatar's bid had sworn it could air-condition its 12 proposed stadiums, five fan parks and 32 training centres with solar-power, to make the tournament playable in the summer, but now the FIFA president was showing the world he had no faith in this promise. Bin Hammam was outraged by the suggestion, on Qatari soil, that his country had won the World Cup race on false pretences. Coming on the heels of the random announcement of a prying anti-corruption committee, this was too much to bear. Why wouldn't Blatter just keep his mouth shut for five minutes and let Qatar enjoy its big moment?

The Asian Cup was supposed to be an auspicious event. This was Doha's big chance to show the world just how wonderful a tournament it was capable of hosting, and the local organising committee had worked energetically for four years to get everything into stellar shape. Issa Hayatou had flown in with his wife along with Hany Abo Rida, Worawi Makudi and many of Bin Hammam's friends in world football, and Amadou Diallo was there to greet the guests.

Mohammed Meshadi had been dispatched to pick up an advance of $100,550 from the AFC debtors' account* so there would be no shortage of cash during the happy occasion. Jack Warner had sent apologies for being unable to come, but he included the bank details of his Dr João Havelange Centre of Excellence 'as requested'. Two days later, he wrote again: 'President and Brother, I hate to bother you, especially at this time re your Congress, but after two days, I am yet to hear from our friend. I know this is not normal.' The reminder had the desired effect: within days Najeeb Chirakal had arranged for Kemco to wire Warner $12,500.

---

* The money was repaid to the AFC from one of Bin Hammam's Kemco accounts shortly after it was withdrawn by Meshadi.

Now the first match between Qatar and Uzbekistan was about to kick off and the Khalifa International Stadium was packed to capacity with local men in white robes and women in black abayas. Sadly, the home team did not stand up under the pressure. The Uzbeks were already 1-0 up when Qatar's Khalfan Ibrahim made a disastrous pass into his own penalty area which allowed the away team to slot in a second goal. The stadium drained of home support before the match had reached its conclusion as the local crowd headed miserably for the exits, with Uzbek drums thundering triumphantly from the away section. The demoralising 2-0 defeat in the opening match was an embarrassing start to a tournament intended to celebrate Qatar's growing status in world football. 'The players wanted to give their best but they forgot everything. Today was a very, very bad day,' the team's distinguished French coach Bruno Metsu told journalists after the final whistle. 'The pressure is huge, but sometimes it is very difficult to play the opening game.'

Bin Hammam was stung by Qatar's defeat, but more than anything he was still spitting feathers about Blatter's suggestion before the match that his proud country was not capable of delivering on its promise to host the World Cup in the summer. He fired off another volley at the FIFA president live on television. Asked if there was any intention to move the tournament to the winter, as Blatter had suggested, Bin Hammam said: 'Not at all ... Our business is to organise a comfortable World Cup in June and July. That's what we have promised the world. And we are sticking to our promise and we are keeping our promise and that is our final word.' He went on: 'I'm really not very impressed by these opinions to ... change the time from July to January. It's premature, it's people's opinions and they're just discussing it on no basis or no ground.'

The public shootout between Blatter and Bin Hammam was beginning to overshadow the Asian Cup and some were already calling the tournament a damp squib. No one could claim it wasn't progressing smoothly: the organisation was flawless, the marketing was slick and every edifice from the gleaming stadiums to the state-of-the-art team facilities seemed to drip with Gulf gold. But the football press were complaining that the stands were half empty and the games lacked atmosphere. After the dispiriting defeat which had sent the home fans packing in the opening game, the locals no longer seemed interested. Qatar's fortunes had briefly recovered with a win over China, but even the resurgent home team wasn't able to fill the stadium for the quarter-final match in which it was finally knocked out by Japan.

Bin Hammam was determined to capitalise on his country's efforts as the tournament drew to a close. 'It's been an extremely well organised event by Qatar,' he insisted. 'Although it is twelve years [*sic*] between now and 2022, it was a very good rehearsal for that competition.' But he couldn't resist using the publicity ahead of the semi-finals to take aim and fire at Blatter. This time, his comments sent shockwaves through world football. 'Everybody is going to accuse us today as corrupted people because maybe people see Mr Blatter has stayed a long time in FIFA,' he told the Associated Press. 'Thirty-five years in one organisation is quite a long time. No matter how clean you are, honest or how correct you are, still people will attack you. You are going to be defenceless. That is why I believe change is the best thing for the organisation.'

If the world was in any doubt, it was now clear that the once golden friendship between Blatter and his one-time Qatari conspirator was well and truly at an end. Bin Hammam refused to comment on whether he would stand against Blatter in the election that June, now that Chung was no longer a contender, saying stubbornly: 'I did not make up my mind yet. I would rather wait and see.' Days later, he used a press conference ahead of the final match between Australia and Japan on 29 January to declare once more that he wanted to see FIFA presidents ejected after two terms. 'I believe that's the right way for FIFA to restructure itself,' he said. 'I don't want to answer any questions about the FIFA elections. But I think, and correct me if I'm wrong, that people today are complaining a lot about how FIFA runs itself as a business. It is not just term limits that need to change, but a lot of changes are needed to FIFA practices, its office business. A term limit will facilitate the rotation of power within the organisation.' There was no backing away from it now. This was all-out war.

No sooner was the FIFA president back in his comfort zone in Zurich than he was preparing to take the biggest pot shot he could at his one-time supporters in Qatar. In an interview with Brian Alexander, a sympathetic BBC journalist whom Blatter would later hire as a FIFA spin doctor, he sensationally revealed that he knew Qatar and Spain *had* colluded in the World Cup ballot after all. 'I'll be honest, there was a bundle of votes between Spain and Qatar,' he said insouciantly.

This was an astonishing admission from world football's most powerful official, after FIFA's own ethics committee had closed the case on collusion between the two countries, citing a lack of evidence. Blatter had just blown the whole thing wide open again. He denied that the deal had decided the outcome of either ballot, insisting: 'It was a nonsense. It was there but it didn't work, not for one and not for the other side.' That wasn't going to cut much ice, given that the votes from Spain and the three South Americans had clearly sealed Qatar's victory. There was no going back from this admission. FIFA's president had just claimed, on camera, that the country which had won the rights to host the World Cup had cheated.*

This could not be borne. The very next day, Chung Mong-joon swung into action. The South Korean had maintained a dignified silence since his shock defeat at the AFC election, but now he took

---

* Qatar and Spain continue to deny that any such collusion deal took place.

to Twitter to declare a threat to Blatter. He wrote: 'I had lunch with Bin Hammam' and 'it seems he will challenge the FIFA presidential election in June.' The Qatari refused to comment on Chung's declaration, but the gauntlet had been thrown down.

Bin Hammam had not forgotten the debt he owed Chung, and he had flown to Seoul soon after the end of the Asian Cup to see what he could do to soothe the pain of defeat for this old foe who had become his friend. When the pair lunched together, Bin Hammam had made Chung a promise. He was sorry that he had been unable to protect the South Korean's seat on the FIFA Exco, but he wanted to offer the next best thing he could. He would see to it that Chung became an honorary vice-president of world football's governing body, granting him unassailable status as a FIFA grandee and most of the perks that came with a seat on the ruling committee. Chung was grateful, and accepted the Qatari's kind offer to make the proposal at the next meeting of the FIFA Exco in Zurich.

The conversation turned next to a dilemma now close to both their hearts: how to stamp out the scourge of Sepp Blatter. Bin Hammam knew how dearly Chung had cherished his own presidential ambitions, so he tiptoed around the subject gingerly. He hadn't decided for certain yet what he should do in the election that June, but Blatter's pronouncements on Qatar's World Cup were increasingly erratic and Bin Hammam felt in his bones that there was only one way to head off the danger. If he did choose to run for the top job in world football, he knew it would be a matter of death or glory, and he would need all the supporters he could get. Bin Hammam was delighted when the South Korean signed up. Chung's own hopes were dashed, but it would be delicious to see Blatter felled. He would do what he could to help his friend in Qatar.

Bin Hammam wrote to him after the meeting in February to thank him for the 'fabulous hospitality' he had received on the visit. 'I will do my best in Zurich and hope it will be successful,' he promised. Chung's assistant, ES Kim, followed up with a letter to Chirakal later that month. 'During his visit to Korea, President Hammam mentioned ... that he would propose Dr Chung as honorary FIFA vice-president at the upcoming FIFA Exco meeting and Dr Chung is deeply appreciative of this kind gesture from the AFC president,' he wrote. 'In relation to this matter, Dr Chung would like to send a letter to some of the FIFA Exco members, who, in his opinion, would support President Hammam's proposal. Before sending out such a request letter, Dr Chung would like to sound out the opinion of the AFC president about his plan.'

Kim had already written to Issa Hayatou asking him to back Bin Hammam's nomination of Chung, and he wanted the Qatari's permission to send similar letters to Jack Warner, Ángel María Villar Llona, Michel Platini, Michel D'Hooghe, Worawi Makudi, Nicolas Leoz, Marios Lefkaritis, Franz Beckenbauer, Rafael Salguero and Vitaliy Mutko. Bin Hammam agreed and, sure enough, Chung got his wish. He was named FIFA's only honorary vice-president later that year, a position he still holds today. The debt had been repaid.

Bin Hammam, meanwhile, had a few favours to return to those who had helped Qatar win the World Cup ballot. Since the month of the big vote, the Qatari had been working with his powerful ally Issa Hayatou to arrange private talks between the leaders of their two countries. Paul Biya, the president of Cameroon, was granted a rare private audience with the Emir in early 2011. In February, an email marked 'Confidential – for President Bin Hammam' dropped into the Qatari's inbox from a senior official at CAF. Attached was a private letter addressed to Hayatou from a Cameroonian government minister, dated 24 December 2010 and headed: 'Visit of the Head of State to Qatar'. It read: 'I have the honour to ask you to kindly relay to his Excellency the Emir of Qatar, the approval of the President of the

Republic regarding this visit, which modalities will be fixed between both parties by diplomatic means.'

Hayatou had clearly played a pivotal role in securing the audience through his relationship with Bin Hammam, and the letter invited him to 'provide us any useful information on this matter'.* Biya's visit to Qatar was arranged secretly and there is no public trace of his meeting with the Emir ever having taken place – or of what the two heads of states discussed if they did come together. But the ability to call in such favours with the ruler of the world's richest country was clearly a big feather in Hayatou's cap back in Cameroon – and it was all thanks to his good friend Bin Hammam.

There was another big state visit in the offing for a second key FIFA voter, too, in the months after the World Cup ballot. Michel D'Hooghe, the Belgian Exco member, had emailed Bin Hammam at the end of January to ask him to meet the president of Flanders, Kris Peeters, who was planning a visit to Qatar the following month. 'Dear Friend,' D'Hooghe had written. 'The Minister-President of Flanders [northern part of Belgium] is planning an official visit to Qatar ... Having knowledge of our friendship and our collegial relationship within the Executive Committee of FIFA, he asked me to examine the possibility of a meeting with you ... I would really appreciate it if this could be possible. Looking forward to your answer and with kindest regards, Michel.' Bin Hammam had been eager to help. 'It'll be my pleasure to meet the Minister and invite him for a dinner or lunch on 10th of February,' he responded. 'Please let me have his itinerary at your earliest.' Jenny Be had then forwarded the email to Najeeb Chirakal in Bin Hammam's private office in Doha with a note to remind the president about the engagement.

* Hayatou denied discussing a meeting between the president of Cameroon and the Emir with Bin Hammam.

The meeting between Peeters and Bin Hammam was a big opportunity for Belgium. Chirakal booked the two men a table for lunch at L'wzaar, Doha's best seafood restaurant, by the long pale stretch of Katara beach. The president of Flanders strode in grinning widely and made his way past the long fish counter heaped with fresh catch to the table where Bin Hammam was waiting. It had already been a good day, and it was about to get better. Peeters had spent the morning with the Emir, and was looking forward to a trip to the Al Shaqab equestrian centre that afternoon to see Qatar's collection of thoroughbred Arabian horses. But there was no doubt about it: this lunch, arranged for him by Belgium's FIFA voter, was the highlight of the whole trip. He was there to make a pitch on behalf of a major consortium of Belgian companies for the multi-billion-dollar contracts to help construct the infrastructure for the Qatar World Cup, and Bin Hammam was the man he most wanted to speak to.

The Belgian Sports Technology Club (BSTC) was an umbrella group covering some 70 firms which wanted to compete for a slice of the $50 billion planned infrastructure spending in Doha over the next decade, and Peeters had been enlisted to make their case. The consortium included the Belgian construction giant Besix Group, which had won a $375 million contract to help build the third phase of the passenger terminal at the New Doha International Airport in Qatar the previous summer. Besix saw itself as a major contender to help build the brand new stadiums Qatar would need to have in place by 2022, and the Belgians wanted to steal a march on the competition. That was why Peeters was lunching with Bin Hammam.

After the pair dined together, BSTC proudly briefed the media that Belgium had been the 'first on the ball' with Qatar's 2022 construction plans. 'Belgian companies were the first to talk with Mohamed bin Hammam, president of the Asian Football Confederation, in view of the organisation of the World Cup in 2022 in Qatar,' the financial magazine *Trends-Tendances* reported after a briefing from BTSC. 'Qatar wants to soon begin preparations for the 2022 World Cup ... Initial contact has occurred ... between the BTSC and Mohamed bin Hammam, as part of the visit to the region of Kris Peeters, Flemish Minister-President.'

There was no doubt in the Belgians' mind that Bin Hammam was the man to come to if you wanted a slice of the World Cup pie, and the contact with the most powerful man in Qatari football was a big boon. A wholly owned subsidiary of Besix, Six Construct Qatar,* went on to win the multi-million-dollar contract to renovate the Khalifa International Stadium ahead of the World Cup – including by building in innovative cooling technology. There was nothing to suggest that the contract had not been won fair and square, but no one knew that the Belgians' first foray into Qatar 2022 had been secretly arranged by the country's FIFA voter thanks to his 'collegial relationship' with Bin Hammam.

Indeed, Qatar's World Cup hero was busily portioning off his own share of the spoils. Bin Hammam had quickly begun lining himself up to win a multi-million-pound contract to supply services to Qatar 2022 days after the vote was won – and the bid's chief executive Hassan Al-Thawadi was ready to help him set up the deal. Bin Hammam was starting a joint venture with Elie and Mona Yahchouchi, a couple of Lebanese television moguls, to provide information technology services for the tournament.

He first met Elie Yahchouchi during the Asian Cup in Doha on 18 January, a few days after holding discussions with officials from Qatar's ministry of information and communications technology (ICT). Yahchouchi wrote to Bin Hammam four days later to 'congratulate you for the great achievement not only for Qatar, but also for the Arab world and Middle East region' of bringing the World Cup to his country. He continued: 'We feel privileged,

---

* There is no suggestion of any impropriety by Kris Peeters, Besix or any of the BSTC companies.

indeed, to be given the opportunity to be part of your vision of what can be achieved to put Qatar at the leading edge, high above the rest, in what it can implement and offer to the world as facilities, services and end to end solution for the Qatar 2022 World Cup.' Yahchouchi concluded by asking Bin Hammam to convey his 'gratitude' to 'your seniors' in the Qatari royal family. Bin Hammam responded warmly: 'It was my pleasure and privilege to meet you and your colleagues. I am looking forward to assist you to achieve your goals with Qatar.'

The two men set about establishing the consultancy firm that would be jointly owned by Bin Hammam and a small consortium of Lebanese businessmen. Yahchouchi emailed Bin Hammam again in February. 'As discussed and agreed, under your blessing, direction and custody, we will start by establishing an IT consultancy company in Qatar based on the initial business plan presented during our meeting.' He said his consultancy firm would look for a managing director to be based in Doha, conduct a prospecting exercise in Qatar to identify opportunities and search for international vendors to partner with. His email concluded: 'Your Excellency, please accept again our gratitude for allowing us the opportunity to be of Service and kindly reiterate our gratitude to your seniors and family as well.'

The documents were soon finalised and, when they were ready to swing into action, Bin Hammam emailed Al-Thawadi asking him to set up a meeting for the Yahchouchis with officials from the government information ministry. The 2022 bid chief quickly ushered Bin Hammam's new business partners in to see the government's executive director of ICT development to discuss the deal, and further meetings with the Qatar 2022 bid committee followed. Bin Hammam was already enjoying the status of a national hero in Qatar after pulling off his World Cup victory, and now he was on his way to reaping the financial rewards too.

*

Everyone wanted a piece of Qatar's victory. Chris Eaton was already enjoying the fruits of his new friendship with the men from the Gulf and he was keen to take the relationship to the next level. FIFA's investigator wrote happily to tell a friend that: 'The emir sent me a wonderful gift following the announcement of Qatar's success. I am sure it was arranged by Mohamed from his protection squad but it came through the embassy in Zurich with a card from the emir.'

The package that had landed on Eaton's desk in FIFA headquarters had contained a luxury watch and cufflinks. This was a generous present from the ruler of the country whose bid he had been investigating only months before, and Eaton was eager to show that the goodwill was mutual. He had pocketed the card bearing Qatar's name that Blatter had pulled out of the envelope at the ceremony in Zurich in December and he intended to turn it into a memento for the country's ruler. He wrote to a friend: 'I have a special gift for the emir (in fact I have the original envelope that contained the card that announced Qatar's success that Sepp Blatter opened on the night – see the picture below). I would like to present it to the emir or someone from his staff while I am in Qatar.' Eaton later asked an aide to 'get something really smart done with the 2022 envelope' and a plan was devised to get it framed with a picture of Blatter declaring the winner.*

At the same time, Eaton was keen to continue his talks with the Qataris about the sports security project they had mooted when he visited Doha the previous autumn. For the sake of decency, he waited until exactly two weeks had passed after the secret ballot before he wrote effusively to Al-Thawadi. 'Dear Hassan, I have waited a reasonable time before sending you this message of my most sincere congratulations to you and your team

---

* Eaton said that the framing never took place and that he had given the envelope to Hassan Al-Thawadi, rather than the Emir.

for Qatar being selected to host the World Cup. I am very much looking forward to working with you and whoever will be the security chief at the LOC [Local Organising Committee]. When I was in Doha the Minister discussed with me the idea of establishing a Sports Security Academy in Doha. I said at the time that it is a very interesting initiative and could place Qatar in a unique position. There is a very real need for such an international academy. On the next occasion I am in the region I would appreciate the opportunity of further discussing this initiative among of course other security issues that are part and parcel of the World Cup. Again Hassan, *Mabrook*, and I hope to see you soon.'

Al-Thawadi responded two days later saying: 'I will mention to the minister the sports academy project and let me know when you will be in town to continue with the discussions.'

By now, Eaton was seriously eyeing a move to Doha. The investigator had stuffed his security team at FIFA with a handful of trusted acolytes, and he called these men together in January to confide that he was pursuing opportunities in Qatar that he hoped would yield a bigger budget, more freedom and much better pay. If it worked out, he wanted them to come with him – but for now their lips were to remain tightly sealed. Shortly afterwards, Eaton discovered that a freelancer who had been brought in to work with his team on a specific project was romantically linked to a senior FIFA official. A stand-up row ensued with his *consigliere* Terry Steans, in which the investigator raged that his plans had been compromised by the proximity of this interloper to his paymasters at FIFA.

After the argument, Steans wrote an emollient email to Eaton, apologising for losing his temper and assuring his boss that he had not breathed a word about the plan to decamp to Doha to the freelancer. 'Today was a bad day for personal reasons, no excuse for unprofessional behaviour ... I had my thumb up my bum and my brain neutral,' he wrote. 'I have been at great pains not to speak to [the freelancer] about the plans we have discussed because I understand he is in a difficult position with [his girl-friend] and he is better off not having any information he can share and discuss with her.'

He went on: 'I have discussed nothing about Qatar or any other potential that presents itself to be capitalised on outside of FIFA as he was not going to be involved in such opportunities. Also if he confided in [his girlfriend] about any such venture you would be compromised ... What I want from you commercially is exactly what you have planned out for me. I am not going to pass up the chance to build a pension pot as you once said, that would be stupid. Outside of the FIFA entity I want what we have agreed, to find an income stream for [the other members of the investigations team], yourself and me.' Eaton was pacified, and soon after tasked Steans with getting Qatar's winning envelope framed, because he was trying to 'arrange a meeting either with the emir or his staff to give him a special presentation'.

Eaton was planning to travel to Doha in March for the International Sports Security Conference, and he emailed Hassan Al-Thawadi to suggest a meeting to discuss 'the concept for establishing an international football (or sports more generally) security academy in Qatar'. Shortly after, he received a tip-off that the exciting new sports security project he had discussed in October with Qatar's interior minister, Sheikh Abdullah bin Nasser Bin Khalifa Al Thani, had come to fruition more quickly than he had expected. He learned that the conference in March would be used by the president of Qatar's International Academy for Security Studies, Mohammed Hanzab, to announce the creation of a sports security centre based in Doha. These were glad tidings indeed.

Eaton immediately fired off an email to Hanzab, attaching his own curriculum vitae 'for ease of reference'. He explained: 'I met with Sheikh Abdullah bin Nasser Bin Khalifa Al Thani during the Interpol general assembly in Doha late last year. At that meeting Sheikh Abdulla [*sic*] raised the possibility of Qatar developing an

International Centre for Sports Security. I said to him at the time, that not only was this an interesting proposal generally, but that should Qatar win the bid for 2022, that on behalf of FIFA I would do my best to promote the concept widely ... I note that you are giving an address at the Conference that appears to be on this subject.' Eaton said he was in the process of developing a holistic security plan for FIFA and would be talking to Al-Thawadi later in the year about arrangements for the Qatar World Cup. He concluded 'I am most anxious to discuss these issues with you when I am in Doha.'

A couple of hours later, he forwarded the same email to Al-Thawadi, along with a short note saying that he hoped they could meet while he was visiting Qatar to 'discuss issues of mutual importance'. Al-Thawadi responded familiarly: 'Chris ... I would very much like to meet with you when you are in Doha.' He was unavailable during the conference, but Eaton extended his stay so that the pair could meet on the following Sunday morning.

Eaton flew into Doha in March, and watched from the audience as Hanzab unveiled the International Centre for Sports Security to the world. The new organisation had the ambitious aim to 'to enhance security and safety in the world of sport', using the Gulf state's oil and gas riches, as part of the grander scheme to make Qatar a global sporting hub. It was also the perfect enticement for FIFA's investigator and his entire team.

Two days after the announcement, Eaton typed an excited email to his underlings back in Zurich. 'I have had a full day with the head of the Qatar Academy for International Security Studies, which has launched the International Centre for Sports Security,' he wrote. 'Lots in this for us I think.' He was right.

Mohamed bin Hammam was an honoured guest at the launch of the International Centre of Security in Doha and he smiled and nodded in all the right places, but his mind was a long way away.

After much deliberation and discussion with his friends in the Qatari royal family and the World Cup bid team, he had decided that the time was right to strike Blatter down. Bin Hammam had been waiting to see if another credible contender would emerge after the loss of Chung and had promised to back Michel Platini if he stood, but now the UEFA president had ruled himself out of the running and there was no one to oppose Blatter unless Bin Hammam stepped up to the plate.

The Qataris had lost all confidence that the FIFA president was on their side, and his capricious pronouncements about their prized tournament had left no choice but to go for the jugular. With Bin Hammam at the top of FIFA, their World Cup dream would remain intact. So later the same day that the ICSS was unveiled, Bin Hammam gave his strongest indication yet that he was preparing to run for the FIFA presidency. 'People have to try change. Change is good,' he told the *Guardian*, adding suspensefully: 'Within ten days I will formally declare whether I will stand or not.'

Behind the scenes, Bin Hammam had already been canvassing for support with the help of Manilal Fernando. The football bosses of Yemen, Sri Lanka, Nepal and Thailand had written to FIFA nominating him as a candidate to oppose Blatter, and the English FA had pledged its support. Junji Ogura of Japan had been asked to back Bin Hammam, and the Qatari had arranged to meet privately with Jack Warner to sound him out, too. Chung had promised South Korea's backing at lunch in February, but Fernando wanted to be sure. The Sri Lankan wrote to Chung on 9 March asking him whether he would support Bin Hammam and suggesting a private chat to reassess his own future in football. He also asked whether Chung intended to continue 'the development programme and assistance programme you promised [*sic*] for persons in my region' and whether it would be possible to help Bin Hammam's ally Ganesh Thapa 'secure a percentage from the Hyundai Car Agency in Nepal'. History does not relate Chung's reply.

Thapa, the president of the Nepalese FA, was one of Bin Hammam's stalwarts in Asia. A total of $115,000 had been paid into his personal bank accounts in the run-up to the World Cup vote, and in the weeks before Bin Hammam announced his presidential campaign, Thapa was busily squeezing more cash out of his contacts in Qatar. He set up a meeting with Sheikh Hamad bin Khalifa bin Ahmed Al Thani, the president of the Qatar FA, and emailed Najeeb Chirakal to report back on the meeting on 8 March. 'He agreed with my proposal for paying US$ 2,00,000 [sic] ... for 4 years. On this regard he had told me to send you a confidential letter for releasing our 1st year's payment which amounts US$ 2,00,000,' Thapa said.

The money, he claimed, was for Nepal's national league, the 'total estimated budget' for which was $800,000, and Qatar had agreed to pick up the whole bill. Thapa followed up with another email on 12 March providing the bank details of the Nepalese FA.* The association would later claim that it had received only $200,000 from Qatar and accuse Thapa of creaming off the rest of the $800,000 he appeared to have secured. He was suspended and is currently under investigation for allegedly embezzling around $6 million from the association during his 19 years as its president.

As word spread that Bin Hammam was preparing a bid for the presidential crown, requests began to roll in again from his friends across Asia and Africa. The day after his interview with the *Guardian*, accounts staff at the AFC recorded in their ledger that he had withdrawn $20,000 as a 'cash advance for Al Musabbir

* Thapa insisted Qatar had only paid $200,000 in 'financial support' for a developing country and said the money had 'no connection whatsoever with the voting process for Mohamed bin Hammam'. He was suspended from his position as president of the Nepal FA after the payment was exposed by *The Sunday Times* and is currently under investigation after the country's Public Accounts Committee accused him of embezzling 582 million rupees (about $6 million) during his 19-year tenure in the office. Thapa maintains his innocence.

Sadi', the president of the Bangladesh FA, and a further $40,000 in cash for an unspecified purpose later the same day.

The irrepressible Seedy Kinteh of Gambia was also knocking on his door once more, this time asking for 'financial assistance' to pay for the West African Football Union's extraordinary general congress in Gambia, including five-star accommodation and meals for all the members, the venue, local transport, dinner and cultural entertainment. 'Please rest assured of our union's support and solidarity always. Find below is my bank details for transfer,' he wrote. Najeeb got on the phone to Kinteh to discuss his needs and then quickly arranged for $50,000 to be wired into his personal account from the funds of Bin Hammam's daughter, Aisha.

It was necessary to shower his supporters in such generosity if he was to have a hope of defeating Sepp Blatter, the ever-bountiful fount of football's gold. With typically exquisite timing at the start of March, the FIFA president had triumphantly disclosed that the organisation had raked in $4.19 billion income from the latest four-year World Cup cycle, declaring: 'I am the happiest man. It's a huge, huge financial success.' The income was all tax-free thanks to FIFA's status as a 'non-profit body existing to invest in football development'. It had ploughed $794 million in that noble cause, and funnelled a further $631 million into its bulging reserves, which Blatter revealed were now standing at a record $1.2 billion, up from just $76 million in 2003. World football's governing body had lavished $707 million on 'expenses' and its wage bill had swelled to $65.3 million, meaning its 387 employees were paid an average of $168,700 each. Football bosses around the globe were waiting eagerly to hear how Blatter would divide up the treasure when he released his manifesto later that spring.

Bin Hammam had scheduled a press conference on 18 March in Kuala Lumpur at which he planned to tell the world that he intended to stand. Blatter, wily as ever, did his best to overshadow the event by jetting in to the Malaysian capital himself the night before on a whistle-stop canvassing tour of Asia. 'I feel still full of energy and I've not yet finished my work in FIFA,' he told his press pack. 'I'm now in my thirteenth year of presidency in FIFA, and the thirty-sixth year to work in FIFA, so I'm available to the congress ... If there is competition there is competition. I have support from different Asian associations, but I must have the support from whole family of FIFA.'

The next morning, Bin Hammam stepped up to the podium in a packed press room at AFC headquarters, spotlessly turned out in a crisp suit, lavender shirt and blue silk tie. Qatar's national hero was a little longer in the tooth than he had been when he set off into the foothills of his World Cup campaign three years ago. Behind him was a larger-than-life photograph of an airbrushed version of the man at the podium, crouching over a bright yellow football in his shirtsleeves, giving a thumbs-up with a faintly strained smile. The word 'FUTURE' was emblazoned in huge white letters overhead. In front of the oversized glossy image of himself, Bin Hammam looked strangely small and shy as he glanced down at the English words his aides had prepared for him to utter. If he hadn't been clutching the podium so tightly, his hands might have been shaking. It was strange to see such a rich and powerful man look so nervous.

Treason did not come easily. The FIFA president had once been his mentor, and there was a time when Bin Hammam would have walked the length of the desert in a sandstorm if it pleased him. He had even chosen Blatter over his own heir, staying at his side in that first election in 1998 when he thought his son was dying back in Doha. Of course, the ambitious Qatari had always dreamed of taking Blatter's place, but he had dearly hoped that the president would one day stand aside and offer his blessing to his protégé as a successor. Bin Hammam knew now that would never happen and the old fox must be destroyed for the sake of Qatar's World

Cup dream. Still, it hurt him to thrust his knife into the heart of a man he could honestly say he had once loved.

Bin Hammam spoke in faltering English as he began his 17-minute speech. 'Armed with my love and passion for football, believing that our game is about fair competition, I have decided to contest the upcoming FIFA presidential election,' he proclaimed softly. There – now he had said it. With those few words, he had engaged Blatter in a fight to the death. The announcement wasn't a surprise to the assembled journalists but they knew this was a significant moment: the man addressing them posed the most serious challenge the FIFA president had ever faced. The rustle of paper accompanied the incessant clicking of camera shutters as the reporters flipped through their notebooks hurriedly jotting down his every word.

The Qatari contender did have some surprises in store. The cornerstone of his campaign was a promise to make the bidding process for future World Cups more transparent. It wasn't fair, he said, that the FIFA executive committee decided such an important matter on their own behind closed doors. It might give the fans the impression that the decision about where to host their beloved tournament was being stitched up improperly.

'FIFA's not a corrupted organisation, but the fact that a few people can take a huge decision affecting millions and hundreds of millions of fans, leaves always that sort of doubt and rumours around the members,' he said. 'The people who are working within the football community, they need as everybody hearing and listening more cooperation, more transparency, more fair distribution of the revenues. These are the changes which FIFA is needing.' For the man who had so expertly exploited the secrecy of the World Cup ballot to stack the deck in his own country's favour, this was an audacious pitch. But Bin Hammam had got what he wanted by wriggling through FIFA's seamy slipways and he was ready to shut the door behind him.

The speech ranged through Bin Hammam's driving 'passion' for football and his desire to usher in a new era of 'ethical, democratic and transparent' governance which would 'keep FIFA ... above any suspicions'. He was confident, he said, that he had done all he could to win the loyalty of enough FIFA officials to decide the vote. 'I hope that Asia is going to be united behind me, but also the other confederations where I enjoy a lot of friendship and relationships, I hope also those people are going to support me. Blatter is an experienced person, he has made significant contribution to football worldwide but I believe there is a time limit for everything.'

The announcement made headlines around the world, and it drew mixed reactions within the FIFA family. Some were withering. Peter Velappan, who had served as the AFC's general secretary for 29 years until 2007, said: 'FIFA will be doomed if Hammam became the president. It would be very detrimental.' The venerable Malaysian official poured scorn on the Qatari's promise to bring in more democracy and transparency in FIFA. 'These are the very things he has not done in AFC. There is no democracy in AFC. He is definitely an underdog but you can't rule out his influence.'

But Bin Hammam had plenty of devoted followers around the world to drown out that sort of naysaying. One was Ismail Bhamjee, the former FIFA Exco member who had inadvertently spilled the beans about corruption in the World Cup bidding race to the undercover reporters from *The Sunday Times* the year before. Bhamjee's son Naeem rushed off a rhapsodic email on his father's behalf. 'I cannot tell you the scenes in the Bhamjee household when we heard that you will be standing for FIFA Presidential election – we were jumping for joy,' he typed. 'Just the thought of you (a man with a heart of gold and the best of characters) leading World football is so exciting.'

Bin Hammam would not have dreamt of taking on the top job in world football without the backing of his beloved Emir and the custodians of his country's cherished World Cup. In the days before his big announcement, he had discussed his presidential hopes in detail with Hassan Al-Thawadi and the pair had devised a plan. The former bid chief executive, who was now enjoying his elevation to an even loftier perch as secretary general of the Qatar 2022 Supreme Committee, had promised to help Bin Hammam by hiring a top Swiss lawyer to mastermind his campaign.

On 14 March, four days before the press conference, Andrew Longmate, general counsel to Qatar 2022, had followed up on Al-Thawadi's promise. He sent an email to Najeeb Chirakal recommending a Swiss lawyer 'as discussed between ... Bin Hammam and Hassan'. Longmate noted: 'He has not been formally approached to represent us but we can do so on request.' The day after Bin Hammam entered the presidential race, Longmate came back to report a small hitch: a professional conflict had prevented the first lawyer he had recommended from working on the project. Instead he proposed 'our number 2 choice' – Dr Stephan Netzle, a Zurich-based attorney who he said 'comes very highly recommended'. He went on: 'Although we have not discussed specifics with Dr Stephan, it is assumed that his instruction will be directly with ... Bin Hammam. Dr Stephan charges at CHF450 per hour plus expenses for his time, which we consider to be reasonable.'

Netzle was a highly distinguished Zurich barrister with a bony face, a crop of thick white hair and a grin so toothy it bordered on a grimace. He had decades of experience in commercial sports law, lectured at the University of Zurich and had served for 19 years in the Court of Arbitration for Sport. Al-Thawadi could hardly have made a superior choice, and Bin Hammam was glad to accept his services.

Netzle received a phone call in March from lawyers acting for the Qatar 2022 committee, asking him to write a report on the legal framework for the FIFA presidential campaign. Once he had completed his task, he was introduced to Bin Hammam, and Longmate took a step back. 'It is probably inefficient for me to sit between you both given the potential dynamic nature of this process, so I would suggest that you communicate directly,' the bid's general counsel wrote in an email. He asked the two men to keep the bid's lawyers 'in the loop' and copy them into all correspondence as the campaign progressed.

The Swiss barrister's engagement letter, sent to Bin Hammam for signature by Longmate, contained a mandate to provide 'legal advice and assistance related to your candidacy of the next presidency of FIFA' and, presciently, 'to represent you before the competent disciplinary bodies ... eg the Court of Arbitration for Sport in Lausanne'. In the fullness of time, Netzle would find himself doing just that. But his work for Bin Hammam began with an assessment of the 'legal framework which governs the election of the president of an association under Swiss law'.

On 29 March, Netzle sent Longmate the report he had commissioned, which was passed to Bin Hammam. At the end of seven pages of analysis came an intriguing paragraph. 'Finally, in Switzerland corruption (eg a bribe payment) in the private sector is not at all part of Swiss criminal law and therefore not generally liable to prosecution,' Netzle noted. 'Although there is a provision in the Swiss Unfair Competition Act which prohibits corruption also in the private sector ... non-profit organisations are not punishable. In documents relating to the respective Swiss legislative procedure FIFA is named as one of those organisations.' FIFA was incorporated under Swiss law in such a way that would in effect give presidential candidates immunity from prosecution if they were caught paying bribes, according to Netzle.

The lawyer would later insist that his advice was 'definitely not' intended to condone corrupt payments by Bin Hammam. He said he had been asked by a Qatar 2022 committee lawyer to examine the law on bribery to see what recourse might be available in case Blatter tried to skew the election with bribes. Still, the document he had produced offered plenty of reassurance for the Qatari contender as he set out to topple Blatter with the same tactics that had won him his World Cup campaign.

The same day as Netzle submitted his report, Bin Hammam sent out his presidential manifesto, including pledges to increase FIFA's annual grants to member associations from $250,000 to $500,000 and payments from its Goal Programme fund for poor countries from $500,000 to $1 million. His announcement on 18 March, ten weeks before the presidential ballot, had kicked off another frenzied vote-buying campaign. The rules in this election were different from the World Cup ballot: now, the presidents of all FIFA's 200-plus member associations had a vote, rather than just the men on the executive committee.

While publicly promising to usher in a new era of transparency if he was elected, the Qatari and his band of loyal sidekicks were tearing around the globe on private jets showering scores of these would-be voters with largesse. The electoral methods were familiar – he hosted a junket in Doha, flew football chiefs in business class to secret summits at five-star hotels, dished out bundles of cash and used the same slush funds that had sealed support for Qatar's World Cup bid. But this time there was a crucial difference. While Bin Hammam's successful 2022 campaign was underpinned by a careful strategy deftly executed over two years, the presidential bid was thrown together in just over two months.

Bin Hammam ordered dozens of payments from his Kemco slush funds as he travelled the globe with Mohammed Meshadi, Amadou Diallo, Manilal Fernando, Worawi Makudi and Hany Abo Rida on board. The group zipped from country to country on their whirlwind campaign tour, travelling the length and breadth of Africa, and stopping off in cities throughout Europe and Asia, from Paris and Tbilisi to Beijing and Phnom Penh.

The campaign was given a significant boost when Bin Hammam was invited to join Sheikha Al-Mayassa bint Hamad Al Thani, the daughter of the Emir, on the royal jet as she travelled between charity projects in Bangladesh, Indonesia and Cambodia at the start of April. Bin Hammam had already withdrawn $20,000 as a cash advance for the president of the Bangladesh Football Federation, back in March, and after the royal visit he received a heartening email from another Bangladeshi official. 'I don't like to take more of your time since your goodself is very busy to turn all stones to win ever the challenge. However, I would like to sincerely pledge my services of any type under your disposal. I would like to acknowledge that I am greatly indebted to your excellency in heart and soul.'

Those who were willing to pledge such unquestioning support were rewarded handsomely. On 1 April, Bin Hammam received an email in which Viphet Sihachakr, president of the Laos Football Federation, provided his personal bank details with the promise: 'Any support from me please call any time Brother.' Makudi* was copied in to the message. Sihachakr had $100,000 paid into his personal bank account, which he would later claim was to pay for a technical centre in Laos. Rahif Alameh, the secretary general of the Lebanese FA, also received $100,000 from a Bin Hammam slush fund. Ganbold Buyannemekh, the president of the Mongolia FA, wrote to enquire whether the Qatari would be kind enough to fund his daughter's university studies for a third year, and his wish was granted. The round sum of $40,000 was wired to his daughter's accounts from Kemco.

Asia was Bin Hammam's heartland, but he knew that Africa was the true battleground. Blatter was campaigning hard across the continent, promising to share the riches FIFA had amassed

---

* Makudi said he understood the money was for a new technical centre for the Laos FA. He did not explain why it was paid directly to Sihachakr.

from the 2010 World Cup in South Africa. First up on the Qatari's African campaign schedule was a tour of Gambia, Cameroon and Gabon in the west. A jet was required, and Bin Hammam turned to Al-Thawadi to pay the bill of Chapman Freeborn, an air charter company. On 6 April, Royston Lasrado, the finance manager at Qatar 2022, wrote to Bin Hammam's assistant: 'Hassan has approved the payment to be processed. We have sent it to the bank this morning and it should be debited from our account this afternoon.' Later that day he sent a second email: 'The payment of USD 142,500 towards Chapman Freeborn was processed at the bank.' The money was sent to Bin Hammam, who later used one of the Kemco slush funds to pay Chapman Freeborn's bill. The money trail would come back to haunt Al-Thawadi, when he needed to deny any connection with Bin Hammam to shield the World Cup from the taint of scandal.

The African trip was a great success. Seedy Kinteh, the Gambian FA president who had already received $50,000 into his personal bank account from Bin Hammam in March, signed up to help the campaign for the presidential bid after the visit in April. The next month, Chirakal paid $9,000 to fund Kinteh's business-class travel around west Africa to drum up support for the campaign among the region's football association presidents. Kinteh wrote: 'I was notified of the transfer you did to my account by my bank the amount is received with thanks and much appreciation. The money will be used to purchase ticket for my trips to my fellow national association presidents to consolidate on our campaign goals for Mr Bin [sic] to be the next president of FIFA.'

As well as visiting voters in their own countries, Bin Hammam used his favoured lobbying technique of flying African football bosses into the Qatari capital for a junket with luxury accommodation at the Sheraton. On 17 April, a delegation of African football chiefs – including Bin Hammam's close allies during the World Cup campaign such as John Muinjo of Namibia, David

Fani of Botswana, Adam 'Bomber' Mthethwa of Swaziland and Kalusha Bwalya of Zambia – were flown in to meet the Qatari. The payments kept flowing. Four days after the junket, Bwalya received $30,000 into his personal account. Said Belkhayat, a top official at the Moroccan FA, also received $100,000. Later that month, Bin Hammam hosted another meeting of football bosses in Nairobi amid the gleaming silver columns of the five-star Panari Hotel lobby. The delegates flew in business class and were told they would have their flight tickets reimbursed by Bin Hammam on arrival.

By the end of April, Sepp Blatter was ready to reveal his hotly anticipated manifesto explaining how he would divvy up FIFA's bumper World Cup spoils among his followers. He did not disappoint. The FIFA president promised he would plough a record $1.6 billion into the development of football around the world if he was granted a fourth term. That investment over the next four years matched the entire sum he had spent on football development so far during his 13-year reign.

In a four-page letter sent to the 208 FIFA member associations on 20 April, Blatter stated the need for 'evolution not revolution' but promised greater transparency in world football. 'In these challenging times FIFA needs first of all stability, continuity and reliability. We do not need revolution within FIFA but the continuous evolution and improvement of our game and our organisation,' his letter said. 'As you all know, today we are living in an insecure and troubled world. After the global financial crises of 2008–09, today we have to cope with other major global challenges including natural and nuclear catastrophes, countries in financial turmoil, the devaluation of leading currencies as well as political instability in many regions. This shows that FIFA as the organiser of global World Cups and world football's governing body has to be prepared for the unexpected when it occurs.'

If Bin Hammam had his way, nothing would prepare Blatter for the shock he was cooking up. The Qatari was digging for dirt on his old mentor and waiting for the right moment to tarnish his name. He had hired a team of private investigators called Naduhl Sports Intelligence who reported back that they were intercepting phone calls and emails to monitor the FIFA president's activities.

On 29 April Bin Hammam was sent an encrypted proposal from Naduhl that offered to provide 'comprehensive intelligence' on Blatter for a fee of €1.5 million. The package of services included 'monitoring and protection' and 'ad hoc integrity testing' of 'promised votes'. A series of intelligence dispatches followed. One reported: 'We have received information about media preparations aiming to bring BH into disrepute. Such media messages would have associated BH with corruption and even terrorism. This kind of attempts have been neutralised with immediate effect.' Another claimed: 'FIFA intends to have the ballots of JB [Joseph Blatter] voters tagged with a certain sign allowing control of election promises. Shortly before the election, the relevant symbol shall be determined and communicated to the relevant community of JB voters.'

Bin Hammam refused to pay the full $1.5 million Naduhl had initially requested and he doubted the credibility of much of the intelligence they provided. But nonetheless he used the private detectives to search for evidence that Blatter was breaking the rules by exploiting FIFA's resources in his campaign. The Qatari was convinced that Jérôme Valcke, FIFA's secretary general, was in league with Blatter against him. One report from Naduhl noted: 'Intercepted phonecalls of the past four days reveal that the FIFA GS spoke to high ranked politicians of two west African states ... The major issue of both conversations was the upcoming election, when the federations of both states are supposed to vote for JB.'

Netzle was enlisted to help Bin Hammam apply pressure on FIFA not to allow Blatter to use FIFA's resources for his own campaign.

With the lawyer's advice, Bin Hammam wrote to Valcke: 'I kindly request you to ensure that none of the candidates use the funds and or resources of FIFA for their electioneering campaign. FIFA staff if they wish to assist Mr Blatter should resign from their positions before taking part in his campaign.' Netzle and Bin Hammam kept the pressure up throughout the campaign.*

Bin Hammam was also developing another line of attack with the aid of Dr Urs Linsi, a former secretary general of football's governing body, who had approached the Qatari with what he claimed was explosive evidence of financial wrongdoing at FIFA's headquarters in Zurich. Linsi had been sacked by Blatter back in 2007 and had walked away after only five years in the post with a payment of $6.8 million dollars which many regarded as hush money. The jowly Swiss official was enlisted to work closely with Netzle on Bin Hammam's campaign, and the men constructed a plot to deploy his information on the eve of the presidential vote to cause maximum damage to Blatter.

One email from Netzle to Bin Hammam reports: 'Dr Linsi has disclosed to me certain financial information which is shocking and certainly works in your favour. I agree with Dr Linsi that it is important that the delegates are informed about these figures in advance of the election. However, the current administration of FIFA should not be given too much time to prepare wordy explanations and defence arguments. Your information especially on the financial situation and the misappropriation of funds of FIFA should rather come as a surprise to the delegates.'

But they never got a chance to drop their bombshell. The entire presidential race was about to be derailed by a firestorm of scandal which would threaten to engulf all of world football.

---

* Netzle said he was entirely unaware that intelligence about Blatter's alleged use of FIFA resources was being gathered covertly by Naduhl.

Eighteen

The Riches of Ruin

Spilling back from the shimmering shores of the Gulf of Paria, Port of Spain is a party city where life bops along to the sound of steel pans, the streets are lined with gingerbread-style fretworked houses and the rum cocktails flow freely. This was where Mohamed bin Hammam had enlisted his old comrade Jack Warner to arrange a two-day lobbying session with Caribbean officials on 10 May.

The presidential pretender had been enraged when US visa problems had blocked him from getting to Miami for the annual congress of the Confederation of North, Central American and Caribbean Association Football earlier that month. His fury had only increased when he heard that Sepp Blatter had used his own address to the congress to announce a special award of $1 million to CONCACAF from the FIFA Goal Programme, in recognition of the confederation's 50th anniversary. He was determined not to be denied his own chance to curry favour with so many voters, and Warner had rolled to the rescue.

The bulk of CONCACAF's membership came from the 31 football associations that made up the Caribbean Football Union, and, happily, Warner was the president of both organisations. He decided to call an extraordinary congress of the CFU and sent a round-robin to the presidents of each of its member associations explaining that Bin Hammam had asked for a chance to make his case. 'In keeping with the principles of our beautiful game, fair play and democracy as well as my obligation to the Member Associations of this region, to ensure we are well-informed and in a position to make a decision in the best interests of our members, I have acquiesced in this request,' he wrote. 'It is therefore my pleasure to invite you to attend a special meeting on May 10th, 2011 from 10am at the Regency Ballroom, Hyatt Regency Hotel, Trinidad.'

Bin Hammam had paid Warner $363,000 to cover the travel, meals and accommodation expenses of the Caribbean football bosses he had invited to the junket at the Hyatt on the waterside in Trinidad and Tobago's capital city. An aide of Warner's would later recall that he had asked her to come up with a realistic budget to cover the cost of the trip, and then told her to double it before sending the bill to Bin Hammam. The travel had all been booked through Warner's own company, Simpaul.

Bin Hammam arrived in Port of Spain on 9 May with his entire campaign team. His loyal FIFA colleagues Hany Abu Rida, Worawi Makudi and Manilal Fernando followed him down the aeroplane steps, with Amadou Diallo and Mohammed Meshadi struggling along behind with the bulging bags. Michelle Chai, the AFC's assistant general secretary, was there too, pinging messages back and forth from her smartphone with the other aides back in Kuala Lumpur. They all knew that winning over the Caribbean delegates would be crucial, and that they would do what their leader told them. 'We just have to pray for Jack Warner,' Chai tapped into one message.

The party was met by Warner's staff and driven to the Hyatt, where they checked into the best rooms overlooking the Caribbean waters. They took a stroll round the city, dined heartily that evening, and turned in for an early night to make sure of being fresh for the big day that followed.

Sonia Bien-Aime was among the delegates who filed into the Hyatt's dated orange and maroon ballroom the next morning to watch Bin Hammam make his pitch for the top job in world football. She was a spark-eyed woman in cherry-red lipstick whose hair was relaxed into long glossy ringlets, and she stood out like a sore thumb in the all-male world of Caribbean football. Bien-Aime had been elected the first ever female secretary general of the Turks and Caicos FA five years before, and though she was quick to smile and joke with her male colleagues, she was deadly serious about her job.

She got on especially well with Fred Lunn, the vice-president of the Bahamas FA, and the pair were knocking around together jovially on the trip. Lunn was a small man with a round, cheerful face and a tidy moustache. He was gentle and unassuming, but every bit as serious as Bien-Aime about serving the game of football. They were equally sick of the series of scandals that continually buffeted FIFA and distracted it from its main business, and they knew Bin Hammam was running for president on a transparency ticket. It would be interesting to hear what the man from Qatar had to say.

The start of the meeting was delayed by half an hour because Warner was running late. When he finally ambled in, Bin Hammam stepped onto the stage dressed soberly in a black suit, grey shirt and striped silk tie. He squared himself at the podium, shuffled his notes, and set off hesitantly into a 40-minute presentation in which he set out his vision for a reformed FIFA in stumbling English. It was the same patter he had repeated many times before, but he was a nervous public speaker and the foreign words did not trip easily off his tongue.

At the end, he took questions from the floor, thanked the

delegates humbly for giving him an audience, and asked them to vote for him on 1 June. Once he had stepped down, the guests were all ushered into the hotel restaurant for a lunch. When they were seated, Warner stood and flashed his infectious grin around the room. He told the delegates that they should head up to the hotel's boardroom that afternoon between 3pm and 5pm where a surprise would be waiting. They would each be given a gift, he said, for attending the conference.

Lunn was curious about what was being offered, and he was one of the first officials to make his way upstairs, shortly after 3pm. When he arrived he found the boardroom locked, so he knocked and waited. A tall, handsome man in a blazer and chinos peered out and asked him to hold on a few minutes. It was Jason Sylvester, the CFU's events co-ordinator. Lunn listened out, trying to discern what was going on inside, but all was quiet. Presently, the door swung open and he was invited in. A prettily plump woman asked him to sign a registration form, and he realised it was Debbie Minguell, an administrator at the CFU. Sylvester was holding out a bulging brown envelope. It was stapled shut, with 'Bahamas' scrawled across the front in biro. Lunn took it, turned it over in his hands, and tore it open. He gasped as four fat rolls of $100 bills tumbled out onto the table.

'What's this?' he asked, incredulously.

'It's forty thousand dollars. It's a gift, from the CFU,' said Sylvester cheerfully. Did Lunn want to count it? He shook his head, momentarily dumbfounded. Then he recovered his poise enough to tell them he hadn't been authorised to accept any such gift, and he couldn't possibly take it back with him through customs when he flew home to the Bahamas via the USA.

'You could mail it,' Minguell suggested, helpfully. Lunn peered at her disbelievingly.

'Are you kidding?' he asked. She wasn't. The officials told Lunn he should relax and accept the gift, but he wasn't to discuss it with anyone else at the conference, or let anyone see the cash. Nonplussed, he decided to take it up to his hotel room and call his boss back in the Bahamas to figure out what to do. He took off his jacket and bundled it around the money before hurrying down the corridor.

When he got back to his room, Lunn pulled out his iPhone and tried to call Anton Sealey, the president of the Bahamas FA, but he got no reply. He sat down on the bed and hastily typed the words 'Pls call URGENT Fred' into a text message, then waited. It didn't take long for the phone to ring. Lunn explained what had happened and asked Sealey if he had heard anything about this gift, which was supposedly from the CFU. Sealey said he knew nothing about it, and told his vice-president that under no circumstances should he accept the money. It must be returned at once, and Lunn should make sure the officials who had given it to him made a note of the fact he had handed it back. Lunn agreed, and hung up. He laid the four rolls of cash out neatly in front of the envelope on the hotel's mottled stone table top, and snapped a photograph on his phone. Then he shoved the cash back into the envelope, slid the package down his trousers to keep it concealed, and made his way rather stiffly back to the boardroom.

Lunn found a small throng officials queuing outside when he got there, so he waited in line. Ahead of him was an official he recognised from one of the other confederations.

'Why is this door locked – are there people getting bribed around here?' the official asked. Shortly afterwards, the same man was ushered into the room. Lunn noticed that when he emerged he was slightly giggling. When it was his turn to go back in, Lunn removed the package from his trousers and handed it over, explaining that he had spoken to his FA president and could not accept the cash.

'We understand,' Sylvester said, obligingly. Lunn was relieved. He took his phone out of his pocket and tapped out another text to

Sealey, confirming that the cash had been returned, and then he went off looking for his friend Sonia, to find out what she had done about the money. It turned out that Bien-Aime had been just as shocked as Lunn to be given a bundle of cash, and had got straight on the phone to her association president, who also agreed she should hand it back. The same was true of David Sabir, from the Bermuda association and officials from the Cayman Islands, whose president Jeffrey Webb had been equally definite that the gift must be returned. The three officials who had refused to be bought watched sorrowfully as their colleagues queued up outside the board room to accept the gifts. A sum like $40,000 was the equivalent of several years' wages for officials from some of the smaller Caribbean islands. Turning it down was too much of wrench for many. Lunn sent another message back to his boss in the Bahamas.

'Sealey a lot of the boys taking the cash this is sad … I'm truly surprise it's happening,' he wrote.

'I am disappointed but not surprised,' came the reply. 'It is important that maintain our integrity when the story is told. That money will not make or break our Association. You can leave with your head high.'

'Should I save the photo for you to see?' Lunn wanted to know.

'Of course. I have never seen that amount of money,' said Sealey. 'I need to see what it looks like. Lol.'

'It hurt to give it back,' Lunn admitted. 'What bill it could pay. But it was the right decision.'

The same day, thousands of miles across the Atlantic, a second scandal was brewing. A committee of MPs at the House of Commons in London had launched an inquiry into the World Cup bidding process following England's humiliating defeat, and today they were meeting to discuss a damning file of evidence which had been submitted by *The Sunday Times* Insight team.

The journalists had sent the MPs evidence gathered during their undercover investigation the previous year, but never before published, that shone a scorching spotlight on Qatar's bid. It contained the claims made by the FIFA men the journalists had approached that Qatar 'had been offering members of the FIFA executive committee large amounts of money for their votes'. The file said that six former and current FIFA officials the journalists had spoken to suggested 'paying huge bribes to FIFA executive committee members as part of a strategy to win the vote'. The newspaper was concerned that FIFA had made no attempt to investigate repeated allegations that Qatar had bought votes despite being handed their package of tapes the month before the ballot.

'The activities of the Qatar bid had come to our attention a number of times during our investigation,' the submission said. Ismail Bhamjee, the former African Exco member who had jumped for joy when Bin Hammam announced his presidential run in March, had been filmed telling the reporters that Qatar was offering the continent's voters between a quarter and half a million dollars each. Michel Zen-Ruffinen, FIFA's former secretary general, had introduced the reporter to the fixer Amadou Diallo and told them Qatar was using him 'to arrange financial deals with the African members in exchange for World Cup votes'. Amadou Diakate, another former African Exco member who had become a member of FIFA's referee committee, had confided that the continent's voters had been offered up to $1.2 million each for 'projects' by Qatar in return for their votes. He said it was normal for a third of such sums to be paid upfront and for the remainder to be collected if the bid was successful.

Worse still, the evidence contained the claims of a whistleblower who had approached the reporters from inside the Qatar bid committee to allege that the CAF president Issa Hayatou and the Ivory Coast voter Jacques Anouma had been paid $1.5 million each. The whistleblower wasn't named in the evidence sent to parliament, but this was Phaedra Al-Majid, Qatar's raven-haired communications advisor who had been discomfited by the activities of her bidding colleagues at the CAF congress in Luanda.*

Al-Majid had told the reporters she had witnessed the money being offered to the voters by senior figures from the bid in two meetings in hotel suites in Luanda. She said a similar deal had been struck with the Nigerian Exco member Amos Adamu, before he was knocked out of the ballot when he was filmed selling his 2018 vote to the phony lobbyists for $800,000. The money would go to the three members' football associations, she said, but in reality it was intended for them personally. 'It was said in such a way that "We're giving it to you". It was going to their federation. Basically, if they took it into their pocket, we don't give a jack,' she was quoted in the evidence as saying. Hayatou, Anouma and Adamu all strongly denied they had been offered or had received any payment from Qatar.

The Sunday Times explained in its letter to the MPs that it had not published the allegations against Qatar because they had been denied firmly by the bid, the whistleblower wasn't then prepared to be identified publicly and none of the FIFA officials they had filmed talking unguardedly would be prepared to repeat the allegations if called as witnesses. But the journalists believed the allegations were credible and that they should have been examined by FIFA. They said it seemed 'extraordinary that such serious allegations by and about such senior officials were effectively swept under the carpet' after being sent to Zurich. Now the MPs had chosen to publish the submission themselves under the legal protection of absolute parliamentary privilege, meaning that the allegations could be repeated with impunity. The claims that Qatar had bribed FIFA's voters to back its World Cup bid reverberated around the globe.

*

*Al-Majid has subsequently chosen to reveal her identity as the whistleblower.

While Lunn stood watching sadly as his Caribbean colleagues queued up to accept the cash, a major breaking news story flashed onto the TV screens around the hotel. The allegations that Qatar had bribed World Cup voters had washed all the way across the Atlantic from the House of Commons in a matter of hours. The shocking news added a whole new dimension of discomfort for the three officials who had just had to hand back bundles of cash after meeting Qatar's most senior football official. Lunn would later recall feeling queasy when he saw officials emerging from the boardroom clutching their envelopes with the story rolling on every screen. 'Witnessing this was particularly troubling because at the same time CNN was running stories concerning allegations of bribes being paid in connection with the awarding of the 2022 World Cup to Qatar,' he would write.

After speaking to Lunn, Anton Sealey had picked up the phone to Chuck Blazer and told him what was happening. Sealey wanted to hear if Blazer knew anything about the gift which was supposedly from the CFU. The CONCACAF secretary general leaned back in his chair in his Trump Tower penthouse office, and ran his fingers through his beard. No, he told Sealey. He knew nothing about the bundles of cash being sprayed around in the Caribbean. And what's more, unless he was very much mistaken, the CFU didn't have anything like the finances to hand out gifts like that. Something distinctly fishy was going on in Port of Spain. Blazer hung up and speed-dialled Jack Warner. The phone rang out.

At dinner that evening, as Lunn, Bien-Aime and Sabir shared their sense of disquiet at the day's events, an announcement came that the meeting the following morning was to be moved forward to 8.30am from the scheduled time of ten. They exchanged glances. What did this mean? After the meal, Bin Hammam made another short speech, asking for the delegates' support. Then Warner escorted the Qatari and his entourage to the airport where their jet was ready for take-off.

When the delegates filed back into the ballroom the next day, Warner was looking twitchy. He opened the meeting by asking whether any reporters were present. Having established that there were no interlopers in the room, he told the delegates sternly that he was disappointed to find out that some of them had squealed to their superiors about the cash envelopes. He had received calls from CONCACAF and from FIFA about the gifts, and it was a shame that the matter hadn't been kept among friends. The money had really been a present from Mohamed bin Hammam, he told them, and it had been his idea to present it as a gift from the CFU. He said he had advised his Qatari friend to hang the formalities and simply give the Caribbean delegates the cash equivalent of whatever present he had in mind for them.

'When Mohamed bin Hammam asked to come to the Caribbean, he wanted to bring some silver plaques and wooden trophies and bunting and so on, and told me to bring for thirty people would be too much luggage. I told him he did not need to bring anything, but if he wanted to bring anything to bring something equivalent to the value of the gift that he brought,' Warner said.

'I said to him if you bring cash, I don't want you to give cash to anybody, but when you do you can give it to the CFU and the CFU will give it to its members. Because I don't want to even remotely appear that anyone has any obligation to vote for you because of what gifts you have given them, and he fully accepted that.'

If, for some unfathomable reason, any of the delegates didn't want to keep the money, they should give it to someone else who did or hand it back, but above all they should keep quiet about it. 'I know there are some people here who believe they are more pious than thou. If you are pious go to a church, friends, but the fact is that our business is our business,' he said. 'You can come in this room here and cuss and disagree and rave and rant, but when we leave here our business is our business, and that is what solidarity is about.'

He went on: 'If there is anybody here who has a conscience and wishes to send back the money, I am willing to take the money and give it back to him at any moment. But don't go and talk of it outside and believe that you're pious and you're holy and you're better than anybody else. I hope that's very clear.' There were nods and murmurs of assent around the room. Lunn looked over at Bien-Aime and sighed.

Warner also counselled the delegates to brush off any allegations that might fly their way when they returned from the visit. 'You will hear the president of Asia came here for your vote and he gave you, a Benz for you, a Benz for you and a Benz for you,' he said. 'You will hear of course that he came from Asia and gave you a barrel of oil. You will hear those things. You will hear he gave you a ship and I am asking you, when you go back home, because the media, everybody believes the worst thing possible. When you go back home, you hold your head high and you will tell your members that you were not part of this international nonsense.'

Once the meeting had broken up and the delegates were heading for the airport, Warner finally returned Blazer's call. The two men had been close conspirators for many years, but relations had recently become strained. Blazer was furious because he had seen Bin Hamman ticking off names in his notebook during the World Cup ballot and believed Warner had betrayed the USA and voted for Qatar. Nor did he like the fact that Warner had arranged an extraordinary congress of the CFU for Bin Hammam, and he had tried and failed to stand in his way. When Warner called to tell him that the Qatari had used the meeting to dish out wads of cash at his own suggestion, Blazer blew his lid. He told Warner he could think of no innocent explanation that he would be able to give for what he and Bin Hammam had done.

The CONCACAF president was defiant. He said that if anyone wanted to ask questions about his actions, they were welcome to ring him. He had nothing to fear because, he said, he had told Sepp Blatter about the cash gifts in advance and the FIFA president had 'no issue' with the plan. The call concluded frostily.

The rolling story about the allegations of Qatari World Cup bribes from the House of Commons was a wounding blow for Bin Hammam. The English FA withdrew its support for his candidacy, saying that it would not back either contender for the presidency until the claims had been properly investigated. The Qatar 2022 team furiously denied the allegations and sought to discredit Al-Majid as an unhinged and 'embittered' ex-employee.

On 12 May, Blatter had a tense meeting with Sheikh Tamim, Qatar's crown prince and now the president of its World Cup organising committee. The royal wanted to know whether his father's World Cup dream was in jeopardy as his country's bid fought off the volley of bribery allegations flying its way. Blatter was said to have reassured Sheikh Tamim of his support, but warned that Bin Hammam's run for the FIFA presidency was adding to the heat around the decision to award the tournament to Qatar. It would be easy to defuse the tension if the country's presidential pretender would only back off. The word was that Blatter hoped Bin Hammam would be forced to drop out after the hint he had apparently dropped with Sheikh Tamim. After more than a week had passed with Bin Hammam still in the race, the FIFA president started to sharpen his knife.

On 21 May, Blatter raised the horrifying spectre of re-running the 2022 World Cup vote. He told the *Independent* that the notion of a re-vote was gathering a groundswell of popular support and 'circulating already around the world'. The prospect was 'alarming', he said, but could not be ruled out. 'Don't ask me now yes or no [for a re-vote], let us go step by step,' he said. This was Qatar's greatest nightmare, and Blatter was dangling it on a thread before their eyes.

Then, two days later, he was back to torment Bin Hammam further. The president piled in to capitalise on the scandal engulfing Qatar, promising to set out proposals to stamp out corruption within FIFA at the upcoming congress. 'We have to make sure that immediately after the election that we rebuild the image of FIFA,' he told the press. 'We need to reinforce the judicial bodies and we shall find a solution how to handle the past in order that we can stop forever in the future all these damaging things about corruption.'

Blatter also confirmed to journalists that day that he would like to see Michel Platini succeed him when he stood down in four years. The UEFA president had emerged as a kingmaker during the campaign as both candidates scrapped for support in Europe. Bin Hammam had promised that he would stand aside after just one term and let the Frenchman take the helm of world football if UEFA backed him. But Blatter would not be outdone, vowing that his next term would be his last and tipping Platini as a worthy successor.

'I have decided to stand for my fourth and final term as president because in these uncertain times FIFA needs stability to secure all that we have achieved so far and to make essential changes to our beautiful game,' he had said. UEFA had now swung its support behind Blatter, and Platini was rewarded. 'I'm sure there are a lot of candidates for president, but Platini is exactly in this trajectory. I'm sure that Europe will make everything to maintain the presidency of FIFA,' Blatter said.

Then, the FIFA president added that he was 'disappointed' to hear that his challenger's close friend, Amadou Diallo, had been named in the British parliament as the alleged 'fixer' of bribes paid by the Qatar 2022 World Cup bid. 'It definitely disappoints me,' the president said. 'He was working for FIFA in the development programmes, he was in the Goal project with the candidate [Bin Hammam]. I knew him because he was around before we started with the Goal project, he was brought in by Bin Hammam. This is a question of character, so ask Diallo if he's happy in his position, what he's doing.'

Blatter rounded off by revealing with a flourish that he had once turned down a bribe when he was handed a cash-stuffed envelope during his days as secretary general. 'I received once an envelope when I was secretary general and in this envelope there was an amount of money. I couldn't refuse because he put it in my pocket. I came home here to FIFA and gave it to the finance director and he put this money on the account of the Swiss Bank Corporation at that time, and informed the guy "the money you gave to the secretary general is in that bank" and a few days later he reclaimed it. Then it was specifically known that, please, don't try to give money to somebody who's in FIFA.' Blatter's timing was as cute as ever.

The weight of the scandal was bearing down heavily upon Mohamed bin Hammam and it seemed his presidential hopes were slipping away on the tide of public opprobrium, but he was determined to stay afloat the best way he knew how. The morning after Blatter's pious speech to the press, the Qatari was busy arranging for a shipment of 'gifts to be distributed at Zurich' before the election. The package was to be sent ahead to the Renaissance Hotel in the Swiss city, ready to be handed out when the FIFA family arrived for its annual congress. Bin Hammam knew he was in choppy waters, but he was not prepared for the tidal wave of disgrace rearing up ahead.

Two days after the CFU delegates had returned from Port of Spain, Blazer had called Jérôme Valcke to tell him what he had heard about the cash gifts Bin Hammam had offered. FIFA's secretary general had asked him to provide a report on what had happened at the CFU's extraordinary congress, so Blazer had instructed John Collins, a Chicago attorney and a member of

FIFA's legal committee, to take depositions from the Caribbean officials who had rejected the money.

The report from the firm of Collins & Collins landed on Valcke's desk on 24 May. It asserted baldly that: 'On March 18, Mohamed Bin Hammam ... announced his candidacy for president of FIFA. Soon thereafter, Mr Bin Hammam began a campaign to buy the votes needed to win the election.' The appendix contained lengthy affidavits from Lunn, Sealey and Blazer himself, as well as the photograph of the cash Lunn had snapped on his iPhone, and copies of text messages, emails and memos about the débâcle. Collins had also interviewed Bien-Aime and Sabir, who had corroborated Lunn's account, and the report included a précis of their evidence. It was a devastating package.

FIFA's secretary general sat down and penned a letter that spelled out Bin Hammam's ruin. 'On 24 May 2011, Mr Chuck Blazer, FIFA Executive Committee Member and CONCACAF General Secretary, represented by Collins & Collins, reported ... that, during the course of a special meeting of the Caribbean Football Union held on 10 and 11 May 2011, you allegedly committed several infringements of the FIFA regulations, in particular, but not limited to, acts of bribery,' it read. 'In view of the foregoing, we are herewith opening ethics proceedings against you.'

Valcke's letter spewed out of the presidential fax machine at AFC headquarters in Kuala Lumpur the following day, when Bin Hammam was in Doha preparing to get on a plane to Zurich for the FIFA congress. Before he had seen the fax, FIFA released a statement to the media announcing that it was opening ethics proceedings against him and Warner, based on allegations of bribery submitted by Blazer. The story exploded onto the news bulletins and Bin Hammam's inbox filled up with emails from journalists begging for his side of the story.

When Valcke's letter reached Bin Hammam, he read it and reeled. It wasn't possible. What was Blazer thinking? He and Jack had been as thick as thieves for years. Some whispered that Blazer had been forced to knife his conspirator by the leaders of the US 2022 bid, who believed Warner had double-crossed them and voted for Qatar in the World Cup ballot. Others even claimed that Warner was in on the scheme to bring Bin Hammam down and had lured him into a trap by telling him to bring bundles of dollars rather than gifts to the Port of Spain. Whichever way you sliced it, people reckoned that Blatter had somehow wielded the knife. His pious remarks about turning down a cash-stuffed envelope appeared just a little too well timed, coming the day before Blazer's depositions plopped through FIFA's letterbox.

Bin Hammam's trio of female aides were aghast.

'This time it really didn't look good,' Jenny Be commented glumly in a message to Michelle Chai. 'Blazer is well prepared.'

'The only thing now is, only those involved knows,' replied Chai, who had been with Bin Hammam in Port of Spain. 'Sometimes you can't believe what you read or even hear. But hopefully there is god ... and justice ... reality seems to be so blurred now.'

'Conspiracy theory abound,' said Be. 'The meeting in T&T is a set up ... but there's also a pouring of sympathies for boss now. All pointing fingers to Blatter pulling a dirty stunt.'

The women agreed that if only Bin Hammam could clear his name before the election, all would be well again. But he had barely any time: he would be summoned to explain himself before FIFA's ethics committee on 29 May – three days before the presidential ballot.

Bin Hammam's scheduled flight to Zurich had been cancelled to allow him to remain in Doha overnight for crisis talks. Late that evening, he issued a defiant statement. 'This has been a difficult and painful day for me today. But, if there is even the slightest justice in the world, these allegations will vanish in the wind.' Then he stepped onto the Emiri jet, which had been specially chartered by government officials to whisk him to Zurich at short notice. He landed at 1.30pm on 26 May, with just three days to go before he would have to appear before the FIFA ethics committee.

Now the race was on for him and Warner to get their story straight. Bin Hammam headed straight for the offices of Stephan Netzle, the Zurich-based lawyer Hassan Al-Thawadi had picked out to assist with his presidential campaign. The Qatar 2022 chief couldn't have chosen a better man for a job like this: Netzle responded to a crisis like a pitbull responds to a bloody bone. He set about drafting a dauntless statement for Bin Hammam to send to FIFA and planning the counterattack.

That day, Bin Hammam issued another press release reiterating his rebuttal of the allegations, and this time dragging Sepp Blatter into the frame. He pointed out that Blazer's deposition cited an assertion by Warner that 'Blatter was informed of, but did not oppose, payments allegedly made to members of the Caribbean Football Union.' If the FIFA president knew that the cash was going to be handed out, why didn't he intervene to stop it? 'Mr Bin Hammam has therefore requested that the investigation by the Ethics Committee be extended to include Mr Blatter himself,' the release said. 'It is no coincidence that these allegations have been made only a few days before the 61st FIFA Congress, at which the new FIFA president will be elected.'

Warner sent the statement he had prepared for the ethics committee over for Netzle's perusal the following morning of 27 May. He wrote to Najeeb Chirakal: 'Hereunder is the final copy of my statement before sending to the FIFA. Pls let your lawyer review and advise within the next four hours.' Netzle was satisfied with what Warner had written, and wrote back: 'I have no amendment suggestions to that statement. It must be sent to FIFA within the next 30 Minutes!!!'

The man from Trinidad flatly denied every single allegation against him in Blazer's bundle of depositions point by point, and he railed against his accuser. He suggested that Blazer was unfairly punishing him and his long-time ally Bin Hammam for America's loss to Qatar in the World Cup race. 'Like the General Secretary, an American, employee of the CONCACAF, I voted for the USA against Qatar for the 2022 World Cup,' he insisted. 'Like the General Secretary ... I am still very hurt over the loss of the USA to Qatar. But, unlike the General Secretary ... I have no intention of conspiring with other Americans to impugn the character of President Mohammed [*sic*] bin Hammam for whom I have the highest regard.'

Bin Hammam's own statement, penned and signed by Netzle and also sent to Warner, made it clear he would fight with all his force to stay in the presidential race. The allegations, it said, were 'completely false', and had been 'submitted to discredit Mr Bin Hammam as a candidate for the upcoming elections to the FIFA presidency'. It went on: 'Mr Bin Hammam expects the ethics committee to see through that paltry and phony manoeuvre and to restore Mr Bin Hammam's honour and reputation as a person of integrity to pave the ground for a fair presidential procedure.'

The statement said Bin Hammam had left Port of Spain on 10 May and had no idea what had happened at the extraordinary congress after that point. He certainly had no knowledge of any cash-stuffed envelopes. The Qatari had 'always and strictly rejected the idea of "buying votes" either directly or indirectly and he never participated in such practices.'

Netzle was good at striking a tone of moral outrage when the occasion demanded it. 'The campaign of Mr Bin Hammam is based on the principles of integrity and transparency,' the statement said. 'He has consistently announced that all efforts must be undertaken to restore the reputation of FIFA, to fight corruption and bribery. It is a negative surprise that this argument is now used against him with the obvious goal of preventing him from fulfilling his mission.'

The same day both statements were submitted, FIFA announced that Bin Hammam had got his wish, and the ethics committee had placed Blatter under investigation, too. The FIFA president would be called upon to explain whether he had known that the cash was to be dished out in Port of Spain, and if so why he hadn't intervened to stop it. Bin Hammam had no intention of going down without a bloody battle, and if he did he would try to bring the whole house down with him.

Nineteen

The Deal

The master suite in Zurich's Renaissance Tower was fraught with the urgent murmur of anxious voices in the 48 hours before Mohamed bin Hammam was due to appear before the ethics committee to fight for his life in world football. The Qatari's aides came in and out of his opulent hotel rooms, gathering on the striped red and gold sofas around the orchid-laden coffee table to fret about his fate. Michelle Chai was furious. The feisty AFC aide thought her boss was wonderful and she hated to see him 'getting screwed', as she put it. Manilal Fernando was also fulminating at the 'low level' to which Chuck Blazer had stooped to discredit Bin Hammam. Sepp Blatter's followers must be getting 'desperate', he spat. Jenny Be was sorrowful to see her employer injured. Amadou Diallo peppered the aides with worried emails from Paris, wanting to know how the boss was faring. Even the ever-affable Mohammed Meshadi was subdued.

These were grave times. Less than six months after Bin Hammam had covered himself in glory by bringing the World Cup home to Qatar, the whole dream had been thrown into jeopardy. But somehow, the man at the centre of the storm was a picture of calm determination. The AFC women were in awe of his composure.

'Boss is just cool about it,' Chai would marvel. 'That's what I think is so great about him. I think he is so controlled because he doesn't want anyone else to worry about him.'

Jenny Be agreed: 'He just doesn't want us to worry.'

Bin Hammam spent hours with his lawyer, Stephan Netzle, preparing his evidence for the hearings on 29 May. Jack Warner would be first in line, then Bin Hammam, followed at the end of the day by Sepp Blatter. The world's media had swarmed into Zurich for the trials of three of world football's most powerful men. The strategy Netzle had devised was to go for Blatter: this was a politically motivated attack designed to crush a presidential opponent promising to clean up the mess he had made at FIFA.

As far as the Swiss lawyer was concerned, there was not a scrap of evidence that Bin Hammam had any knowledge of the brown envelopes that were handed out in Port of Spain. On the contrary, the person who was clearly alleged to have known was Blatter. Blazer's deposition said Jack Warner had told him on the phone that he had informed the FIFA president about the plan to distribute cash gifts, and he had been 'fine' about it. Jack denied saying any such thing, so there were two possibilities. Either the allegation was right, in which case Blatter should be punished for failing to stop the illegal act from taking place. If it was wrong, then the credibility of all the accusations was undermined. This was a stitch-up, and the key to survival was to pull off a successful counter-attack.

The day before the hearings, Bin Hammam was mostly absent. He had much work to do readying himself for his appearance the following day, and he had a private appointment that afternoon in London. He had been contacted by associates of Franz Beckenbauer the day before the allegations from Port of Spain had surfaced. The German football legend was firmly in the Blatter camp and he had been critical of Bin Hammam's bid for the presidency, warning that it threatened to tear football apart. But his agent, Marcus Hoefl, had got in touch out of the blue on 23 May and asked to speak to Najeeb Chirakal.

The pair talked on the phone the same day news of the allegations against Bin Hammam broke, and Hoefl's secretary followed up with an email. 'As discussed by phone with Marcus we would propose a meeting on Saturday between Mr Bin Hammam and Franz Beckenbauer,' she wrote. *Der Kaiser* would be staying at the Hilton Metropole Hotel on the Edgware Road in London, and he wanted Bin Hammam to join him there at 4.30pm on 28 May, the eve of the ethics committee hearings. The Qatari was happy to make the trip from Zurich. 'Mr Bin Hammam acknowledges the message and he confirms that he can meet Mr Beckenbauer at Hotel Hilton between 4.30-5.30pm,' Chirakal wrote, once the group had landed safely in Switzerland. It was agreed that the pair would meet in the lobby, but no one else knew what they were there to discuss.

Michelle Chai and most of her colleagues had said goodbye to Bin Hammam the night before. They had left him in fighting spirit, steeling himself for the biggest test of his professional life. One thing was certain: he was not going to let this politically motivated attack derail his presidential campaign. Blatter had to be stopped, for the good of Qatar, and for the good of world football as a whole. They waited anxiously in the more modest rooms of their own hotel a few kilometres away from the Renaissance, unsure whether they would hear from their master or be summoned to see him again before his big appearance the next day.

Meshadi confided to the others that he had a sense of foreboding for Bin Hammam. The trusty bagman had always been wary of the idea of his master making a run for the presidency so soon after Qatar had won the rights to host the World Cup.

Blatter was a wily old fox, and he would use any weapon he could find to crush his opponent. Meshadi had always worried that the president would use the threat of derailing the country's cherished World Cup as leverage to destroy Bin Hammam's candidacy. The aides knew Blatter had met the crown prince Sheikh Tamim weeks before, and they had heard he had been whispering in the Emir's ear too, putting pressure on the royals to force Bin Hammam to withdraw and dangling the threat of a 2022 revote. So far, Qatar's rulers had stayed loyal to the man who had won them the rights to host the world's most prized sporting tournament. Meshadi and the others just hoped that wouldn't change now these allegations were swirling over Bin Hammam's head.

The hour hand was progressing agonisingly slowly around the face of the clock on the wall of Michelle Chai's hotel room. It was nearly 10pm and she had heard nothing from her boss all day. She wondered what he had been doing. It was strange to be out of contact for so long. Then her smartphone began vibrating. She leapt up and dashed across the room to pick it up.

'Michelle,' Bin Hammam's voice sounded sombre. 'I need to see you. Can you come to my hotel, please.' Something in his tone unnerved her, but it would be impertinent to ask questions.

'Yes boss, I will come straight away,' she said.

Chai hurriedly pulled on her coat, threw her phone into her handbag and sped out of the door. She ran out into the street and flagged down a taxi, directing the driver to take her to the Renaissance Tower. The ten-minute journey seemed to take ages. What had happened? Why did he need her so late at night? Please, oh please, don't let anything bad have happened to Mohamed.

Finally, the taxi eased to a stop outside the imposing grey skyscraper. Chai shoved a bundle of Swiss francs through the hatch and jumped out, hurrying through the revolving door and across the lobby to the lift which sped her up to the 15th floor. She hastened down the corridor to the master suite, knocked, and waited. After a few moments, Bin Hammam came to the door, and greeted her calmly. Inside, the side lamps suffused the sitting room with pinkish light and the curtains were open a fraction, giving an inky glimpse of night sky and the glowing cityscape far below. Bin Hammam was alone. He asked Chai to sit down, and handed her a piece of paper.

'This has been drafted for me. We must release it tonight,' he said flatly. 'Can you check it, please?' She stared down and saw that he had given her a printed email, sent from someone with a Qatari address and a name she didn't recognise. Chai spoke the best English of anyone on Bin Hammam's team, and he frequently asked her to check over his press releases and blog posts before he sent them. She began to read the words on the page, and the colour drained from her flushed cheeks.

'I made the decision to run for the FIFA presidency because I was and remain committed to change within FIFA,' the email said. 'However, recent events have left me hurt and disappointed – on a professional and personal level. It saddens me that standing up for the causes that I believed in has come at a great price – the degradation of FIFA's reputation. This is not what I had in mind for FIFA and this is unacceptable. I cannot allow the name that I loved to be dragged more and more in the mud because of competition between two individuals. The game itself and the people who love it around the world must come first. It is for this reason that I announce my withdrawal from the presidential election.'

Chai felt like she'd been hit by a truck. How could this be? She looked up at Mohamed, who had turned away and was pacing contemplatively, with his head bowed and his hands loosely joined at his back. A flood of questions and protestations rushed through her mind. She loved her master as much as Jenny Be or any of the other aides who were always at his side. He was the finest, kindest, noblest man they knew. And he was also the most determined. What had happened that day to make him give up so suddenly? Who was this strange person in Qatar, who had drafted this terrible statement? There were a hundred thousand things she wanted to say. But as she studied his countenance, she saw it was no good. His jaw was set, his expression was opaque. She knew this look well. When Bin Hammam had made up his mind, he was implacable. He was the master, she was the servant, and nothing she could say would do any good.

'So?' he asked. 'All is OK with the statement?'

'Yes boss,' she said quietly. 'The English is all fine.' He gave her a faint smile of gratitude.

'Thank you, Michelle. Then we will send it.'

The world woke up on the morning of 29 May to the news that Bin Hammam had pulled out of the presidential race. The reaction was one of astonishment, with Fox News reporting his decision to bow out as a 'dramatic twist in the battle for the top job in football' which left Blatter sailing unopposed towards re-coronation. Over in London, Franz Beckenbauer took to the airwaves to welcome Bin Hammam's withdrawal and call upon FIFA to unite behind Blatter. The Qatari corruption scandal was, he said, 'a disaster for football'. He went on: 'I hope when the first of June comes and the election will be over, then all the discussion about corruption is finished and FIFA can go back to normal. I don't know what's going on in the next days, but in general it's my opinion it's very, very bad.' For Beckenbauer, Blatter was a hero who had steered FIFA through choppy waters and must be allowed to continue on his course. 'He did a wonderful job. It's not easy. FIFA is like the United Nations – we have two hundred and eight members. It's not easy to handle, but I think Blatter and his staff are doing a wonderful job,' he said.

Bin Hammam's aides and supporters were beside themselves. What could possibly have happened to make the boss throw in the towel in this way? Bin Hammam was slow to explain. His decision was made, and he preferred to maintain his silence. There were, at that stage, just a very few trusted friends who he let in on his secret.

Bin Hammam told them that, the previous day, he had received a summons to visit Blatter on the FIFA hilltop. The invitation had taken him aback, of course. The two men had not spoken for months, except to exchange volleys of tactical vitriol in the media. But now Blatter wanted to see him, alone. Bin Hammam didn't say whether he'd still made it to London to see Beckenbauer that afternoon, but at some point during the day he had found time to make his way to FIFA headquarters, as requested, with some trepidation. What did he want now?

When he arrived at the president's office, knocked, and entered, he told his friends he was astonished to find Blatter chatting easily with a senior member of his country's royal family. He was invited to sit down, and Blatter was all smiles. He sensed instantly that some awful accord had been reached without him in this room, with its huge window giving out onto the playing fields outside, where in years gone by he had spent so many hours giving counsel to the president. Was it Blatter who first broke the news, or was it the man in the gold-trimmed robes? The memory of the meeting was a blur.

He was told that these allegations of bribery were bad for FIFA, and they were bad for Qatar too. His candidacy was threatening to divide world football just at the time when it was more important than ever to maintain unity. It was time to put a stop to all this unpleasantness. Just as he feared, a deal had been done in his absence to make the whole mess go away. Bin Hammam was being ordered to do the decent thing for his country and withdraw from the FIFA presidential race.

In return, Blatter would see to it that no harm would come to Qatar's World Cup dream. There would be no re-vote, as the president had hinted days before, and the 2022 tournament would be untouched by the allegations swirling on all sides.* Bin Hammam was aghast. He would do anything for his country, of course. He loved his Emir even more than he loved this game. But he had spent decades building up his reputation in world football, and he could not bear for his name to be dragged through the mud. The ethics committee was investigating him. How could he bear to stand down in shame with that hanging over him?

'What about the case against me?' he asked tremulously. 'The case before the committee?'

On this point, he said, Blatter was magnanimous. 'If there is no candidate, then there is no case,' he recalled the FIFA president had told him.

Those words would linger in Bin Hammam's mind for years to come. He repeated them to his friends often. 'No candidate; no case.' That was the deal, as he understood it. Blatter would see to it that nothing would come of the following day's hearing. The ethics committee would find no cause to open a full investigation into Bin Hammam, and the case would be dropped. But only if he pulled out of the race that very night.

Bin Hammam had later appealed to his Emir, he told his friends, but his country's ruler was adamant that he should do as he was told. His candidacy was badly damaged and if he refused to go now then the country's World Cup would be at Blatter's mercy when he lost the election. Withdrawing would be a noble sacrifice for his country. He would be cleared of all wrongdoing and would emerge with his honour and dignity intact. It was the

---

* A spokesman for FIFA said the organisation had 'verified internally' that no such deal had been made, but Sepp Blatter declined to respond to questions personally. The Qatar 2022 supreme committee did not reply to the allegation.

best thing for everyone – he *had* to see that. It felt to Bin Hammam like his world was collapsing, but if the Emir wished it then it must be done. So he told his friends he had no choice but to assent to the deal, allow his resignation statement to be drafted for him from Doha, and bow out of the race.

Up on the FIFA hilltop, a shallow morning fog was slowly dissolving. Late spring sunlight trickled through the haze onto the landscaped lawns where the media scrum was waiting eagerly for the accused men to arrive. Inside, Petrus Damaseb was flicking one last time through the bundle of affidavits from Collins & Collins which would be the subject of the day's hearings. The portly Namibian judge would be at the head of the ethics committee today. Its usual chairman, Claudio Sulser, had recused himself to avoid accusations of bias arising from the Swiss citizenship which he shared with Blatter. The events inside the committee room would take place in absolute secrecy, and the tapes and transcripts of the hearings would be kept under lock and key inside FIFA. They were meant never to be scrutinised by prying eyes outside.

In his suite on the top floor of the Renaissance Tower, Bin Hammam was eyeing his reflection in the mirror as he lifted the collar of his starched white shirt and looped a deep red tie around his neck. This garment would always remind him of the most glorious moment of his life. It was the same as the one that he, the Emir and Sheikh Mohammed had all sported for the announcement of Qatar's World Cup victory six months before. Their ties had been chosen to match the striking silk dress Sheikha Mozah wore that night, in the rich burgundy of Qatar's national flag. That had been his proudest hour, standing shoulder to shoulder with his country's royals in a display of national pride as they reaped the rewards of his devoted efforts. And now it had come to this: he had been sacrificed to save the dream he had delivered. The Emir's words from the night before were still echoing in his ears. His hopes of leading FIFA were over. All that remained was to clear his name.

Jack Warner was the first to appear before the committee that morning. The president of CONCACAF had already made it clear he would bite, kick and scratch if the hearing did not go his way. His parting shot before boarding the plane to Zurich the previous day was to tell reporters in Trinidad: 'In the next couple days you will see a football tsunami that will hit FIFA and the world that will shock you. The time has come when I must stop playing dead so you'll see it, it's coming, trust me ... I have been here for twenty-nine consecutive years and if the worst happens, the worst happens.' Warner had been caught entirely off guard by Bin Hammam's resignation that morning, and he wondered what it all meant. Perhaps his friend from Qatar wasn't made of such stern stuff as he'd thought, but there was no way Warner was going down with him.

Once the CONCACAF president had settled into his chair and finished conferring with his lawyer, Judge Damaseb introduced himself and the rest of the committee, and opened the hearing. He explained that their job that day was simply to establish whether there was a *prima facie* case that the code of ethics had been infringed pending a fuller hearing at a later date, and then he set out the allegations from Blazer's deposition. As soon as the opening formalities were over, Warner got onto his soapbox. 'I want to talk about a thing called respect, sir,' he told Damaseb grandly. 'Respect, because that in some way impinges on why we're here this morning. I want to say to you, sir, that the minute we as a people, as a nation, no longer honour respect as a virtue it is the beginning of the end of civilisation.' Warner felt his general secretary, Blazer, had displayed a shameful lack of respect for him, ever since forming the conclusion that he had betrayed the US bid and voted for Qatar.

'I have a general secretary in America paid full time for the last twenty-one years, and twenty-one years he has been with me as general secretary until the vote for the last World Cup,' Warner fumed. 'He sat next to President Bin Hammam and he told me that he was watching him and his book and he was seeing him ticking off people whom he saw supported his bid.' A row had ensued after the ballot because Blazer thought Warner had voted for Qatar, and he blamed this falling out for the allegations about the cash gifts in Port of Spain. 'He made the point to me that USA had a better bid than Qatar and he will never forgive Bin Hammam. He told me that and I said to him, that's not my business ... but if the general secretary had an allegation or allegations against me one would have thought that if from the fundamentals of good law, good principle, is for the accuser to confront the accused ... That is the first thing about respect and I'm saying this because of lack for respect.'

Warner rushed on to explain that he had arranged the extraordinary meeting of the CFU for Bin Hammam after Blatter had used the CONCACAF congress in Miami to announce a gift of $1 million to the confederation from FIFA. Recalling the scenes when Blatter announced the gift, Warner told the committee: 'He said that he has given CONCACAF one million dollars to spend as CONCACAF wishes and we applauded and so on, and Michel Platini objected brutally afterwards because that was not given with any approval of the finance committee, of which I'm deputy chairman. I went to him [Blatter] quietly and said, President, that was good, but please go back and have it ratified by the finance committee because it is not correct that you have just given them one million dollars just so.'

Warner thought it was unfair that Bin Hammam had been prevented from making his case to CONCACAF by visa issues, so he had organised the special meeting of the CFU. But neither he nor his friend from Qatar had given out any cash. In fact, he said, the only gifts on offer at the special meeting had been laptop computers and projectors which had been sent for each association by FIFA. Warner addressed Damaseb directly: 'I felt it was wrong for

FIFA to use Mr Bin Hammam's meeting to give delegates FIFA gifts but, be that as it may, I said, you have to receive from FIFA a laptop and a monitor and sign for having received it ... That's the only mention I made of a gift.'

The man from Trinidad was still racing on without a pause, more than 15 minutes into his speech. This sorry affair was all the result of sour grapes. 'I understand Mr Blazer's point, I understand the pain he suffers over the US loss to Qatar. I feel it here too,' he said, beating his chest, 'but I will not allow my office or me to be used to carry out any campaign against Qatar and or Mr Bin Hammam as a consequence; that's not my business.'

At last, Warner was running out of steam. 'Finally, before I take your questions ... I will tell you that I did not know that Mr Bin Hammam would have resigned until this morning. I'm sorry, I'm sorry he has in some ways,' he said. 'I remain firm and intransigent in my view, my statement, I received nothing from Mr Bin Hammam to give delegates, I know nothing of any money, I never spoke about any cash gifts to collect and I am therefore saying today, that I don't even know why I'm here. Despite all the regulations and points there, I wish I really knew why I'm here. Do you see the points I made? I repeat here, I don't know why I am here. I thank you.'

Damaseb was flawlessly polite. 'Thank you very much, Mr Warner, for your very important statement,' he said, before moving on briskly. 'I just want to emphasise a few things. The first one is to repeat what I said at the beginning of this procedure. That is, the reason we are here as a committee for FIFA ethics committee, is based on the file that has been handed over to us to determine whether there appears to be an infringement of the FIFA code of ethics. That's the only reason we're here. We want to guarantee you whichever way this thing moves forward ... that you will be given every right to give all the evidence at your disposal, every right to confront those who accuse you of wrongdoing to determine at the end of the day your guilt or innocence.'

Warner leapt back to life: 'I'll get a chance to confront the accusers?'

'Yes.'

'Which I have not done so far!' he cried, and he was off again. 'Sorry to butt in. For twenty-nine years I wore the FIFA uniform with pride. Yesterday I had to hide it in my suitcase because I don't want people to see Jack Warner, vice-president of FIFA, because I would be embarrassed. Today I landed here in Zurich as a common criminal trying to avoid the media ... what have I done to deserve that? All I've asked for is to ask you to practise fair play, let us hear Mr Bin Hammam, what is wrong with that, sir?'

The tirade continued for some time. Once Warner had settled down again, his lawyer was invited to present his formal submission rebutting each of Blazer's claims point blank, and then it was time for the members of the committee to ask their questions. Robert Torres, a small floppy-haired judge from the tiny Pacific island of Guam, was intrigued by Warner's falling-out with his accuser.

'How would you describe your relationship with Chuck Blazer before the events outlined in his affidavit and report occurred?' he asked.

'Up to the World Cup, just before the vote for the World Cup, it was excellent,' Warner replied. 'After that it was atrocious. In fact, the president of the US Soccer Federation, who is a member of the executive committee, stopped talking to me the day after.'

Then Sondre Kaafjord, a startlingly sallow Norwegian football official, wanted to know what had happened at the end of Bin Hammam's speech to delegates in Port of Spain.

'After the meeting on the tenth of May, the delegates were told to – according to the papers – they were told to go to a board-room ...' he began.

'Told by whom?' Warner jumped in.

'That was my question ... In the papers it's written that they were told to go to the boardroom to collect gifts. You have ...'

Warner butted in again. 'That never transpired, sir!'

'Just let me finish,' Kaafjord snapped.

'Okay, sorry. My apologies.'

'You have denied that there were any gifts,' Kaafjord continued. 'Do you also deny that there was such an arrangement after the meeting that the delegates had to go to a room to collect something ... Could you describe what really ... happened?'

'There was never anything said while I was there, before Mr Bin Hammam or after, or while the lunch was taking place about any gift, any room at any time,' Warner insisted.

There were a smattering of further questions before Damaseb reiterated that the committee's only task was to determine whether, on the face of it, the ethics code had been broken. If they thought it had, a full investigation would follow. Before he could end the hearing, the irrepressible Warner leapt in again.

'May I?' he interjected. Damaseb was a patient man.

'Yes, you may,' he replied.

'In normal jurisdictions one is innocent until proven guilty. In my part of the world one is guilty until proven innocent. You have no idea what my family and I are going through!' Warner protested. 'You have no idea, you have no idea. You have no idea what my party and my government are going through, you have no idea. So whatever happens it will take years, years to overcome this and that is the legacy that Mr Blatter and the FIFA have given me after twenty-nine years. Me!' He sat back in his chair with an expression of wounded outrage.

Damaseb felt the time had come to be firm. 'Yes, I understand the depth of the offence you feel,' he told Warner. 'But one thing I want to emphasise is we are a judicial body and, Mr Warner ... what I do every day for a living is take judicial decisions which affect the lives of people ... I am never scared to do that because that's the oath that I've taken. However unpleasant the consequences, a judicial function must be performed. Always bearing in mind the rights of people, weighing all the evidence and so on. So I can only assume that what you say about what you go through is a true reflection of what is happening and how you feel, but that again does not take away the responsibility that we have as a committee to deliberate on this matter.'

Warner was subdued. Before the hearing finished, Torres had a couple more questions.

'Do you recall having a meeting with President Blatter in Guatemala on the tenth of April?'

'Sure,' Warner said.

'Did you tell President Blatter that CFU was having a special meeting?'

'I told him then and I told him at the congress in Miami.'

'Did you ever mention to him that the delegates would be given cash by President Hammam?'

'I couldn't tell him that, that was not the case.'

'So you don't recall President Blatter telling you at that meeting that no gifts should be provided to any of the attendees?'

'I swear to you here today we never discussed that,' Warner said.

'Thank you,' said Torres. The meeting drew to a close, and Damaseb made a note of the telephone number of Warner's hotel so that he could be contacted later that day when they made their decision. Next, it was Bin Hammam's turn to face the inquisitors.

By the time the AFC president's black limousine rolled down the drive at just after noon, the late spring light had been greyed by gathering clouds. Hunched in the back seat in a black suit, his red tie and dark glasses, Bin Hammam stared out reproachfully at the cameramen clamouring at the window, his tight-lipped frown captured eerily in the blaze of flashbulbs which threw half his face into shadow. The driver forced his way through the throng and the car eased down the ramp into the privacy of the underground car park, where Bin Hammam took a moment to gird himself before stepping out. Netzle accompanied him upstairs to the committee room.

'I'd like to welcome you, Mr Bin Hammam,' Damaseb began, when the Qatari and his lawyer had taken their seats before the panel.

'Good morning, Your Honour, and good morning gentleman; lady. My name is Mohamed bin Hammam Al-Abdulla,' the accused man said softly. Damaseb introduced the panel, and asked Bin Hammam if he was happy to proceed.

'Your Honour we are, have a full confidence in yourself and all the members existing here,' Bin Hammam said, with a courteous inclination of the head. Damaseb shuffled his papers and prepared to begin.

'A complaint has been submitted to us by the FIFA general secretary, relating to allegations that involve you, Mr Bin Hammam, which I'm sure, by now, you are aware,' the judge said. 'Now given the gravity of the allegations made ... the reason we are here this afternoon with you Mr Bin Hammam, is to determine this sole question: does there appear to be an infringement of the code of ethics?' The charges were read. Bin Hammam stood accused of violating articles three, six, nine, ten, eleven, twelve and fourteen of the FIFA code of ethics relating to conduct towards government and private organisations, loyalty and confidentiality, accepting and giving gifts and other benefits, bribery, commission and duty of disclosure. Damaseb invited him to give his account.

'Dear members, I have introductory personal remarks I want to make to you,' Bin Hammam began. 'First of all, Your Honour, I don't know why I am here. Mr Blazer alleges that I try to buy votes. This is outrageous and simply not true. I never bought any votes. I confirm again that I paid the cost of the extraordinary meeting in Trinidad and the travelling and accommodation costs and the daily allowances for the participants. The banking transfer of $360,000 was based on estimate by my staff. I learned that after our arrival in Trinidad my staff paid another amount of $50,000 in cash to the staff of CFU to cover any additional expenses when they learned that the numbers of the attendees was higher than we have estimated.'

Netzle interjected: 'May I add that we expected you, Your Honour, to ask specific questions to Mr Bin Hammam and that he will be ready to answer, that was our expectation for this proceeding. How do you want to proceed?'

'We will ask some questions but what I've decided to do is to afford as much opportunity as possible to you to state your case,' Damaseb said. 'Please use this opportunity to tell us as much as possible about your side of the story.'

Bin Hammam went on to explain that his friend Jack Warner had arranged the CFU meeting to give him a fair hearing after he was shut out of the CONCACAF congress in Miami. He had simply attended to make a speech, and had no part in handing out any gifts. 'I was really very surprised to learn about the allegation against me later on,' he said. 'I confirmed to you that . . . no cash, no transfer made by me or by any of my staff or delegations.'

Once he had stated his own denials, Bin Hammam was at pains to extinguish any suggestion he might previously have appeared to make that Sepp Blatter may have condoned the payment of bribes by Jack Warner.

'I asked to include Mr Blatter in the proceeding to demonstrate by his own statements that he did not consent to any cash payments and that all such remarks in the report of Mr Blazer's are false.' He elaborated: 'Regarding Mr Blatter, it wasn't my saying that I wanted to bring Mr Blatter today as a committee, but when I read the report of Mr Blazer, it referred to a statement of Mr David Sabir who said that Mr Warner told the delegates that he had informed Mr Blatter about the gift and he had no issue with it. I want to make this very clear. I cannot imagine that Mr Warner said so or that Mr Blatter acknowledged any cash payment, but I want this to be confirmed by the ethic committee that this is not true. For me it is a further indication that the entire allegations are not true. All I wanted was a level playing field for the election. The ethic committee shall investigate all allegations made by this report and not only some of them. I am sure that these allegations are unfounded whether they are aimed at Warner, me or Mr Blatter. I don't know whether there is anything else, Your Honour, I can say in this regard.'

Netzle stepped in to overlay the point, in case there was any room for doubt. No allegations were being made about Blatter by Bin Hammam. 'We had no goal to create more harm to anyone else but when we read this document which ... is the basis of this proceedings then we stumbled over two or three sentences in which Mr Blatter was mentioned. The only reason why we asked you to include him was because of these sentences. We do not have additional evidence. We do not bring any allegations against him but we say, this has been mentioned and if this is not true, this should be determined by your court, by your commission. It also gives an indication about the credibility of all other allegations which have been made under the same headings and which are directed against Mr Bin Hammam. That's the reason why we included that.'

After some further discussion, Sondre Kaafjord pitched in with a question. 'After meeting the tenth of May in the congress in CFU, there obviously had been a follow-up in a smaller room. There are very different opinions on what happened there ... Did you hear during the meeting or at the end of the meeting ...

anyone saying anything to the delegates about to proceed to a room to get daily allowances or whatever? Did you hear anything from anyone?'

'Never, sir.'

Now it was Juan Pedro Damiani's turn. The Uruguayan official was well known to Bin Hammam – the pair had served together on FIFA committees for years.

'Why would you think that Mr Blazer, after designation of Qatar for the World Cup, why do you think the relationship with you changed?' he enquired.

'I cannot comment, sir,' Bin Hammam replied. 'I don't want to believe that such a relationship should be affected when Qatar and the United States were in a fair competition and Qatar won over the United States.'

Next, Les Murray, an Australian broadcaster who sat on the ethics committee, piled in.

'You say in two of the paragraphs in your statement to the ethics committee, that there are attempts to discredit you in this process. You do that in paragraph three where you claim that your candidature is obviously, you say, is being besmirched by these allegations, deliberately and also in paragraph seventeen where you accuse, I gather, Mr Blazer of doing this. I mean, are you talking here about some kind of broad conspiracy? If you are, is there any other evidence you have, beyond this particular case, of that going on?'

'Definitely I have been very much affected by these allegations,' Bin Hammam replied sadly. 'I don't want actually to wish that there is a huge conspiracy, but some evidence is there. For example two or three days earlier, there was the Qatar bid and my name was always connected to bribery and for, you know, to bribe another members from FIFA executive committee. So this connection, and after that this has come, it means one thing. There is some people trying to damage my name and the public, prior to the election. Well, if you say it's conspiracy, I think it is. But I don't know whether these are evidence or not enough.'

The committee made no comment. There were a few more general questions about the reason for asking for a special meeting with the Caribbean officials, and then Damaseb asked Bin Hammam whether he had anything to add in conclusion.

'Your Honour ... just to repeat what I have said in the beginning. I really don't know why I am here and why – what is all this about, and nothing more. Thank you.' Damaseb asked Bin Hammam whether there was any aspect of the procedure he had been unhappy with. The accused gave a small smile of humble gratitude.

'Your Honour, dear members, I believe that I have received a fair treatment and a fair hearing in your committee. I'd like to thank you very much for that.'

Damaseb gave a nod, satisfied. 'Thank you very much, sir, and I want to assure that moving beyond this, we shall respect your rights fully, afford you every opportunity to state your case, to present evidence and to challenge whatever evidence there may be against you. You are going to leave us now, but I want you to know that we are not here to determine your guilt or innocence and we don't want anyone to suggest to you otherwise ... That is a process that will come at a much later stage and, as I said, after you, we are going to listen to the next accused person who is the president of FIFA and after that we'll make our determination on the limited purpose for which we are here.'

Netzle interjected again: 'Excuse me, the timing. Just to know ... It has been announced that there is a media conference at six o'clock?'

'Well, I know because of the intense public and media interest, they have to announce whatever decisions the committee takes,' said Damaseb. 'I'm personally not aware of times that they've been given or anyway but ... before anything is announced, you will be informed about the outcome. That I can promise you.'

'Good,' said Netzle.

'If the contrary happens, I would like to know that,' said Damaseb, who had learned a thing or two about working for FIFA by now. 'Whatever decision that is taken affecting you and your client must be informed to you before anybody knows. If the contrary happens, I'll be very surprised and in fact angry.'

'Yes,' the lawyer said gratefully. 'We don't want to learn your decision from the media.'

'No. That's not how I function,' the judge replied.

And then it was all over. Bin Hammam left the room in a daze, just 55 minutes after he had entered. He and Netzle exited the building swiftly and directed the chauffeur back to the lawyer's office on Falkenstrasse, by the mouth of Lake Zurich, to await news of the decision that afternoon.

Finally, the most powerful man in world football strolled into the committee room, and took his seat alone before the ethics men. He graced the panel with an indulgent beam.

'Welcome, President Blatter,' said Damaseb. 'Everybody before you was accompanied. I assume you are unaccompanied – you are alone?' The accused nodded nobly.

'Chairman ... yes, I am alone.'

'Thank you very much, sir. President Blatter, as you are aware ... The circumstances under which we convene relate to, as you know, the forthcoming elections for the presidency of FIFA and the allegations that have been made around that. The reason you are present here is that Mr Bin Hammam, who is in his own right an accused, has asked that a case be opened against you and that was referred to the ethics committee.'

Damaseb introduced the panel. He explained: 'Allegations have been made by Mr Bin Hammam that, in seven of the documents that have been brought against him in the context of the inquiry against him, an allegation was made that it had been reported to you by Mr Jack Warner that certain payments were going to be made by Mr Bin Hammam to national associations and that, to the extent that it is alleged that you are aware of those payments, you are under a duty to disclose that fact. That is the basis for the allegation.' If this was true, Blatter would be guilty of article fourteen of the FIFA code of ethics, which requires all officials to report 'any evidence of violations of conduct to the FIFA secretary general'.

Blatter licked his lips, and began. 'Thank you Chairman, thank you gentlemen, lady, around this table. I have listened carefully to the introductory remarks and the accusation that has been brought towards me.' The FIFA president said he had met Warner on 10 April in Guatemala, and had been informed of the plan to hand out cash to delegates at a special meeting of the CFU. But Blatter said he had put his foot down.

'When he was speaking the aspect of money I told him ... don't speak about that. Then, for me, the situation was closed. My message has been given very clearly and when I am looking on this article fourteen, then I should report if any evidence was there. There was not evidence because this was a declaration of Mr Warner and I thought that he will understand my message. It is only when I came back the other day from travel from Japan, on the twenty-third of May, that I was informed by the secretary general that he has received some evidences. So, between the time I spoke with Mr Warner in April and this time there, I personally had no evidence that something had happened and I was of the opinion that Mr Warner would have understood my very clear message. First to not organise this special meeting and secondly to not speak about money.'

'When he talked about the money, did he give some indication about amounts or what they would be for, or anything of that nature?' Blatter was asked.

'No, he has only mentioned what I put there. It would be good for some of the associations. I told him, stop speaking about money, but he didn't speak about any amount or the number or whatever.'

'Did he mention where the money was coming from? Did he mention Mohammed bin Hammam being the supplier of this money?' Les Murray enquired.

Blatter said no. 'We didn't speak about ... from who the money was coming.'

Sondre Kaafjord had a question: 'Did you ever, after that meeting on the tenth of April, discuss this matter or mention Warner's intention to Mr Chuck Blazer?'

Blatter said he had. 'I think I spoke with Mr Blazer before this meeting because he told me that the northern part and the central part of the CONCACAF is against this meeting. So it was before I met Mr Warner.'

And then the questioning was over. 'President Blatter,' said Damaseb. 'Anything you want to say in conclusion at this point in time in your defence?' Blatter seized the opportunity eagerly to remind the men on the panel that they owed their jobs to him. It was he, after all, who had introduced the ethics committee to FIFA, in the first place. None of this would have been possible without his vision and leadership.

'Yes, I have a lot to say in my defence in such a case. I have to tell you, Mr Chairman, if I am happy to be once with the ethics committee, I didn't know that I shall be here as an accused. I present my defence, but I have to say it's a sad day. It is a sad day for me to be here but it's a happy day that I can defend myself in front of you. So I'm happy to be here, I'm honoured to be in a constitutional committee that I have had the initiative to put in FIFA after having served so many years in FIFA and having seen that we are not able to go on what happened outside of the field of play ... That's why, in 2006, in the congress of Munich we have installed the FIFA ethics committee with the FIFA Code of Ethics.'

That wasn't all. Not only was Blatter the sole reason that the ethics committee existed at all – when he was re-elected he planned to continue his good works to make FIFA a better, cleaner organisation. Not only that: one of his main proposals was taken from the lips of the wise men before him themselves. 'Mr Chairman it's not my defence but I tell you at the congress – on the forthcoming congress I have on the agenda, and this is since two months, zero tolerance. Zero tolerance was, by your committee you said zero tolerance. I take it off from you, I put it on the agenda and this will be one of the key points of the next congress. For my defence I don't say more than what is the truth. I had no evidence what I am accused. Why should I have had a problem? If there is a problem somewhere I am the number one to go into these problems. Here, for me, there was not a problem because the problem had been created by the other parties.'

He rounded off with a bit of well-timed flattery. 'Thank you for your dedication for the good of the game ... I congratulate you, I thank you what you are doing. Thank you for your attention Mr Chairman, members of the committee.'

Damaseb thanked him for his kind words, and asked: 'Have we treated you fairly, are you unhappy with the way in which anything has transpired here this afternoon, sir?' Blatter couldn't have been more delighted with the conduct of his committee.

'Definitely, Chairman. You and the committee members, you treated me fairly. This is exactly what we want. It is respect; it is discipline and fair play. Thank you so much.' And how would the ethics committee be able to reach Blatter to communicate their decision to him later that day?

'I am in my office, I am working,' he said.

'I would like to thank you for your cooperation in coming,' said Damaseb. 'As I have done with others, of course given your pivotal position in the organisation and a senior official of FIFA, we assume that you will continue to provide your cooperation to the committee with its continuing investigation of this matter?'

'Definitely, yes,' said the president. 'You can count on one hundred per cent of this zero tolerance, definitely. I thank you for your help.'

'Thank you, Mr President,' the ethics judge said. 'You are excused now.'

It took next to no time for the men on the ethics committee to reach their decision once the hearings were over. Damaseb saw things clearly: the meeting in the Caribbean had been arranged for the sole purpose of enabling Bin Hammam to promote his candidacy; the photographs proved that bundles of dollars *had* been dished out to the delegates, and the CFU plainly didn't have the funds to hand out cash gifts totalling more than $1 million. On the face of it, they thought there was little room for doubt that the Qatari billionaire had been trying to bribe voters in the presidential election, with help from his friend Jack.

Warner was clearly up to his neck in the mucky business, with multiple witnesses giving consistent accounts of his role in the scheme. When it came to Blatter, though, the panel agreed that his evidence had been exemplary. There was no reason to believe that the president had condoned Warner's plan to help bribe the members of his association at the midnight meeting in Guatemala. Warner said he and Blatter had never discussed any such thing; the president said he had been told about the plan but had instructed his errant official to desist from paying bribes. There was every reason to believe the latter account, they agreed. So, they decided, the *prima facie* case against Bin Hammam and Warner was clear, and the two men would be suspended. Blatter survived unscathed.

Bin Hammam was waiting in Netzle's office with small cluster of aides around him when the fax from FIFA headquarters began sputtering out of the machine. He was characteristically calm. His closest confidants knew he feared nothing from the ethics committee after the meeting he described with Blatter and his royal masters the previous day. He had kept to his side of the bargain by pulling out of the presidential race, and in return the trumped-up charges Blazer had orchestrated would be dropped. 'If there is no candidate, there is no case.' That was what Blatter had said. So Bin Hammam was serene as Netzle tore off the strip of fax paper and glanced down at the words on the page. The lawyer pursed his lips and nodded gravely. Then he handed the sheet to his client.

When Bin Hammam began to read, his face contorted in consternation. He sat down heavily and continued scanning the page. The committee had found against him. A full-blown investigation would follow. And then, the terrible words: 'The official Mohamed bin Hammam is hereby provisionally banned from taking part in any kind of football-related activity at national or international level . . . . until the FIFA ethics committee will reach a decision in the merits of this matter.'

This wasn't the deal! Blatter had double-crossed him again! How could he have been so stupid as to trust him to be true to his word? The aides were furious. How dare Blatter screw Mohamed like this? How could the royals have allowed it to happen? Bin Hammam quickly recovered his poise, reassuring them that it was not over, and he would keep striving to clear his name. Netzle would begin putting together the appeal at once. But the accused man knew he had thrown away all his bargaining chips, and now Blatter was in the clear and sailing towards re-election unopposed. The cold hand of fear was closing around his heart.

At 6pm sharp, Damaseb emerged to address a packed press conference alongside Jérôme Valcke. The air crackled with anticipation. FIFA's day of reckoning had dominated the headlines and bulletins all day, with broadcasters and live-bloggers struggling to feed the beast of 24-hour news with what scraps they could glean as the hearings progressed in secret on the hilltop. The reporters were champing at the bit, desperate for something substantial to report to follow all the filler they had churned out manfully in anticipation of this moment.

The judge infuriated the journalists further by spending 20 soporific minutes explaining the procedures of the ethics committee without reference to the fate of the three accused men. Eventually, he cut to the chase. With regards to the allegations against Bin Hammam and Warner, Damaseb said: 'We are satisfied that there is a case to answer. There is going to be a full inquiry.' Two of FIFA's most powerful men, together controlling the game across all of Asia and the Americas, were to be suspended while the bribery allegations were properly probed. The announcement exploded like a mushroom cloud billowing skyward from the FIFA hilltop. Twitter lit up instantly and within minutes the breaking story about the suspensions was flashing up on every TV bulletin and newswire.

Damaseb concluded by dismissing the charges against Blatter. He told the press conference that he accepted the president's evidence that he had told Warner not to hand out cash in Port of Spain. 'No investigation against Blatter is warranted,' the judge said. As for the other two, their final fate would be known some time in late June or July. Then, the ethics judge handed over to Valcke, who confirmed that the presidential election would go ahead as planned on 1 June. The room filled with angry murmurs.

'Surely FIFA must postpone this election?' a British journalist called out.

'Why?' Valcke shot back. 'The allegation against Blatter has been cleared by the committee. Why should we postpone the election?'

Soon after the press conference wrapped up, FIFA released a

statement making its position plain: 'The Ethics Committee considered that a provisional suspension was required while the investigation continues, taking into account the gravity of the case and the likelihood that a breach of the FIFA Code of Ethics and the FIFA Disciplinary Code has been committed. Regarding the proceedings opened against FIFA president Joseph Blatter, at the request of Mohamed bin Hammam, for a potential breach of the FIFA Code of Ethics – all charges were dismissed in full. The Ethics Committee found that no breach of the Code of Ethics had been committed and they will meet again in due course in order to take a final decision on the matter after gathering more information and evidence on the cases.'

Bin Hammam watched in horror as his dreadful fate unfolded. It was as if his whole world was crumbling around him. Things were about to get much worse. Jack Warner was on the warpath, and he was ready to unleash the 'tsunami' of scandal he had threatened before the hearing, even if it engulfed his friend Bin Hammam. In the early hours of the following morning, Warner sent Najeeb Chirakal an email containing a statement he was about to release to the world.

'I have learned this evening via the media that I have been provisionally suspended by the FIFA ethics committee. This has come both as a shock and surprise to me,' he raged. 'At the conclusion of the enquiry I specifically requested that I be notified of any decision as I had learned via the media before attending the hearing that a decision would be handed down at 5.00pm. Despite leaving my contact details, up to this point, I still have not received any notification from the FIFA.' The statement continued with a rambling diatribe against the ethics committee, who he said had treated him unfairly in every possible way.

It was at the end that Warner dropped his bombshell. He revealed a private email exchange with Jérôme Valcke, in which the FIFA secretary general had given a devastating assessment of

Bin Hammam, and Qatar's World Cup campaign. 'On May 18 when I realised that the political battle between Blatter and Bin Hammam was getting out of hand I wrote Secretary General Valcke,' Warner had written, 'telling him, among other things, that the outcome of the elections may cause some fracture in the Arab world which we can ill afford now and that I will like to ask Bin Hammam to withdraw from the race.' Then came Valcke's response.

'For MBH, I never understood why he was running. If really he thought he had a chance or just being an extreme way to express how much he does not like anymore JSB. Or he thought you can buy FIFA as they bought the WC.'

Those few short lines were to cause mayhem. The secretary general of FIFA had accused Qatar, and Bin Hammam, of buying the 2022 World Cup. Warner's statement concluded ominously: 'I intend to say a lot more on this matter shortly. In the meantime, I will vigorously defend my reputation as well as the reputation of the rest of the Caribbean members.'

Valcke's incendiary email shattered FIFA's attempt to screen off the corruption scandal ahead of the presidential election. The proof that the secretary general privately believed Qatar had 'bought' the World Cup had all the hallmarks of a smoking gun. Coming in the wake of the bribery allegations from the House of Commons and the downfall of the country's most senior football official in a blizzard of brown envelopes, this looked like an obvious *prima facie* case for scrutiny by the ethics committee.

When Blatter announced a surprise press conference the following day, the assembled journalists were certain a big announcement was coming. Surely the plan for a 2022 World Cup in Qatar could not sail blithely on with such grave allegations swirling? Blatter himself had mooted a re-vote only days before. Wouldn't the tournament at least have to be suspended while the matter was investigated? Paul Kelso, the *Daily Telegraph*'s chief sports writer, tweeted a 'hunch' about what was to come. 'The 2022 World Cup will not take place in Qatar. See me in 2021 if I'm wrong,' he wrote a few moments before the press conference began.

The journalists piled back into the auditorium, and their editors were poised for another newsflash from Zurich. They saw that a single podium had been placed at the front. Jérôme Valcke was the first figure to emerge, striding in alone. The secretary general faced the press pack and explained gruffly that he just wanted to straighten out a few little things about his email to Jack Warner before Sepp Blatter came in to address them.

'I'd like to clarify, I may use in an email a lighter way of expression by nature,' he began. 'A much less formal tone.'

'Oh, that's all right then,' one journalist muttered. Valcke continued.

'Having said that, when I refer to the 2022 FIFA World Cup in that email, what I wanted to say is that the winning bid used their financial strength to lobby for support. They were a candidate with a very important budget and have used it to heavily promote their bid all around the world in a very efficient manner. I have at no time made, or was intending to make, any reference to any purchase of votes or similar unethical behaviour.' The journalists exchanged incredulous glances. Sometimes, FIFA's fancy footwork when dodging a scandal was a wonder to behold.

The secretary general disappeared and the journalists were left to wait for Blatter's appearance. More than 15 minutes passed, with the suspense heightening with every second. 'Genuine anticipation here,' Paul Kelso tweeted. 'Don't think anyone in this room is certain what Blatter is going to do or say. Stick, twist or fold?' While the journalists were waiting impatiently, their smartphones began to ping with an email sent out by the Qatar 2022 bid team. 'Mr Valcke's statement was clearly taken out of context but again Qatar's name has been dragged through the mud,' it said. All wrongdoing was categorically denied, and the bid leaders were outraged that their reputation had been so besmirched.

At last, the FIFA president appeared at the side of the auditorium and crossed the floor, wearing a jet-black suit, a chrome-coloured tie and a theatrically sombre expression. Blatter squared himself with both hands on the podium and told the journalists he wanted to address them alone, like this, and not as he usually did from a dais flanked by his officials. He began with the sorrowful tone of a father whose children have strayed.

'I regret what has happened. In the last few days and weeks, great damage to the image of FIFA but especially also a lot of disappointment to football fans,' he said. But a new dawn beckoned. The scandals of the past were behind; the FIFA family was ready to reunite and sally forth to the sunlit uplands of another four years under his leadership. 'What we have to do is in the congress to get a unity in solidarity and to look forward for the next four years. Will not be an easy task, but together we can do it . . . We go together for the good of the game, and . . . for the fans of football and for the perception of the game in our society.'

Eventually, Blatter turned to the matter of the moment. The allegations *The Sunday Times* had sent to the House of Commons about Qatar buying World Cup votes. The journalists' pens were poised above their pads, ready for the big announcement – but Blatter's words confounded them all. 'We were happy . . . that we have not received any evidence whatsoever from *The Sunday Times* or from any announced whistleblower with regards to allegations made,' he said. 'Therefore, what shall we do?' The president paused for emphasis, scanning the room with an indomitable stare. 'Nothing,' he said, with a clench of the jaw. 'The World Cup 2022 is not touched by that.'

Even for Blatter, this was a breath-taking piece of duplicity. The evidence *The Sunday Times* had sent to the House of Commons came from the package of undercover tapes which FIFA had been sitting on since last October. The newspaper had put its whistle-blower in touch with FIFA, and she had been ready to testify on the basis of conditions of anonymity and legal protection, which the organisation was in the middle of negotiating. Now, Blatter was dismissing her evidence out of hand and extinguishing any possibility of a proper investigation into the allegations that Qatar had rigged the ballot with massive bribes.

'I believe that the decision taken for the World Cup in 2022 was done exactly in the same pattern and in the same way as the 2018 tournament,' he told the press conference. 'There was no problem for FIFA or the Exco to act in this direction. I say, as I said in the beginning, there is no issue for the 2022 World Cup.' There was bewilderment among the assembled journalists. Only a week ago, Blatter had been talking about a re-vote. Now, suddenly, he was telling them the tournament in Qatar was set in stone. What had changed?

The FIFA president had maintained his studied tone of sombre dignity thus far, but when the time came for the journalists to ask questions the mask quickly slipped. Confronted with the suggestion that FIFA was in the grip of a crisis, Blatter scowled and snapped off his translation headset.

'Crisis? What is a crisis?' He waved his hand irately. 'If somebody of you would describe to me what is a crisis then I would answer. Football is not in a crisis ... We are *not* in a crisis, we are only in some difficulties,' he said, adding firmly: 'These difficulties will be solved *inside our family.*'

Next Tariq Panja from Bloomberg wanted to hear Blatter's thoughts on Valcke's email, which 'seems to allege that Qatar bought the World Cup'. Did the president think his secretary general's comments were appropriate? Blatter stonewalled him.

'I do not answer this question.' There was a cacophony at the back of the hall. Matt Scott from the *Guardian* had become enraged.

'You must answer that question!' he was shouting repeatedly. 'You are the person who is responsible!' Scott was quickly silenced by a spin doctor, but Blatter bit back. He raised his arm and wagged his finger censoriously.

'Listen gentlemen. I accepted to have a press conference with you alone here. I respect you. Please respect me, and please respect the procedure of the press conference ... Don't intervene. We are not in a bazaar here, we are in FIFA house and we are in front of a very important congress, so please.'

The president's answers became increasingly fevered. 'There are devils in the world but we have to fight against these devils,' he frothed. The 'survival of FIFA is at stake'. Without him at the helm, the organisation would suffer 'irreversible damage', and even 'disappear into a black hole'.

Another journalist at the back began shouting that Blatter had refused to answer important questions about corruption in FIFA and the world deserved answers. The spin doctor ordered silence, but again Blatter barked retorts into his microphone, drowning out the unamplified journalist who was still thundering at the back.

'I have asked for respect. I have only asked for respect, nothing more. I have been respectful to you,' he snarled.

'Have the respect to answer questions! You do not answer questions!' the journalist shouted. The spin doctor ordered silence and passed the microphone to another member of the pack. But he had chosen badly.

'This is a press conference and I thought it was for asking questions,' the new inquisitor said. 'There are so many more people here who want to ask questions, and it's not about respect!'

'I have answered the questions, and now I thank you for attendance,' said Blatter, snatching up his black leather folder and preparing to leave the podium.

'But you have said this is about ethics ...'

'Thank you,' Blatter said emphatically, turning to go.

'... and this is about FIFA ...' The reporter's microphone was shut off, but he carried on almost inaudibly: 'Warner has come up with new allegations ...' Blatter had left the podium and taken a few steps towards the door, but he turned back and grabbed the microphone.

'Listen, listen,' he hissed. 'I will not go into discussions individually with people – they like to create problems.' Gripping the top of his upturned folder, he balanced on the podium and hunched forwards with his eyes narrowed. 'I just want to tell you one thing,' he said, but one of the reporters close to the front was now emitting a loud, hollow laugh. Blatter shot him a piercing stare. 'Yeah, you can laugh,' he spat, with a dismissive flick of the wrist. 'That's also an attitude. Elegance is also an attitude! Respect is also an attitude!' He jabbed his hand angrily between clauses. 'Yeah, sure. I think that something I have learned in my life ... when I was in a press conference and it was said it was finished, then I said, thank you.' He spun sideways and bolted towards the door. There was a smattering of sarcastic applause.

The press conference had been a PR disaster, but Blatter didn't much care about that sort of thing. The world's media could think what they liked – the fact was he was adored by the children of the FIFA family and with Bin Hammam gone they would re-elect him unopposed in two days' time, come what may. That little bun-fight at the end notwithstanding, he had delivered the main message he needed to get across. The World Cup was staying in Qatar, and that was final.

Bin Hammam was already heading home to Doha, but Blatter's remarks gave him cause for relief when they reached him. At least that part of the deal had been honoured, he thought. At least the Qatar World Cup was in the clear.

*

The disgraced Qatari football boss had demanded that the ethics committee provide him with its reasoned decision in time for him to lodge an appeal ahead of the FIFA congress. Their failure to do so meant he was barred from entry, and there was therefore no point remaining in Zurich. Before he took off, he released a statement vowing to clear his name. 'I am very sad and disappointed over what has happened in the last days. I will never accept how my name and my reputation have been damaged. I will fight for my rights. I thank all the people who have supported me during the last weeks and will support me further. Good days bring you happiness, bad days bring you experience.'

The presidential election went ahead at the congress on 1 June. It was a cool, drizzly morning in Zurich. Blatter stood up and opened the day's proceedings with his customary platitudes about unity in the FIFA 'family'. There was a faint nod to the choppy waters buffeting the organisation from all sides. 'The FIFA ship must be brought back on the right route,' he said. 'And I am the captain. And I can only do it with your help.'

Jérôme Valcke appeared next, to take a roll call of member associations from Afghanistan through to Zimbabwe. After ten minutes of anaesthetic tedium, he announced that 'The two hundred and eight member associations are all present, Mr President,' and the room filled with relieved applause.

A brief upset followed. David Bernstein, the chairman of the English Football Association, took the stage and made a short but assertive speech calling for a delay in the FIFA presidential election. 'A lot of people have warned me I shouldn't be making this speech,' he began, 'but FIFA is a democratic organisation.' Or, at least, it should be. 'The election has turned into a one-horse race. Only with a contested election will the winner have . . . a proper, credible mandate. We are faced by an unsatisfactory situation and universal criticism from governments, sponsors, media and public.' Such impudence was simply not to be borne in the FIFA family. Bernstein could not have anticipated the savagery of the lashing his daring remarks would provoke.

His speech was followed by a series of endorsements for Blatter and a barrage of attacks on Bernstein. A delegate from Haiti stood first to deliver a sugary five-minute ode to Blatter. Next came the head of the Congo FA, who praised Blatter and lashed out at the English. 'He who accuses must provide evidence ... A single candidate sometimes proves that people are satisfied with that candidate,' he bellowed, to loud applause from the floor. The delegate from Benin declared: 'We must be proud to belong to FIFA. We must massively express our support to President Blatter. Please applaud!' and the hall erupted. An official from Cyprus was the next to stick his studs into Bernstein. 'Allegations – what a beautiful English word,' he scoffed. 'Someone stands up says a few things ... without a single shred of truth.' At the end of the verbal stoning of England's now cowering FA chairman, a vote was taken on his proposal to postpone FIFA's presidential election. It was torpedoed with 172 votes to 17.

Satisfied at seeing an opponent so comprehensively crushed, Blatter climbed back onto the stage to offer some more pearls of wisdom from the bridge of the FIFA ship. 'I personally have had to face the public's anger,' he said. 'But I am the captain weathering the storm!' The nautical metaphors came thick and fast. 'This has been a difficult period in FIFA's history, and I have admitted it readily. Not only is our pyramid shaking but our ship has taken water.' The solution was another four years of Blatter's presidency. 'This is the reason why we must put the ship back on course. We need a leader, someone who will accept his responsibility,' he said.

The president went onto unveil his heavily trailed programme of 'radical' reforms. He proposed that future World Cup hosts should be selected by FIFA's full congress of 208 people, and not by the executive committee alone. He promised to make the ethics committee more professional and independent, with the catch that its members should be elected by the congress. Another committee would be established to examine FIFA's corporate governance. 'Football belongs to everyone and we are in charge,' he shrilled. 'I have found my voice again. If you agree with me, say it!' The delegates applauded long and hard.

It had been a while since anyone insulted the English, and Julio Grondona wanted to put that right. 'We always have attacks from England which are mostly lies with the support of journalism which is more busy lying than telling the truth,' Argentina's executive committee member declared. 'This upsets and disturbs the FIFA family.' He went on: 'It looks like England is always complaining, so please I say will you leave the FIFA family alone, and when you speak, speak with truth.'

The day before, Grondona had given an interview to a press agency in which he called the English 'pirates' and added: 'Yes, I voted for Qatar, because a vote for the US would be like a vote for England. And that is not possible.' He revealed what the price of his vote for England would have been. 'With the English bid I said: "Let us be brief. If you give back the Falkland Islands, which belong to us, you will get my vote." They then became sad and left.'

When Grondona had finished ranting, Valcke stepped up to announce it was time to adjourn to lunch. As soon as the delegates returned, the Spanish Exco member Ángel María Villar Llona was on his feet decrying FIFA's critics and praising Blatter amid thundering applause. 'The problem of some comments in the paper came from some people who may have lost in the World Cup elections ... They associated us with crimes we have not committed, they insult, they attack our freedom. It's enough!' he declaimed. 'Let's talk about the main issues ... for the last twelve years this gentleman,' – he gestured towards Blatter – 'has done them. He is a great president and I respect him.' The Spaniard poured scorn on the notion of any independent investigation into the corruption allegations surrounding the 'the football family'. 'You are fathers,' he said to the delegates. 'Would you let people from the outside into your family to sort out problems?'

Now, at long last, it was time for Blatter's re-election. The president was applauded when he announced graciously that he would leave the room while the votes were cast. After all, this was a democracy, and it was a secret ballot. Before he left, Blatter offered a last piece of advice to the voters on how to make up their minds. 'It is a question of trust and confidence,' he counselled.

Each delegate was invited to go to a booth one at a time and submit his secret vote. The results were due in ten minutes. At the end, the announcement came that 203 ballot papers had been deposited in the urns and five officials began solemnly sorting through them. The result was recorded and passed to Julio Grondona, who stood to announce the winner. Blatter was re-elected with 186 of the 203 votes cast. Victory music filled the hall and the president returned to the arena clutching a bouquet of flowers and blowing kisses.

'Ladies and gentlemen ... I thank you for your trust. I thank you from the bottom of my heart,' he said. 'And together we will have four years, provided the Lord gives me life, the energy and the strength to continue on our path and to do our job. I'm happy that we were able to bring today into FIFA this solidarity, this unity, that enables us, with sufficient courage and a positive standpoint, to move forward ... We are going to put FIFA's ship back on the right course, in clear, transparent waters. We will need some time, we cannot do it from one day to the next, but our pyramid is intact because the foundation is solid, just as solid as our game. I would simply like to tell you that I am touched and honoured and I thank you. But at the same time this is a challenge for me, and I accept it. Let's go together. Something marvellous has happened today.'

Chapter Twenty

I Have Seen the Ugly Face of Football

Precisely six months had passed since Mohamed bin Hammam's great triumph amid the snow fields of Zurich and his circumstances could not have been more changed. Everybody had wanted to be his friend in those months after Qatar's improbable victory when he bestrode the football world like a colossus, jetting from handshake to handshake in the four corners of the earth as his whirlwind presidential campaign had gathered momentum.

And now this. Bin Hammam had never been a man to lounge around his home, but here he was in Doha, excluded from the theatre of intrigue and politics in Switzerland where he belonged. He should have been there at the FIFA congress challenging Sepp Blatter to a proper contest – instead of watching him being crowned unopposed on the television. It had been a nauseating spectacle. Now he was languishing in Qatar wondering how to fill his afternoon with the temperatures reaching over 40°C, as they had done fairly consistently since the beginning of May. It was, of course, a reminder to Bin Hammam that this was the time of year that the World Cup would be played. Despite his new lowered personal circumstances, he had to keep his eye on the main prize for the sake of his country.

Something had to be done about Jack Warner. His 'only brother in football' was an ally when times were good, but Warner was clearly out to save his own skin and his method of doing it was by flaying others. Bin Hammam had been furious when Warner had released the Jérôme Valcke email speculating that his countrymen had bought the right to host the World Cup. That had been unforgivable and no way to repay a friend. Now the whole of FIFA was trembling at the possibility that Warner might unleash the 'tsunami' of scandal he had threatened, whatever it might be.

There were plenty of skeletons lying beneath the FIFA hilltop and the man from Trinidad was someone who knew exactly where most of them were buried, having spent the last three decades grubbing around in the dirtiest corners of football administration. Warner had been close at hand throughout Bin Hammam's World Cup campaign and was privy to many secrets – not least the payments into his own account from the billionaire's slush funds. He had to be silenced. The best way to do that was to give him what he wanted, and Jack only ever wanted one thing. Money.

This one had to be a big payment. On 8 June, a week after Warner had threatened the tsunami, a message pinged on Najeeb Chirakal's smartphone: 'Could you please let Mr bin Hammam know that I am trying to contact him with an urgent message. I believe he has my number.' It was from a kindly, bespectacled middle-aged woman called Joanne Mora, who acted as Warner's assistant and described herself as the 'chief administration officer' in the football official's group of private companies. It was clearly an important call. Mora had been up at 5am to send the email Chirakal.

The subject of the call to Bin Hammam was a $1.2 million

payment to Warner from the Kemco slush fund. Within a couple of hours, Mora sent Chirakal the first of several emails that day which were to give details of how the cash should be paid. In order to disguise the payment, Mora asked for $412,000 to be paid into her own account, $432,000 into an account controlled by Warner's son Daryl and a further $368,000 into a company called We Buy Houses Ltd, owned by the FIFA official. All three accounts were in the same branch of the First Citizens Bank in the northern fishing district of Tunapuna, Trinidad. Chirakal dutifully arranged for the money to be paid through Kemco in the following days.

Now that Jack was getting paid, any fractures in the relationship with his brother in Qatar were quickly plastered over. The two men were planning to fight the ethics committee's decision to suspend them and they set about getting their stories straight over a string of calls and emails. FIFA had announced that there would be an independent investigation by the Freeh Group, a US company owned by the former FBI director Louis Freeh, into the bribery allegations, and both Bin Hammam and Warner were outraged. They were simply not prepared to deal with these American interlopers. FIFA's internal problems should be kept inside the FIFA family. Wasn't that what Blatter was always saying? Both Bin Hammam and Warner resolved to refuse to speak to Freeh and his sidekick Tim Flynn.

The contract had been a breakthrough for Freeh, who had been attempting to persuade FIFA to hire him as its 'independent ombudsperson' for some time. In an email back in February to Valcke and FIFA's director of finance, Markus Kattner, he had set out his vision for the role he could play. 'I believe that the time is ideal now for the President to announce a new, comprehensive plan to establish the strongest ethical and anti-corruption governance structure for FIFA,' he wrote. And he, Louis, was just the man for the job. 'One recommendation would be for him to appoint me as an independent "Ombudsperson" who would function as a public "clearing house" for corruption or ethical complaints alleged against FIFA and its associated officials. (As an option, this could also be established to be an investigative facility which would report its findings/recommendations directly to the President. However, the Ombudsperson role can be simply a "reporting channel" for the President).'

The benefits of such a scheme would be endless. 'The costs associated with its operation (eg, a "hot line," minimal staffing, administrative, etc.) are very minimal and, conversely, the "reputational" and PR benefits are very immense if rolled-out properly and personally endorsed by the senior leadership. We realise how busy you are but I am convinced that such an action, taken now (when the public media has quieted a bit), would be a "win-win" for the President and FIFA.'

Blatter had decided that the time had come to claim that 'win-win', now he wanted Bin Hammam and Warner buried, and so his officials had picked up the phone to Freeh and asked him to come and sort out the former presidential challenger and his friend in the Caribbean. Flynn was now tearing around the world on a bottomless expense account, visiting officials in the Bahamas, Zurich and New York, piecing together their accounts of what had happened in Port of Spain.

Dozens of football officials were prepared to speak to them and they collected a whole raft of new affidavits corroborating the original accounts by Fred Lunn, Sonia Bien-Aime and David Sabir about what had occurred in Trinidad. Some of the officials had handed over records showing they had deposited their $40,000 gift in bank accounts straight after the congress. Others had been given letters by the CFU confirming that they had been given the cash for football development to enable them to carry it through customs. One had kept the original brown envelope, matching the one in Lunn's photograph, which he handed over.

The investigators had even managed to recoup about $80,000 of the cash that had been disbursed. But for all this industry, every effort they made to speak to either of the accused men themselves was frustrated.

While Bin Hammam refused to co-operate, the companions who had been with him on the Port of Spain trip were happy to leap to his defence when they had their collars felt by Flynn. Manilal Fernando remained a loyal champion of Bin Hammam throughout his suspension. On 16 July, he emailed his friend to say he had been contacted by the investigators. 'I would be happy to have a copy of your Statement for my personal guidance,' he said. Later, he sent Bin Hammam the statement prepared by Worawi Makudi, who had also been on the trip. Among his many talents, Fernando was the proud owner of a law degree, and he offered his friend in Qatar unlimited free legal advice. At the end of June, he asked Bin Hammam to send over his entire file and urged him to take a strong stance because 'the American lawyers will try to fix you.'

Back in Port of Spain, Mora was having trouble with the bank holding the accounts into which Bin Hammam had paid the $1.2 million for Warner. On 16 June she was forced to contact Chirakal again. 'The funds have hit the all respective accounts,' she wrote, 'but the banks are all asking for a letter from you stating that the funds came from you and the purpose.' She provided Chirakal with the wording for three letters to cover each of the payments. The first said: 'This is to advise that monies in the amount of US $412,000.00 was wire transferred to Ms Joanne Mora by Khalid Electrical and Mechanical to offset expenses associated with meetings held in Trinidad and Tobago, Zurich, Switzerland and New York, USA of delegates and officers of the Caribbean. Such costs include but are not limited to airfare, accommodation, meeting logistics, interpretation equipment and services, etc.' The other 'Kemco letters', again written on Mora's computer, were along similar lines but mentioned legal costs for an 'on-going matter'. Kemco's general manager sent the letters back to Mora that day.

While Warner was waiting to collect the $1.2 million waiting in the bank, a short statement appeared on FIFA's website on Monday 20 June which sent a shock through the global game. The president of CONCACAF had resigned all his positions in FIFA, ending his 29-year career as a football administrator. One of the game's biggest and most controversial beasts had gone. Since Warner was no longer involved in FIFA, the investigators from the Freeh Group were deprived of any right to pry into his affairs. He would not have to answer any questions or submit his financial accounts, which would have shown his past payments from Bin Hammam.

FIFA's statement accompanying his resignation left the world – and its own investigators – baffled. Warner was leaving while under investigation for bribery and yet Blatter showered him with praise. 'Mr Warner is leaving FIFA by his own volition after nearly 30 years of service, having chosen to focus on his important work on behalf of the people and government of Trinidad and Tobago as a Cabinet Minister and as the Chairman of the United National Congress, the major party in his country's coalition government,' the FIFA press statement said. 'The FIFA Executive Committee, the FIFA President and the FIFA management thank Mr Warner for his services to Caribbean, CONCACAF and international football over his many years devoted to football at both regional and international level, and wish him well for the future.' And then world football's governing body waved the magic wand and made all charges against Warner disappear. 'As a consequence of Mr Warner's self-determined resignation, all Ethics Committee procedures against him have been closed and the presumption of innocence is maintained.'

FIFA's own in-house investigator Chris Eaton had been away from Zurich and was intrigued to learn of Warner's resignation. He forwarded a Press Association report to his old friend Tim Flynn, who soon pinged back a reply.

'That got out quickly,' Flynn wrote. 'It will be interesting to see what he has to say if he talks to us.'

'He won't talk to you mate – that's why he resigned,' Eaton scoffed. 'He's fighting for his life now – and I don't care!'

'I agree,' said Flynn. 'If he does it will all be self-serving.'

'But he's also taken out his evidence against BH [Bin Hammam] – so chances are he has had an inducement to resign,' Eaton came back.

'I think he may come to Zurich to talk to us but it will be interesting to see what the terms were. They wont [*sic*] give us the agreement,' said Flynn. Eaton had been unaware of the negotiations with Warner, but his ears pricked up at the mention of an agreement.

'I've been out of the loop for a couple of weeks ... so if there has been a "pre-resignation" agreement, as there should have been, then good,' he wrote. 'And I would hope part of the condition of FIFA saying such things as: "Mr Warner is leaving FIFA by his own volition after nearly 30 years of service," [is] that full and frank disclosure is required, because I don't know how you (I mean, Louie and you guys) can write up this without inculpating Warner. So much then for his (temporary) presumption.'

'I agree,' said Flynn. 'That will be an interesting dance that will take place later this week ... Warner is trying to save his political life but I don't see it unless he tries to put it all on Bin Hammam. Unless of course, they take over the questioning from us. I will keep you in the loop.'

The two men had got at least one thing right: Bin Hammam had indeed paid Warner a large inducement, but the $1.2 million was still sitting in a Trinidad bank while its officials assessed whether any money-laundering laws had been broken. They were still unhappy, despite receiving the letters Mora had requested from Kemco. She once again wrote to Chirakal: 'Dear Najeeb, Please inform Mr bin Hammam . . . that all the funds have been or will be returned to source. No reasons were given.' It was a problem that was to bedevil the attempted transfer of funds for a few more weeks.

Warner had to find a new way to receive the money. He suggested an alternative route: the cash could be paid as a single sum of $1.2 million into his company J&D International, which had an account in Salt Lake City, Utah. He told Bin Hammam he was getting desperate. 'My dear brother,' Warner wrote in an email. 'We have a serious problem in paying all our legal bills since the local bank did not release the transfer but instead returned it to your bank. In the circumstances, can you be kind enough to have the full sum wired to the under-mentioned account for which I do thank you kindly. Time is of the essence.' Later the same day, he sent Bin Hammam a $20,000 bill from his lawyer, with the subject: 'Help'. However, the Salt Lake City transfer failed too, and Warner's staff turned to the Cayman Islands as a way to transfer the cash from Qatar. When Chirakal wrote to say he believed the money had finally been paid, Warner's delighted response read: 'Allah is great ! ! !'

But the joy was misplaced: that transfer too eventually bounced back. 'Just got a rude shock from our Bankers that your Bank has again returned the funds,' Mohammed Farid, Kemco's financial controller, wrote to Mora on 7 July. Mora responded: 'We are working feverishly on our end to address this distressing situation,' and quickly came back with a suggestion. The money should be sent 'in parts rather than the entire amount, within at least one week of each other (500K, 212K, 500K) [or] be sent from another account, possibly one that is more directly related to football and the reason for sending same could be payment for advisory/professional services rendered.' Three days later, Warner chimed in with an email directly to Bin Hammam. 'I'm financially desperate re the legal bills,' he pleaded. The following day, on 14 July, another failed attempt was made to pay the money – this time into an account held by Warner in New York.

A false invoice for 'professional services provided over the period 2005-2010' was then concocted as a fig leaf for the corrupt payment, and dated 15 December 2010. This time, the attempt to pay the cash appeared to have been successful. Warner had gone for good, and his tsunami had subsided far from the Doha shore in the clear blue waters of the Caribbean Sea.

As Jack was being taken care of, there was more good news for the Qatar bid as it sought to fight off accusations that it had bought the World Cup. It came curiously from Phaedra Al-Majid, the whistleblower who had alleged that she had witnessed the African executive committee members taking bribes from her bid team colleagues at the Luanda congress. On 1 July, she signed a witness statement completely retracting her allegations and publicly apologising to her former employees, and the three men she alleged had taken bribes: Issa Hayatou, Jacques Anouma and Amos Adamu. The barely believable U-turn by Al-Majid was a major coup for Qatar which instantly claimed she had wiped clean a major stain on its reputation. Although, as it happened, Majid's *mea culpa* moment had all been orchestrated by the Qatar 2022 supreme committee.

Blatter had already dismissed the allegations by the whistleblower on the eve of his re-election, claiming that she had not come forward with any evidence and promising that the Qatar World Cup would therefore remain untouched. In fact, Al-Majid had been negotiating with Eaton, through a London lawyer, to give her full account to FIFA under conditions that it maintained her anonymity and protected her from a legal action. Eaton had contacted *The Sunday Times* after Majid's allegations had been included in the newspaper's submission to Parliament the previous month, to see if its journalists would be willing to let him talk to the whistleblower. The newspaper sought permission from Al-Majid and provided her with a lawyer to make sure that any interview with FIFA did not expose her to any risk. She was a single mother with two children and she was anxious about being thrown to the wolves. She had every right to be nervous.

Al-Majid's lawyer had first contacted Eaton on 20 May and began discussing terms under which she could give evidence. Two days later a FIFA security colleague emailed Eaton confidentially about ways they might be able to discredit the whistleblower. He suggested that the investigator should: 'Ask the Qatar contact for her name and any background,' and 'We should research her background too. It may be there is something in it to use.' FIFA had proposed a meeting with Al-Majid on 25 May and she was still considering her position when, out of the blue, Blatter announced to the world's media that FIFA hadn't 'received any evidence whatsoever' from the whistleblower and the matter was closed.

Shortly after Blatter's surprise pronouncement, Nasser Al-Khater, the communications chief of the Qatar supreme committee, had contacted his old colleague at her home in Washington and told her he knew she was the whistleblower. Al-Majid would later say Qatar had threatened to invoke a non-disclosure clause in her employment agreement to sue her for $1 million if she didn't sign a statement retracting all her claims. This would have ruined her financially and put her children's future in jeopardy. She buckled. Al-Khater accompanied Al-Majid to an attorney's office in Washington on 1 July and sat next to her as she swore an affidavit confessing to her 'lies'. The Qatar supreme committee invited the BBC to do some filming of their preparations for 2022 and then offered an exclusive interview with Al-Majid by phone when they arrived in Doha.

'There was never anything suspicious or any wrongdoing on Qatar's part,' she told BBC's *Newsnight*.*

As for Chris Eaton, within a few months he was on his way to live and work permanently in Qatar. In January 2012 he announced to FIFA that he was taking his entire security team to work for the Doha-based International Centre for Sport Security (ICSS) – the multi-million-dollar contract he had been lining up in his talks with the Qataris. Eaton sent his new boss, Mohammed Hanzab, a briefing note setting out a detailed time-line of the intelligence his team had built up over the past two years at FIFA and took with him a detailed knowledge of every in-house FIFA investigation before and after the World Cup bid.

Eaton penned himself a note titled 'Reasons for leaving' as he pre-pared to go to Doha. The top item read: 'It's more salary, responsibility (all, not limited integrity issues) and greater potential for success.' He also wrote an excoriating intelligence 'brief' on FIFA as he departed for his new job in Qatar in which he branded 11 of the 24 men on the executive committee 'untrustworthy' or 'com-pletely untrustworthy' and was scathing of the men at the very top. The president, he wrote, was 'the epitome of a political leader. Compromises on all for ambition. No evidence of personal com-promise. Greedy and manipulative. Maintains relationships and loyalty mostly through largesse. Manages FIFA like it's a small club of colleagues. Ruthless.' As for Jérôme Valcke, the secretary general: 'Has a difficult post under the grace of the President ... Had visions of replacing Blatter. Not now. Is charmingly arrogant and carless [*sic*] of integrity, but not directly complicit. Ruthless.'

The departure was greeted with amazement by Valcke, who had first brought Eaton into FIFA. 'Dear Chris, It takes me as a

---

* Qatar said that although Al-Majid had withdrawn her allegations, she had been given a 'full and fair' opportunity to repeat them later to FIFA's investigators and that they had been 'tested, considered and dismissed'.

surprise! Why?' Valcke asked. When Eaton's departure leaked to the press, the secretary general finally lost his rag with the investigator. 'Again we are the stupid people having to react. I have asked to keep this information until we can communicate positively and again and again we are fucked. Nice. So do whatever you want. I am going home,' he fumed.

While Bin Hammam awaited the outcome of the Freeh Group investigation in Doha, there was a final little favour to attend to for one of the FIFA voters. Franz Beckenbauer was bringing a group of German shipping magnates to Qatar to discuss trade deals with the Gulf state in June 2011, and Bin Hammam would be their host. *Der Kaiser* had retired from the FIFA executive committee in the spring after the World Cup vote and, since April, he had been working as a consultant for Erck Rickmers, the owner of the German shipping firm ER Capital Holdings. His contacts in Qatar from his days in world football were part of the big attraction. The firm owns companies which transport oil and gas on the high seas and, thanks to their new star hire, they were coming to Doha to discuss 'a possible cooperation ... with Qatari investment funds and investment opportunities in the maritime sector'.*

Beckenbauer went back a long way with Rickmers. They were so close that his wife, Heidi, had been chosen to christen one of the firm's new supertankers – named *ER Bayern* after the footballer's old club – in a ceremony in Korea in August 2010. The shipping boss had followed up with a donation of $250,000 to Beckenbauer's charitable foundation. Now he was accompanying the football legend to Doha, along with three other executives from his firm.

* ER Capital Holdings confirmed that Beckenbauer worked for the firm as a 'consultant and ambassador' from April 2011 until March 2014 but said 'no contract resulted with any of the interested parties' from its trip to Doha and 'Mohammed bin Hammam was not present at these talks.'

They were joined by Marcus Hoefl, the sports agent who had arranged Bin Hammam's mysterious rendezvous with Beckenbauer in London on the eve of his withdrawal from the presidential race the month before. Najeeb Chirakal booked the group's flights and put them up in fine style in the Four Seasons Hotel.

The delegation arrived in Doha on 28 June, enjoyed Bin Hammam's hospitality and attended talks with the dignitaries in charge of Qatar's sovereign wealth funds. No deals were signed, but the ability to arrange such high-level access for his new employer was a big feather in Beckenbauer's cap – and it was all thanks to Bin Hammam. Rickmers wrote personally to the Qatari at his home address to thank him for all he had done a month after the group returned to Germany. That would be the last favour he would do for one of FIFA's World Cup voters.

On 1 July, Bin Hammam finally received a letter from FIFA enclosing the full report put together by Louis Freeh's team of investigators and informing him that the final hearing of the ethics committee would take place on 22 July. He hurriedly opened the attached document and began to scan through the pages. 'There is substantial credible evidence that cash was offered to and accepted by attendees of the CFU meeting held in Trinidad and Tobago on May 10-11, 2011,' the report said. 'This evidence comes in the form of witness statements, documents, and more than $80,000 worth of payments received at the conference that three football associations are willing to disgorge.'

It went on: 'There is no direct evidence linking Mr Bin Hammam to the offer or payment of money to the attendees of the Trinidad and Tobago meeting. However, there is compelling circumstantial evidence, including statements attributed to Mr Warner, to suggest that the money did originate with Mr Bin Hammam and was distributed by Mr Warner's subordinates as a means of demonstrating Mr Warner's largesse. Indeed, the funds were offered to attendees shortly after Mr Bin Hammam's campaign speech.'

The Freeh report noted that, although Warner's resignation letter had promised 'cooperation with the FIFA Ethics Committee in the resolution of the ongoing investigations into alleged irregularities pertaining to the recent visit of Mohamed bin Hammam to Port of Spain,' he had subsequently told reporters he would 'die first' before speaking to the investigators. Their numerous attempts to speak with him had been unsuccessful, and he had finally confirmed his refusal to cooperate in writing on 26 June, accusing them of being part 'of a trans-Atlantic cabal' which was trying to destroy him.

The report noted that Bin Hammam had also 'refused to speak with Investigative Counsel working for the FIFA Ethics Committee'. He had also refused to provide his bank statements for review and claimed that telephone records the investigators had demanded did not exist.

The report made grim reading, but here was a small glimmer of hope for Bin Hammam. It said in plain black ink that there wasn't *actually* any evidence that he had anything to do with the cash envelopes. Almost all the Caribbean officials recalled Warner telling them to collect their gifts upstairs, and later saying they came from him, but no one could remember anything linking Bin Hammam to the payments beyond what Warner had said. Worawi Makudi, Hany Abu Rida, Manilal Fernando and Michelle Chai had all spoken to the investigators to confirm they had not seen any evidence of money being transported into Port of Spain on Bin Hammam's private jet, or distributed in the hotel. Surely no court would convict on that basis? Netzle was already hard at work using all his forensic legal brainpower to tear the Freeh report to shreds.

A week after Bin Hammam received his copy of the document, on 7 July, he was appalled to see it extensively quoted in a flurry of press reports. There had been a leak. 'FIFA find evidence of

Jack Warner and Mohamed bin Hammam corruption,' the headline in the *Daily Telegraph* blared. That day, Najeeb Chirakal
forwarded the entire file to Hassan Al-Thawadi.

The secretary general of the Qatar 2022 supreme committee
was keeping a close watch on Bin Hammam's case. He found
himself in a terrible bind. Al-Thawadi revered this wise elder who
had taken the bid committee's young leaders under his wing and
taught them so much about the world of football politics. They
knew how much they owed him. Everyone had expected Bin
Hammam to play a huge part in the preparations for the World
Cup he had worked so hard to bring to Doha, and Al-Thawadi
had been looking forward to working alongside his mentor to
bring the bid's grand plans to fruition over the next decade.

Only ten days before the scandal had broken in the Caribbean,
he had been busily negotiating with Elie and Mona Yahchouchi,
the partners in Bin Hammam's new IT company, which was in
line for a multi-million-dollar contract to deliver digital services to
the tournament in 2022. He had done all he could to get Bin
Hammam's presidential push off to a flying start, too –
bankrolling a private jet from the supreme committee's central
funds and engaging Netzle to advise on the campaign. He had
grown close to Bin Hammam, but not so close that he couldn't see
the full horror of the situation when he read the Freeh report.

Al-Thawadi was the chief custodian of the Qatar World Cup
project, and it was his job to keep the poison of scandal away
from the Emir's 'big cake'. Much as it pained him, he knew that
Bin Hammam had become toxic and he needed to be kept at
arm's length now more than ever. That IT deal would have to be
junked, for a start. And Al-Thawadi thought it would be best if
Bin Hammam retired from world football altogether. After Bin
Hammam had pulled out of the presidential race to protect the
World Cup bid, the Emir had generously granted him a long
enough leash to allow him to fight to clear his name – as long as

Qatar 2022 didn't get dragged into the mess. Al-Thawadi hoped very much that he would succeed, but when he read the Freeh report, he didn't feel hopeful. It was better for everyone if the wounded old timer accepted that his days in football administration were over, so Qatar could look to the future.

The secretary general of the 2022 supreme committee gave an interview to the *Guardian* from his office high up in Doha's Olympic tower at the start of July to try to polish away the dirt accumulating around his bid. Al-Thawadi was an accomplished media performer: engaging, assured and articulate. Perhaps sometimes he could be a touch abrasive, but today he was showing the reporter his soft underbelly, confiding that he had broken down and cried when Qatar won. 'So much good can come out of this World Cup,' he insisted. 'Breaking down prejudices between the Arab world and the rest of the world, bringing people together, a profound legacy.' The corruption allegations whirling around Qatar's bid were just a figment of the imagination, fuelled by anti-Arab prejudice, he said. 'I'm asking the world to look at us rationally. There is no evidence behind any of these claims, not a sliver ... Even if we had wanted to do anything improper, which we did not, we could not risk it because if it ever came out, the reputation of our whole country would be in tatters, the absolute opposite to what we are trying to achieve.'

Then, Al-Thawadi took his first tentative steps towards disowning his mentor. Bin Hammam had not, he said, been integral to Qatar's World Cup bid, and they should not be tarnished by the scandal which had brought him down. 'We never went and gave him instructions. There is no connection to what is happening to him now, and what happened with us,' he said. He couldn't bring himself to jettison the man completely – not yet. 'Also remember: he too is innocent until proven guilty,' Al-Thawadi said. 'And in our nature, as Arabs, as Qataris, we are not just going to abandon people for the sake of others in the world saying we should.' Within a few short months, he would find himself with no option but to do just that.

On 17 July, Al-Thawadi was taking one last look over a statement that had been drafted for Bin Hammam by the Qatar 2022 team, for the greater good of the World Cup dream. It was five days before the accused man was due to appear one last time before the ethics committee. Satisfied that the right tone had been struck between protestations of innocence and resignation to the inevitable, he sent the statement to Najeeb Chirakal, with an instruction to 'Please forward the below statement to Mr Bin Hammam'.

It read: 'On the 22nd of this month, I will travel to Zurich for my hearing in front of the FIFA Ethics Committee. It is no secret that the last two months have been disappointing. My hopes of a fair trial have been jeopardised by continuous leaks of information and public comment from certain people involved in the process.

'In spite of this, my years serving football and FIFA give me confidence that the Ethics Committee will give me the fair hearing that I deserve, uninfluenced by political agendas or other interests. I trust that the committee will base their decision on factual evidence and come to a reasoned decision. I will fight my case to the end. If this means taking the matter to CAS or the Swiss Federal Courts – I am prepared. I will not rest until I clear my name.'

Then came the punch. 'Continuing the battle to prove my innocence and clearing my name will eventually allow me to retire from all football-related affairs. It is disappointing to leave a game behind that I truly love and am committed to. The majority of my life has been dedicated to serving the game and in particular the Asian Football Confederation. I intend to conclude my career on a high and am convinced I will be fully exonerated from the charges made against me.'

Bin Hammam read the statement, and his jaw set defiantly.

The Emir had promised him he would be allowed to clear his name *before* he was made to retire from the game. He knew it was inevitable at the end of all this, but announcing it now looked all too much like conceding defeat. He was a realist and he could see that his chances of surviving the ethics committee hearing unscathed were almost nil, with all the odds stacked against him, but he didn't want to admit it was all over. Not yet.

Two days later in Kuala Lumpur, Jenny Be was chatting to Victoria Shanti, a secretary in the AFC president's office. They hadn't seen their boss, whom they called 'P', for ages. He had been in Doha since his suspension – and they were sick with worry. But on 19 July, Be had news for her colleague.

'I spoke to boss on the weekend,' she said.

'Oh . . . how is he?' Shanti was eager to know.

'He is worried coz no matter what, they will pin it to him,' Be replied.

'Yeah, I thought so too,' Shanti said sadly. 'But the Emir not pressuring P to leave football?'

'No, this time, they backed off, coz he is fighting for his name,' Be explained. 'In their culture that is more important than life and death.'

'I see. But they might reopen the bid,' Shanti worried.

'No, Blatter gave his word.'

'Yeah right. I don't believe a word he says.'

'It is not that smart to go against a country's Emir, and one of the richest men at that,' Be reminded Shanti.

'Yes, money is everything,' she responded. 'Even Blatter knows that.'

The next day, Bin Hammam released an altogether more defiant version of the statement Al-Thawadi had sent him on his website. Some parts of the secretary general's draft had survived. Bin Hammam had assented to saying that: 'My years serving football and FIFA lead me to think, and presume, that at the very least the ethics committee will give me the fair hearing that I deserve, uninfluenced by political agendas or other interests.' But much of the statement struck a more strident tone, and all mention of retirement had been excised.

The evidence against him was 'weak and unsubstantiated', the allegations were 'flimsy and will not stand up to scrutiny in any court of law'. Bin Hammam was gloomy about his prospects – 'I am not confident that the hearing will be conducted in the manner any of us would like ... So, none of us should be completely surprised if a guilty verdict is returned' – but he vowed to 'travel a long and hard road to clear my name of the stain of this politically motivated affair'.

Bin Hammam chose not to go the hearing on 22 July – he had been booked into the Baur au Lac, but had cancelled his trip at the last minute. Instead, he was represented by Netzle and a formidable team of lawyers from Zurich, London and Washington. Eugene Gulland, his lead US counsel, arrived at FIFA headquarters under gunmetal skies sporting large round orange-rimmed spectacles under his helmet ofiron-grey hair. Bin Hammam had some of the finest legal minds in the world on his team, and they gave Damaseb's panel a run for their money. The first day of the hearing lasted 13 hours, running on till 10pm, and reconvened at 9am the following day. But it was no good. The ethics men were convinced that the Qatari presidential contender had been the source of the $1 million that had been handed out in cash in Port of Spain. At the end of the second day, the ethics judge emerged before a crowded press room and announced: 'Bin Hammam is hereby banned from taking part in any kind of football-related activity at national and international level for life.'

Gulland was quick to shoot out a statement. 'Mr Bin Hammam rejects the findings of the FIFA ethics committee hearing and maintains his innocence,' it said. 'He will continue to fight his case through the legal routes that are open to him. The FIFA ethics committee has apparently based its decision upon so-called "circumstantial" evidence, which our case has clearly demonstrated was bogus and founded on lies told by a senior FIFA official.' The next step was to take the case to the FIFA appeals committee, and the team got to work preparing their submissions right away.

Bin Hammam was desolate, but had known this was coming ever since his shock suspension the day after his deal with Blatter. 'I was expecting it actually,' he said glumly in an interview by phone from Doha. 'The ban for life, that shows how much these people are angry, how much they are full of revenge.' Asked if he meant revenge for standing against Blatter, he replied: 'Exactly. There is nothing else.' That evening, he sat for many hours brooding over what had come to pass. Riffling through some old papers, he happened upon a letter which brought the old days flooding back – the days when he had basked in the golden light of the president's gratitude and brotherly friendship. He read it and raged.

The next morning, the letter appeared on his website in a posting headed: 'The Reward.' It was the message Blatter had sent him back in June 2008, to mark his tenth anniversary as FIFA president. 'Without you, dear Mohamed,' he had written, 'none of this would ever have been possible.' It was an acknowledgement of all Bin Hammam had done to pave his path to the presidency with slabs of Gulf gold. Under the letter published on his website, Bin Hammam had written one line. 'This is only the battle, not the war,' it said.

In Kuala Lumpur, Bin Hammam's empire at the AFC was crumbling. Zhang Jilong had taken over as acting president when he was suspended, and the Chinese official had got his feet under the table with what some considered indecent haste. Manilal

Fernando had railed against seeing his friend so quickly supplanted. When Jilong had called an emergency meeting of the AFC to set the confederation's new course just a week after Bin Hammam's suspension, Fernando snapped. He sent a round-robin email calling for a freeze on any changes to AFC activities till its true leader was back at the helm. 'We must all stand behind our President Mr Mohamed bin Hammam Al Abdulla who has done so much in reforming and improving the AFC,' he said. 'We do not need any acting revolutions, what we need is stability and strength. The President I knew in Mr Hammam is an honest man, sincere in his beliefs, perhaps arrogant sometimes but never vicious and has been a good friend to me, to Football and therefore, we should stand united with him. There is no need to create any fuss or have meetings regarding this. Let him seek legal relief.'

There was no longer any hope of holding back the tide. Jilong had reacted to Bin Hammam's life ban by vowing to wash away corruption in Asian football, and the Qatari's enemies in the AFC were quick to capitalise on his ruin. 'It is the best news for Asian football and FIFA,' Peter Velappan, the confederation's former secretary general crowed. 'I have worked with bin Hammam. He totally polarised the Asian football family.' He went on: 'It is a fair decision. Justice is done. There is no better alternative. Now the whole world will know how Qatar won the hosting rights of the 2022 World Cup.'

Suddenly, the loyal cabal of aides inside the AFC were feeling very exposed. In the days after the ban, Jenny Be orchestrated a frenzied effort to shred all the evidence from the three years in which Bin Hammam had waged his World Cup campaign and then his presidential bid. Victoria Shanti was her main accomplice.

'Vic, I need you to take all P's correspondence (misc ones, i.e. via emails) except for letters and start shredding them,' Be wrote to the secretary in mid-July.

'Oh,' Shanti said, crestfallen. 'So soon.'

'Start from now,' Be urged. 'There are three years of filing to be shredded . . . also, please do it quietly.'

'So only official letters that he replied, don't shred?' asked Shanti.

'Yeah.'

'But all others such as emails and those from Peter Hargitay, shred?'

'Yes.' The shredding went on for days.

'Do I shred every email sent to P directly?' Shanti later asked.

'Yeah. Just from 2008 onwards. No need before.'

'There is an email from Moscow for P to consider a Russian for position on the AFC. Shred?'

'Yes,' said Be.

'For P's personal file,' Shanti asked, 'should I just keep it aside first or need to shred most of it?'

'Personal file contains what?' asked Be.

'Mostly from 2004 to 2007 . . . correspondences . . . invoices.'

'Keep that,' said Be. Back then, there had been nothing to hide. 'Only from 2008 to shred,' she told Shanti.

'The list of nominees from tech com from Hassan with P selecting them, should I shred?'

'Yes,' came the inevitable reply. 'Shred anything that you feel is sensitive . . . or could be used to tarnish him.'

By the end of the month, Bin Hammam's loyal aides were being forced out of the door. Jenny Be was marched out on 26 July. She wrote hastily to Michelle Chai before she went.

'They have come to collect my laptop and access card . . . I deleted all my emails and files except those in the server (official AFC business). Have you received your letter yet?'

'Not yet la,' said Chai. 'Of course delete all la. That's normal.'

'Don't leave anything easy for them. Let them work it out for themselves. Hehhehehee.'

'Hahahahahah,' Chai wrote back.

'Have some fun, life is too short,' Be told her friend. 'If you don't get your letter today then you have more time and can come help me carry my boxes.'

'Aiya … more time for what? Hahahahahaa.' Those were the last messages the pair would ever exchange as colleagues.

Chai and the AFC's finance director Amelia Gan were sacked soon after. Two days after her departure, Be wrote on Facebook: 'The measure of a man is the way he bears up under misfortune. I am proud to walk out of AFC having worked with a great man and true leader.' Two weeks later, she was still ruminating over the terrible fate that had befallen her beloved president. 'Never does the human soul appear so strong as when it foregoes revenge and dares to forgive an injury,' she wrote. 'So true,' Shanti commented underneath.

FIFA rejected Bin Hammam's appeal on 16 September. A month later, a tape was passed to the *Daily Telegraph* in London. It had been recorded on 11 May, and showed Warner telling the CFU delegates in Port of Spain that the cash gifts had come from their Qatari visitor. Bin Hammam's legal team was now preparing for his next appeal to the Court of Arbitration for Sport, and this latest leak gave his reputation yet another battering he could do without. Bin Hammam fumed. This was all part of Blatter's conspiracy to bury him for good, he was certain of it.

The man who had brought the World Cup to Doha was feeling increasingly isolated at home. By now, Hassan Al-Thawadi was at pains to disown his former mentor in public. At the start of October, he told the Leaders in Football conference at Stamford Bridge that Qatar 2022 had nothing to do with Bin Hammam and did not condone his appeal. 'Mohamed bin Hammam is his own man,' he said. 'He and Qatar 2022 are completely independent and separate. The appeal is his decision and his steps. We have to ride it out as patiently as having to ride out the whistleblower allegations and others.' Perhaps Al-Thawadi had forgotten the statement he had written for Bin Hammam back in July, declaring his intention to fight his appeal all the way to the Court of Arbitration for Sport if he couldn't clear his name before the ethics committee. Such disavowals were a very far cry from the happy days when the bid leaders had described Bin Hammam as their 'biggest asset'. How far he had fallen since then.

Meanwhile, back in Zurich, Blatter was busily implementing his electoral promise to set up an independent governance committee to lead the reform of FIFA. On 30 November, it was announced that he had appointed Mark Pieth, a professor of Criminal Law and Criminology at the University of Basel, to lead the new body. If Qatar's World Cup delivery team had cause for concern when they first heard the news, they needn't have worried. Blatter was no fool. It was soon announced that Pieth's panel would be looking to the future; he would 'not be supervising investigations into the past'.

Pieth showed he was the man for the job at his first FIFA news conference, saying: 'I don't care to rake up all that muck. I think I can be much more use looking into the future.' The law professor conducted a quick review of FIFA's practices and published a report in the spring which said its reaction to past scandals had been 'insufficient and clearly unconvincing'. He believed he had the remedy. The organisation should split its ethics committee into two chambers, one to investigate allegations and another to adjudicate them. Blatter sensed an opportunity. He hailed the idea as 'historic' and vowed to implement Pieth's suggestion forthwith.

Bin Hammam's growing team of lawyers had submitted his appeal to CAS, and they were feeling confident. They remained convinced that the charges would not stick in a court that was not controlled by FIFA. The tape of Jack Warner claiming the cash had come from Bin Hammam didn't prove anything against their client. The man from Trinidad was hardly renowned for his honesty and who knows what scam he might have been trying to pull off.

By February 2012, it was time for FIFA's own lawyers to respond to the appeal. They filed a 99-page submission to the Swiss court, which was never meant to be seen by outside eyes. It was a potentially incendiary document. Contrary to Al-Thawadi's claims that Bin Hammam had no part in the country's 2022 campaign, FIFA's own lawyers had noted: 'He played an important role in Qatar securing the 2022 World Cup.' They also highlighted the 'striking similarity' between the allegations against Bin Hammam and those against the Qatar bid which had surfaced in the House of Commons.

The submission said the messages Fred Lunn sent to Austin Sealey as the allegations about Qatari World Cup bribes broke on CNN were evidence that he believed the cash he had just been offered had come from Bin Hammam. Citing the 'SMS exchanges between Mr Lunn and Mr Sealey on 10 May,' FIFA's lawyers noted: 'The breaking story on CNN was about Qatari bribery in football, and they plainly believed that the payment was made by Mr Bin Hammam. There can be no doubt that the very striking similarity was being made by Mr Lunn ... between these bribery allegations on CNN and what had just happened to him only moments earlier in the CFU boardroom.'

FIFA's submission quoted extensively from the video recording of Warner claiming Bin Hammam had been the source of the cash, which had been leaked in October, and contained a section headed: 'If Mr Bin Hammam was not the source then who else was?' The lawyers argued: 'It is self-evident that no other body or person had any motive to provide the gifts. Still less did anyone else have the motive to do it at Mr Bin Hammam's Special

Meeting.' Bin Hammam's lawyers scoffed when they read FIFA's submission. It was laughable to expect a court to convict a man with no hard evidence just because no other culprit had been identified. They were confident of victory.

Zhang Jilong was watching events unfolding closely from the AFC headquarters in Kuala Lumpur. He had been acting head of the confederation ever since Bin Hammam's suspension, and the spectre of the former president's return if he overturned his ban was distinctly unappealing. The AFC had already turned a corner under Jilong, and the vast majority of staff who had not been part of Bin Hammam's trusted cabal found the interim regime a breath of fresh air. The fact was, however carefully the Qatari's loyal aides had tried to cover up for their departed boss, Jilong knew there were bombs under the carpet in Kuala Lumpur. So the AFC had quietly commissioned its own investigation into the activities of its former president as he prepared to make his appeal to CAS. The auditors from PricewaterhouseCoopers had arrived in force in February and were trawling through the sundry accounts Bin Hammam had used to make so many payments to his friends in world football.

The CAS hearing went ahead behind closed doors on 18 and 19 April in Lausanne. Bin Hammam did not attend, but once again sent his team of lawyers in to make his case. At the end of the hearing, Eugene Gulland issued a confident statement. This had been 'Mr Bin Hammam's first chance to answer charges against him in front of a court that is not controlled by FIFA'. The US lawyer was hopeful for a better outcome for his client.

Bin Hammam would have to wait for three months for the judgment, which was due on 19 July. Two days before it was handed down, he was hit side-on by an unexpected broadside from his old fiefdom. The Asian Football Confederation had announced his suspension. The PwC auditors had handed Jilong an excoriating report earlier that week, flagging up Bin

Hammam's 'highly unusual' use of the sundry debtors' accounts at the AFC.

'Our review indicates that it was common belief that this account was for Mr Bin Hammam personally and that all funds flowing through it were his personal monies,' the auditors noted. 'We question why Mr Bin Hammam would conduct his personal financial transactions through the AFC's bank accounts when the documents we have seen indicate that he already has several personal bank accounts in various countries.' The auditors had also found that 'payments have been made, apparently in Mr Hammam's personal capacity, to a number of AFC member associations and associated individuals ... Significant payments (totalling $250,000) have also been made to Mr Jack Warner for which no reason has been provided.'

In reality, what PWC had uncovered was just the tip of the iceberg, but it was more than enough to sink an already listing ship. By happy coincidence for FIFA, the same day as Bin Hammam's AFC suspension was announced, it had just unveiled the twin heads of its new ethics chamber, the former US prosecutor Michael Garcia as the investigatory chief and the German judge Hans-Joachim Eckert as the adjudicator. The PwC report from the AFC was the first item in their in-tray. It was time to bury the menace of the man from Qatar for good.

When the Court of Arbitration for Sport finally overturned the life ban imposed on Bin Hammam by FIFA's committee on 19 July, the joy of hard-fought victory was somewhat muted. CAS said there was 'insufficient evidence' against him, so it 'upheld Mr Bin Hammam's appeal, annulled the decision rendered by the FIFA Appeal Committee and lifted the life ban imposed'. But the panel said the decision was not 'an affirmative finding of innocence' because, although there was 'insufficient evidence', it was after all 'more likely than not that Mr Bin Hammam was the source of the monies'. They feared that his conduct, 'in collaboration with and most likely induced by Mr Warner, may not have complied with the highest ethical standards that should govern the world of football and other sports'.

Bin Hammam was weary. 'My wish now is just to quit and retire,' he told the BBC afterwards. 'I've served football for forty-two years – this last year I have seen a very ugly face of the sport and of football.' He said he had 'one mission' and that was 'to clear my name and then I say goodbye'. Almost exactly a year after Al-Thawadi had drafted a statement to that effect, Bin Hammam had finally accepted it was time to go. But first, he wanted to purge the stain that had now been placed on his reputation by his traitorous successor at the AFC.

A week later, on their first day in their new jobs, FIFA's new ethics double-act Garcia and Eckert announced that Bin Hammam was to be provisionally suspended while the new investigator sought further evidence of his role in the Port of Spain scandal and probed the new allegations from the AFC. Eckert handed down his reasoned decision for the suspension in August, citing several *prima facie* breaches of the code of ethics identified by Garcia. He noted that the PwC report listed payments 'out of the AFC sundry debtors' account ... controlled by Mr Bin Hammam to delegates of the Confederation Africaine de Football ... and a payment made to Mr Jack Warner ... in the amount of USD 250,000'.

Garcia had also advised that the report was 'of relevance to the recently closed proceedings before the Court of Arbitration for Sport' because 'contrary to what Mr Bin Hammam had stated in the course of the respective proceedings ... it results from the PwC report that Mr Bin Hammam had more than only one single bank account at his personal disposal.' With the new suspension in place, Garcia had the chance to get his teeth into his first big case.

Bin Hammam was disconsolate. To be shut out again a week

after being vindicated by CAS was too cruel a torment for an already badly beaten man. He wrote a letter to the member associations he had once ruled over in Asia, saying that the payments he had made had come out of his own bank accounts and were driven by a desire to help those in need. His letter cited five people from Bangladesh, Nepal and Kyrgyzstan whom he said he had helped, including two who had since died of cancer, one who had open-heart surgery, another for tuition fees for a FIFA programme, and the family of a 16-year-old from Nepal who died while playing football.

'Let me declare that as a human being with the personal means to help and coming from a culture and society where this is seen as a duty, I am proud of these accusations, and I welcome them,' he wrote. This was, he said, 'yet another attempt by Zurich through the infinite tools and power of FIFA to diminish and insult Asia's name by attacking me directly following the annulment of my previous FIFA ban by the Court of Arbitration for Sport'.

A second appeal to CAS, this time to overturn the temporary ban, failed in September. And now Garcia and the investigators at the AFC were pulling Bin Hammam's world apart piece by piece. News reached him that Amelia Gan, his former AFC finance director, had come under investigation by the Malaysian police over the theft of a financial document relating to a payment he had received. The AFC had informed police that the document was missing, and Gan's husband Kong Lee Toong was arrested and charged with theft. Bin Hammam's AFC trio had all taken refuge in the Gulf since they had been forced out of their old jobs in Kuala Lumpur: Gan and Jenny Be were both now employed by the Qatar Stars League, headed by Sheikh Hamad bin Khalifa bin Ahmed Al Thani, while Michelle Chai was director of club licensing for the professional league in the United Arab Emirates. Bin Hammam hated to see them dragged into this awful mess.

He was relieved when Malaysian prosecutors eventually dropped the charges against Lee Toong, without explaining their reasons, but things got worse at the start of October, when FIFA announced that Najeeb Chirakal had been banned from football. The unswervingly faithful aide had refused to co-operate with Garcia in any way when the investigator demanded information and documents about his master. Chirakal was 'banned by the FIFA Ethics Committee from taking part in all football-related activity, at any level, due to his lack of collaboration with the ongoing investigation proceedings opened against Mohamed bin Hammam', the official statement read. 'This failure to cooperate constitutes a breach of the FIFA Code of Ethics. The ban is effective immediately and will last for two months or until Chirakal cooperates with these proceedings as requested, whichever is earlier.' Bin Hammam's right-hand man never buckled under the pressure, and so his ban was never lifted.

Then, on 12 November, a new storm broke over Qatar's World Cup bid. *The Sunday Times* had obtained documents proving that the Al-Thawadi brothers had offered the son of Amos Adamu $1 million to host a dinner. All parties claimed the payment had fallen through, but the newspaper's damning documents were sent to FIFA headquarters and passed to Garcia. It was the last thing Qatar, or Bin Hammam, needed. After the latest scandal broke, the Emir pulled the plug on any further attempts to clear Bin Hammam's name. Sheikh Hamad had told him it was time to give in. Qatar couldn't fight on so many fronts. The battle had to come to an end, and he didn't want to hear any more from Bin Hammam on the subject of world football.

Michael Garcia submitted his final report to Eckert on 6 December. He had not found a scrap of extra evidence implicating Bin Hammam in the Port of Spain bribery scandal beyond that which had already been rejected by CAS, and so the case of the mysterious brown envelopes that had dashed his presidential hopes had been closed. But, now, FIFA was armed to the teeth with documents from the AFC which were enough to annihilate him. The Emir had made his wishes clear, and so before FIFA had a chance to ban him for life again, Bin Hammam quietly resigned on 15 December 2012. But FIFA was not taking any chances. This time, they were going to kill him off for good.

Two days after his resignation, world football's governing body released a statement on its website. 'In view of the fact that under the new FIFA Code of Ethics, the FIFA Ethics Committee remains competent to render a decision even if a person resigns, the Adjudicatory Chamber decided to ban Mohamed bin Hammam from all football-related activity for life,' it said.

'This life ban is based on the final report of Michael J. Garcia, Chairman of the Investigatory Chamber of the FIFA Ethics Committee. That report showed repeated violations of Article 19 (Conflict of Interest) of the FIFA Code of Ethics, edition 2012, of Mohamed bin Hammam during his terms as AFC President and as member of the FIFA Executive Committee in the years 2008 to 2011, which justified a life-long ban from all football related activity.'

And then, for the avoidance of any doubt, the statement made it clear he was never coming back. 'Mr Mohamed bin Hammam ... will never be active in organised football again.'

Twenty-One

After the Story, the Civil War

The moment had arrived. Summer had set in, the rulers of world football were about to descend on São Paulo ahead of the Brazil World Cup, and it was time for the journalists to push the button on the biggest story of their lives. Blake and Calvert had been frantically writing all week, pulling together the mountains of material they had gathered into a series of long articles, graphics, timelines, fact-boxes, document 'rag-outs' and side-panels for *The Sunday Times* edition of 1 June 2014.

The amount of space which had been made for the stories in the paper had swelled as their editors back in London had come to comprehend the enormous scale of the evidence. On Tuesday they had been asked to write enough to fill four full pages. That was already way in excess of the usual amount of room given to an Insight investigation, but by the end of the day it had grown to six. On Wednesday it was eight pages, then ten, and by Thursday morning it had been decided that the first 11 pages of *The Sunday Times* would be devoted to the astonishing story of the FIFA Files. That sort of coverage of a single topic was, as the paper's head of news Charles Hymas told the reporters, 'unprecedented outside a war'.

The stillness that had hung over the little attic bunker while the journalists had searched through their vast haul of documents was blown away by the mounting sense of urgency as the deadline approached. The source looked on in bewildered amusement when he popped in to find the attic suddenly full of the frenetic activity, raised voices and hammering of computer keys of a miniature newsroom on deadline. Calvert, who had learned to type on a metal Olivetti, had bashed out the tens of thousands of words he had to write so hard that his keyboard had to be junked and replaced halfway through the week. Blake sat bolt upright, her fingers flying over the keys, with a clenched expression of controlled panic as she reeled off page after page of copy with the deadline rushing ever closer.

The reporters fielded a constant flurry of calls from executives, colleagues and lawyers back in London. Martin Ivens, the editor of *The Sunday Times*, was backing the story all the way and throwing all the might of the publication's considerable resources behind it. Still, the FIFA Files remained a closely guarded secret, even inside newsroom, so Hymas had prepared a dummy news list with no mention of the Qatar World Cup to maintain the pretence that there would be nothing unusual about the 1 June edition of the paper. Only a select group of people were brought into the secret on a 'need-to-know' basis.

Ivens had deputised Bob Tyrer, the paper's toughest editor, to run his iron rule over the reporters' copy. Hymas was in charge of coordinating the stories, jig-sawing all the content onto the 11-page spread and working with selected designers, photographic staff, graphic artists and sub-editors to produce a package which landed a big visual punch. The newspaper's lawyers, Pia Sarma and Pat Burge, combed through the stories the journalists had sent down from the bunker, checking every word for fairness and accuracy against hundreds of supporting documents which had been couriered to London on an encrypted hard disc.

The paper's chief reporter Jonathan Ungoed-Thomas and its

defence correspondent Mark Hookham had been filled in on what their colleagues were up to. They were now digging up background on Mohamed bin Hammam's deals and assiduously contacting the scores of officials the newspaper intended to name to give them their right to respond to the evidence in the files. For secrecy's sake, they had been moved from their usual desks in the newsroom to sit in the Insight team's locked box office in a quiet corner on the floor below. Very few reporters had ever been in there before, and they gazed around at the jumble of mug-shots, wall-charts, target lists and scrawled findings plastered all over the walls from past investigations and chuckled.

'Not sinister at all,' Ungoed-Thomas joked to Hookham.

Blake and Calvert had written to Bin Hammam detailing the findings they planned to publish that weekend and setting out the questions they wanted him to answer. 'We are preparing to write a series of articles this weekend concerning new evidence about your central involvement in Qatar's successful World Cup bid,' the letter began. 'We will be publishing evidence of payments you made to senior football officials in exchange for supporting the bid.'

Soon after pressing send, they received a polite email from Bin Hammam's son, Hamad. 'Thank you for allowing us the opportunity to respond to the upcoming articles. However, my father and my family have no comment regarding this matter,' it said.

The journalists had also sent detailed questions to Hassan Al-Thawadi, and were amazed by the response that came back. The Qatar 2022 chief did not reply personally, instead instructing the law firm Schillings to send a threatening letter, which arrived at 4.10pm on Saturday. The solicitors wished to inform *The Sunday Times* that: 'Mr Bin Hammam was at no time officially or unofficially a member, employee, agent or consultant' of the World Cup bid, it said.

Blake and Calvert exchanged an incredulous glance. Officially *or unofficially*? Sheikh Mohammed had called him the bid's 'biggest asset' before the vote, for heaven's sake. The letter went on: 'At no time was he acting under instructions or with the authority of our client or any official individual or organisation on behalf of Qatar's bid for the 2022 FIFA World Cup™. As Mr Al-Thawadi has previously stated "[Mr Bin Hammam] and Qatar 2022 are completely independent and separate".' In fact, it said, officials on the committee had to devote a good deal of time to trying to convince *him* to vote for Qatar. 'Our client's activities in relation to Mr Bin Hammam were ... primarily directed towards obtaining his support for Qatar's bid. It is not a secret that ultimately our client was successful in winning his support, as it was with a majority of the FIFA Executive Committee members. All of our client's dealings with Mr Bin Hammam at all times were entirely above board and Mr Bin Hammam did not have a secret role in our client's bid as you seek to suggest.'

The bid's lawyers accused the journalists of 'a desperate attempt to find a new angle to criticise our client in order to serve what appears to be a pre-determined agenda intended to discredit our client, and the State of Qatar.' Their sole aim, the letter said, was to 'depict our client in a deliberately negative light with a view to pursuing Times Newspapers' long-standing objective of discrediting its successful bid'. It said 'any attempt to link our client to any alleged activities that may have been undertaken independently by Mr Bin Hammam would be false, entirely without merit and grossly defamatory of our client'.

It was a bizarre response. Calvert and Blake had expected the Qatar 2022 committee to distance themselves from Bin Hammam and point out that he had not been an official member of their bid team, but to claim he had no role *at all* in promoting the country's World Cup effort was preposterous. There was no evidence showing Al-Thawadi and his men knew Bin Hammam was making illicit payments, but the reporters had documents proving they had worked closely at numerous key moments in the campaign. Nonetheless, they wrote up the denials and inserted them into their stories.

By 7.30pm on Saturday evening, all the stories had been filed, approved by the lawyers, edited, sub-edited and placed on the page. The reporters had printed the 11 final page proofs as they were emailed through from London and ran across them with red pens poised, weeding out any last tiny slip-ups in the headlines or picture captions. Then, it was time. The chief sub-editor pressed the button and the first edition of *The Sunday Times* was sent off to the printers. The secret was out and an eerie calm descended on the little attic in the moments that followed. Blake and Calvert staggered out into the soft shadows of an early summer evening, punch drunk with tiredness, nerves and elation. There was nothing left but to wait.

The story splashed across the front of *The Sunday Times* under the headline 'Plot to Buy the World Cup' ricocheted around the globe before the paper had even hit the newsstands. The sub-heading read: 'Huge email cache reveals secrets of Qatar's shock victory' and the FIFA Files were puffed as a 'World Exclusive' revealing the 'bribes, bungs and slush funds' that helped buy the world's most-prized sporting tournament for a tiny Gulf state in the desert. The splash revealed how Bin Hammam had funnelled more than $5 million into the accounts of football officials across Africa from his ten secret Kemco slush funds to buy support. It also disclosed that Bin Hammam had bunged $1.6 million to Jack Warner and bankrolled Reynald Temarii's legal and private detective bills to stop votes for Qatar's rivals.

As soon as the story went live online, it exploded on social media and shot to the top of the television news bulletins, first in Britain, and then all around the world, reaching an audience of hundreds of millions.* Calvert and Blake felt like they had

---

* Centaur media estimated the 'Plot to Buy the World Cup' story had reached a potential global audience of 1.3 billion people.

detonated a nuclear bomb from their dark little cluttered bunker in this anonymous British suburb. Back at their hotel that evening, they huddled in the corner of the hotel bar with a bottle of prosecco, watching their story roll on the BBC News. Sometime around midnight, they were both jolted awake by a tap on the shoulder. It was Sam, the hotel barman. They had fallen asleep in their armchairs in front of the television. It was time to stumble downstairs to bed.

They woke the next morning to find the story still leading the television and radio news bulletins, and dozens of missed calls on their mobile phones from broadcasters around the world who wanted to interview them about the FIFA Files. The revelations had caught FIFA in the full glare of the world's media as its hundreds of delegates prepared to swarm into Brazil ahead of the 2014 World Cup. Many of the men who would be flying into São Paulo for world football's annual congress that month had hoovered up Bin Hammam's cash before his disgrace. The story was met with near-universal outrage. Political leaders, national football association bosses, players, anti-corruption campaigners and fans around the world called furiously for Qatar to be stripped of the right to host the tournament and for the World Cup vote to be re-run. There was mounting pressure for Sepp Blatter's resignation. The reporters – and the world – waited expectantly to see what FIFA would do. And the breathtaking answer was: nothing.

The morning after the story broke, Calvert and Blake picked up the phone to FIFA's ethics investigators. Michael Garcia had launched an inquiry into the Qatar 2022 World Cup bid in November 2012, after the journalists passed him their documents revealing Samson Adamu's million-dollar dinner deal. Two months later he had widened the probe to encompass all nine countries in the competition for the 2018 and 2022 tournaments, and Tim Flynn had been hired in from the Freeh Group to assist with the project. Blake and Calvert had met Garcia and Flynn when the investigators flew into London the previous year. The former US attorney in charge of FIFA's investigatory chamber was courteous and charismatic, and the reporters liked him. They had done all they could to help him get to the bottom of the mysterious $1 million offer from Qatar to the son of a voter, handing him documents and putting him in touch with sources. His sidekick, Flynn, was a man of few words, but he had stayed in touch with the Insight team, calling occasionally to ask them questions or request more evidence.

Calvert and Blake were aware that the investigators had become increasingly frustrated as they toured the globe trying to unravel the World Cup web. In many ways, their hands were tied. Only 11 of the men who had been on the executive committee at the time of the vote remained in place, and those who had gone were out of Garcia's reach. He had no power to compel anyone who was no longer part of the 'FIFA family' to speak to him or supply evidence. That included Bin Hammam and Jack Warner. Nor would FIFA allow the investigators to offer witnesses indemnity against future legal action by anyone they accused, and many would-be whistleblowers were too scared to tell them what they knew without protection.

By the summer of 2014 Garcia and Flynn had spent 18 months and £6 million on their investigation into the most corrupt bidding process in sporting history, but try as they might, they just couldn't find a smoking gun. That was the message the journalists had received when they had spoken to Flynn a couple of weeks before. The investigator had told them he and Garcia were still months away from finishing their work. Jérôme Valcke had recently issued a statement saying he wanted to see their report before the Brazil World Cup, but Flynn was adamant that wasn't possible. There was too much still to be done. The reporters couldn't tell the investigator that they were sitting on an explosive cache of documents containing enough dynamite to blow the whole probe sky-high, but they were sure Flynn and Garcia would be delighted when they eventually learned of this smouldering mound of evidence they could finally get stuck into.

It was strange, then, that when the call was connected to Flynn the morning after the FIFA Files went public, he was oddly cool with the reporters. He told them he had not read their stories, and neither had Garcia, but they were going to make a statement later that afternoon. Calvert and Blake were taken aback. Why wasn't their evidence of Bin Hammam's covert World Cup campaign of interest to FIFA's investigators?

Flynn's tone was world-weary. He told the journalists that he and Garcia did not believe that Qatar's most senior football official had played any significant part in his country's victory. In fact, he said, the official bid team had to work hard to convince him even to vote for Qatar and he only promised his vote in the last months before the ballot. Blake and Calvert looked at one another, agog. Could Flynn be serious? He was parroting exactly what Al-Thawadi's lawyers had said in their statement the day before. Why was Flynn drinking the Qatari Kool-Aid? They told him they had millions of documents proving Bin Hammam's pivotal role in securing the Qatar World Cup and Garcia should look at them. Flynn sounded unenthused. He advised the reporters to wait and see what the investigator had to say later that day.

When Garcia finally released his statement that afternoon, the reporters read it in stunned silence. 'After months of interviewing witnesses and gathering materials, we intend to complete that phase of our investigation by June 9, 2014, and to submit a report to the Adjudicatory Chamber approximately six weeks thereafter,' it said. 'The report will consider all evidence potentially related to the bidding process, including evidence collected from prior investigations.' That date was just a week away. Garcia was shutting down his inquiry early and closing the door on new evidence the day after learning that *The Sunday Times* was sitting on a database of hundreds of millions of documents with direct relevance to his work. What had happened? Why didn't he want to get to the truth?

The Sunday Times dropped its second FIFA Files bombshell on 8 June, as football's global elite touched down in Brazil for the annual congress ahead of the World Cup. It revealed how Bin Hammam had exploited Qatar's vast oil and gas wealth to garner World Cup support. 'Gas deal turns heat on World Cup,' the front-page headline read, over a picture of the famous trophy engulfed in flames. Now the first major FIFA sponsor, Sony, had broken ranks and called for the FIFA Files to be investigated properly. Blatter had still said nothing. The FIFA president and his executives arrived in São Paulo amid the biggest crisis in the organisation's history, with the revelations about the Qatar 2022 World Cup bribery scandal blaring from every airport television screen. Their air-conditioned limousines pushed through streets clogged with angry protests against the exorbitant cost of hosting the tournament in a country where millions live in poverty. It was a perfect storm for the cosseted officials on the Exco, and lesser men might have blanched. But they were soon delivered to the safe haven of the best hotel in town, where waiting in their suites was a goody bag to make them feel more wanted.

Inside were the usual football trinkets Blatter and his executives are showered with as they travel the globe – but nestled between the Brazilian national team shirt and mascot, they found a gift of extraordinary value. It was a limited-edition commemorative watch created by Parmigiani, the luxury Swiss brand that sponsors the Brazilian football federation (CBF), and it was worth $25,000. The gift should have rung alarm bells for Blatter and his Exco, who had voted in the code of ethics that bans them from accepting gifts of more than 'symbolic or trivial value'. But while three took a principled stand and reported the 'excessive' gift to FIFA, the majority quietly kept the watches. By slipping the Parmigiani timepieces to the bottom of their luggage rather than sending them back, FIFA's rulers had just buried another land-mine which would later blow up in their faces when it came to the attention of the Insight team three months later.

For now, though, the family was in fighting spirit. Sepp Blatter stood up at the congress in São Paulo and, at last, faced up to the avalanche of filth tumbling out of the FIFA Files. Would he announce a re-vote on the hosting of the 2022 World Cup? Would he order Garcia to examine all the evidence? Would he apologise to the fans for allowing the face of football to be stained once again with such disgrace? Not a bit of it. With a familiar tone of fatherly disappointment, Blatter told the delegates: 'Once again there is a sort of storm against FIFA relating to the Qatar World Cup. Sadly there's a great deal of discrimination and racism and this hurts me. It really makes me sad.'

Later that day, the president appeared again before the Asian delegates at the congress. 'We have seen what the British press has published,' he said. 'I don't know what the reasoning is behind this but we must maintain unity.' He was gearing up for re-election the following year having, once again, reneged on his promise to stand down at the end of this term. The president was nothing if not a deft opportunist and there wasn't anything quite like a corruption scandal to remind the children of the FIFA family why they needed such a benevolent patriarch at the helm. The room was dotted with men who had grown rich on Bin Hammam's riyals and not one of them wanted FIFA to change.

'I still have fire inside me and if we show unity that is the best way to deal with those in the world that want to destroy FIFA,' Blatter told them amid cheers. 'They want to destroy us. They don't want to destroy football but they want to destroy the institution. Because our institution is too strong and is so strong, we are sure they will not destroy it!'

Blake and Calvert watched open-mouthed from their attic hideout as the miniature Blatter on their computer screens brushed away their evidence and accused them of being nothing more than a pair of racists, his voice a shrill whine on their tinny speakers.

'This is too ridiculous for words,' Blake said. 'The man has become some sort of ludicrous parody of a dodgy dictator clinging to power.' It would have been funny if it wasn't so deeply insulting. And then it got worse.

Blatter rounded off his response to the corruption crisis by promising a cash bonanza to his bedrock of supporters across Asia and Africa. At a meeting of CAF officials that morning, he promised to use the billions of dollars FIFA was raking in from the Brazil World Cup to bump up their bonuses. 'It's for you, for us, for everyone,' he declared. Speaking to the Asian congress, he promised: 'I will give bonuses to you – actually two . . . The confederations also deserve it. I'm sure you will be very happy with it.' The delegates erupted in wild cheers and applause.

Blatter received a far frostier reception when he popped up before the UEFA congress the following day. The defiance which had so delighted the delegates from Africa and Asia had gone down like a lead balloon in Europe. There was muted applause after Blatter announced he had decided to stand for four more years because he was best placed to lead FIFA through the 'storm'. Then Michael van Praag, the Dutch FA president, stood. 'Mr Blatter, this is nothing personal, but if you look at FIFA's reputation over the last seven or eight years, it is being linked to all kinds of corruption and all kinds of old boys' networks things,' he said gingerly. 'You are not making things easy for yourself and I do not think you are the man for the job any longer.'

Blatter's nostrils flared. What was this impudence? How dare this jumped-up Dutchman question the father of the family in public? Then Greg Dyke, the chairman of the hated English FA, stood too. 'Mr Blatter,' he said, 'many of us are deeply troubled by your reaction to these allegations. It is time for FIFA to stop attacking the messenger and instead consider, and understand, the message … I read the articles in *The Sunday Times* in great detail, the allegations being made were nothing to do with racism. They are allegations about corruption within FIFA. These allegations need to be properly investigated and properly answered.'

Two days later, Michael Garcia stepped up to the podium on the eve of the first World Cup match. The investigator had been flown in to head off the growing storm over the organisation's failure to respond to the evidence in the FIFA Files. World football's spin doctors had flatly ignored requests for comment from *The Sunday Times* and were now deflecting all calls about the crisis to the office of Garcia's law firm in New York. The beleaguered investigator was being used as a human fireguard by his employers, and he looked like he knew it.

The journalists watched as the speech was streamed live. Garcia looked like the man they remembered meeting the year before, with his sharp suit and his curly hair gelled into submission, but his manner was strikingly altered. He had lost his air of easy self-assurance and his face appeared to be fixed in a permanent wince. Standing there in the spotlights, he looked like a shifty schoolboy hauled before the assembly for forgetting to do his homework.

'Is it me, or does he look like he's about to be sick?' Blake asked.

'He's definitely looking a bit green about the gills,' Calvert said. 'I sort of pity him, being dragged out like this to defend the indefensible.'

Garcia had written perfunctorily to *The Sunday Times* the previous week, after receiving a volley of criticism for shutting down his investigation without examining the files. He had asked the newspaper to send him 'any information and material you have that you believe may assist our inquiry'. The newspaper's lawyer Pia Sarma had responded explaining that the evidence was voluminous, comprising millions of files, and the journalists were only beginning to mine their wealth of material. They would continue publishing fresh revelations in the coming weeks and they hoped he would review the underpinning documents. He had not responded. What would he say now?

The investigator began. He said that his team had examined the reports and published documents in *The Sunday Times* and concluded that the evidence wasn't new. The 'majority of that material has been available to us for some time, since well before the recent wave of news reports,' he claimed. The reporters shook their heads. There was no way he could have seen all their material. Their source had told them it was impossible. Still more bafflingly, he continued by claiming that he had approached 'what appears to be the original source' of that data and would be reviewing all the information in the files before issuing his final report. As it happened, the source was reclining in a chair a few feet away, and he let out an exclamation of protest.

'I haven't heard a word from anyone,' he said indignantly. 'The nerve!'

Garcia was pushing on. 'What we cannot do and what I will not do is postpone indefinitely our work on the possibility someone may publish something we may not have seen ... we will follow our process, the process being considering the greatest number of allegations and issues in as thorough manner as possible.'

The journalists later spoke to Flynn again, who remained adamant that there was no evidence that Bin Hammam had any real role in Qatar's campaign. Garcia hadn't interviewed him and he had been ruled out of the enquiry. The reporters were genuinely perplexed. On the one hand, the investigators claimed to have seen all their evidence. One other hand, they said they had not seen anything linking Bin Hammam to the 2022 bid. The two positions were plainly contradictory. From that point on, it was clear that FIFA's internal investigation was a busted flush.

It was only after the journalists had published the first two weeks' stories that Blake suddenly stumbled upon another incendiary document within the files. It was the assessment by Andrew Pruis which named Qatar as the only bidding country with a 'high risk' of the tournament being shut down by a terrorist incident, and it made spine-chilling reading. 'FIFA ignored its own terror alert,' *The Sunday Times* splash headline read that weekend. The edition also revealed how Qatar had poached Chris Eaton and his entire investigations team to new jobs in Doha, and exposed Hassan Al-Thawadi's secret involvement in Bin Hammam's doomed presidential campaign.

FIFA had refused to respond to questions from *The Sunday Times* in the previous two weeks, but this time its head of communications Walter De Gregorio had not been able to resist firing off an irascible reply. 'As you might have noticed, we have a World Cup to run in Brazil and have therefore slightly different priorities then [*sic*] you,' the email read. 'We are answering your request in due course next week. On a confidential basis: England is playing tonight (just a head up for you).' FIFA never did respond to the questions.

The week after, the reporters revealed how FIFA's executives had all pocketed bumper World Cup rewards of $200,000 each in South Africa. They had since announced amid fanfare that they would comply with new ethics recommendations to scrap all future bonuses, but had secretly doubled their salaries at the same time to make up for it. The newspaper also named and shamed a dozen FIFA officials who were still in power despite having taken Bin Hammam's cash.

This time, De Gregorio's email was even more fevered. 'We cannot comment on every single paper you pick out of the hundreds of millions of emails you have as you say. This could go on and on. First please kindly check all the hundreds of millions of emails you have, send us a summary of your findings and then you might get a statement from FIFA. But not before you do your homework. And for sure not before Judge Eckert has come to his conclusion based on the investigation report due to be delivered to him by Michael Garcia. We cannot play this game every weekend, you know well. This is ridiculous.'

Blake read it to Calvert in fits of giggles. 'Oh how wrong you are, Walter. Nothing would give us more pleasure than to play this game every weekend,' she laughed.

'Seriously,' he said, 'they pay this man to do their communications?'

As the journalists were preparing their final stories, they received a startling phone call. It was from a man who had once held great power and influence within FIFA – one of the many casualties of Blatter's changeable loyalties. He had been sent down from the hilltop and was now one of the characters who hung around in the shadows of world football, fixing deals, lobbying and trading on his knowledge of the inner workings of the game. By now, the journalists knew his name well. He had been a close friend of Bin Hammam's for many years, and his emails had cropped up in the inbox many times. They always made for a lively and interesting read, full of gossip and intrigue. During Bin Hammam's presidential campaign, this man had helped fix him up with a private surveillance outfit to monitor Blatter's every move, and they had read the intelligence reports which came back with great interest. Hearing this voice on the end of the phone was uncanny – like getting a call from a character in the book on your bedside table.

The lobbyist had been watching the FIFA farrago unfold over the past two weeks. He had seen Blatter stand up and denounce the journalists as racists and the Qatar World Cup bid team disowning Bin Hammam. He had since spoken to his friend in Qatar, and now he had something to say to Blake and Calvert, on condition of anonymity.

'When I spoke to Bin Hammam about your story, he was laughing,' he said. 'The problem is that he has been bound to silence and he can't defend himself.' The lobbyist asserted that 'Bin Hammam was the key person' in the World Cup bid and 'that's why they won', but the victory had incurred the wrath of the FIFA president. Blatter had been 'very much afraid when Qatar was named as the host' because he knew 'if Bin Hammam was so powerful he can make an election in favour of Qatar for the World Cup, he could do it again in the presidential race.' Then, the lobbyist told the journalists why Bin Hammam had pulled out of the presidential race so suddenly. 'There was a deal between Qatar and Blatter. Blatter blackmailed Qatar and they forced him out.'

Blake and Calvert were tantalised by this extraordinary claim which might explain so much about Bin Hammam's mysterious retreat from the presidential battle and Blatter's subsequent unwillingness to countenance any challenge to the Qatar World Cup. They were eager to find out more, and they agreed to meet the lobbyist in Zurich in two days' time. As soon as the paper had gone to the printers on Saturday night, they drove straight to London to pick up their passports and headed to the airport.

The journalists had arranged to meet the lobbyist for breakfast in a hotel on the shores of Lake Zurich. The Swiss air was crisp and the sun glittered on the gently rippling water as they sipped their cappuccinos and tucked into a basket full of fresh croissants with butter and jam. After months cooped up in the attic, it was nothing short of blissful to be abroad in the bright light of the world again, amid the hubbub of ordinary human chatter and the tang of freshly ground coffee in the air. The man who had phoned them out of the blue strolled in a few minutes late and gripped both their hands firmly. He was dressed in jeans, a navy blazer with brass buttons and an open-collared white shirt. They couldn't help but notice the enormous glinting Rolex protruding from his cuff. This man had walked straight out of the dark world they had been scrutinising – a living, breathing character from the story of Bin Hammam's corrupt campaign. And yet, as he began regaling them with his outrageous stories, it was impossible not to begin to warm to him.

The lobbyist told them he had once been close to the FIFA president, but the relationship had soured and he had been forced out. 'Blatter is a liar,' he said in a lilting mid-European accent, tearing cheerfully into a croissant and beckoning to the waitress for coffee. 'He has not a good character or a bad character. He has no character.' Bin Hammam had been kind to him after his fall from grace, offering him ongoing work as a consultant and bringing him often to Doha. He had become close to the Qatari football boss and his kindly aide Najeeb Chirakal, and remained in touch with them both today. The journalists asked him what he knew about Qatar's World Cup campaign.

As far as he was concerned, Qatar had secured the 2022 tournament simply by playing the corrupt FIFA system, and who could blame them? 'What Qatar did,' he said, 'was they excessively applied the rules of FIFA. They always did that. What they did was the way in FIFA. They were playing by FIFA's unofficial rules.'

'But what about Bin Hammam?' Calvert asked. 'What was his role?' The lobbyist leaned forward confidentially.

'Bin Hammam brought the World Cup to Qatar,' he said

firmly. 'And they say publicly he had nothing to do with it. They set up two separate organisations: Bin Hammam and the bid were separate, but Bin Hammam was the coach of the Qatar bid. He brought the votes to Qatar. He was the one with the relationships … The rainmaker was Bin Hammam. That was his job … Blatter didn't vote for Qatar because he did not want to give Bin Hammam any more power. Then when they won he got a shock and from then on his one thought was to destroy Mohamed bin Hammam. He provoked a death penalty by collecting those fourteen votes.'

He looked wistful when his friend's name came to his lips. 'Society in Qatar is very cruel,' he mused. 'Once you are dropped, you are dropped.' He explained that Bin Hammam was 'forbidden to speak' by his country's royals after he was banned from football. 'You don't go against the Emir, but it's a big joke to say he had no role … Bin Hammam fell into disgrace … Always when we talk about that, Najeeb points out how cruel the system is in Qatar.' He looked up, engaging them with his pale grey eyes. 'It's like: "The Moor has done his duty, the Moor can go",' he said, quoting the 18th-century tragedy *Fiesco* by the German playwright Friedrich Schiller.

Blake was still scribbling in her notebook under the table as she jumped in with the next question. 'You said on the phone that there was a deal to make Bin Hammam pull out of the presidential race. Can you tell us more about how that happened?'

'Blatter had told Qatar that he would expose their bid unless they made Bin Hammam pull out,' he said simply, licking a trace of cappuccino froth from his upper lip. He said he had visited Bin Hammam at home some months after his final retirement from world football and heard the whole sorry story.

'Can you describe what happened when you went to see him?' asked Calvert. The lobbyist nodded and leaned back in his chair, gazing momentarily out across the water.

'It was in the majlis, a room where men met,' he began. 'Ten or twenty people would always be there, all local Qataris, personal friends of Bin Hammam. You left your shoes outside. It was a big room with warm beige sofas along the three sides. On the fourth side there were two TVs. People would come in and ask for help. They watched football on TV and chatted … It was a very relaxed, comfortable situation. Just to be with him is nice. He is quiet, with a sense of humour. Not showy. Male servants came round pouring coffee from on high into golden cups. There were hand gestures to tell the servants when you wanted coffee. In the house there were no shoes. Everyone was wearing the arabic dishdashas. There was only me in a suit. It was very cosy. Very nice.'

'And what did he tell you about why he pulled out of the presidential election?' Calvert urged.

'He told me there was a deal and he was forced to withdraw. Blatter promised him that the ethical committee case would be dropped if he pulled out, and Bin Hammam pulled out of the race overnight. Later that day he was suspended. Blatter promised: "If there is no candidate, there is no case," but not surprisingly, he lied. Blatter was very quick to betray him … This was especially hurtful for Bin Hammam. Having a case in front of the ethical committee and being condemned was very painful … When he told me he was strong. He is a very strange person. He doesn't show a lot of emotions. But I knew how hurtful that must be for him.' The reporters nodded and scribbled furiously in their notebooks, on the edge of their seats.

'How was this deal communicated to Bin Hammam?' Blake asked eagerly. The lobbyist told them that Bin Hammam had been called into a meeting between Blatter and a very senior member of the Qatari royal family on 28 May 2011, and told his presidential bid was over.

'Blatter put Qatar under pressure – Bin Hammam told me

this – to destroy Bin Hammam. It's very sad for Bin Hammam. Now he has nothing. There was a deal between Blatter and [the Qatari royal]. It was here in Zurich in Blatter's office ... First they had a meeting and then Bin Hammam was called in and they told him to step down ... Bin Hammam asked: "What about the case against me before the committee?" And Blatter says: "If there's no candidate, there's no case." ... Blatter knows how to blackmail people. For Qatar, this is normal life. It was more important that they can keep the World Cup. Qatar only had one concern – to get rid of Bin Hammam as a candidate.'

The reporters were riveted. If this was true it was a seismic story, and it would explain so much. They wanted to know if there was any conceivable way the lobbyist might be able to persuade Bin Hammam to speak to them about what had happened. He laughed.

'You are perhaps not his favourite people. Bin Hammam would never admit that he is forbidden to speak.'

The journalists begged him to try to persuade Bin Hammam or Chirakal to talk to them directly. For three months they had been trawling the FIFA documents without the time to try to reach out to the characters involved. Now they wanted to talk to anyone who could shed light on this extraordinary new chapter in the story, about the alleged deal between Qatar and Blatter.

They flew back from Zurich and returned to the bunker. It was time to pull down all their scribbled notes, charts and diagrams from the walls, pack up all their papers and vanish. They went out for a farewell dinner with the source at a local Indian restaurant, and they all marvelled at the whirlwind events of the past month. It was not over. Now he knew he could trust them, the source had agreed to allow Blake and Calvert to access the files remotely from two heavily encrypted laptops so that they could continue to mine the evidence back in London. After dinner, Calvert shook his hand warmly and Blake gave him a hug. They would always be grateful for his immense bravery in risking everything to blow the whistle.

The next morning, the journalists climbed into Blake's Polo and set off home to London. They would soon see their families and friends for the first time in months, and sleep in their own beds. Then it was time for a holiday. Blake disappeared to a remote France farmhouse with a group of friends and Calvert went to visit his daughter in Rome. They came back at the end of the summer refreshed, and ready to plunge back into the files.

At the end of September, the white-haired German judge in charge of FIFA's adjudicatory chamber took delivery of the most hotly anticipated document in international sport. Michael Garcia had finally submitted his report, and Hans-Joachim Eckert reached for a highlighter pen in his Munich office as he began to leaf through its 350-pages, occasionally dipping into the 200,000 pages of supporting evidence. There were only four copies of this document in existence – Garcia and his deputy Cornel Borbély had retained theirs, and the other two went to Eckert and his deputy, the Australian lawyer Alan Sullivan.

Millions of fans around the world had been eagerly awaiting the delivery of the document, which they hoped would finally provide an answer to the allegations of corruption that had swirled around the decision to hold the 2022 tournament in Qatar. But Eckert was going to disappoint them sorely. When he had finished flicking through the document and marking a few passages he wanted to return to, he crossed the room to his safe and tapped in the combination. He slid Garcia's report and the weighty sheaf of accompanying evidence inside. Then, he slammed the door.

News that the report was finished was briefed out amid fanfare by FIFA's spin doctors. Their strategy for batting off the allegations from the files had been to remind anyone who asked that there was an ongoing investigation into this matter, and that the ethics chamber must be allowed to do its work in peace. 'The report sets forth detailed factual findings; reaches conclusions concerning further action with respect to certain individuals; identifies issues to be referred to other FIFA committees; and makes recommendations for future bidding processes. Pursuant to the FIFA code of ethics, the adjudicatory chamber will now make a final decision on the report and supplemental reports, including publication,' the official press statement said.

Shortly after the report was handed over to Eckert, the journalists received a secret read-out of its contents from a well-informed source close to the ethics committee. They were told Qatar had been cleared of any serious wrongdoing and Mohamed bin Hammam's role had been airbrushed out as they had feared. Russia had a clean bill of health, too. England and Australia had come in for the worst criticism. They were nonplussed. How could that be? Days later, officials who had been with Jérôme Valcke at a private meeting told the journalists the secretary general had briefed them that both World Cup hosts were in the clear and the 2018 and 2022 tournaments would go ahead in Russia and Qatar exactly as planned.

Two weeks later, the reporters were in Zurich. In a peerless act of self-satire, FIFA had decided to play host to an international conference on ethics in sport, and both Garcia and Eckert were due to be there. Blake and Calvert were looking forward to the encounter. They had thrown another grenade up the hilltop the Sunday before, revealing that almost the entire executive committee had broken FIFA's rules by taking the $25,000 Parmigiani watches left in their São Paulo hotel rooms by the Brazilian FA that summer.

Sunil Gulati, the new US member, the Australian Moya Dodd and Prince Ali bin Al-Hussein of Jordan had unwittingly caused acute embarrassment by handing back the gifts and alerting

FIFA's ethics committee when all their colleagues had simply pocketed the present. Garcia had been called in to investigate, but nothing had been done by the time *The Sunday Times* found out about the watches three months later.

Four days after the paper published the story, Garcia rushed out a statement. 'The CBF should not have offered the watches, and those who received gift bags should have promptly checked whether the items inside were appropriate and, upon discovering the watch, either returned it or ... reported the matter to the investigatory chamber. The FIFA code of ethics plainly prohibits such gifts.' This sounded like remarkably stern stuff from FIFA's usually meek ethics investigator. But would anyone be punished for breaking the rules? There was no need for any such unpleasantness. 'The investigatory chamber will not pursue further formal ethics proceedings in this matter against officials who submit the Parmigiani watch they received from CBF to the secretariat of the investigatory chamber by no later than October 24, 2014.'

The story of how almost every single member of FIFA's ruling committee had flouted the organisation's own rules in the midst of the biggest bribery and corruption scandal in sporting history flew around the world. Lesser men than Sepp Blatter might have felt a touch abashed, standing up to address an international conference on ethics in sport days after it had emerged. But the FIFA president was unflappable. He opened the conference by claiming, without a hint of irony, that world football's governing body had the best ethics structure in the world. 'Since the reforms, we have had an exemplary organisation in ethics ... we have two chambers ... with independent chairmen. We are the only sports organisation which has this independent body for ethics, nobody else.' There was a smattering of polite applause.

Shortly afterwards, Judge Eckert came to the stage. Small, smart and snowy haired, he was a picture of judicial rectitude peering down over steel-rimmed spectacles from the podium. He began speaking in German, sending the reporters scrambling for translation headsets, and after some general remarks about the importance of proper ethics procedures, he turned to the burning topic of the hour. Eckert announced that there would be no final outcome to the World Cup corruption investigation until the spring, at which point he would publish *only* the names of anyone found to have broken the rules and the sanctions imposed on them. No details of the specific breaches or the reasoning behind the sanctions would be released.

In short, the report Garcia had delivered to him earlier that month would remain under lock and key forever. 'There is an obligation for secrecy for all members of the ethics committee and we will comply with this. You cannot expect anything to be disclosed from this report,' Eckert said amid murmurs of consternation. 'Nobody else has seen this report. Neither FIFA nor any other organisations have got this report and this is how it was meant to be ... You can rest assured that we professionals know how to safeguard the report, and not give anyone access to it.'

For months, FIFA had been hiding behind Garcia's forthcoming report to deflect questions about why they were disregarding the evidence produced by *The Sunday Times*, and now Eckert was saying that only he and his deputy would ever know what the investigator had found. After the speech, as the judge tried to leave the stage, he found himself caught in a media scrum being pelted from all sides with questions from reporters who had travelled from all over the world to find out what Garcia had discovered. He stalled and stonewalled and then his upper lip began to curl. 'I understand, the media are greedy like that,' he snapped eventually, starting to push through the crowd. 'I will not start an ethics discussion now.'

Blake piped up from the middle of the scrum: 'Mr Eckert, I work for *The Sunday Times* and we have a very large volume of

evidence which shows that Mohamed bin Hammam made corrupt payments in order to win support for his country's World
Cup bid, and Mr Garcia has not looked at our evidence. Would
you be prepared to consider the evidence that we have?'

'Well I, I will not comment. Sorry. I will not comment, I, I ...'
the judge stammered.

'Can we show you our evidence?'

'Not to me,' he said.

'Will you look at it, if we send it?'

'No, no, not to me.' He was now firm.

'But you have the power to consider additional evidence, apart
from the evidence that Mr Garcia has given to you,' Blake urged.

The judge was stony faced. 'I have to look what he is writing,
and if I need there is more evidence to take, I will do it, but
please, let me have the time to read it.'

Blake did not give up. 'Mr Garcia has ruled out the role of
Mohamed bin Hammam. He does not believe that Mohamed
bin Hammam was working for the Qatar bid ...'

'No comment,' Eckert cut in.

Blake pressed on: ' ... and we can show you that he was working for the Qatar bid.'

'No comment. But you know, I have banned Mr Hammam,
lifelong. That was me. So ...'

'But you have not examined his role in the Qatar World Cup
bid. That hasn't been examined, and it needs to be examined
because he played a critical part,' Blake persevered.

Calvert joined in. 'And as a result Mr Garcia hasn't interviewed
Mr Bin Hammam as we understand it, so therefore how could
you ever get to the bottom of these allegations? It seems to us that
the investigation itself is flawed,' he said.

'I will please you, let me say no comment,' said the judge,
making to go.

Watching in the wings, Garcia was enraged by Eckert's clumsy pronouncements. He could see exactly how badly all this was going to play in the press. FIFA had placed a heavy load on his shoulders by telling the world for the past three months that his report would answer every question about the Qatar World Cup. Now it was going to be kept secret and he was going to look like part of the whitewash. It was a horribly invidious position. When the investigator stood up to address the audience himself that afternoon, he decided to vent his frustration with FIFA's culture of secrecy.

'What we need at this point is more transparency into the process ... into charges, into decisions, into the basis for those decisions and into the facts,' he said pointedly. 'The goal has to be instilling confidence ... that the process is working in a fair way.' He warned that 'there could be little support from a public that was so little informed,' and then, sensationally, he called on world football's governing body to publish the report that Eckert had just vowed to keep secret. 'The more that is public and the more people can see what was done and disagree with what was done, then those issues can be resolved and the organisation can move on.' Journalists swarmed after Garcia when he tried to leave the auditorium. Seeing the advancing throng, the investigator turned and sprinted down the corridor into the safety of the anteroom where the press could not enter.

The cosy relationship between the twin chairs of FIFA's ethics chamber had just been shattered. When *The Sunday Times* reported Eckert's remarks that weekend, there was an outcry. Prince Ali of Jordan began a small rebellion when he broke ranks to declare on Twitter: 'In the interest of full transparency, I believe it is important that the much-anticipated report on the ethics investigation that is crucial to ensuring good governance at FIFA is fully disclosed and open to the public.' A further five members of the executive committee followed suit and called for the report to be published. Then Garcia himself joined the fray, dispensing with ethics committee protocol to issue his own statement taking a pop at the judge. 'Given the limited role Mr Hans-Joachim Eckert envisions for the adjudicatory chamber, I believe it is now necessary for the FIFA executive committee to authorise the appropriate publication of the report on the inquiry into the 2018/2022 FIFA World Cup bidding process,' he wrote.

The growing tumult made for a stormy encounter when the executive committee met in Zurich at the end of September. Blatter had wanted to stamp down on the insurrection and initially tried to propose that only the 11 remaining members who had voted in the World Cup ballot should be allowed to decide whether Garcia's findings should be made public. When this met with angry opposition from the rebels, the president offered an olive branch. He agreed to explore the possibility of persuading Eckert to produce a summary of the investigator's work which could potentially be published if the names and identifying details of suspects and witnesses were removed.

Once peace was restored by this promise and FIFA's rulers were heading for the airport, Blatter held an impromptu press conference giving his own wacky version of what had happened at the meeting. 'Most of the requests coming for the publication of this report were from people [who] were not there on December the second when the decision was taken for the World Cups 2018 and 2022,' he said dismissively. 'And today in the meeting there was not any longer any requests from any of these members in FIFA to publish this report,' he claimed.

Blatter then insisted that it was not possible to release the report because FIFA were 'bound by the regulations', and therefore it would stay under lock and key. Prince Ali and his supporters were infuriated to see the headline 'Blatter insists World Cup bid corruption probe must stay secret' when they checked their smartphones in the airport departures lounge. They got on the phone to FIFA instantly seeking a statement correcting Blatter's remarks. Over the following weeks, the true picture emerged. Blatter was forced to concede that his executive committee wanted a heavily censored summary of Garcia's evidence to be published, and Eckert would be its author. Some arm twisting had clearly taken place.

The familiar figure of one of FIFA's rulers was half way through a glass of prosecco when the reporters arrived to meet him. Blake and Calvert were busy bottoming out the lobbyist's claim that Blatter had done a deal with Qatar and the trail had led them to this meeting on a sunny afternoon in a foreign city. The man from the FIFA executive committee had agreed to see them on condition of strict anonymity. He enjoyed Blatter's trust and was not prepared to risk his position at world football's top table, but he could see that the Qatar World Cup decision was tearing FIFA apart and there were things he knew that he wanted to share. He ordered a fresh round of drinks and the reporters filled him in on their work so far on Qatar. Then Blake slipped in the first key question.

'When the Qatar World Cup bid says Mohamed bin Hammam had nothing to do with their World Cup bid and was not working for them, do you believe them?'

He snorted. 'Look at these people! They live on cloud nine,' he scoffed. 'They are wealthy, they are powerful, and they believe, which happens often when you are too powerful ... that everybody has to agree with them ... This decision was taken with active support from Bin Hammam in whatever role he was fulfilling.' The reporters nodded as they took notes in shorthand and the football boss went on. 'I am convinced that Bin Hammam also used financial means to get the necessary votes for Qatar. So the role he was playing in this entire game, and whether it's possible to assign blame to the official Qatar bidding team, this is exactly a question which Garcia has to sort out.'

He moved on to the fallout from Qatar's victory in the World Cup ballot. 'At that point the question of the relations between the FIFA president and Qatar had to be clarified from the point of view of Qatar. So from their point of view, we either have to have a FIFA president or Blatter has to play our game. So as a consequence, many talks were held between the old buddies, the Qatar Emir and Blatter, and the result was that Bin Hammam had to be neutralised ... Obedience is simply a duty there. So Bin Hammam does not do any act which is not in line with the Emir's will. He might have a certain freedom but he fulfils the role of the Emir. And so, consequently ... when they realised that Bin Hammam was a threat, they disposed of him. He had done his job so they disposed of him.'

'And the Emir met with Blatter? There was a deal with Blatter?'

'Yes, because in 2011 Blatter wanted to run as president, then suddenly there was another candidate coming up from Qatar ... Blatter of course he knew of the danger of the threat. And it was clear to him that he had to make some peace with the Qataris, and this resulted in his encounters with the Emir, and as a result Bin Hammam was disposed of and this paved the way of Blatter to be elected in 2011.'

'What did Blatter have to promise to Qatar to get them to make Bin Hammam withdraw?' Blake asked.

'It's obvious. To push through with the World Cup decision. To promise not to do anything which would question this decision.'

Since they had met the lobbyist on the shores of Lake Zurich two months before, the reporters had tracked down three other friends and allies of Bin Hammam who recounted a near-identical story about the deal between Qatar and Blatter. One was a close aide who was with him in Zurich at the time the deal was done. Another was a second Westerner who had heard the story over coffee in the majlis. The third was formerly one of his staunchest allies within FIFA. The trail of evidence lit up further when they found the messages between Jenny Be and Victoria Shanti discussing how Blatter 'gave his word' to the Emir that he would not re-open the vote when Bin Hammam withdrew. And now they had confirmation from inside FIFA's ruling committee that a pact had been made to save Blatter from a presidential challenge and protect the Qatar World Cup forever.

On 13 November, Judge Eckert produced a 42-page summary of the evidence in Garcia's report. FIFA's spin doctors had hit the phones furiously the day before to spread the line that Blatter wanted everyone to hear. That morning the BBC news bulletins were reporting on a loop that Qatar and Russia had been cleared of any wrong-doing during their World Cup campaigns and, in a delicious twist, the English and Australian bids had been singled out for the most criticism. Eckert's summary was eventually released along with a short statement saying: 'FIFA welcomes the fact that a degree of closure has been reached.' But the moment of respite was short.

The critics barely had time to utter the word 'whitewash' before Garcia did it for them. Within a couple of hours of the release, FIFA's investigator put out a statement disowning Eckert's summary of his work, which he said contained 'numerous materially incomplete and erroneous representations of the facts'. The whole inquiry had descended into farce and FIFA's attempts to stem the crisis by putting a limited amount of information into the public domain had backfired completely.

Reading Eckert's assessment of the evidence on Qatar was a deeply frustrating experience for Calvert and Blake. The summary contained glaring omissions and snap judgements which smacked of expediency rather than rigour. Eckert said Garcia's report had found that Bin Hammam only became a supporter of the Qatar bid as the ballot neared on 2 December and 'the relationship between him and the bid team appeared to be somewhat distant.' Bin Hammam's payments to the African officials was explained away with the claim that the cash was intended to 'influence their votes in the June 2011 election for FIFA president' rather than the World Cup ballot. Of course, the summary made no mention of the many emails quoted in *The Sunday Times* which directly linked Bin Hammam's largesse to the World Cup campaign, and not to the presidential race.

The judge inexplicably ignored the $450,000 Bin Hammam paid to Jack Warner before the World Cup ballot. Nor did he address the evidence that the Qatar 2022 bid had offered $1 million to Amos Adamu's son to host the Legends' Dinner. Eckert acknowledged in his introduction that Garcia's two-year investigation started as a result of this story in *The Sunday Times*, but his summary never returned to the topic again. FIFA's investigators had clearly found no answer to its central mystery: who eventually stumped up the cash for the dinner after the official Qatari bid pulled out?

Eckert did accept that Bin Hammam had persuaded Reynald Temarii to appeal against his ethics ban in order to 'eliminate a vote for Qatar's competition' with the huge payment for legal fees and that his actions had therefore 'influenced the voting process'. But this straightforward example of vote-rigging was waved aside on two grounds. First, the judge pointed out that there was no 'direct link' between the payments and the Qatar bid. Second, he reasoned that the illicit deal was just a trifling matter because it affected only one vote out of the 13 needed to win.

Eckert also acknowledged that the financing and contracts relating to the Brazil vs Argentina friendly game in Doha 'raised concerns' under the ethics rules, particularly in relation to payments to Julio Grondona's Argentine Football Association. But the judge didn't find a clear breach because the cash had been paid through an unnamed conglomerate owned by a wealthy 'private individual' in Qatar and he saw no connection to Qatar's bid or its football association. Eckert's summary neglected to mention that the individual in question was Ghanim Bin Saad al Saad, a key agent of the Qatari royal family as both a director of its sovereign wealth fund and the managing director of its giant property company.

The upshot was that four members of the executive committee would come under further investigation over their behaviour during the World Cup contest, but the Qatar and Russian bids were in the clear. Franz Beckenbauer, Worawi Makudi, Michel D'Hooghe and Ángel María Villar Llona were all facing individual scrutiny. Blatter was content that the matter was now finished, despite Garcia's protestations. He was quoted on FIFA's website a few days later saying: 'There is no change to Judge Eckert's statement that the investigation into this bidding process for the 2018 and 2022 FIFA World Cups is concluded.'

FIFA's investigator was still furious with the judge for twisting his work and made a complaint to the FIFA's appeals committee in an attempt to have Eckert's findings overturned. Ironically, one of the committee members was Ahmad Darw, the president of the Madagascan football association, who had picked up a wad of Bin Hammam's cash from Amadou Diallo in Paris in 2010. It was no surprise that Garcia's appeal fell on deaf ears and in December the committee ruled that it had no power to alter Eckert's findings.

This was the final straw for Garcia. He quit FIFA on 17 December and issued a scalding resignation statement. 'No principled approach could justify the Eckert Decision's edits, omissions, and additions,' he wrote. 'And while the November 13, 2014, Eckert Decision made me lose confidence in the independence of the Adjudicatory Chamber, it is the lack of leadership on these issues within FIFA that leads me to conclude that my role in the process is at an end.'

The next day, the executive committee met in Marrakech, Morocco, to address the crisis. After two days of wrangling, they agreed that an 'appropriate' version of Garcia's report would be published in a heavily redacted form at some time in the future. 'We have always been determined that the truth should be known,' Blatter said piously afterwards. 'That is, after all, why we set up an independent Ethics Committee with an investigatory chamber that has all necessary means to undertake investigations on its own initiative.' He said for what felt like the thousandth time the troubles of the past were at last behind and now it really was time for the FIFA family to reunite and move forwards. Qatar was keeping its World Cup, and that was final. 'The report is about history and I am focused on the future. We will not revisit the 2018 and 2022 vote,' he said.

The sins of the past could never be swept aside so easily. FIFA had become a toxic brand, synonymous with corruption, greed and duplicity the world over. The revelations in the FIFA Files had shaken the very foundations of world football's governing body and the edifice was still crumbling. The European leagues were up in arms at the prospect of having to move the World Cup to the winter to avoid the height of the scorching desert heat, and the presidents of UEFA associations had started calling for Blatter's head. They were even ringing him directly to tell him to resign.

There was mounting international fury about the deaths of hundreds of migrant workers in appalling labour conditions in Qatar, with predictions that 4,000 more could perish before the 2022 construction work is complete. FIFA's sponsors were deserting in droves – already five had withdrawn their multi-million-dollar sponsorship deals since the story of the Qatari plot to buy the World Cup was exposed. The calls for reform grew louder and louder. But, for once, Blatter was sticking to his word. He had promised the Emir that the World Cup would remain in Doha, and he was not backing down.

The FIFA president was all smiles in Marrakech, pink cheeked and giggling with misplaced excitement throughout the press conference in which he announced that the 2018 and 2022 World Cups would remain untouched. There was always at least one journalist who had to rain on his parade, but Blatter was in robust spirits.

'Do you believe that FIFA is in a crisis right now,' the tired old question came, 'and are you the right man to lead FIFA into the future past the next election?'

Blatter beamed. 'I am not a prophet,' he said modestly. 'But I repeat what I have said today. We have *been* in a crisis. With the decision of the executive committee today, the crisis has *stopped*.' A thrust of the hand gave emphasis to his words. 'Because we have again the unity in our government.' He gestured heaven-wards. 'I believe in the Lord ... If they give me health, and let's say good luck, *yes*. I will bring back the FIFA. But not alone. I need my executive committee and then I need also the football family ... I trust in myself and I trust in my colleagues. And together, we will do it.'

Epilogue

Mohamed bin Hammam is at the window of his majlis, wondering who might arrive to take coffee with him tonight. Outside, the light is dimming and the sky is as grey as the wing of a desert dove. The dissolving sun tinges the distant shore with a coral haze, and the air cools. A little wind is whipping up. Today the memories took hold and he could not shake them. It is best to forget, he knows. But this afternoon, he has been leafing through his old letters again; taking out the commemorative watches one by one to weigh them in his hands; lingering in the hall lined with old photographs. By the grace of God, he is a lucky man and there is much to be thankful for. But solitude is a strange thing for one who was once so rarely alone.

In his heyday, Bin Hammam was abroad much more than he was ever at home, jetting from city to city to be greeted so graciously, always accompanied by his attentive entourage. Now he has no reason to travel and has not left Doha for a year. His beautiful young wife Nahed has tired of him and left, and Fatima is the only wife who remains at his side. So many of the children have gone abroad. At least his pretty Aisha is at home still, doing her charitable work in the local Indian school and helping out with the clerical affairs at Kemco. Jenny Be is here too, and so is Amelia Gan. They work in the city and dine at his table, and both are kind enough to call him Mr President, even now. Michelle Chai phones as often as she can, to see how he is faring. And then, of course, there is gentle Najeeb Chirakal. Bin Hammam hopes his kindly aide will never leave him, but as old age draws nearer Chirakal begins to pine for the Keralan backwaters where his life began, and one day soon he may wish to go home.

Soon Meshadi will be here, he hopes, and the servant will bring in the cardamom coffee. Maybe a few other locals will grace him with a visit, too. From time to time, some of his friends in world football still get in touch. Not often, but it is pleasant to hear from them when they find time. His brothers in Africa and Asia still need a bit of financial assistance on occasion. A little help funding their national leagues, or their children's school fees, or this new artificial pitch, or that new car. He gets so few letters these days, but the presidents of a smattering of associations write to him once in a while. Sometimes, rarely, they will even come to dinner – if he arranges the jets and the hotels to get them here. There's nothing to be gained now, but he still helps them when they ask, just out of the goodness in his heart. Michelle tells him she does not understand it.

She asked him once: 'President, when these people come to you always asking for things, don't you think that they are taking advantage of you, always wanting more?'

'No, Michelle.' He shook his head and gestured around. 'God has given me all this wealth. It's my responsibility to help people if I can.'

She tutted. The trouble with Mohamed, she knew, was that given his time at the top again, even after everything, he would do exactly the same things. He didn't know another way to be. When he saw what *The Sunday Times* had written about him, he just laughed.

There is nothing he can say. A new Emir is in the palace now – Sheikh Hamad stepped down to make way for his heir, Sheikh Tamim, and the son runs an even tighter ship than his father. Bin

Hammam has no quarter. It is his job to stay in the shadows, not to cause any more fuss. Outside, a whole new city is being built for the World Cup he brought to Doha, but a storm is raging at the gates and his country's ruler wants no more trouble. So Bin Hammam must stay silent. Still, he is proud of what he achieved. He is proud to have turned his country's daydream into a real future. He is proud to have brought the old Emir his big cake. That is enough.

Outside, the wind is stirring up faint eddies of the fine dust that blows in from the desert. It dissolves as it swirls in the thick grey air so when it reaches the rooftops it is almost invisible – a phantom shamal. Bin Hammam watches the dust diffusing. You can hardly see it but, like the man in the majlis, it is still there. It hangs in the air and when the trade winds catch hold of it they will carry it across the whole world.

A single gust sweeps it seaward over the Doha cityscape, past the Diwan Palace where the new Emir stalks the corridors and across the shoreline where little Mohamed once watched the riggers play. The dust drifts across the bay to the north shore where the Olympic Tower glints in the setting sun and, in his sky-high office, Hassan Al-Thawadi is slotting a sheaf of stadium plans into his briefcase after another long day at the helm of the 2022 supreme committee. It floats on northwards to Lusail, where the foundations are being laid for a brave new world. This will be the home of the World Cup finals: a gleaming city of 19 districts with lagoons, marinas, hotels, golf courses, zoos, fine restaurants and designer stores.

At its beating heart will be the Lusail Iconic Stadium, its 90,000 scarlet seats glistening like the flesh of a sliced fig. Qatar's crowning moment is just seven years away and Lusail is one of nine sparkling new football stadiums which will soon bejewel the tiny country. Now night is falling, the migrant workers who have toiled away all day building the World Cup city are retreating to their grim camps on the outskirts of Doha. They have flocked there in their thousands from India and Nepal, but their dreams of joining a land of golden opportunity were soon dashed. They often go unpaid for months and the desert heat is harsh. They must labour all day under the scorching sun, often with no drinking water or food. Their employers have taken their passports so there is no escape, except in a coffin. In the summer, the migrant workers in Qatar can die at a rate of around one a day, mostly of heart attacks in the fierce temperatures. More than 1000 fell in just two years. There have been warnings that thousands more will perish before the World Cup arrives in Doha.

When borne high on the trade winds, the fine dust from the Arabian desert will blow across the whole of Africa. Far below in Cameroon, Issa Hayatou still rules the continent's football confederation, having seen off a presidential challenge from the ambitious Jacques Anouma in the Ivory Coast. The two officials still regularly fly to Zurich to pick up their salaries as FIFA executive members alongside Bin Hammam's one-time stalwart, Hany Abo Rida from Egypt. Qatar's three voters from Africa emerged unscathed from the corruption scandals which claimed so many of their colleagues. Their Nigerian colleague Amos Adamu had been an unfortunate casualty of the World Cup race, but now he had come out of his three-year suspension a reformed man. 'I went through some transformations which have been worthwhile. I am now a different person, wiser than before,' he swore. Adamu saw the light as he reflected at home in his pink Park View villa. It is time to shun football administration for good and devote his energy to making serious money from the business side of sport.

When the wind picks up again it buffets the dust high into the turbulent weather systems of the Atlantic. It swirls in seemingly endless circles over Central and North America, falling in invisible particles over the land and the sea. Down in Port of Spain, a resurgent Jack Warner is marching along the beach under the hot midday sun, at the head of a troop of youths in matching green t-shirts and baseball caps. Warner has reinvented himself as an 'agent for change' in Trinidadian politics after being forced to quit his government job when the full scale of his CONCACAF fraud was exposed. The 'Youths for Warner' brigade is the junior arm of the new Independent Liberal Party which Jack set up as a vehicle for his own ambitions. Today, his teenage followers are bopping along behind him singing their Calypso anthem 'Rockin' with Jack' on a litter-picking excursion along the windy shore. Their t-shirts carry the 'Y4W' logo on the front and the slogan 'Dawn of a new era' on the back. 'I rockin' with Jack, one step forward, one step back!' the group chants. 'Hear what I say! Jack's the man to lead the way!'

On the northern edge of the tropics, the winds have ceased and the sun is shining. At an elegant hacienda in the grounds of the Palm Beach Polo club in Florida, another of Qatar's World Cup voters lolls on a lilo and toasts his wonderful life with an ice-cool caipirinha. Ricardo Teixeira left football and the Brazilian tax authorities behind in 2012 when things became too hot to handle during FIFA's investigation into the ISL scandal. His secret is now out – the world knows about the millions of pounds in bribes he had gladly pocketed from the company which bought the World Cup TV rights. The bad publicity had been a bitter pill to swallow, but it was more than amply sweetened by the fact that he got to keep the money. What's more, he slipped away from FIFA without facing any censure because he'd taken the kickback before the ethics code had been introduced. So no rules had been broken! Teixeira takes another sip of his cocktail. '*Saúde* FIFA!'

On a bench in a shady plaza of Asuncion, an elderly man sits in deep contemplation, his features frozen in a frown. After the glory years and the countless honours, it all ended badly for Nicolas Leoz in April 2013 when was forced to resign 'because of

ill-health' a week before he was criticised for taking bribes in
FIFA's report into the ISL affair. The investigators had seemed
sceptical about Leoz's story that he had donated his bribe to a
school, eight years after receiving it. One thing had softened the
indignity of having to leave world football under a cloud.
Paraguay's national football association had kindly made him its
'honorary' president for life. Another accolade to add to his long
list of cherished titles.

The third member of the South American collusion deal lies in
a grand marble mausoleum in the Avellaneda Cemetery in
Buenos Aires. Julio Grondona died aged 82 of an aortic aneurysm
shortly after the 2014 World Cup in Brazil. Sepp Blatter joined
the long cavalcade for his funeral and tried to capture the spirit of
the sharp-tongued Argentinian football boss: 'He was a man of
few words,' the FIFA president eulogised, 'but when he did speak
he always got to the point and made sense.' Were he alive to read
it, Grondona would certainly have a few angry words to say about
the claim in Judge Eckert's report that his federation received
irregular payments from Qatar for its friendly match with Brazil
just before the World Cup vote.

On the east coast of America, a large bearded man huddles in
his Trump Tower apartment, straining to hear a muffled audio
recording crackling through the speakers. When Chuck Blazer
realised the net was closing in after years of creaming off millions
of untaxed dollars from the CONCACAF coffers, he had signed
up to work as an undercover informant for the FBI to get off the
rap. He had travelled the world secretly recording his fellow FIFA
officials with a keyfob specially wired for sound to help his new
friends from the Bureau with their ongoing investigation into
football corruption.

Blazer was hoping to save his neck by betraying his colleagues,
if he could only get them someone to say something incriminat-
ing. The trouble was, it had been hard to get people to open up

ever since he was forced out of all his football positions in 2013 when that CONCACAF 'integrity report' had exposed his embezzlement of the confederation's funds. As Blazer scans through his barely audible tapes, the already-muffled sound is drowned out by the din of that pestilential parrot. 'You're a dope!' it squawks. 'You're a dope! You're a dope!' That goddamned bird is even more abusive than his ex-wife. Why can't he get a minute's peace?

The tiny molecules of Arabian dust swirl high in the atmosphere, spreading further and further into the slipstreams drifting across oceans and continents. In the middle of the Pacific, on the tiny island of Tahiti, Reynald Temarii leans back in his leather chair in the offices of his football association, tapping away on his MacBook in a pastel blue and peach Hawaiian shirt. His pleas of innocence fell on deaf ears and his ban from football was upheld, despite the hundreds of thousands of euros he took from Bin Hammam to fund his appeal in exchange for blocking Oceania's World Cup votes. The three-year exile is over but Temarii's jet-set days in FIFA boss class are behind him and now he is reduced to running his tiny island's lowly football association from this little office close to the turquoise shore.

Sweep east across the ocean to Tokyo and the gentle Junji Ogura is fast asleep, dreaming of the delicious rack of chicken yakitori skewers he has left marinating in the fridge for his family's lunch tomorrow. He has all the time in the world to pursue his hobbies of cooking and reading these days, having retired from the Exco at 72 the month after finally backing Qatar in the World Cup vote. A short leap across the Sea of Japan and Chung Mong-joon is shifting restlessly under silk sheets in his Seoul mansion. He is still smarting bitterly after his political ambitions were thwarted once again, when he lost his campaign to become mayor of South Korea's capital city in June 2014. Still, it is some small consolation that he remains an honorary vice-president of FIFA, thanks to the efforts of his friend Bin

Hammam. Chung's vote in the final round was crucial to Qatar's victory, after all. He knows he will always have a friend in Doha.

A southeasterly swoop and, on a riverside rooftop in the bustling metropolis of Bangkok, Worawi Makudi and his chief confidant Joe Sim are sipping short drinks at a well-stocked bar and contingency planning. Thailand's executive committee member survived the furore over his role in Qatar's collusion deal with the Iberian bid and then the scandal in Port of Spain without a scratch but, unsettlingly, FIFA's investigators have suddenly started digging around in his business four years later. Makudi's nerves took a knock when he opened Michael Garcia's letter informing him that his activities before the World Cup vote were under investigation back in November 2014. But his equilibrium was somewhat restored when the investigator abruptly resigned a month later, leaving a big question mark over his ongoing inquiries. Who knew what would happen to Garcia's caseload now he had shipped off to New York, where he belonged? His Swiss deputy Cornel Borbély had since stepped into the breach but, whatever happened, Sim assured Makudi, they would duck and dive their way through it like they always had.

Across the Bay of Bengal, Manilal Fernando sits on the veranda at home in Colombo with his eldest son and his little team of bespectacled lawyers, sharing a bottle of chilled white wine as the insects hiss in the hot night air. He has taken his appeal against his eight-year ban from world football all the way to the Court of Arbitration for Sport, and now the hearings are finished and the team are awaiting the outcome. His ascent to the FIFA executive committee was the realisation of a lifetime's ambition for the friendly Sri Lankan hustler, but sadly it lasted only two years before he was brought down in the collapse of Bin Hammam's Asian empire. Despite all the assiduous shredding by Jenny Be and Victoria Shanti, those meddling FIFA investigators found all sorts of unfortunate pieces of paper when they stormed into

Kuala Lumpur looking for trouble after Bin Hammam's ban, and they threw the book at Fernando for the cash he doled out to help his friend hang on to power in the AFC elections. He likes to keep his lawyers close these days. They travel with him, dine with him and drink with him. He is as sociable as ever and, though he is busy fighting to clear his name, he is one of the few friends from FIFA who still visits Bin Hammam in the majlis, when he can find the time.

The sand atoms in the sirocco winds which gust across the Mediterranean from the Arabian desert drizzle down over Europe like a gentle mist. The sea-moistened clouds blow in over the plains of the Sierra de Guadarrama, where Ángel María Villar Llona maintains his stand-off with FIFA's ethics men. From his offices in the Spanish football association's sprawling Ciudad del Futbol campus by the foothills of the mountains outside Madrid, the co-architect of the Iberian-Qatari collusion pact has steadfastly refused to cooperate with the World Cup corruption investigation. He scorned Garcia and Flynn as American interlopers with no business intruding into the private grief of the FIFA family and wilfully flouted his obligation to be interviewed and hand over any information they requested. Garcia's last act before resigning was to launch a fresh investigation into Villar Llona's failure to cooperate with the first one. Gazing out across the playing fields where his country's future football superstars are perfecting their game in the blue evening light, the Spaniard wonders whether he ought to be more helpful this time.

Now the warm fog is rolling in over the quaint medieval Belgian town of Bruges, where Michel D'Hooghe is rooting around in his attic. Up here, along with all his football gifts, photographs and trinkets, is that landscape painting wrapped in brown paper that his friend Vyacheslav Koloskov gave him when he was garnering votes for Russia 2018. The dreaded painting had caused so much fuss, but thankfully FIFA's investigators had accepted it was worthless. He was in the clear now and could go back to playing his accordion with peace of mind.

Not far to the east, in Germany, Franz Beckenbauer is also feeling the heat. When Garcia first sent *Der Kaiser* a long list of questions about his relationship with the lobbyists Fedor Radmann and Andreas Abold, he had thought it best to dodge the issue by telling the investigator he did not speak good enough English to respond. That excuse had not cut much ice and Beckenbauer was temporarily banned from world football until he agreed to cooperate. He had done his best to answer the questions before Garcia submitted his World Cup report to Judge Eckert, but it had been to no avail. Beckenbauer's heart sank when he received the letter in November telling him he was under individual investigation for his role in the World Cup vote. He hoped he would come out of it clean. This grubby business was no way to end a glittering career.

The Russians had an altogether neater way of dealing with FIFA's investigators. First they used a diplomatic spat with the US to ban Garcia from entering the country. Then, when his Swiss deputy Cornel Borbély showed up instead, they regretfully informed him that all their computers had been destroyed and they had no records to show for their campaign. The bid was given a clean bill of health by Garcia on the basis of no evidence, and its chairman, Vitaly Mutko, still has his feet comfortably under FIFA's boardroom table.

In Nyon, Michel Platini takes a drag on his cigarette and knocks back another half-glass of robust red. It is wearing work, trying to calm the growing tumult within European football over the chaos caused by the Qatar World Cup decision. He sees how the continent's football bosses look at him askance since he did the decent thing and confessed that he had voted for Qatar. He knows some of them will never forgive him for sending the tournament to the desert, and they are even more furious now they know that the event will have to be moved to the winter, causing catastrophic disruption across their leagues. There is open revolt now, across much of Europe, and Platini is struggling to steady the buffs. He could not quite find the mettle to challenge Blatter for the FIFA presidency, but such was the disquiet in UEFA that he has steeled himself and called publicly for the old man to step aside.

A storm is blowing in towards the FIFA hilltop as Sepp Blatter sits in his den, oblivious to the first light taps of rain on the dark pane. He is hunched forward over his desk squinting at the screen with a fond smile, winding back and re-watching his favourite movie scene of all time. Two men are on a small boat floating on the waters of a vast lake under a brooding sky. The mood is tense. If this were a mafia movie, someone would be about to get shot and pushed overboard. But this isn't *Godfather II* – it's a film about the FIFA family! Now shhh – it's about to get to his favourite bit. Tim Roth, playing Blatter with all the dignity he can muster, turns to Sam Neill, in the role of his mentor João Havelange. The former president has just offered a veiled apology for all the mess left behind for his protégé to clean up after his years of bribery, corruption and nepotism. The young Blatter throws him a magnanimous smile. They are both men of the world, after all.

'I knew I wasn't joining the chess club,' he says, with a macho shrug.

Blatter sits back delighted by his big line. Such grace! Such elegance! Such loyalty to the family. If you ask him, *United Passions* is a masterpiece, and worth every cent of the $27 million he took from FIFA funds to pay for it. Okay, so it grossed only $200,000 at the box office, but since when was football administration expected to be popular? It's a lonely life, up here on the hilltop. Nobody knows what he suffers for his love of this office. When he travels to matches in almost any city in the world, there is such hatred to contend with. Sure, he flies in first-class and stays in the best hotels known to humanity, but it's not easy being greeted with deafening boos on all sides of the stadium. He is an old man now, at 78. He is less sure-footed than he used to be. More doddery, some might say. They are whispering in the corridors that he's losing his grip. His daughter, Corinne, wants him to stand aside for the sake of his health, but he won't hear of it.

Then the phone rings, and it's yet another European football president telling him to resign. There's pandemonium in the European leagues over the prospect of a winter World Cup and an angry army of human rights do-gooders is advancing on Zurich, demanding action to save the migrant workers dying by the dozen in Qatar. Now that damned investigator has made a spectacle of himself by disowning FIFA's summary of his work and resigning, and the baying mob is demanding the publication of his full report. The calls for a re-vote grow louder every day. Worse, the sponsors are deserting FIFA one by one, taking their multi-million-dollar contracts with them. Yes, it's lonely being in charge, up on the hill. Even when dark falls, he's still here, in the office, holding on. The FIFA ship needs a firm hand on the tiller to steer its course through another storm, and Blatter won't let go. The rain is lashing down now and the winds are raging at the window. But he is safe and warm within the impenetrable shell of his Zurich bunker. There's no good in going outside in such filthy conditions. He draws the blinds and clicks rewind, one more time.

Back in Doha, night has fallen and the wind has subsided. Bin Hammam remains at the window, deep in thought, imagining the distant world he left behind. The servant has lit the lamps and the coffee is on the table. The scent of cardamom steam snaps him back to his senses and when he looks up the city outside is black with shadow and there are no stars. The only image in the window is his own reflection, and he turns away from it. He has seen the ugly face of the game. Now, perhaps, it is time to forget.

Afterword

We wrote *The Ugly Game* in two frantic months over Christmas and New Year 2014-15, hurrying to get the book onto the shelves ahead of the election for the FIFA president on 29 May. The core the story was, of course, Mohamed bin Hammam and his corrupt campaign to secure the 2022 World Cup, but the book was also intended to be a wider exposé of Sepp Blatter's FIFA. If it made some of the FIFA delegates think twice before voting to give the Swiss president a fifth term in office, then that was a good thing. Blatter had presided over a thoroughly rotten organisation for too long and had turned a blind eye to the egregious activities of his executive committee colleagues because, in the end, clinging on to power meant more to him than anything else. It was important to show how the absurd decision to hold the World Cup in the desert was a product of a corrupt regime – and to expose the fact that Qatar may never be stripped of the right to hold the competition because of an equally crooked back-handed deal done by Blatter with the country's royals to stay at the helm of FIFA.

Producing a book in such a short time required an intensity of effort which was not dissimilar to our time in the bunker six months earlier – except that we did it from the comfort of our own homes. We would write a chapter each and come together once a week on the comfy leather sofas of the Century Club in Soho, London, to review each other's work. FIFA was our obsession for those two months. Our Christmas film was *United Passions* – Blatter's $27 million vanity project. It was unintentionally funny because it was so leaden, but we also found it weirdly gripping because it revealed so much about Blatter's world view: his acceptance of João Havelange's dubious *realpolitik*; his reliance on African votes; his belief that the administrators were more important than the players or the fans; and his bristling hatred of the English. The film would later be disowned by its own director in the summer, after becoming the lowest-grossing film in US box office history ($918 in its opening weekend). Blatter must have completely lost the plot to have spent so much money on such a turkey.

A constant topic of conversation over coffee at the Century was the question of whether Blatter's regime was about to topple. We certainly felt that the ground had shifted, leaving the previously impenetrable FIFA in a perilously vulnerable position. The revelations from the FIFA Files and our subsequent stories in the autumn had been a game-changer. The public perception had hardened against FIFA. If the image of world football's governing body was ragged before, it was now in tatters. Its own ethics investigator Michael Garcia no longer wanted to be associated with such a toxic brand and increasingly the sponsors appeared to be feeling the same way.

FIFA hadn't helped itself by arrogantly refusing to engage with the questions we'd raised about Qatar in the files. It had cleared Qatar without sharing the evidence with the public and, as we described at the end of this book, Blatter had attempted to draw a line under the scandal with his speech declaring 'the crisis has stopped' in Marrakech. While we were writing *The Ugly Game*, we thought maybe the old man might pull it off again and ride out yet another crisis. But we could see the cracks were there and it felt as if all that was needed was one more small push. We didn't realise it at the time, but in a way we had already done enough. The chain of events that would eventually be the undoing of Blatter had already begun.

In March this year, a Swiss prosecution team based in Bern launched a secret investigation code-named Operation Darwin into corruption in the bidding contest to host the 2018 and 2022 World Cups. Its origin can be tracked back to our Legends' Dinner story more than two years earlier which had, in effect, pushed over the first domino. The article and our previous stories had raised such serious questions about the activities of the Qatar bid that Garcia had decided to look into the whole process leading up to the ballot on 2 December 2010. The results of his two-year investigation were spun by FIFA as giving the two winning bids, Russia and Qatar, clean bills of health. However, his work had unearthed a number of awkward pieces of evidence which suggested possible criminal acts. Since FIFA was under intense pressure in the late autumn of 2014 after being buffeted by the aftershocks of the FIFA Files revelations, it could not risk sitting on the evidence and felt obliged to hand it over to the Swiss police. That was to prove disastrous for Blatter.

In more benign times, the Swiss authorities might have been relied upon to deal with the narrow matters referred to them by FIFA and not delve deeper. But FIFA had become an embarrassment in Switzerland and had lost its political protection. The prosecutors were given licence to poke around where they wanted, and they were soon seizing documents and email accounts from within FIFA. The lead prosecutor, Olivier Thormann, was later to tell us that he had read our stories from the FIFA Files and the first edition of this book as part of his extensive research. As spring turned to early summer, he and his team set their sights firmly on the men from the executive committee who had voted for Russia and Qatar. Two men were of particular interest: Blatter and Michel Platini.

Meanwhile, a second investigation had also been sparked by Qatar's victory and by early 2015 it too was coming to a head. FIFA made a powerful adversary on the day that its executive committee decided Qatar was a better place to hold a World Cup than the United States. He was Eric Holder Junior, the United States Attorney General, who was in Zurich for the ballot alongside Bill Clinton in December 2010, and watched in stunned silence as the tiny Gulf state recorded its improbable victory. The bidding process had already been exposed as corrupt by our undercover journalism and so there was every reason for the Americans to ponder what lay behind this eyebrow-raising result. By coincidence, a small team of agents in the FBI's Eurasian organised crime unit in New York had already been taking an interest in FIFA as a by-product of an inquiry into Russian money-laundering. When Holder returned from the humiliation of Zurich, a wider trawl was launched to look into FIFA and its American connections. Significantly, it was run from the US attorney's Brooklyn office headed by Loretta Lynch, who was to be Holder's eventual successor as Attorney General.

The FBI began casting around for new evidence in early 2011. They tracked down the whistle-blower Phaedra Almajid after her allegations had been made public in the British parliament and offered her equipment to tape-record her telephone conversations with her ex-colleagues at the Qatar bid. This lead didn't take them anywhere, but they were to get lucky. The spat between Chuck Blazer and Jack Warner over the latter's suspected vote for Qatar had a number of ramifications which were catastrophic for the two men. In the tit-for-tat that followed, Blazer's financial records were leaked and they provided just the leverage the FBI had been looking for. Blazer had been earning millions of dollars over many years, but had paid hardly any tax. He was going to do a long stretch in jail unless he cooperated with the authorities. So he turned informant. The clock was ticking.

The corridors of the Baur au Lac were so quiet you could hear the gentle lapping of Lake Zurich in the early hours of 27 May. Liveried footmen in freshly polished shoes crept quietly along from door to door, putting out the day's newspapers as their guests slept silently inside. The back pages were filled with FIFA news as the election for its new president was just two days away. Blatter was standing against Prince Ali, and his recoronation was already a forgone conclusion, even though the Jordanian would pick up the anti-Blatter protest votes from the European federations. So the hotel was packed full of voters that morning. When the clock struck 6am, a dozen Swiss policemen in jeans and trainers swept through the revolving doors and presented a warrant with a list of names to the reception desk. Then they stormed upstairs and plucked seven members of FIFA's ruling elite from their beds – arresting them on behalf of the FBI. The officers brought out their quarry one by one and covered their heads with the hotel's crisp, white linen sheets as they helped them into the waiting police cars.

This was a watershed moment. For so many years, FIFA had batted away scandal after scandal as if it was above it all; as if public opinion didn't matter, and openness and transparency were for others. But now the years of grubby backhanders and shady deals were being laid bare for all to see and world football's governing body was being held to account by not one, but two judicial authorities. The Swiss had arrested the seven FIFA executives – all from the Americas – on behalf of the FBI, which was looking into corrupt football television and marketing deals involving officials and businessmen with some connection to the United States through bank accounts or tournaments. The most notable of the men arrested that day was Jeffrey Webb, the man who had succeeded Warner as head of CONCACAF. But on the other side of the Atlantic, there were even more high-profile arrests.

The US Justice Department announced that 14 FIFA officials and related executives were under investigation worldwide over the payment of more than $150 million in bribes and kickbacks dating back to the early nineties. At a press conference on the day of the arrests, Lynch, who had taken over from Holder as Attorney General a month earlier, launched a blistering attack on the indicted FIFA officials. 'They were expected to uphold the rules that keep soccer honest and protect the integrity of the game. Instead they corrupted the business of worldwide soccer to serve their interests and enrich themselves,' she said. The tax aspect of the inquiry was being handled by the Internal Revenue Service and the knock-out quote which appeared in all the media the next day was from its chief criminal investigator, Richard Weber. 'This is really the World Cup of fraud and today we are issuing FIFA a red card,' he said.

It was no surprise that the most prominent name of those indicted was Blazer. He was the FBI's key cooperating witness and it emerged that he had already pleaded guilty to racketeering, wire fraud, income tax evasion and money laundering at a court hearing which had been held in camera two years earlier. The big news was that a warrant had also been issued for the arrest of his long-time co-conspirator and FIFA's most notorious scoundrel, Warner. The man from Trinidad and Tobago had probably been expecting such a move for months, if not years. His two sons, Daryll and Daryan, had been cooperating with the American investigation after pleading guilty to a series of ticketing scams and illegal money transactions. Warner was taken into custody but was quickly released on bail. Typically defiant, he held a press conference accusing the United States of carrying out a 'witch-hunt' because they had lost out to Qatar. After delivering his statement, he began singing Bob Marley's 'Don't Worry About A Thing' while doing a little jig. You can't keep a bad man down.

The third big FIFA name to be indicted was Nicolás Leoz, who was placed under house arrest at his home in Asunción, Paraguay. At the time of writing, both Warner and Leoz remain on Interpol's most wanted 'red list' as they await extradition to the United States where they will face charges for alleged racketeering conspiracy, wire fraud and money laundering.*

If FIFA's Zurich hierarchy took some small crumb of comfort from the fact that the FBI was focusing on crimes far away in the Americas, then that would be soon swept away. The Swiss police were not just acting as go-betweens for the FBI. It was announced that they were formally investigating the 2010 ballot for the hosting rights to the 2018 and 2022 World Cups – a move that spelt more imminent danger for Blatter and his cronies. As well as making the arrests at the Baur au Lac, Thormann's team also raided FIFA's headquarters and came out with documents and electronic correspondence belonging to leading figures such as Jérôme Valcke, the secretary general, and Blatter himself. Perhaps more worrying for the football executives was the fact the prosecutors had access to the normally impenetrable Swiss banking system, where most of FIFA's secrets were supposed to lie dead and buried.

Blatter can often appear indestructible – some might say shameless. If the timing of the arrests was bad for his election campaign, it certainly didn't knock him off his stride. Two days later, he went before FIFA congress as if nothing had happened and was reinstated as the president after polling 133 votes to Prince Ali's 73. The messages of congratulations flooding in included a warm note from Vladimir Putin. The next day, Blatter was unrepentant in his victory press conference, describing the reasons for the arrests as mere 'infractions' relating to marketing companies in the Americas and protesting sulkily that FIFA couldn't be responsible for everything that happened in football.

* Leoz says he has 'nothing to hide' and denies the FBI charges.

When asked by a reporter whether he was the official who had allegedly allowed a $10 million bribe from South Africa to Warner to be channelled through FIFA's own bank account, he answered 'definitely that's not me' without elaborating. Next to him, Valcke shifted in his seat and said nothing.

The new bribery allegations had emerged from Blazer's testimony and possibly also from one or both of Warner's two sons. They opened up a couple of new cans of worms for FIFA as they suggested corruption in the bidding for 2006 and 2010 World Cups. The first allegation was that one of Warner's sons had travelled to Paris to meet 'a high-ranking official' from the South African bid committee for the 2006 World Cup. The son reportedly returned to his father with a suitcase stuffed with cash in '$10,000 stacks'. Despite the alleged bung, South Africa did not win, but it bid again for the 2010 competition in a ballot that was held in 2004.

According to Blazer, his former friend Warner was initially offered $1 million for his vote by South Africa's rivals Morocco ahead of the ballot for 2010. But the South African government and its bid committee allegedly made a much better offer to capture the votes of Warner, Blazer and a third Exco member. The $10 million payment to the Caribbean Football Union was ostensibly to support 'the African diaspora'. But, according to Blazer who admits to accepting the bribe, the money was to secure the trio's votes for South Africa in the ballot to host the World Cup. All three men voted the right way and the 2010 World Cup went to South Africa. It took some time for the money to be paid out as it couldn't come from central government funds but, in the end, South Africa asked for $10 million of the grant it was given by FIFA to prepare for the World Cup to be transferred instead to Warner. Most of the cash was rerouted into Warner's own accounts and businesses, and Blazer was slightly put out he received only three-quarters of the $1 million cut he had been promised.

This episode dominated the headlines on the weekend of

Blatter's re-election. The South African government admitted paying the cash, but denied it was a bribe. Matters then came to a head on the Tuesday morning when FIFA was forced to publicly deny that either Blatter or Valcke had been the 'high-ranking' official referred to in the FBI evidence who 'caused' the payments to be made to Warner. But later that very morning, a letter was leaked revealing that it was Valcke who had been asked by the president of the South African football federation to transfer the money to Warner.* FIFA was spinning out of control, but nobody could have quite foreseen what would happen that afternoon.

The rumours began to swirl when the media were notified that an emergency press conference would be held within hours. Back in London, we all tuned in to the live screening. Heidi was watching from the offices of BuzzFeed News in Soho, where she had just started a new job, while I sat glued to the screen in the Insight room at *The Sunday Times*. When Blatter appeared, he spoke confidently and slowly in French, but it was clear from his portentous opening line – 'I have been reflecting deeply about my presidency' – that it was all over. I picked up the phone to Heidi and we sat on either end of the line in stunned silence as he went on: 'While I have a mandate from the membership of FIFA, I do not feel that I have a mandate from the entire world of football ... Therefore, I have decided to lay down my mandate at an extraordinary elective congress. I will continue to exercise my functions as FIFA president until that election.'

As he rambled on, he did not actually say in simple words that he was resigning and it was left to his spin doctors to make that plain after he had finished speaking. His reasons for going were equally opaque. Quite what happened to change his mind in the

---

* A statement by FIFA said the South African payment had been properly authorised and Valcke was not involved with the 'invitation, approval and implementation' of the project.

four days between his election and resignation still remains a mystery. Had the public-relations disaster over Valcke and the South African payment been the final straw that rattled him? Had his lawyers advised him that he could not continue exposing himself to public questioning when he might one day be cross-examined on such matters in court? We may never know. True to form, Blatter's resignation was not straightforward. The old fox could not quite let go just yet and he was going to remain in post for another eight months until his successor could be chosen. This was, however, a seismic moment in FIFA's history. As soon as Blatter had finished speaking, I raced over to Soho to dissect the day's astonishing events with Heidi – over a delicious Swiss fondue.

Once the president had rendered himself effectively powerless by announcing his departure, the dam broke and FIFA's ethics committee took over. It began attending to the carnage that had followed the extraordinary decision to award the World Cup to Qatar, and the ramparts of world football's governing body really began to crumble. When we finished writing this book earlier this year, Bin Hammam was the only member of the original 2010 FIFA executive committee who had been banned for life from football. Now, 13 of the 24 members on that committee have either been banned for life, suspended, fined or are the subject of an ongoing investigation by the ethics committee. Astonishingly, a quarter of those men are also being investigated for alleged crimes. Even the man who counted the voting slips at the 2010 ballot, Jérôme Valcke, has been stripped of his role as secretary general pending inquiries into allegations that he was involved in a ticketing scam.*

The two new life bans from football were handed out to Warner and Blazer. It is difficult to be certain – because as ever

---

* Valcke denies the allegations that he sought to profit from ticket sales for the 2014 World Cup.

FIFA will not say – which of the many allegations against Warner finally led to him being kicked out of football permanently. Was it the $1.6 million he took from Bin Hammam before and after Qatar's victory, the $10 million he allegedly solicited from South Africa for his vote, or the routine pilfering from CONCACAF and FIFA which amounted to many millions over the years? Warner protests his innocence and is currently fighting against extradition to America. Blazer has already admitted to ten counts of fraud, bribery, tax evasion and money laundering in a secret deposition in November 2013 and is awaiting sentencing. He must rue the day he fell out with Warner over the Qatar vote.

Another of Bin Hammam's close allies, Reynald Temarii, has paid heavily for his involvement in the 2010 ballot. Temarii had been suspended ahead of the vote and banned from football for a year. In May this year, he was kicked out of football again for eight years following the revelations in the FIFA Files that he was paid €305,000 by Bin Hammam towards the legal and other costs of contesting his original suspension – a move which effectively knocked out votes for Qatar's rivals Australia and the United States.

A six-year ban was also handed out to another of the men Bin Hammam arranged to vote for Qatar. In September, the South Korean Chung Mong-joon's high ambitions of standing to become Blatter's replacement were dashed when he announced he was facing a suspension in relation to a proposal for a Korea-backed football development fund linked to the contest to win the 2022 World Cup, adding that the move was intended by FIFA to block his bid for the presidency. The ethics committee has not specified the precise details of the billionaire's misdemeanours.

Our story about the Legends' Dinner continued to have ramifications. Amos Adamu, who was suspended following our first 'World Cup Votes for Sale' story alongside Temarii, is now being investigated again by the ethics committee. The investigation relates to Adamu's role in the negotiations, which ended up with the Qatar bid committee drawing up a contract to pay his son Sampson $1 million to organise the dinner six months before the 2010 ballot.

At the same time, somewhat unspecified allegations have appeared in the German media about Franz Beckenbauer. The football legend is separately coming under scrutiny for his role in securing the 2006 World Cup for his country. The magazine *Der Spiegel* has alleged that Germany bought votes of key Exco members using a £4.9 million fund. A subsequent inquiry by the Deutscher Fussball-Bund has found that Beckenbauer, a leader of the bid, agreed a contract with one of the voters four days before the 2000 ballot to provide a series of services, including friendly matches and coaching support. The voter was, unsurprisingly, Jack Warner.*

Warner's name was also to crop up in the most breathtaking suspension of them all. In September, Blatter became the first president in FIFA's 111-year history to be investigated for criminal offences. Swiss police again raided his offices looking for evidence on separate financial deals which were made by Blatter and benefited both Warner and Michel Platini. The two FIFA vice-presidents had been key power brokers for Blatter over the years, as they held sway over more than 80 of the 105 votes he needed to retain power.

The most surprising of the allegations related to Platini. According to the Swiss investigators, Blatter improperly used FIFA's funds to pay Platini 2 million Swiss francs (£1.3 million) in February 2011. The men claimed the payment was for work Platini had done as a special adviser many years earlier, between January 1999 and June 2002, but the significance of its timing was not lost on the Swiss prosecutors. It came as Blatter was campaigning for his fourth term as FIFA president and just two months after the World Cup had been granted to Qatar. Blatter had gone back on his promise to stand aside in 2011 and let someone else take over the presidency. This had infuriated Bin Hammam. Documents from

---

* Beckenbauer has denied sending 'money to anyone in order to buy votes'.

the FIFA Files show Platini flew to Kuala Lumpur on 29 January 2011, with UEFA's general secretary, to lunch with Bin Hammam.

A close friend of the Qatari told us: 'Bin Hammam was tired of Blatter breaking his pledges to step down and he wanted to find a viable candidate to stand against him. So he was pushing Platini to be a candidate in the presidency election due to take place in June that year.' Platini had initially agreed to give the proposal some thought, but by March 2011 he had decided not to run against Blatter. 'As a result, Bin Hammam decided that he himself would have to stand against Blatter. He didn't like doing it because he preferred to be behind the scenes pulling the strings,' said the friend. At the beginning of May, with the election only weeks away, Platini signed an endorsement from UEFA's executive committee that urged all 53 member associations to vote for Blatter.

Both Blatter and Platini deny that there was anything wrong with the payment. The delay, they claim, was because FIFA could not afford to pay Platini his full salary. However, their cause was not helped by the fact that no paperwork existed to prove the payment, there was no note of it in FIFA's accounts and Platini had already been paid a reasonable salary of £123,000 a year for acting as a special adviser to Blatter. Questions were also asked about why it took nine years to pay the money when FIFA had netted billions of pounds from two World Cups in the intervening period. FIFA immediately suspended both men – a move that has almost certainly dashed Platini's hopes of taking over from Blatter as the president. Platini was questioned as a witness by the Swiss, but French prosecutors have launched a criminal investigation into the matter. Platini's lawyer revealed that FIFA are gearing up to ban him for life if he cannot prove his innocence. At the time of writing, his lawyer claimed to have a document which exonerates him, despite which the ethics committee banned both men for eight years on 21 December. Blatter and Platini said they intended to appeal to the Court of Arbitration for Sport.

The second criminal allegation against Blatter concerned a deal in which he handed over World Cup television rights to Warner's Caribbean Football Union (CFU) in 2005 at an apparently preferential rate. According to Swiss prosecutors, Blatter is suspected of acting against his fiduciary duties by entering into a contract with the CFU that was 'unfavourable for FIFA'. Suspicions about the deal were first alleged in a Swiss television documentary, which claimed that the CFU bought the TV rights to the 2010 and 2014 World Cup finals for $600,000 (€536,000). Warner is alleged to have then passed on the rights to his own private company and sold them on for $20 million. FIFA says it should have received 50 per cent of the profits from the resale of the rights. However, it did not write to Warner asking about its share of the money until after he was forced to resign in June 2011 over the Caribbean bribery scandal.

Richard Cullen, an American lawyer acting for Blatter, has strongly denied the allegations of criminal mismanagement, arguing that the contracts with the two vice-presidents were properly negotiated and involved the appropriate members of staff within FIFA. However, the criminal investigation is likely to go on for some time and may mean that Blatter will never walk through the doors of FIFA headquarters again.

The stress on Blatter proved to be too much. In November, he was rushed to hospital after suffering what was described as a 'small emotional breakdown'. In exile from the job that was his life, he couldn't help stirring up trouble. In candid interviews with a Russian news agency and the *Financial Times*, he said there had been a 'gentlemen's agreement' among FIFA's leaders that the next two World Cups would go to 'two superpowers', Russia and the United States. 'It was behind the scenes. It was diplomatically arranged to go there,' he said. So the votes for the 2018 and 2022 World Cups were a stitch-up anyway. At least, they should have been a stitch-up, but it didn't work to plan because of Qatar.

And what was happening about the Qatar 2022 World Cup? It

was significant that the co-conspirators in the vote-swapping pact between Qatar and Spain-Portugal also fared badly, with only Hany Abo Rida from Egypt and the late Julio Grondona of Argentina escaping any censure. The deal was the bedrock of Qatar's success, providing a guaranteed seven votes. Yet when it was revealed ahead of the vote, FIFA's investigator Chris Eaton – who later took up a lucrative job in Doha – was unable to find any evidence that any such agreement existed.

Bin Hammam's right-hand man in the deal was Worawi Makudi. In October, it was announced that he had been suspended by the ethics committee pending an investigation into allegations relating to the 2010 bids. It was not the least of Makudi's woes. In July, he was convicted of forgery in his 2013 election campaign to retain the Thai football federation's presidency and was given a 16-month suspended sentence, which he said he was appealing. Leoz, one of the South American members of the pact, is also currently suspended after being indicted for multiple crimes by the FBI in May.

When Garcia had attempted to reinvestigate the pact, he met with a wall of silence. Bin Hammam refused to cooperate and so did the other lynchpin, Spain's Ángel María Villar Llona. Most normal organisations would have shown the door to an employee who failed to cooperate with an internal disciplinary inquiry. But this was FIFA, and Villar Llona was fined just £16,000 and allowed to continue as the acting president of UEFA.

However, his troubles may not yet be over. For all that Eaton and Garcia could not find evidence of the pact, it has been finally confirmed by one of those who took part. Once one of the most powerful men in football, Brazil's Ricardo Teixeira has returned from Miami to his home country, where he was out of the reach of the FBI. It was the lesser of two evils for Teixeira, as the Brazilian police are also looking into how he amassed his personal fortune and failed to declare money he kept abroad, including €30 million in a secret account in Monaco. To add to his woes, he too is the subject of an ongoing investigation by FIFA's ethics committee. Beset by bigger problems, Teixeira finally came clean about the illicit voting pact in an interview in June. It could not have been a fuller confession.

These are his words translated from Portuguese: 'People say that I personally voted for Qatar or that the CBF [Brazilian football federation] voted for Qatar, but that is not strictly accurate. It's more precise to say that South America voted for Qatar and I will explain why. Think back to the 2018 vote. Was there ever any doubt whose bid South America would support? Of course it would be Villar. Argentina and Paraguay were very close to Spain. Argentina and Paraguay had a deal with Spain. Who was linked to the Spanish candidacy? Wasn't it Portugal? Yes, they were proposing a shared cup. So, with Portugal in the running, it was obvious that the Brazilian vote would be for them.

'Here's the thing. Spain needed votes. It had three from South America and possibly one more from Europe. It wasn't very much. So we had a meeting, me, Villar and Grondona, and we managed to get some votes from Asia [Bin Hammam, Makudi and Abu Rida], thanks to Qatar.

'And what was the deal? Qatar would vote with us for 2018 and in return would receive our support in 2022. That was the deal. It was just that deal. And what happened? Spain got through to the last round of voting but lost to Russia. The history does not differ one millimetre from this.'

In other words, seven members of FIFA's ruling executive broke specific rules forbidding collusion between the bidders for 2018 and 2022 that they themselves had introduced. When they were investigated for this rule breach ahead of the vote, they all denied that any such deal was in place, even though Blazer reported seeing the note that passed between Villar Llona and Bin Hammam discussing the pact. Along with the corrupt payments and other deals struck by Bin Hammam, the seven votes were the key to Qatar's success. The contest was unfairly won, by Teixeira's own admission. So will FIFA now seize on this to rerun the competition for the 2022 World Cup? Only time will tell.

So much has happened in the ten months since we wrote *The Ugly Game*. The majority of those who voted for Qatar have been banned, suspended or are under investigation for disciplinary offences. Evidence is continuing to emerge about corruption in previous World Cup ballots involving the very same men. The president has fallen and with it Qatar's greatest protector. Warner may save his neck by finally telling the authorities everything he knows and there is more to come from Blazer's testimony. The Swiss police are homing in on the bribes and bungs in the bidding process, and the FBI is digging into the same quagmire with another major announcement expected imminently. A news agency recently reported that the Swiss investigators have now identified more than 120 suspicious transactions relating to the 2018 and 2022 bids. None of the Qatar bid team has been interviewed so far but, inevitably, there is one man the prosecutors wish to talk to. 'The former head of the AFC is particularly welcome to deliver a statement,' a spokesman for the Swiss attorney general's office was quoted as saying last month. If the prosecutors can ever make Bin Hammam tell them what he knows, then the remnants of FIFA will turn to dust and Qatar's dream of hosting a World Cup will remain just that.

— *Jonathan Calvert, 21 December 2015*

The Ugly Game Cast List

Mohamed bin Hammam's entourage

Jenny Be Siew Poh *the director of the president's office at the Asian Football Confederation (AFC)*

Michelle Chai *assistant general secretary at the AFC*

Najeeb Chirakal *his personal assistant in Doha*

Amadou Diallo *the African bagman*

Amelia Gan *the director of finance at the AFC*

Manilal Fernando *the Asian fixer*

Mohammed Meshadi *his Qatari companion and bagman*

Victoria Shanti *a secretary in the AFC president's office*

In Qatar

Sheikh Khalifa bin Hamad Al Thani *the old Emir (1972–95)*

Sheikh Hamad bin Khalifa Al Thani *the ruling Emir (1995–2013)*

Sheikh Tamim bin Hamad Al Thani *the Crown Prince (Emir from 2013–)*

Sheikha Mozah bint Nasser Al Missned *the wife of Sheikh Hamad*

Sheikh Abdullah bin Nasser Bin Khalifa Al Thani *an interior minister, later prime minister*

Abdullah bin Hamad Al-Attiyah *the energy minister, deputy prime minister and chairman of Qatargas*

... and the Qatar 2022 bid committee

Sheikh Mohammed bin Hamad Al Thani
the chairman
Hassan Al-Thawadi *the chief executive*
Ali Al-Thawadi *the deputy chief executive*
Phaedra Al-Majid *an international media officer*
Sheikh Hamad bin Khalifa bin Ahmed Al Thani *the president of Qatar FA and a bid member*

FIFA

Sepp Blatter *the president (1998–)*
Chris Eaton *the head of security (2010–12)*
Judge Hans-Joachim Eckert *the ethics judge (2011–)*
Michael Garcia *the ethics investigator (2011–14)*
João Havelange *the former president (1974–98)*
Jérôme Valcke *the secretary general (2007–)*

... and the executive committee voters in 2010

Hany Abo Rida *a member, Egypt*
Amos Adamu *a member, Nigeria*
Jacques Anouma *a member, Ivory Coast*
Franz Beckenbauer *a member, Germany*
Chuck Blazer *a member, USA, and the secretary general of CONCACAF*
Michel D'Hooghe *a member, Belgium*
Şenes Erzik *a member, Turkey*
Julio Grondona *a member, Argentina*
Mohamed bin Hammam *a member, Qatar, and the president of the AFC*
Issa Hayatou *a vice-president, Cameroon, and the president of CAF*
Marios Lefkaritis *a member, Cyprus*

Nicolas Leoz *a member, Paraguay, and the president of Conmebol*
Worawi Makudi *a member, Thailand*
Chung Mong-joon *a vice-president, South Korea*
Vitaly Mutko *a member, Russia*
Junji Ogura *a member, Japan*
Michel Platini *a vice-president, France, and the president of UEFA*
Rafael Salguero *a member, Guatemala*
Reynald Temarii *a member, Tahiti*
Ricardo Teixeira *a member, Brazil*
Geoff Thompson *a vice-president, England*
Ángel María Villar Llona *a vice-president, Spain*
Jack Warner *a vice-president, Trinidad and Tobago, and the CONCACAF president*

The consultants

Andreas Abold *an adviser to Australia*
Peter Hargitay a *former Blatter aide and adviser to Australia*
Fedor Radmann *a business partner of Beckenbauer and adviser to Australia*
Michel Zen-Ruffinen *a former FIFA secretary general*
Joe Sim *an adviser to the Thai Football Association*

The confederations

AFC *the Asian Football Confederation*
CAF *the Confederation of African Football*
CONCACAF *the Confederation of North, Central American and Caribbean Association Football*
Conmebol *the South American Football Confederation*
OFC *the Oceania Football Confederation*
UEFA *the Union of European Football Associations*

The 2018 bidders

England
Netherlands–Belgium
Russia
Spain–Portugal

The 2022 bidders

Australia
Japan
South Korea
USA
Qatar

Acknowledgements

Both authors would like to thank their editors at *The Sunday Times* for throwing the newspaper's full weight behind the FIFA Files investigation. Charles Hymas instantly saw the vast potential of the documents and backed the project throughout with huge energy and dedication. It was Martin Ivens's boldness in devoting the first 11 pages of the paper to the story in the first week of the series that gave the scoop its massive impact. We are indebted to our fearless and forensic lawyers Pia Sarma and Pat Burge for copper-bottoming every word we wrote against the original documents from the files and providing constant advice and guidance.

Georgina Capel and Rachel Conway at our literary agency Capel & Land saw the potential for a book and got this show on the road with great aplomb. Ian Marshall, our editor at Simon & Schuster, seized the moment and spirited this volume onto the shelves at double speed. Thanks to David Hirst, our barrister, for bullet-proofing every paragraph before publication.

We are so grateful to the friends and family who read this manuscript as it came together, sharpening it with their shrewd observations and fortifying two tired authors with their kind words. Matthew Lacey pruned through every sentence deftly honing the language and testing each fact against the scarily vast store of knowledge in his 'memory palace'. Andy Rutherford enriched our work with his deep understanding of world affairs and foreign cultures, his love of football and his limitless enthusiasm. We're thankful to our dear friend Michael Gillard for inspiring us by his own example as a brave and brilliant investigative journalist, and for countless late-night pep talks over far too much tequila.

Heidi would like to thank Libby Blake for being her biggest inspiration and showing her how to kick the doors down in a man's world. Ruth and Bob Overy provided essential reading for a sports novice. Melissa Harteam Smith kept the home fires burning. Jamie Blake was always on hand to buck her up with a beer and a brotherly hug. And Nathan, Dominic and Gabriel Blake will always be her favourite little football fans the world over – in her heart, wherever she goes.

Jonathan would like to thank his children, William and Grace Calvert, for being their lovely selves and putting up with a father who has spent far too much time with his laptop lately. William for lighting up the room with his cheerfulness and infectious laughter and lifting weary spirits with his exquisite jazz guitar. Grace for being such an inspiringly bright and beautiful young woman and providing so much warm support and lively chatter.

And finally, both authors are forever grateful to our sources for their bravery and conviction in risking so much to make the truth known. You are the heroes of this story.